T0285048

VALLEY SO LOW

VALLEY SO LOW

ONE LAWYER'S FIGHT FOR JUSTICE IN THE WAKE OF AMERICA'S GREAT COAL CATASTROPHE

JARED SULLIVAN

Alfred A. Knopf · New York 2024

THIS IS A BORZOI BOOK
PUBLISHED BY ALFRED A. KNOPF

www.aaknopf.com

A portion of this book first appeared, in different form, in *Men's Journal.*

Library of Congress Cataloging-in-Publication Data
Names: Sullivan, Jared, author.
Title: Valley so low : one lawyer's fight for justice in the wake of America's great coal catastrophe / Jared Sullivan.
Description: New York : Alfred A. Knopf, 2024. | Includes bibliographical references and index. |
Identifiers: LCCN 2024006434 (print) | LCCN 2024006435 (ebook) | ISBN 9780593321119 (hardcover) | ISBN 9780593321126 (ebook)
Subjects: LCSH: Scott, James Kidwell (Lawyer) | Tennessee Valley Authority—Trials, litigation, etc. | Pollution—Law and legislation—Tennessee. | Coal-fired power plants—Law and legislation—Tennessee. | Coal ash—Health aspects—Tennessee. | Coal—Combustion—By-products—Environmental aspects—United States. | Coal—Combustion—Waste disposal—United States. | Discrimination in criminal justice administration—United States. | Environmental disasters—Law and legislation—United States.
Classification: LCC KFT354.S85 2024 (print) | LCC KFT354 (ebook) | DDC 344.76804/633—dc23/eng/20240214
LC record available at https://lccn.loc.gov/2024006434
LC ebook record available at https://lccn.loc.gov/2024006435

Jacket photograph courtesy of Appalachian Voices / Dot Griffith
Jacket design by Jenny Carrow

Manufactured in the United States of America
First Edition

For Caroline, of course

Down in the valley, valley so low
Hang your head over, hear the wind blow.

—American mountain ballad

Contents

A Note to the Reader

This is a true story. All the people and events described in the pages that follow are real. Most of the material comes from court documents; from records I obtained through Freedom of Information Act requests; or from interviews I conducted with sources over a period of five years. (Some of these sources requested anonymity.) All quoted dialogue in the deposition, hearing, or trial scenes comes from official court transcripts or from audio recordings of the proceedings. Quoted dialogue in other scenes was, in most cases, recalled to me by primary sources, and I reproduced it word for word. Jacobs Engineering and TVA dispute much of my reporting. See the Notes section that follows the text for more information on sources.

—Jared Sullivan

PART I

2008–2013

On December 22, 2008, Ansol Clark woke to a ringing phone. It was sometime before 6 a.m., far earlier than he had intended to get up. He drove construction trucks for a living, but he'd been furloughed recently, leaving him little to do in the three days before Christmas except wrap gifts and watch movies with his grown son, Bergan. The house was dark. Janie, Ansol's wife of thirty-six years, slipped out of bed, stepped across the bedroom, and disappeared through the doorway that led into the kitchen. A light clicked on, and the ringing stopped. She returned to the bedroom. "It's for you," she told Ansol.

In the kitchen, Ansol, groggy, picked up the landline from its place atop the bread box. You need to get up, a man told him, and you need to get up right away. Ansol recognized the caller's voice: it belonged to his supervisor, a general foreman named Tim Henry. "Get to Kingston," Henry added. "They've had a blowout down here."

Ansol, needing no further explanation, hung up. Janie rushed to brew a thermos of coffee and wrap up biscuits while Ansol pulled on his work clothes: jeans, a blue down jacket, a neon hard hat, muck boots. At fifty-seven, he was a bull of a man, strong from hauling around equipment all day and from spending much of his free time hunting on the Cumberland Plateau; he liked to pick off squirrels with a .22 Magnum rifle. He, Janie, and Bergan lived in Knoxville, Tennessee, in a one-story brick home three miles from the farm where Ansol grew up. Within half an hour of receiving Henry's call, he was pulling his Chevy

S10 pickup truck out of the driveway and heading toward the Kingston Fossil Plant.

He made his way by headlights, following I-40 west out of town. He knew the route well. After a decade crisscrossing North America in a tractor trailer, he'd joined the Teamsters labor union in 2000 and had spent much of the past five years working at the Kingston Fossil Plant, a coal-fired power station forty miles outside downtown Knoxville, in Roane County. Built and managed by the Tennessee Valley Authority (TVA), a giant federally owned power company, the Kingston facility was, at the time of its completion in 1954, the world's largest coal-fired power station. It burned fourteen thousand tons of coal a day, enough to fill one hundred and forty train cars and to power some seven hundred thousand homes.

With no traffic, Ansol reached the plant within thirty minutes. He met Henry in a parking lot; a few other Teamsters and some equipment operators showed up around the same time. In a shipping container used to store tools, the group waited for sunrise, anxious to see what they were up against. Ansol had something of an idea. Each day, the Kingston plant generated a thousand tons of coal ash, the sooty by-product of burning coal to produce electricity. Much of this ash ended up in an unlined pit in the ground, known as a holding pond. But Kingston's "pond" was not really a pond, at least not anymore. In the 1950s, TVA started flushing coal ash into a spring-fed swimming hole, and, in the decades since, the ash had displaced the water and grown into a mountain, sixty feet tall, covering eighty-four acres, and situated at the confluence of two rivers, the Emory and the Clinch. It was a precarious setup, one made more so by the dike that contained all this ash—an earthen embankment made not of concrete or steel but of clay and bottom ash, a coarse, sandlike component of coal ash.

By that December morning in 2008, the ash mound had become a topographical feature so large that marathoners ran up it for training. TVA planted grass over it, so it resembled a hill, and bulldozers sculpted neat tiers into the sides, reminiscent of those of a stepped pyramid. But the mound lacked the sturdiness that its size suggested. Two years earlier, Ansol had helped to repair a minor breach in the dike that had sent coal ash rushing into a ditch. When he walked on the mound, the ground had jiggled like a water bed; when he drove his truck along the dike's

Homes along the Emory River,
near Kingston, Tennessee, in December 2008

sloped sides, he went as slowly as possible, to avoid causing another rupture. He'd once told a coworker that the dike would surely fail one day. Now, it seemed, that day had come.

At first light, Ansol and Henry climbed into a pickup and drove up the back side of a large wooded bluff that overlooked the coal-ash mound. The sight at the top would stick in Ansol's mind until the day he died.

Hours earlier, as the clock approached midnight, a stiff wind blew over the rolling countryside that surrounded the Kingston Fossil Plant. It was the winter solstice, and, in the quiet of that long night, the old farmhouses, country churches, trailer homes, and lakeside estates that dotted the hills and coves around the power station were dark and still. Christmas trees glowed in living rooms. *The Year Without a Santa Claus* played on TVs. Outside, the temperature hovered around 14 degrees Fahrenheit, cold enough to freeze the pipes at the McDonald's in town. Then, shortly before one o'clock, the north section of the coal-ash dike suddenly and almost wholly collapsed. When it did, more than a billion gallons of coal-ash slurry—about fifteen hundred times the volume of liquid that flows over Niagara Falls each second—broke forth. A black wave at least fifty feet high rushed northward with the power and violence of water punching through a dam.

A backwater inlet separated the coal-ash pond from a small peninsula along the Emory River. A few dozen homes sat along the water's edge. As the black wave roared ahead, shaking the earth, it overwhelmed the inlet and slammed into the peninsula. Most of the slurry, nearly six million tons in all, forked right around the obstruction and rushed into the Emory River, filling in a forty-foot-deep channel. The rest of the ash, nearly three million tons, filled in two sloughs on either side of the peninsula, hurling fish forty feet onto the riverbank. The wave kept going. It downed trees, covered roads, and knocked out power lines. Docks were inundated; boats were carried away; soccer fields were smothered.

The wave first collided into the home of fifty-three-year-old James Schean. With a thundering boom, it ripped Schean's vinyl-sided place off its foundation, upturning furniture, crushing door frames, and knocking over Christmas presents. The rafters cracked.

Down the road, Chris and DeAnna Copeland, a married couple with two young daughters, were awakened by the din. Chris, a firefighter, glanced out a window. A black torrent was flowing across his backyard in the moonlight. Trees bobbed in the muck. He got up and flipped a light switch. No power. In the dark, he pulled on a T-shirt and pants. Downstairs, he called 911 on his cell phone. There was a landslide, he said, or maybe something else. It was hard to tell. Then he hung up, grabbed a flashlight, and bolted outside.

Then, as now, the Kingston Fossil Plant had twin thousand-foot-high smokestacks that towered over the forested countryside. Far across the inlet that separated Copeland's home from the plant property, he could see flashers blinking, as always, at the top of the two stacks, but there was no other light beyond that of the moon. He swept the ground with his flashlight. Debris and mud everywhere. A musty smell. Then he realized: it wasn't mud; the coal-ash dike had failed. He owned a white Suzuki Sidekick. He climbed in, cranked the engine, drove into the backyard, and pointed the high beams toward the plant. A sea of coal ash had inundated the inlet. The black wave had dissipated within a minute, but smaller slides would continue for an hour or more.

Copeland's next-door neighbor, Jeff Spurgeon, soon emerged from his home carrying a flashlight. The two men had known each other for years. The ash had washed within feet of their homes, but somehow it hadn't touched either. Copeland jumped out of his Suzuki, and together he and Spurgeon hurried toward the river, knowing that their neighbors would need help.

The first 911 calls poured in shortly before one o'clock, and emergency personnel took swift action. By 1:06 a.m., police had blocked off the long, curving, tree-lined road to the Kingston Fossil Plant. Members of the county emergency-management team arrived minutes later. The TVA staffers who were on shift at the plant quickly realized that the dike had at least partly collapsed, but they had no idea how severe the blowout might be. Someone needed to check. A shift supervisor hurried to the plant's loading dock, climbed into a TVA pickup, and rattled toward the coal-ash pond, a mile or so down the road. It was impossible to see much as the truck's headlights carved through the darkness. Leafless trees, heavy shadows. Then the high beams fell upon something in the road—a deer, half buried in sludge, struggling to escape. The supervisor threw the truck into reverse. He knew that the dike had not sprung a leak or suffered a minor breach, as it had in the past. The dike, and nearly all the coal ash it held, was gone. "This is unbelievable," another TVA employee scribbled in a log that morning. "We did not expect this."

The two neighbors, Copeland and Spurgeon, reached a white, two-story home at the tip of the peninsula, directly across from the holding pond. A Christmas wreath hung between two windows, but little else was normal. Sludge had buried the home nearly above the porch, shattering the front windows. The place belonged to an elderly couple named Janice and Perry James. As Copeland crossed the yard, he called out to them, then he took another step and sank—muck to his waist. He struggled for several long moments to free himself. Once he recovered his balance, he was able to see Janice James upstairs, shining a flashlight through a window—a relief. She would later tell reporters that she had watched as dark slurry poured in under the front door, filling her living room and sunroom. Through a window, James shouted to

Copeland and Spurgeon that she was okay and that her husband was away on business. Copeland asked her not to go downstairs. A rescue squad was en route, he said, and he and Spurgeon needed to check on Mr. Schean.

In the Suzuki, Copeland and Spurgeon sped toward Schean's place, a quarter of a mile down the road. It was here where the black wave had first collided with the land. Sludge and tree limbs and debris covered the asphalt. Soon gray mounds of ash, at least ten feet tall, blocked the way. Copeland parked at the top of a hill, then he and Spurgeon bushwhacked through a dark wood to the house. The wave had dragged Schean's little home sixty-five feet off its foundation and thrust it against an embankment. The red-shingled roof had partially caved in, and boards and concrete blocks littered the ground. Schean's shed was gone, along with the tree where he chained his dog, along with the dog itself. The wave had tossed around Schean's two-door pickup as if it were a child's plaything.

The two men hollered out for Schean, and a voice yelled back. They followed the sound to a bedroom window and shined in their lights. Schean, sitting in the dark and somehow uninjured, wore a blank, dazed

More than a billion gallons of coal-ash slurry inundated the East Tennessee countryside.

look. He worked as a boilermaker at the Kingston plant, and yet he said he had no idea what had happened, and he hadn't dared to venture outside alone.

After offering a brief explanation, Copeland and Spurgeon tried to open the window, but it wouldn't budge. The house popped and cracked, as if it might collapse. The two men found a board and shattered the glass and lifted Schean to safety. He had on a shirt and pants but neither shoes nor a coat. With the temperature still well below freezing, the sludge would soon crust over with ice. They needed to go.

Hours later, standing at the top of the wooded bluff, Ansol Clark wasn't aware of any of this, but, as he surveyed the ruined landscape, it was clear that TVA had made a tremendous mess. By sunup, helicopters whirled overhead, as local, state, and federal agencies assessed the biblical scope of the breach. Three hundred acres lay buried in ash, a foot deep in spots, six or more in others. The spill would prove to be nearly a hundred times larger than the 1989 *Exxon Valdez* oil spill, and it would rank as the single largest industrial disaster in U.S. history in terms of volume. The sludge could have filled the Empire State Building nearly four times over.

Wanting to see more, Ansol and Henry, the general foreman, drove around the site's perimeter. Thirty-foot chunks of ash towered over the sludge. Fish flopped on the ground. Police officers shot deer trapped in the ash. Geese writhed crazily; their carcasses would soon pile up. Ansol had never seen anything like it.

Motoring slowly, he and Henry reached the crushed home of James Schean. First responders had already delivered Schean to a nearby community college to sleep and warm up. Ansol and Henry climbed from their vehicle and waded across the yard, hunting for firm footing in the muck. They entered through the kitchen to silence. Dishes lay shattered on the floor. In an adjacent room, a Christmas tree was submerged in ash; wrapped gifts floated in the slurry. *How could this happen?* Ansol wondered.

All told, the breach damaged or destroyed twenty-six homes, and rescue teams had to evacuate twenty-two people. TVA staff quickly reserved hotel rooms for them and handed out gift cards to be used in restaurants and to replace ruined Christmas gifts. But the biggest concern in the first chaotic hours that morning was finding whoever might be buried under the coal ash. Nearly everyone on-site, including Ansol Clark, expected to find bodies.

The attorney Jim Scott had a routine. He liked to wake up at four or five in the morning, fire off a few emails, and then go for coffee. He preferred the Starbucks on Kingston Pike, in a Kroger parking lot next to a Chick-fil-A. He liked the coffee but also the drive, since it afforded him a few precious minutes of solitude before he returned home to take his two young sons to school. In the predawn darkness, he sped through the empty streets of Knoxville, a "scruffy little city of 180,000," as *The Wall Street Journal* once called it. To Scott, it often felt like a tiny Appalachian village. He could hardly go to a restaurant without seeing someone he knew from college or from his years practicing law. The lady at the Starbucks drive-through had even given him a nickname: Two Equals and Extra Cream Boy.

On December 22, 2008, Scott kept his ritual, making the two-mile drive from his home. He was forty-one years old and did not intimidate in either size or disposition. He stood five foot eight and had a soft, expressive face and a black tumbleweed of hair. He seldom wore a suit when he wasn't due in court. After a few mild days in the 50s, Knoxville was now wrapped in frost, but the weather didn't deflate Scott's mood. He was looking forward to some time off for his birthday, on the 24th, and to Christmas. This year, like every other, his parents had invited about twenty relatives—uncles, aunts, nieces, nephews, Scott's two sisters—to their home to celebrate. They lived in Oak Ridge, twenty-five miles west of Knoxville, in the same one-story home they bought when Jim was nine, after his dad, James "Buddy" Scott, was elected Anderson County district attorney. Buddy went on to serve as a circuit judge for nearly thirty years and in that time became a legend in local legal circles, as much for helping to rewrite Tennessee's constitution as for his long-standing feud with a local prosecutor, whom he jailed four times for contempt of court. Jim admired his father's public service and had felt fated to follow his lead into law. Besides, what else was he going to do with a poli-sci degree?

Scott lived with his wife and their two young sons in Sequoyah Hills, one of Knoxville's best neighborhoods, comprising a collection of Craftsman-style cottages and Georgian Revival mansions, encircled by a greenway. Theirs was a quaint, white-painted home on a half-acre lot, less than half a mile from the Tennessee River. Jim and his wife, Mary, had bought the house shortly after the birth of their first son, Jack, about six years earlier, as Jim began to pull a solid income.

Once back home from Starbucks that December morning, he pulled into the driveway and walked down to the basement-level living room. He sank into a brown leather couch and clicked on the TV. He could hear his sons stirring upstairs, but Knoxville public schools had already let out for winter break, so he didn't need to rush anywhere.

Over the past few days, President George W. Bush's proposed auto-industry bailout, following the global financial meltdown, had dominated headlines, as had the Blagojevich scandal;* Barack Obama, recently elected president, was vacationing in Hawaii. But that morning, as Scott sipped his coffee, watching as the images flickered past, the reporting's focus had shifted. A helicopter had flown over and filmed the Emory River in Kingston, forty miles away. Except, in the footage, there was no longer a river. In its place, a gray, unbroken plain stretched toward the horizon. Half-submerged roads, downed trees, brown standing water glinting in the morning sun: it was hard to tell where the destruction ended. The local news reported that a mudslide of some sort had destroyed several homes near Swan Pond Circle Road, but details were scarce.

Scott booted up his laptop and read whatever stories on the event that he could find. Few had been published yet, but the *Roane County News* reported that coal sludge had broken loose after a dike collapsed at the Kingston Fossil Plant. The disaster was no mudslide.

Scott knew Kingston well. He had lived there on a family farm until he was four years old, and it formed the backdrop of his earliest memories: catching salamanders in a creek that flowed through his grandmother's property; watching as his dad bird-hunted in gold autumn fields. As a teenager, Scott had played football against the local high-

* Rod Blagojevich, former governor of Illinois, was convicted of trying to sell Barack Obama's vacated Senate seat after Obama was elected president.

school team, attended church just outside Kingston, and water-skied near the spot of the coal-sludge disaster.

His connection to the town extended into adulthood. When he was twenty-five and fresh out of the University of Tennessee law school, he took a job as an assistant district attorney in the judicial district that encompassed Kingston. (His father had held the same position after earning his degree from UT.) Jim worked out of the Kingston courthouse. For many young lawyers, a job in the DA's office—the public sector—wouldn't have held much appeal. He earned $26,000 a year, and after taxes and student loans, he had $1,400 a month to live on. But, to him, the position was a golden opportunity. He started to argue cases before juries almost immediately. There would be no years of waiting in the wings to try big cases, no years stuck in traffic court. He handled cases in four counties and often litigated three jury trials a month; he put sixty thousand miles on his Chevy Blazer in his first year.

In short order, he learned how to connect with jurors and think quickly. And, in time, he proved to be something of a law savant, albeit a scattered one. He was able to remember nearly every detail about a case, along with the names of his clients' children and which college team they pulled for. Yet he constantly misplaced his wallet and keys, and he was hopeless at returning phone calls. In depositions—pretrial testimonies conducted by lawyers—he often leaped from one topic to the next and then back again. He swore that the approach was by design, but his friends and colleagues weren't convinced. He sent late-night emails to opposing counsel riddled with typos, and sometimes wore white athletic socks with his leather dress shoes and suit. Later, when he entered private practice, he sported shorts and baseball caps to meetings. "It is a chore to deal with that man," one Knoxville lawyer said of Scott. "He's a mess," another attorney added.

But Scott didn't care what other lawyers thought of him, or he tried not to. His clients were his priority, and, by all accounts, he did commendable work on their behalf. He revised briefs late into the night and worked nearly every weekend and holiday. Perhaps his greatest strength was that he excelled at imparting hope to his clients, making them feel as if, despite how little money or stature they had, the legal system would produce a fair result if they had truth and the law on their side. And he mostly believed that to be true.

In time, Scott grew to love Kingston as much as his job in the DA's office there. The town, perched on a bend in the Clinch River, among the cave-pocked Appalachian foothills, originated as a federal outpost, and, with a population of about six thousand people, it remained something of an outpost. On North Kentucky Avenue, the sole thoroughfare, a Sonic drive-in sat across the street from the First Baptist Church, the town's largest congregation. Around the corner, the Roane County Courthouse faced a cash-advance place and an empty storefront that, a few years later, would house a business that sold gold, coins, and collectibles. While driving on I-40 between Nashville and Knoxville, you would miss Kingston altogether if not for the thousand-foot smokestacks of the TVA power plant, rising from the forested hills. The town was insular and cliquish in the way that every tiny East Tennessee hamlet has always been, but folks treated Scott well and respected his efforts on the public's behalf.

By 2008, he had been in private practice for a decade. After spending a few years at a local law firm, he went into business with his sisters, who were also lawyers, and two other partners (one of whom, Michael Pemberton, was his brother-in-law). Scott, like many Knoxville attorneys, worked a grab bag of cases to stay afloat: food poisoning, medical malpractice, DUIs, wrongful deaths. He could do criminal cases in his sleep, he once told a friend. Still, he tried to avoid any case he disagreed with personally or professionally, even when he assumed he could win. Raised in the Presbyterian Church and still religious, he had morals he tried to live by. Throughout that December, he and his firm had been helping a couple reach a settlement with a local Days Inn after one of its employees murdered their daughter, a twenty-one-year-old former homecoming queen. It was bleak work, and not the sort of case that Scott typically sought out, but he wanted to help the family. Surely, they deserved *something* for their loss.

Even with such worthy cases, Scott missed public service, and he not infrequently wished that he still worked in the DA's office. He had a knack for it, and he would have stayed had the pay been half decent. A former clerk still talked about a time in general-sessions court when Scott bought a coloring book and a Coke for a mistreated little girl who was at the center of a child-abuse case. He spent a few minutes talking to her eye-to-eye, a rare gesture in a legal environment that didn't reward such kindness. Another time, a hysterical mother showed up at the DA's office after her daughter was murdered, demanding that Scott, and no one else, prosecute the killer. Word had spread in Roane County that if you wanted justice and respect, you went to the young, short, curly-haired attorney. Scott considered it a compliment that many of his clients still came from the area.

That year, leading up to Christmas, he wasn't looking to take on any big new cases. He liked working sprawling, messy suits, sure. But he already had a heavy caseload and saw little of his wife and two sons. Sam, his four-year-old, especially needed his attention. Two years earlier, Scott and his wife were in Anguilla, enjoying a rare vacation, when their babysitter called. "I don't know what's going on," she told them. Sam had started flopping around on the floor. The couple packed their bags and flew home. The diagnosis was Tourette's syndrome and, more controversially among the family, perhaps autism as well. (Mary would later deny that Sam had the disorder.) A specialist told Scott that Sam might need to live at home for the rest of his life, a prognosis Scott refused to accept. Now, for him, every moment that he spent away from Sam felt like a missed opportunity to help him confront, or perhaps overcome, his disorders, even as the cost of therapy and specialists necessitated a full caseload.

Still, frustrated by the lack of information about the disaster in Kingston, Scott called B. R. Ladd, a criminal investigator he knew in the Roane County DA's office. How bad is it? Scott asked. Ladd used Scott's old nickname in response. "Studley," he said, "it's worse than you could ever think."

In 2008, there were approximately six hundred coal-fired power stations scattered throughout the United States, and the Kingston Fossil Plant operated much like any of them. Coal traveled up conveyor belts into the plant, where it was pulverized into a powder as fine as cosmetic makeup. Then the plant burned this powder to heat boiler tubes to a thousand degrees. The steam from these boilers drove a turbine that, in turn, spun generators thirty-six hundred times a minute. The process created not only alternating electrical current but also boiler slag—coarse chunks of melted coal—and coal ash, of which there are two types: fly ash, which is dustlike and "flies" in the air; and bottom ash, which has a texture akin to sand. In the U.S., coal-fired power stations produced one hundred and thirty-six million tons of such waste in 2008, and the Environmental Protection Agency (EPA) did not require power companies, like TVA, to store any of it with special care—by disposing of it in lined dump sites, say, to prevent the ash's toxins from leaching into the ground. Instead, in nearly all cases, power producers simply poured their coal ash into large holding ponds—typically bare holes in the earth—and then hoped that these ponds wouldn't leak or break. What distinguished the Kingston plant was that its pond failed, and did so catastrophically.

In the hours after the disaster, Ansol Clark and about fifty other men raced to clear the roads and find vehicles or people trapped beneath the coal slurry. The sludge released from the holding pond—overloaded and poorly constructed and maintained—included large earthenlike chunks, but most of it was thick and soupy. The bulldozers and track hoes onsite proved almost useless; they kept getting stuck in the slop. The workers, able to do little else until more equipment arrived, moved debris by hand at times.

A group of fifteen or so people, composed mostly of TVA and county employees, established a command center in a portable office trailer near the power plant. They needed to secure the site and identify any imminent dangers, and then restore power and test the toxicity of the ash. No one knew why the dike had failed, or if the coal ash contained severe hazards, or whether the county's drinking water was affected. The Coast Guard closed off the Emory River, while TVA rushed to sample water intakes near the power plant. Within days, teams would begin building a weir, or an underwater dam, six hundred and fifteen feet long, to prevent ash from migrating downstream.

Union representatives worked the phones. They needed bodies, a lot of them, to clear away and haul off the coal ash. Come to Kingston, they told nearly any truck driver or equipment operator who answered their calls. In the days and weeks ahead, nine hundred workers flocked to Roane County from Knoxville and from backwoods hamlets scattered throughout East Tennessee, but also from as far away as New York and Florida. They belonged to the International Brotherhood of Teamsters, to the International Union of Operating Engineers, to the Laborers' International Union. They loathed wearing a suit. They liked to hunt and fish, and almost all the locals rooted for the University of Tennessee Volunteers in football. They were family men, fathers, sons. One laborer, Ernest Hickman, sketched in his downtime. Danny Gouge, an equipment operator, had a little pet ape. At least one man cooked moonshine. Some attended church, some not, but they all bowed their heads when someone prayed aloud. Few had much schooling beyond high school. They wouldn't die rich, but they earned enough to raise their kids and pay their mortgages and get by generally well enough. Or they had until recently. Earlier that year, they'd watched as work dried up after the stock and housing markets imploded, bringing the global economy to its knees, and they had seen President George W. Bush on TV blame the fiasco, in part, on borrowers—that is, on the American public, on *them*. But that didn't really matter now. What mattered was that they needed to work.

At 4 p.m. on the day of the disaster, Ansol was assigned to drive a fuel truck. He spent the rest of the day gassing generators, portable lights, and vehicles. Following the spill, he worked for ninety-four days straight, driving a fuel truck in fourteen-to-eighteen-hour shifts. The hundreds of other men and women who took jobs at the cleanup site logged similar hours, with the work continuing day and night. Some guys slept in their trucks rather than drive home between shifts.

Adding to TVA's problems, the torrent of sludge had ripped out, twisted, and covered train tracks that led to the power plant. Then, in the early-morning hours after the dike failed, a train had inadvertently plowed into the ash-covered tracks and gotten stuck. The plant needed coal to generate power, but it couldn't receive any shipments until the train was moved and the workers laid new track. The plant had coal reserves, but they wouldn't last long.

Within a day or two of the disaster, about thirty amphibious track hoes, essential for clearing the wet coal-ash slurry, arrived on-site. These excavators had been disassembled for shipment, so the workers had to put them together before they could do much else. One relief was that they discovered no people or vehicles buried under the muck, a miracle by any measure. But it would take crews nearly four days to clear the roads and almost two weeks to remove and replace the mangled train tracks.

Ansol and Janie Clark's home sat on a grassy slope overlooking a busy highway, about half a mile from a Kroger shopping center, a Walgreens, and a fast-casual American restaurant called Aubrey's. At eleven o'clock on Christmas night, Ansol pulled into his driveway, having spent the entire day, and most of the past three, working in Kingston. He took off his boots in the garage, where he parked an old blue Mustang that mostly collected dust. He had coal ash on his face and in his ears and up his nose; it caked his work shirt and his vest. He would arrive home equally filthy every workday onward. He thought little of it.

Janie had stayed up waiting for him. She stood five foot two and had straight silver hair and luminous dark eyes, and she was impossibly sweet. She offered to bake cookies for new acquaintances and kept careful track of friends' birthdays, so that she could email or call them first thing the morning of. But, for all the kindness she showed friends, her world revolved around Ansol. Earlier that evening, her mother and her younger brother had come over and spent a few hours at the house. Each Christmas, they made oven-toasted sub sandwiches, Janie's specialty, and exchanged presents. This year, Ansol missed everything. That night, once he was in clean clothes, he sat in the living room with Janie and unwrapped his gifts as a ceramic Christmas tree glowed on a table near the door. He couldn't complain about missing the holiday, because he knew, as far as his employment went, the disaster was a godsend.

He took orders from TVA but technically worked for G-UB-MK Constructors ("GUBMK"), a contractor that was effectively TVA's private construction outfit. A few weeks earlier, he had been helping to dig a holding pond to store chemical slurry, but then an unusually wet winter halted all progress, hence his furlough. He guessed the cleanup project would keep him and the Teamsters busy for years, and he would be paid well for his time. In a good year, he might clear $55,000. At Kingston, he could easily earn six figures with overtime. The spill had caused serious environmental damage, to be sure. But with the money he'd make maybe he and Janie could finally save for retirement, or at least buy a new lawn mower. Janie told Ansol it felt as if they had won the lottery.

Ansol agreed. He liked that he was helping the residents of Roane County and that the job was close to home. Back when he drove a tractor trailer, he had hauled shipments as far as Montreal and California, and he always missed Knoxville on the long trips. He grew up outside town on a fifteen-acre farm with his mom, dad, and five siblings. As a boy, he spent his free time in the woods, climbing trees and running around with his beagles. Money was tight. His family butchered their own sheep, rabbits, and chickens, and their farmhouse had neither indoor plumbing nor electric heat. Ansol and his twin brother, Edsol, chopped firewood all summer to stock up for winter. Once a year, their father would sell some cattle for extra cash, then pile the family into a 1957 Chevrolet and strike out for the Great Smoky Mountains National Park, forty miles southeast of Knoxville. Ansol and his siblings swam in cold mountain streams, teeming with wild brook trout, until their skin turned blue. At night, they pitched old canvas tents at Chimneys, a campground along a little river high in the lush, green mountains.

The main reason Ansol liked working at Kingston, though, was that he could drive home to Janie every night. They'd met in high school after he returned from a short stint in the Navy during the Vietnam War. She sold tickets at a movie theater at the time. Nearly forty years later, they still adored each other. Janie, now a professional housekeeper, baked homemade blueberry muffins for Ansol to take to work every day, and she always had a hot meal waiting in the evenings: spaghetti, beef stew, pot roast, fried chicken, barbecue, greens. Her mother had cooked that way for her father, and she considered it a privilege to do the same for Ansol. She would tell friends that she'd never met a better man.

With Christmas approaching, national news outlets had been slow to respond to the Kingston disaster and dispatch reporters to East Tennessee. But by the time Ansol returned to work the morning after Christmas, newspaper reporters and TV crews had descended on the site. James Schean's daughter, a waitress, told a *New York Times* reporter that, though TVA had apologized for the disaster, it meant little to her. "I don't need your apologies," she explained. "I need information." She and other residents had pressed TVA to answer some important questions—about whether it planned to buy them new homes, and what caused the disaster, and whether the sludge was hazardous. But TVA had few answers.

On the night of December 26, Anne Thompson, a television journalist, reported from the disaster site for *NBC Nightly News*. Dressed in a lime-green coat and matching scarf, she explained to viewers that the volume of coal ash released was "enough to fill more than thirteen hundred Olympic-size swimming pools." The segment cut to Chris Copeland, the firefighter. "I've lost my past, my present, my future," he said, almost tearfully. A gray river of sludge loomed over his shoulder. "I've been hearing people talk and seeing reports about the heavy metals, the arsenic, the lead, the beryllium," he went on. His family had lived on the lake for thirty-seven years, he said, but he planned to send his wife and daughters to Florida until he felt sure the ash was safe.

Other residents shared Copeland's concerns about the sludge's potential toxicity, Thompson told viewers. But, she added, the federal government didn't regulate coal ash, so there was no independent data about the waste's hazards. Anda Ray, a TVA senior vice president, appeared on camera, sporting safety glasses and a white hard hat. "As far as the inert material in the ash," Ray said, "there's not a significant health effect." (A TVA spokesman told the *Times* the same thing.) TVA had found high levels of lead and thallium near the collapsed dike, but, allegedly, nowhere else. The drinking water was safe, Ray assured viewers. There was nothing to worry about.

A week or two after the Kingston disaster, Jim Scott drove his Ford Explorer out of Knoxville. The winter had been especially cold and wet, and the distant hills were gray and lonesome as he motored down I-40, past the strip malls, big-box stores, and truck stops of the west Knoxville suburbs. On the morning the dike collapsed, he knew that there was potential for a lawsuit against TVA, but state bar associations largely restrict attorneys from soliciting clients directly—they had to come to him. And they had already begun to.

Jim Scott

Scott's dad, Buddy, the former judge,

had cautioned him against getting involved in a suit against TVA. "Son, you can't beat that money," he warned. But Scott couldn't ignore Kingston, a community that had treated him with so much respect and kindness. He was also not inclined to turn down what seemed like easy-to-win, and potentially career-defining, cases. No earthquake or other act of God had caused the dike's collapse. Fault seemed to fall entirely on TVA. Still, Scott did worry about the cases' potential time demand. Loud noises debilitated Sam, his youngest, so on weekends, Scott drove him to an airport parking lot, in hopes he'd grow accustomed to the din of the jets roaring overhead. (Sam also ate next to nothing.) Scott didn't want to break the routine. Then again, he figured that, if he had to work and spend time away from his sons, he might as well help people.

As he approached Kingston, he tried to glimpse the spill site where I-40 crosses the Clinch River and overlooks the Kingston power station, but the view was limited and fleeting. He pulled off at the Midtown exit and drove toward the main route into the power plant. Within two minutes, he hit a roadblock. TVA has its own federally commissioned police force, and several officers told Scott that only residents were permitted through. That, or "you have to know somebody back here—by name," as one cigar-smoking local cop sternly told the driver of another vehicle. "Only family members are allowed back there."

Scott tried other routes, only to encounter more roadblocks. Irritated, he headed back to Knoxville. Surely, he had the right to see the disaster zone, he thought. He knew that, with a catastrophe like this, a large number of Roane County residents were bound to seek representation, and he wanted to see for himself what had happened in the likely event he took some of their cases. Over the next week, he learned that TVA and local police had kept out more than just lawyers. Officers briefly detained members of United Mountain Defense, an environmental group, after they tried to enter the disaster area and collect samples. Reporters were also largely denied entry after the national news crews cleared out. None of this exactly surprised Scott: footage of dying birds and fish flapping around in the muck wouldn't exactly help TVA's public-relations crisis.

• • •

Jeff Friedman was a fifty-two-year-old trial lawyer, with straight, neatly parted dark hair. He usually kept an overloaded schedule, but around Christmas and New Year's, his law practice typically enjoyed a short lull, so Friedman was having a quiet morning at home, outside Birmingham, Alabama, watching TV with his wife and their three children. Then his phone rang. It was Jeff Hagood, a college buddy from Knoxville who specialized in personal-injury law and white-collar criminal defense. Had he seen the news? Hagood asked.

"About the coal ash, right?" Friedman replied. He had caught some coverage on CNN.

Yes, Hagood said. He explained that some Roane County residents had approached him and a few other local attorneys about suing TVA over property damage. He might need Friedman's help. "How fast can you get to Knoxville?" Hagood asked.

Friedman had a warm voice and, even in casual conversation, spoke with few false starts, a gift even among veteran trial lawyers. He grew up in Clarksville, Tennessee, outside Nashville, and for his undergraduate degree, he'd attended the University of Tennessee at Knoxville, not far from the Kingston plant. After finishing law school at Samford University, he made a name for himself at Starnes & Atchison, a prominent Birmingham law firm. He guessed that, in his fourteen years there, he'd had a case in each of Alabama's sixty-seven counties, and a jury trial in about half of them. Friedman performed so well that, in the late 1990s, he left Starnes & Atchison and cofounded his own firm, Friedman, Dazzio, Zulanas & Bowling, expressly to focus on environmental cases of the exact sort now taking shape in Roane County.

He wasn't the type of lawyer to race to scenes of disaster. Still, he had disdained bullies ever since childhood. And TVA, he knew, was the consummate environmental bully, not just in Tennessee but throughout the Southeast. It regularly sparred with the EPA over federal Clean Air Act violations, and it was notorious for polluting rivers. What's more, since 2006, it had been battling the state of North Carolina in court over its emissions; the state's attorney general alleged that pollutants from TVA's coal-fired power plants traveled eastward, sickening residents and contributing to the premature deaths of some fourteen hundred people annually across the region.

Friedman's father, a prominent Jewish entrepreneur in Clarksville, had owned and operated a shopping center and several dry-cleaning businesses. He died of a heart attack before Jeff entered grade school, and the shopping center burned not long after that, but his mother somehow kept the family business going. Jeff grew up helping out, but he never shared his father's entrepreneurial ambitions. In his view, the most respected people in Clarksville were attorneys, so, from a young age, he intended to practice law. His father's early death, at age forty-three, inspired Jeff to try to live meaningfully, in the event that he didn't live long, either. The impulse added appeal to representing the Roane County landowners.

Friedman told Hagood that he would visit Kingston and meet with some of the property owners after the holidays. First, though, he wanted to see the destruction up close.

About two weeks after the dike failed, he drove two hundred and thirty miles from Birmingham and encountered the same roadblock that Jim Scott had. Undeterred, he wove up and down the Kingston back roads in a Ford pickup, searching for other entrances.

Over two or three days, Friedman found a few spots where he was able to drive close to the ocean of sludge without the police stopping him. He parked as close as he could to the muck, then, dressed in jeans and boots to look like a local, he eased down to the riverbank. In backyards that once overlooked the Emory River, beach chairs, patio tables, and bird feeders were surrounded by a stagnant gray slurry. A pontoon boat, ripped from its mooring, lay strewn atop the sludge. Friedman was amazed. *This kind of thing isn't supposed to happen*, he thought.

At the water's edge, he snapped photos with a digital camera. He hadn't litigated a case against TVA before, but he knew that it wouldn't be easy sledding. If TVA's legal department were a private law firm, it would be one of the largest in Tennessee. Its offices occupied a top floor in one of TVA's twin twelve-story office towers, which rose over downtown Knoxville. More daunting even than the agency's legal manpower was that TVA was not just a standard power company, like Duke Energy or Pacific Gas & Electric. Created in 1933, as part of the New Deal, TVA was, for almost a quarter of a century, the single-most ambitious public-works project in the world. At the height of the Great Depression, it brought electricity to the Tennessee Valley, a rural, forty-one-thousand-square-mile region of three million people, and, in doing so, it transformed the poor countryside into the nation's energy lab.

Friedman knew that, decades later, TVA still held tremendous sway in the South. In East Tennessee it was almost a religion, as much for the ten thousand people it employed as for its cheap power. There was no chance, Friedman felt sure, as he slogged through the slurry back to his truck, that TVA would readily admit to having mismanaged its coal waste. TVA operated twenty-nine hydroelectric dams, one pumped-storage plant, and three nuclear power plants, but 60 percent of its power came from its ten active coal-fired power stations. TVA couldn't afford to stop burning coal, no matter how much flak it caught for its waste.

More problematic for Friedman, TVA was almost legally untouchable. In the U.S., federal agencies, such as TVA, are shielded from most private lawsuits under sovereign immunity, a doctrine derived from English common law that's rooted in the idea that the state cannot commit a legal wrong. In most instances, the U.S. government and its agencies must consent to be sued. In practice, this meant that, with few exceptions, plaintiffs and their attorneys could neither seek punitive damages from TVA nor get a jury trial against it. Friedman would have to convince a judge to make an exception in both regards, and TVA's famously stubborn, hubristic legal department promised to make neither easy.

On a map, the Tennessee River system resembles a crooked, child-drawn smile. The headwaters form six thousand feet above sea level, in the emerald virgin forests of the Great Smoky and Unaka Mountains, along the Eastern Continental Divide—the ancestral home of the Cherokee people. Cold streams drain these weather-worn mountains, which are older than the rings of Saturn, and race through deep, wild gorges, cut away over the course of some three hundred million years. The streams collect hundreds of tributaries as they fall through the timbered mountains, gathering strength and volume, before they tangle to form the Holston River and the French Broad. Once out of the mountains, the two tributaries meet at Knoxville, to create the Tennessee—the Big Tennessee—and then take in the Little Tennessee and the Clinch, the latter at Kingston. The fat river pushes southward through the Tennessee

Valley, a geological trough that measures fifty-five miles wide at spots and runs north to south through East Tennessee, with the Cumberland Mountains to the west and the loftier Blue Ridge to the east. Quiet woods line the riverbank. Once past Chattanooga, the Tennessee abandons its southern trajectory and veers curiously westward, forming a giant crescent that spans the upper fifth of Alabama. The river keeps veering until it flows northward. After kissing the state of Mississippi, it slides into the flat red farmlands of West Tennessee, running parallel to but in the opposite direction of the Mississippi River, one hundred miles to the west. In Paducah, Kentucky, the Tennessee terminates into the Ohio, at almost the exact same latitude of its headwaters, four hundred miles due east, high in the mountains. Then the Ohio marries the Mississippi and heads to the Gulf.

In the 1770s, when the first European settlers ventured into the Tennessee Valley, they thought they had stumbled into paradise, into a land of endless abundance. Cool springs and strawberry fields dotted the landscape, and thick hardwood forests teemed with elk, black bear, turkey, and deer. But just as communities took shape and began to grow in this wilderness, the Civil War made a wasteland of the valley, and Reconstruction and the decades that followed brought few improvements. In the mountains, families survived in crude shacks clustered along creek bottoms or hillsides, walls plastered with newspaper and flour paste to keep out winter's cold. Relatives slept three or four to a bed. Babies died of "summer complaint"—diarrhea or heat exposure or some combination of both. People caught typhoid from drinking bad water. Malaria was endemic. Three-quarters of homes lacked indoor plumbing. The Tennessee River, wild and almost unnavigable, regularly brought catastrophe. In 1867, the river rose fifty-eight feet above its normal level, drowning the city of Chattanooga in eight feet of water and leaving bodies littering the streets. Industry was almost nonexistent outside a few cities. The timberlands were overcut. Six million acres of farmland were eroded. By the time the stock market crashed in 1929, the typical person in the valley earned $317 a year, about 65 percent less than the national average at the time and the equivalent of about $6,000 in 2024 dollars when adjusted for inflation.

The Tennessee Valley might have remained mired in poverty, doomed to lag behind the rest of the nation, had Franklin D. Roosevelt not contracted polio. Beginning in 1924, Roosevelt, reared in New York, began making regular trips to Warm Springs, Georgia, for treatment, and he witnessed firsthand the valley's destitution as he traveled through the Southeast. The region's crushing poverty challenged whether a democracy could care for its people, and whether the American experiment had vigor and vitality.

After Roosevelt won the presidency in 1932, he raced to prove that democracy could meet the South's needs, as the region reeled from the Great Depression. In April 1933, while visiting Muscle Shoals, Alabama, Roosevelt called on Congress to create the Tennessee Valley Authority, which he described as "a corporation clothed with the power of Government but possessed of the flexibility and initiative of a private enterprise." Roosevelt's expansive vision drew on the urban-planning ideas pioneered by Alfred E. Smith, his predecessor as New York governor, who pushed for the creation of the Port of New York Authority and the New York Power Authority. Roosevelt, in his message to Congress, argued that TVA, a cornerstone of his New Deal public-works program, should have the power to oversee planning and development not just in a single state, like New York, but throughout the entire Tennessee Valley region—to prevent flooding and soil erosion and to conserve and develop the natural resources "for the general social and economic welfare of the Nation."

A month after Roosevelt's Muscle Shoals speech, Congress passed the TVA Act of 1933, officially creating the agency. And, with FDR's backing, TVA's early leaders did exceptional work on a grand scale. In 1933, only 3 percent of farms in the valley had electricity. Within two decades, about 70 percent of them would, thanks to TVA. To achieve this, it employed an army of some forty thousand workers to dam and control the Tennessee River and its tributaries, which spanned an area roughly equal in size to Cuba. This army—composed of men from across the valley, almost all in desperate need of employment, and almost all white*—worked at an incredible clip, completing sixteen

* During the first several decades of TVA's existence, Black workers seldom made up more than 10 percent of TVA's labor force. In 1935, the NAACP's magazine, *The Crisis*, wrote of TVA jobsites, "For the most part skilled work is denied Negro workers."

dams and seizing control of ten others in about a decade. TVA finished twenty-three more dams in the years to come, bringing its total fleet to twenty-nine hydroelectric facilities and twenty non-power-producing impoundments.

These dams radically changed the region's topography, bloating the rivers of the valley to create more than six hundred thousand acres of new lakes and reservoirs and eleven thousand miles of new shoreline. There are fewer miles of shoreline around the Great Lakes than in the Tennessee Valley. Before the waters rose, TVA used eminent domain to force out twenty thousand families whose homesteads would disappear beneath the rising reservoirs; their stories of losing their land would become part of Southern folklore. Despite whatever ill-will these evictions engendered, TVA won ecstatic praise in the South and beyond. The TVA dams "should make one prouder to be an American," the critic Lewis Mumford wrote in *The New Yorker* in 1941. The dams—bold, unadorned Art Deco giants—recalled the Pyramids of Egypt in their scope, Mumford added. But whereas the ancient tombs grew out of slavery and celebrated death, TVA's colossi were "produced by free labor to create energy and life for the people of the United States." The dams

TVA's Norris Dam, circa 1936, near Andersonville, Tennessee

bore no bronze tablet listing the names of engineers or architects or the TVA board; instead, they featured a simple inscription: BUILT FOR THE PEOPLE OF THE UNITED STATES. "Here is modern architecture at its mightiest and its best," Mumford concluded his review. "The Pharaohs did not do any better."

The folk singer Pete Seeger went further, recording a song about Roosevelt's Southern experiment, in which he sang, "We saw democracy's future when we built TVA." Indeed, TVA's early leaders championed "grassroots democracy," or the belief that the government should actively engage with and measurably improve the lives of its lowliest citizens. TVA aimed not just to electrify the valley but also to uplift, educate, and empower its people. It launched a mobile-library service that loaned tens of thousands of books. It leased lands around its lakes to state and county parks departments. It created thirteen thousand demonstration farms, where it taught locals how to maximize crop yields and prevent soil erosion. It distributed hundreds of millions of seedlings. It started a ceramics laboratory. It built bunkhouses where at night its dam builders played Ping-Pong, boxed, and watched movies. And, in perhaps the purest manifestation of TVA's utopian vision for the South, it built a planned community, called Norris, which included a school, a drugstore, a library, a recreation building, and comely homes with stone chimneys and cedar shingles.

As TVA reshaped the Tennessee Valley, it became not only emblematic of good, benevolent government but also core to democracy's defense. During the Second World War, TVA outproduced every other U.S. power system, supplying a tenth of the electricity used by the nation's defense industries, electricity that helped to manufacture dive-bombers and to produce the uranium fuel for the atomic bomb dropped on Hiroshima. TVA later became, and remains, the federal government's sole producer of tritium, a radioactive isotope that's a critical component of every warhead in the U.S. nuclear arsenal.

The cheap, abundant power that TVA generated with its dams spurred industry that benefited the valley. Per capita income rose from about 45 percent of the national average in 1933 to roughly 60 percent less than two decades later. For TVA, the trouble was that, after the Second World War, it needed more electricity than its dams could produce. This partly owed to several sprawling uranium-enrichment facilities that the federal government had built in Oak Ridge, Tennessee, as part of the Manhattan Project, for which TVA supplied power. The Cold War and the Korean War spiked demand for the bomb fuel produced in Oak Ridge, and the need for TVA electricity rose accordingly.

In short order, TVA constructed eleven of the world's largest, most technologically advanced coal-fired power plants throughout Alabama, Tennessee, and Kentucky. (It acquired a twelfth, from the Army Corps of Engineers, but shut it down in 1966.) Just three of these coal-fired power stations produced more electricity than all twenty-nine of TVA's hydroelectric dams. But these new plants were expensive to build. Republicans in Congress, incensed over the billions in appropriations that TVA needed for construction, repeatedly withheld public funds from the agency, never mind that roughly half of TVA's power went to the federal government's bomb-making facilities in Oak Ridge. In 1959, Congress agreed to let TVA, desperate for cash, issue bonds and self-finance its operations through electricity sales. This decision meant that TVA no longer needed taxpayer dollars, but this change—this grave compromise—put profits, instead of the public interest, at the center of its concerns for the first time.

As TVA's coal-fired power plants came online, it gradually lost interest in or outright abandoned its other efforts. The library service, the ceramics laboratory, the demonstration farms: all soon gone. Contributing to this shift, several early TVA leaders—namely the idealistic Arthur E. Morgan, the agency's first chairman and the former president of Antioch College, "the most liberal of liberal arts colleges," *The New York Times Magazine* would later call it—had left by then, and TVA's new leadership struggled to replicate the successes of the FDR era. Instead, they turned TVA into an electricity behemoth.

In the mid-1950s, TVA, already the nation's largest power system by output, became the country's largest coal consumer, and the skies over the valley darkened as proof. In Chattanooga, soot blackened men's white shirt collars. In Nashville, boys rode bikes with handkerchiefs tied over their faces to prevent choking on coal smog. On the Cumberland Plateau, pine trees twenty miles from the nearest TVA power plant lost their color. In northeast Alabama, TVA's Widows Creek Fossil Plant sprayed two counties with sulfurous smog in concentrations "that most private industry would not dare," *The Nashville Tennessean* reported in 1967. Three years later, the federal government ranked three Tennessee cities—Nashville, Chattanooga, and Knoxville—as having some of the country's worst air quality. But, of all the towns forced to endure TVA's pollution, few had it worse than the little hamlet of Kingston.

In the months following the Kingston disaster, the cleanup went on day and night, seven days a week. Some evenings the temperature dropped to single digits and hardly rose by the time Ansol Clark turned off the interstate in the predawn darkness. His shift started at five o'clock, an hour before most of the other day-shift workers'. When he pulled into the parking lot, the air would sparkle in his truck headlights—owing, he later learned, to fine metal particles suspended in the dust.

The cleanup workers were racing to dredge more than four million tons of fly ash from the Emory River, partly so that it could be reopened, partly to prevent ash from migrating downriver. The night crew always left Ansol's fuel truck at the bottom of a hill near the parking lot. TVA had set up six or seven mobile offices a short walk from the jobsite. The workers called the area Trailer City. After Ansol poured a cup of coffee, signed some paperwork, and collected the fuel logs from one of the temporary offices, he would walk down the hill, crank the thunderous engine, turn on the headlights, and then drive through a fence into the exclusion zone, ground zero of the disaster.

It was the mouth of some kind of hell. Mounds of ash towered and rolled on in every direction. It was a world of lifeless gray, droning motors, and muck and grit—grit in your mouth and in your eyes and in your ears. Most of the ash was soupy. It swallowed men to the knees and to the waist, but big chunks of ash stood as tall as two-story homes. Vehicles tipped and rolled without warning trying to drive over the stuff. The air tasted like aluminum foil. Geese and coyotes writhed around dying in the mess.

In the frigid blackness, Ansol and a partner sloshed and stomped through the sludge, with only an hour and a half to pump some fifteen hundred gallons of diesel fuel into dozens of track hoes, bulldozers, and articulated dump trucks. Whenever Ansol reached a vehicle, his partner would jump out and pull the fuel hose through the muck and unspool it from a reel. Once the vehicle was filled, Ansol would climb out and hold the fuel hose with an absorbent rag to keep it from gunking up as they reeled it back in.

As Ansol and his partner rushed, the other day-shift workers—a mix of operators, laborers, and truck drivers—usually met for a safety meeting at a home that TVA bought after the disaster, which now served as a makeshift office for TVA staff and for employees of Jacobs Engineering, a California-based construction and environmental-cleanup firm. Hired by TVA in February 2009, Jacobs Engineering was one of the twenty largest U.S. government contractors, generating more than $11 billion in annual revenue and employing some fifty-three thousand people. The company, which was founded in 1947, got its start mining and recovering potash, a potassium-rich salt used to make fertilizer. But over the years it had transformed into a do-it-all construction and engineering firm. It regularly won multimillion-dollar contracts from the U.S. Army and NASA, and it had worked for the government of Jordan. The company's conservative, Brooklyn-born founder, Joseph Jacobs, once wrote that "environmentalists, in their elitist arrogance, often do more harm than good." Yet his company earned billions of dollars remediating environmental disasters. It had cleaned up radioactive waste at Department of Energy sites in at least ten states, including Tennessee, and it responded to environmental emergencies with, and wrote reports for, the EPA. The Kingston cleanup, Jacobs's first major project for TVA, expanded the company's footprint in East Tennessee considerably. Based on the terms of its contract, Jacobs would oversee safety at the site on a day-to-day basis, while TVA and the EPA oversaw the cleanup more broadly. Jacobs, for its efforts, would receive almost $64 million by the project's end, which TVA expected to take years. The estimated cost of the entire cleanup: $1.2 billion.

Jacobs had about a dozen employees at Kingston. At the morning safety meetings, Tom Bock, a top Jacobs safety officer, often addressed the cleanup workers from a wooden deck of the repurposed home.* He was thirty-something, with close-cropped hair, glasses, and a broad forehead. On numerous occasions, he told the group that they could eat a

* Bock declined an interview request in 2019, and the author's subsequent attempts to reach him were unsuccessful.

pound of fly ash—the dusty component of coal ash that "flies"—each day and be fine. It was that safe. Bock repeated the spiel often enough that it became something of a joke among the workers: *Don't worry, man, you can eat a pound of ash a day!*

The workers, kidding aside, trusted Bock. He was a conservative family man. He lived in the Knoxville suburbs and, in the years to come, would share Ronald Reagan speeches and church-sermon clips on social media. He held a degree in safety technology from Marshall University, in West Virginia, and had previously worked for a Jacobs subsidiary, Bechtel Jacobs, at the demolition site of the K-25 Gaseous Diffusion Plant, an Oak Ridge facility built during the Manhattan Project to enrich uranium-235 for atomic weapons. That Bock had overseen site safety at K-25 lent him credibility, since it was the sort of place, one might assume, where lax protective protocols weren't tolerated, given the risk of radioactive exposure.

At Kingston, Bock led new-hire orientation in a makeshift classroom in an office trailer. Trust me, he reassured the new hires. I want to protect myself as much as you do. "I've got a wife and kids that depend on my income, too," he once put it. If there was a hazard, he would take care of it, if not for his sake then for his family's. TVA also insisted that the coal ash posed no legitimate health concerns, stating on its website that thousands, and eventually hundreds of thousands, of air-quality tests had all fallen within the EPA's acceptable safety limits. TVA attributed this feat to "aggressive dust suppression."

About two months after the disaster, Billy Isley, a thirty-five-year-old truck driver from LaFollette, Tennessee, took a job at Kingston. He lifted weights five days a week; loved heavy metal, especially Metallica; and had a tattoo of an eagle on his arm. Some guys thought he was an asshole, since he talked openly and loudly if he thought another worker screwed up or slacked on the job, but Ansol Clark liked him immediately. Each morning, they chatted as Ansol fueled up Isley's rig. Isley drove what was known as a water truck, a vehicle equipped with a large water cannon for spraying down fly ash that could turn dusty and blow into the air. As many as eighteen of these trucks operated at Kingston. The Jacobs Engineering team said that, by keeping the ground wet, the trucks stopped fly ash from migrating off-site, partly to avoid upsetting the community further. Jacobs staff instructed truck drivers to rumble across the jobsite slowly, to avoid flare-ups. "Dust suppression is EVERYONE'S responsibility," a Jacobs manager wrote in an email to TVA project leaders and contractors.

One day, though, Isley mentioned to Ansol that a Jacobs staffer had asked him to spray down an area near the Emory River that was close to some stationary monitors that sampled the air for hazards. Isley had also hosed off some trees dusted with fly ash. The orders came from Jacobs,* but Isley suspected they originated elsewhere: TVA. Isley told Ansol that the whole thing struck him as odd. Tom Bock had told the workers that the coal ash was basically innocuous. A TVA spokeswoman had said much the same shortly after the disaster, telling reporters that, for the ash to cause harm, "you'd have to eat it. You have to get it in your body." Even the EPA's on-scene coordinator, Leo Francendese, had described fly ash as an irritant at worst. "It's primarily sand," he explained during a public meeting. So why bother spraying around the monitors, then? Isley asked Ansol.

Knoxville is a famously ugly town, a fact that residents have come to embrace with a certain degree of contrarian civic pride. T-shirts bearing the words KEEP KNOXVILLE SCRUFFY caught on for a while. Kingston Pike, the main commercial corridor, has done much to win the city its unsightly reputation. The road runs from the outskirts of downtown Knoxville to Kingston, forty miles west, loosely following an old Cherokee trail, a route now cluttered with car dealerships, churches, fast-food places, and acres upon acres of mostly underused parking lots.

Jim Scott's office occupied a low-slung brick building on Kingston Pike, next to an Old Time Pottery and a Burlington Coat Factory. He shared the space with his four partners and his father, Buddy, who'd retired in 2005, around the time he turned seventy, but he continued to help Jim and his sisters with cases. Early each weekday morning, Buddy, white-haired and pink-cheeked, arrived promptly in his old maroon Buick Regal, sporting a suit. One morning, Jim, after working late the night prior, went for a seven-mile jog. He showed up at the office shortly before noon, sweaty and still in his running clothes. "How

* Jacobs denies that its staff directed the workers' activities on the jobsite.

the fuck do you expect to run a law office coming in here at eleven-thirty in the morning?" Buddy asked. "Dad," Jim snapped, "I worked till eight-thirty mediating a case for $900,000. How much fucking money did you bring in?" Jim's point was clear: he was the boss now.

Generally, though, Jim and Buddy got along. Jim respected his father. When Jim was a kid, Buddy often drove him to pick up one of his friends, whom everyone called Spoon, in a poor, mostly Black section of Oak Ridge—not something that every white father would do in the 1970s in rural Tennessee. Decades later, Spoon still talked about how Buddy and Jim's mother, Mildred, welcomed him into their home and treated him with genuine kindness. When presiding over cases, Buddy, who was a longtime Democrat—as was Jim—tended to side with individuals over companies, especially in workplace-injury suits. Buddy seemed to believe that, with limited job opportunities in the area, it was a serious matter whenever a worker got hurt, and he awarded injured persons as much money as he was able. Or at least many defense attorneys held that opinion. "He would hammer us," one lawyer recalled. Jim admired his old man for that.

In the months after the Kingston disaster, Jim met with dozens of Roane County residents at his office. Before he could file complaints against TVA on their behalf—and then hope that a judge would let the cases proceed, despite TVA's immunity—he needed to know exactly how the blowout had wrecked their properties and how much money they hoped to recover in damages. He listened as they explained how the black tide of ash had flooded their waterfronts, ripped apart their boat slips, poured into their garages, and inundated their swimming pools. Many were middle-class folks who, without his help, might never recover.

One client, a middle-aged statistician named James Crichton, owned a riverfront home a mile south of the Kingston Fossil Plant. A few months before the disaster, Crichton had listed the property for sale. After coal ash deluged the waterfront, he'd expected TVA to buy his property. By April 2009, TVA had spent some $20 million acquiring seventy-one properties affected by the disaster (including the home of Chris Copeland, the firefighter). It would buy at least one hundred and eight more properties in the months to come. But far more locals wanted a buyout than were offered one. TVA refused to buy homes as far downriver as Crichton's. In rejection letters to residents, TVA stated that, based on its review, "we have found no reason for TVA to purchase your property or offer compensation for any diminished value of your property." That left Crichton stuck with a home he hadn't even wanted before the disaster, much less now.

"You've got a case here," Scott told Crichton, as they sat in his office, "a good, legitimate case, because you're not going to be able to sell your house and get what you want for it."

Crichton, struck by Scott's confidence, explained that he hoped for a settlement of at least $100,000, roughly equal to his equity in the property. No, Scott said. "We're going for $250,000," the home's value had the spill never happened—or the 2008 housing and financial crisis, for that matter. Crichton shrugged: "Whatever you think."

After work, Scott often jogged or rode his bike along his neighborhood greenway to keep his high blood pressure in check. His dad had suffered his first heart attack at thirty-seven, and Scott didn't want to take after the judge in that regard. He followed the greenway for miles, passing grassy fields along the Tennessee River. Inevitably, as he pedaled or ran, his thoughts turned to the tsunami of sludge—how it had enveloped the countryside that cold December morning, swallowing land where his clients had raised kids, launched fireworks, thrown block parties. It angered him. But something that Crichton had told him, unrelated to property damage, nagged at him the most.

A few months after the disaster, Crichton had waded waist-deep into the Clinch River to free a tree branch stuck under his dock. He told Scott that he hurried out as soon as he freed the limb. Strangely, though, within a few hours, he felt pain in his chest, and he struggled to breathe. Scott assumed that, as with any industrial waste, a person would be ill-advised to handle, much less wade through, coal ash. This seemed different. Crichton compared the sensation to being stunned, shocked even. He went to the hospital, where doctors assured him that a brief exposure to coal ash couldn't have caused such a reaction, and Crichton felt fine the following morning. Still, the episode rattled him, as it did Scott after he heard the story.

In the summer and fall of 2009, Scott happened to be in Roane County often, dealing with a few minor cases. Like most personal-injury attorneys, he worked on a contingency-fee basis, earning money only when he won or settled a case. He usually relied on small suits to keep cash flowing in, while larger ones, like the coal-ash cases, came together. Following the spill, TVA held several public meetings to address residents' concerns over the coal ash. Scott didn't attend any of them, to avoid appearing as if he were soliciting clients, but he kept tabs on what was happening.

On the evening of October 1, 2009, TVA held a public meeting at the First Baptist Church in Kingston. At previous such events, residents had packed into gymnasiums and community centers to berate TVA executives; some held signs reading CLEAN COAL IS A MYTH and CLEAN COAL? Now, nine months after the disaster, the fifty or so people who filed into the church made no such commotion, but tensions nonetheless ran high, with the cleanup still years from completion.

The meeting was held in the church's family center, a multipurpose space that doubled as a gym and a banquet hall. Anda Ray, of TVA, was among a handful of TVA, EPA, and state officials who sat behind a table at the front of the beige-walled room. At a little past six o'clock, Ray, who was in her early fifties, greeted the crowd. Though she had promised in several newscasts in the spill's immediate aftermath that coal ash was safe, she now acknowledged, albeit elliptically, the material's potential dangers. Since the cleanup crews were "working right in the ash," she said, their health was a "top priority." She admitted that she checked her boots and vehicle for coal ash when she arrived home each night. That way, she wouldn't track the material inside.

Kingston residents were already troubled about the coal ash's potential dangers, and Ray's admissions ignited tempers. "We've been exposed to this for decades," one local told Ray during the night's public-comment period. "Some of us are terrified of cancer." Another man complained that no single government agency seemed to be overseeing the cleanup and asked Ray who was ultimately in charge. "The president of the United States," she replied curtly, sparking indignant chuffs and eye rolls throughout the audience.

For Kingston locals, the meeting, and the coal-ash disaster in general, compounded decades of resentment toward the agency. It had started in the 1950s, when TVA forced hundreds of families to relocate when it "eminent-domained the shit" out of Roane County, as one local put it, to build the Melton Hill Dam, Watts Bar Lake, and the greatest nuisance of all, the Kingston Fossil Plant.

In 1956, two years after the plant opened, TVA boasted that it used "as much water as the city of New York" and that its "boilers consume a 50-ton carload of coal in six minutes." What TVA kept quiet was that each day the plant also pumped four hundred and fifty tons of fly ash and seven hundred tons of sulfur dioxide, the chief pollutant in acid rain, over the community and surrounding countryside. In Kingston, ash settled over homes, blew through clotheslines, and blanketed rivers and streams. Trees withered, grew discolored, and lost their leaves. In May 1957, a five-year-old boy was hospitalized and nearly died after inhaling sulfur fumes while playing outside his home in Kingston. By 1973, the plant there and TVA's other coal-fired facilities contributed 53 percent of all toxic sulfur-dioxide emissions in the southeastern U.S. and 14 percent of all such emissions nationwide, though its customers comprised less than 1 percent of the population.

Before the coal-ash disaster, TVA had either ignored or half-heartedly addressed complaints about its pollution—though, in internal reports, it speculated that public pressure would eventually force it to control its emissions. For decades, the president and Congress, both officially tasked with overseeing TVA, did little to intervene and let the agency more or less operate autonomously, since it no longer depended on federal funds. But, after the Kingston disaster, legislators threatened to step in.

In a congressional hearing days after the spill, California senator Barbara Boxer had blasted TVA, not only for its disastrous handling of coal ash but also for fighting the EPA over orders to reduce its pollution. TVA had recently agreed, albeit reluctantly, to install emission-cleaning devices, known as scrubbers, at its Kingston and Bull Run facilities, after two years fighting in court with the state of North Carolina over whether its pollutants sickened its residents. The scrubbers weren't enough. The Kingston disaster, Boxer said, highlighted the need for stricter coal-ash regulations broadly, and for closer oversight of TVA specifically. "You have got to clean up your act there, literally," she told TVA's chief executive, Tom Kilgore. Underscoring her point, a day after the hearing, ten thousand gallons of coal sludge broke from an impoundment at TVA's Widows Creek Fossil Plant, in Alabama.

The congressional lashing put pressure on TVA leadership to clean up its billion gallons of coal sludge as quickly and with as little fanfare

Janie and Ansol Clark outside their home, in Knoxville

as possible. And they needed to keep Roane County residents happy in the process. TVA couldn't risk locals whining to the newspapers or to their local representatives if the cleanup wasn't going as they thought it should. "We recognize there's a trust issue," Anda Ray conceded to the crowd that October evening. But she swore that TVA would take every step to make things right, no matter how drastic.

On a living-room shelf, Janie Clark kept a few framed photographs on display. One was of her and her son, Bergan, around the time he turned two. Dressed in a blue Superman T-shirt, he sits smiling on a tricycle as Janie crouches and hugs him. She's still a young woman. Thirty-two, probably. Her straight dark hair falls past her shoulders. A warm, delighted smile lights her face. Nearby on the shelf, another framed photo, taken around the same time as the first, showed Ansol sitting in a railroad car, dressed in a shirt unbuttoned at the neck. The light behind him is warm and bright, with a summer ease to it. He's young, too. Long, shaggy hair covers his ears and flops down his forehead. His lips are slightly parted, as if he's beginning to grin. These snapshots captured a time in Janie's life that she liked to think about most, a time that divided her old life from the one she knew now.

Janie was born in Knoxville in 1952, and grew up in a white, vinyl-sided home in a working-class community north of downtown called

Alice Bell. Her parents had married less than a year before her birth. Janie never asked how they met, and no one ever told her. Her mother, Margaret, was seventeen the day of her wedding. Her dad, Joe, was fifty-one. The age gap was significant but not scandalous. In that era in southern Appalachia generally, and in Tennessee specifically, young women customarily married before they turned eighteen, and they not infrequently wed much older men. A Baptist reverend performed the couple's ceremony.

Janie's father was thin and had straight black hair and deep-set cheeks. He worked for Southern Railway, moving locomotives in and out of a train yard. Janie later learned that, owing to his advanced age, he never expected to have children, and he treated her as if she were a tiny, brilliant miracle. He read to her, held her hand on walks, and never raised his voice in anger toward her. Once, when Janie was a toddler, she stuffed the family cat into a drawer, where, terrified, it pooped on the deed to the family home and other important documents. Her father just laughed. Most children in the neighborhood walked to school together each morning. But when Janie reached school age, her father insisted that he drive her the few blocks in his old Studebaker. He didn't want her feet to touch the ground, she would recall to friends later. Whenever he arrived home from work or from running an errand, he would remove his hat as soon as he spotted Janie, as if she were a lady of great distinction, then he would throw open his arms and wrap her in a hug. She would never forget that.

Janie's mother hailed from Valley Creek, Tennessee, a tiny mining settlement in the mountains near the Kentucky border. One evening, in March 1955, when Janie was two and a half years old, her mother had an awful dream. In it, she tried to phone her parents—Janie's grandparents—back home in Valley Creek. But the line broke. "I don't know why I was calling them," she later told *The Knoxville News Sentinel*. But she woke from the dream frightened, certain something bad had happened, and it had.

Her parents' home sat in a narrow valley, and at the head of this valley stood a slate dam—a jumble of rocks, twenty yards high and fifty yards thick, that had been discarded by coal miners. Over several decades, a lake had grown behind the improvised dam, and that spring a heavy rain filled it to the brim. Water spilled over the rocks into the valley. Then, one March morning, the dam burst. A wall of water blasted through the rock heap and traveled six miles down the valley, flipping cars, downing telephone lines, drowning or carrying off everything. Four houses stood in the wave's path. One belonged to Margaret's parents, who lived there with her younger siblings. The family tried to flee, but the surge swept away Margaret's eight-year-old sister, Carolyn—Janie's aunt. Janie's grandmother, age forty, held tight to her two-year-old daughter, Peggy, as she ran. But the thundering current knocked down and dragged away the pair, ripping the toddler away from her mother. The family's barn, livestock, personal belongings—all gone in the roar.

The lake behind the failed dam drained within forty minutes. Once the water receded, a bystander found Janie's grandmother two hundred yards from where the family home had stood. Alive but barely conscious, she was pinned beneath debris and logs. Carolyn drowned after the water trapped her in a tree. Peggy's body remained missing for nearly a full day before Janie's grandfather found her small corpse under a mound of slate. Janie's grandmother later said that the loss of her daughters and the head injuries she sustained left her mentally unwell and unable to function fully.

Newspapers across the state carried stories about the disaster. Two days afterward, the family memorialized the girls in a double service at the Valley Creek Baptist Church. Janie's parents drove up from Knoxville and brought her along. The two girls, each wearing a dress and jacket, looked like angels lying next to each other in their open caskets. Years passed before Janie realized that, had her mother not married her father and moved to Knoxville, she might have easily died, too.

As dreadful as the dam disaster was, the biggest blow to Janie came eleven years later, in 1966. Her family was at home one spring evening when her father stepped outside to catch his breath. He had been forced to retire, having damaged his lungs inhaling dust and exhaust in the train yard where he worked. He often strained to breathe, but now, standing on the front porch, he gasped and gripped his chest. The family didn't own a telephone, so Janie sprinted to a neighbor's house and begged them to call an ambulance.

Her father was taken to St. Mary's Hospital, three miles away, where he declined over six long days before dying of heart failure. He was sixty-five years old. The family held a funeral two days later at Woodlawn Cemetery, on Knoxville's south side. Janie was in eighth grade. Her father's headstone, flat and small, bore the inscription "Beloved Father," and he was.

For Janie, not yet fourteen at the time, it was disorienting to think that one moment someone she loved dearly could be there, then the next moment that person could be gone. Her relationship with her dad had given her confidence, rooted her in love and grace. Now the source of all her assurance had disappeared.

The family had almost no money, and Janie's mother, thirty-one by then, had no marketable skills. But even if she'd landed a job, she didn't have a driver's license or an easy way to get to work. Years later, Janie and her brother, eight years younger, would consider it something of a miracle that the three of them survived. Janie's best explanation was that they ate a lot of canned soup.

Janie learned to fend for herself. In high school, she took a job at the Tennessee Theatre, an ornate movie palace on Gay Street, downtown Knoxville's main thoroughfare. It had a gold-painted ceiling, red velvet curtains, a Wurlitzer organ, and French-style chandeliers, but it was long faded from its Jazz Age heyday. Janie loved it all the same.

She didn't have a car, so she walked two miles to catch a bus downtown for her shifts. At first, she sold popcorn and candy, then was promoted to the ticket booth. Downtown Knoxville had been in decline since she was in diapers, if not before, mostly owing to white flight and poor city leadership. Smoke and soot hung in the air, and litter blew through alleyways. Cigarette butts collected on the sidewalks. When President Lyndon Johnson had visited Knoxville a few years earlier, he said that the city's Black slum held the worst poverty he'd seen in the United States. By the late 1960s, state and federal employees, including TVA staffers, were among the few professionals who regularly ventured downtown. Janie didn't mind. Alone in the box office for hours, she chatted with passersby or commuters waiting for the bus. The Ku Klux Klan marched down Gay Street one day, which frightened and sickened her, but most people were nice and chatty in a familiar, small-town way.

To keep her job at the theater, Janie enrolled in Knoxville Evening High School, a public outpost that held night courses in an aged, three-story brick building. Veterans, working mothers, and recent immigrants made up the student body, as did young kids like Janie who worked daytime shifts. During breaks between classes, students bought sodas and snacks from vending machines and stood outside and smoked or talked. One classmate who didn't smoke, and who drew Janie's attention, was a strong, clean-cut guy with a wide smile and a big blocky head: Ansol Clark.

Ansol was fresh out of the Navy, having spent ten months in Hawaii, giving tours of the USS *Arizona*, a battleship that the Japanese had sunk during the attack on Pearl Harbor, in 1941. Girls liked him, Janie noticed, and she understood why. Strong, well traveled, gainfully employed: he commanded respect. He'd dropped out of school to serve, and now back home, he wanted to earn a few missing credits in order to graduate. Janie sat next to him in class. The trouble was that another girl did too, an attractive one. "I was nothing outstanding," Janie later recalled. But, whereas the other girl fawned over Ansol, telling him he looked handsome, Janie teased him and jokingly copied answers off his assignments. Her humor had an effect.

On their first date, he picked her up in his white Dodge Charger and drove her to Pizza Palace, a drive-in parlor a few miles from downtown. They ordered a pie and sat together without saying much. Ansol didn't fill gaps in conversation with empty chitchat, Janie would learn. If he had something to say, he said it. If he didn't, he didn't. Still, as they ate, Janie felt comfortable with him. Whenever he did talk, he spoke ill of almost no one, and he didn't complain about work or family or play up his Navy service to seem more demanding than it was. "It was a vacation," he said of his time in Pearl Harbor. As a boy on his family farm, he often began working at five in the morning. Then he would go to school, come home, and then work until nine at night. Compared to that, he said, giving tours of a sunken battleship wasn't work at all.

In the coming months, the couple spent more and more time together, until one day Ansol asked Janie, "When are we getting married?" Janie replied, "I don't know! You never asked me!"

A few days later, they drove to Maryville, Tennessee, a little town at the base of the Great Smoky Mountains National Park. A justice of the peace married them in the courthouse. They could have waited and planned a proper ceremony, with family and friends, but Ansol didn't want her to get away. Or that was Janie's joke. In truth, she admired his decisiveness. She was eighteen; he was twenty. The ink was still fresh on their high-school diplomas. They had almost no money, so, after signing their marriage license, they celebrated at Burger King. Two Whoppers set them back fifty-nine cents each.

Ansol later explained some of his initial attraction to Janie, and it only partially owed to her playful teasing. "I wanted to save you," he told her. "I wanted to protect you." And he did protect her, she believed. He worked for the local utility company at the time, and he would drive by and wave to her in the ticket booth of the Tennessee Theatre whenever he had a chance, to make sure she was okay. About a year after they married, they bought a ranch home in west Knoxville, with a facade of stone and yellow siding. Janie found it darling.

When she and Ansol were newlyweds, the local radio stations kept Helen Reddy's 1974 hit single "You and Me Against the World" in regular rotation. The lyrics concern a single mother and son enduring life's hardships together, but the chorus, in which Reddy belts the song's title, reminded Janie of her and Ansol, especially a lyric about the characters having only God on their side.

Neither she nor Ansol came from money, and neither earned a college degree. And yet, as the years ticked by, they secured increasingly better jobs and built respectable careers. When Janie had Bergan, in 1979, their finances were stable enough that she was able to stay home and take care of him full-time for a few years. She drove him to the library and taught him to swim at the YMCA. She enrolled him in piano and violin lessons. Later came golf and karate. And, partially thanks to her efforts, Bergan turned out well, she was proud to say. He grew up, earned a two-year degree, and landed a job in telecom.

A few years after Bergan was born, Janie picked up some part-time housekeeping jobs, at first ironing clothes and later cleaning homes, which would become her main line of work as Bergan grew older. She and Ansol saved up for a couple of decades, then, in the late 1990s, built their dream home: a one-story, tan brick house in the west Knoxville suburbs. Their place sat on an acre and a half of land. It had a sunny dining room near the front door, a master bedroom off the kitchen, and a rear sunroom. It was altogether something to be proud of, Janie believed. By the spring of 2010, she and Ansol had been married for thirty-eight years. Thirty-eight good years.

Along with the photos of her and Bergan and Ansol, Janie had a few framed snapshots of her father that she took out and looked at from time to time. In one, Janie, about seven years old, with a beaming smile, pulls on her father's hand as they stand in front of a thick, ivy-covered tree. He wears a dark suit and hat—the perfect image of a gentleman, in her mind. She's a toddler in another photo. Her father kneels beside her, with a hand on her round little belly, as if he's ready to scoop her up, as if he'll never let her go. Janie loved her father and mother, and cherished her old photographs of the two, yet she and Ansol had been together for such a long time now that anything that occurred before they married almost seemed to have happened to a different person. She was okay with that, mostly. It did her little good to dwell on the past, she believed. Her mother and brother still lived in Knoxville, but Ansol was her family now. She didn't know life apart from him, nor did she want to.

Ansol wasn't as expressive as Janie, but he shared many of her feelings regarding their years together. He loved her without question, and he looked forward to retiring and going on adventures together. The trouble was that he would have to endure a few more years at Kingston first, and that task grew harder by the day.

In the spring of 2010, Ansol caught a cold he couldn't shake—a cough, a runny nose, an endless headache. He hadn't felt great since the start of the cleanup, a year and a half earlier, but the cold marked a new low. It wasn't his nature to complain at work, but the cold irked him enough to bring it up. When he did, Jacobs's staff assured him that allergies, probably because of high pollen counts, were to blame. Ansol bought some over-the-counter medicine, but it didn't help.

The cleanup project had grown mildly less frantic in recent months, affording Ansol some mild relief. During his first year on the job, he'd worked nearly seventy hours a week, every week, logging more than thirty-six hundred hours in 2009. The busyness had kept him and Janie in a "tailspin," as she put it. They hardly saw each other. Ansol left for work before sunup, came home late, took a shower, and climbed straight into bed, then repeated the cycle the following day. But now, with the cleanup project reasonably on track, he worked more manageable twelve-hour shifts, rather than fourteen- or sixteen-hour ones.

At the end of the day, as other workers stood around and talked, Ansol would head straight for his pickup. He wanted to be home. When he arrived at five or five-thirty, he would kick off his boots and pull off his soiled clothes in the garage, shaking off muck that Janie would inevitably sweep up. He would wash, slip on a pair of Crocs, and eat whatever Janie had fixed for dinner. Then he would settle into his maroon easy chair to read the local paper, *The Knoxville News Sentinel.* He savored this tiny margin of downtime at the end of the day, but whenever he leafed through the *Sentinel,* his eyes burned and stung. He rubbed them constantly.

At four o'clock one March morning, Ansol woke up feeling still worse. He lay in bed feeling dizzy, looking up at the stippled drywall ceiling. "You need to call and tell them you can't come in," said Janie. She was already up and readying for the day. He couldn't work, much less drive a fuel truck, in such condition, she told him.

He sat upright. "I have to go," he said. He couldn't make a habit of calling in sick, he said, not as an easy-to-replace subcontractor. He had to show up to stay employed.

He swung his strong legs over the edge of the bed. But when he tried to stand, he wobbled and reeled backward, crashing into a bedside table. He met the hardwood floor with a thud. Janie dashed over. He moaned and held his right shoulder as Janie tried, and failed, to lift him up. Minutes passed. She had no clue what to do. At last, Ansol, looking dazed, sat up, and Janie helped him into bed. He'd briefly blacked out. It was as if someone had turned off a light switch in his brain, he said. But he felt somewhat stable now.

"I got to get the phone," Janie told him. She ran into the living room, grabbed the cordless, and ran back. She told him he had to see a doctor, and he agreed. Before she called to make an appointment, she dialed his foreman. "Ansol won't be in today," she blurted when the foreman picked up. She explained what had happened, then called the couple's family doctor. "We got to get him in," she told the receptionist. But the doctor's first opening wasn't until later in the week. For a moment, Janie contemplated driving Ansol to the hospital but decided against it. Surely it was just a freak spell, she told herself. Irritated but seeing no other choice, she told the receptionist that later in the week would be fine.

Ansol, feeling too unwell to sit in his easy chair and watch TV, spent the rest of the day in bed with sheets pulled over him. Janie checked on him regularly, ensuring that he was comfortable and that his cold, or whatever it was, hadn't worsened. When he woke up the next morning, he didn't feel much better, and his shoulder ached from the fall. But he climbed out of bed and went to work anyway, knowing that he would need to take another day off to see the doctor and wanting to minimize his time away.

A few days later, at a little past nine in the morning, Janie drove Ansol to an office building near the interstate. She waited at reception while Ansol met with the doctor. Since they had always enjoyed good health and had rarely needed medical care in all their years together, she didn't know that typically spouses are allowed to accompany each other in a physician's exam room.

The doctor looked Ansol over, then ordered a chest X-ray, blood tests, and an EKG. The results were clear: Ansol had atrial fibrillation—a fast, almost chaotic heartbeat. Fatigue, dizziness, shortness of breath: his symptoms were classic. The condition could cause further problems if left untreated. The doctor prescribed Ansol a calcium channel blocker called diltiazem that would help lower his blood pressure and control his heartbeat. Ansol didn't know what to make of the diagnosis. It sounded serious, but how serious? He had never stayed sick for long, so surely, he figured, his health would rebound once the diltiazem kicked in.

Janie shared Ansol's optimism, and some of his confusion. Atrial fibrillation didn't seem to explain Ansol's cold symptoms, but she took solace in the fact that at least a doctor had caught the problem before it grew serious. And maybe Ansol had allergies after all.

After the examination, Janie paid Ansol's insurance copay at the front desk, handing over $20 in cash. As she turned to leave, a staff member handed her a form that the doctor had scribbled on throughout Ansol's exam. In a box labeled "Diagnosis," the doctor had written that Ansol's atrial fibrillation owed to "exposure to toxic substances." Janie froze. *Toxic substances?* she thought to herself. *Ansol doesn't work near toxic substances.* The form didn't elaborate, and Janie didn't turn back and ask for clarification. Ansol had pushed himself too hard, she told herself. That had to be the reason for his blackout and heart troubles. If Ansol was working around hazardous material, he would have told her, and he hadn't said a word.

• • •

The same month that Ansol Clark collapsed, Jeff Brewer, a dump-truck driver and part-time Baptist preacher, took a job at the Kingston cleanup site. He was a quick-to-smile guy in his mid-thirties, with thinning brown hair and a mole on his left cheek. He spoke softly and had a gentle, good-natured temperament. He lived in New Market, Tennessee, a town of about thirteen hundred people sixty miles from Kingston. He had recently lost his job at a local trucking company that had been hit hard by the recession. When a union rep from Teamsters 519 called Brewer and mentioned an opportunity at Kingston, he readily accepted. He had three young daughters and a wife depending on him.

On his first morning, Brewer drove not to the spill site but to the Kingston Fossil Plant itself. There, TVA staff led him and other new hires to a conference room and told the men to empty their pockets, take off their hats, and line up for drug tests. They peed in cups. The workers who passed took a seat. Those who didn't left. Brewer watched as they filed out.

He grew up about thirty miles west of Knoxville, in a town called Dandridge. His mother sewed hosiery and pocketbooks, and his stepdad mostly farmed. Brewer had driven or worked on trucks since finishing high school. In 1998, after four years of driving a beer-delivery truck, he rededicated his life to Christ and devoted himself fully to his family. While in a convenience store shortly thereafter, he overheard a young girl ask her father for a candy bar. No, the man told her. He couldn't afford it. Yet the guy bought booze for himself. Brewer turned in his keys and quit at the end of his shift. "The Lord broke my heart that day," he later explained.

Brewer spent his first few days at Kingston riding with another driver in an articulated dump truck, known as an arctic. The spill had reportedly covered three hundred acres, but, if Brewer had to guess, he would have put the total closer to a thousand. Towering mounds of coal ash stretched before him in every direction. Workers had carved roads through the ash, and driving over it felt like rolling over a wet sponge. Men in rubber boots and overalls stood knee-deep in the muck, their faces smeared with ash. When heavy machinery rumbled past, the ground rippled like gelatin. *What is this stuff?* Brewer wondered. He had never seen such a thing.

By the spring of 2010, TVA and its legion of contractors had sucked roughly four million tons of coal ash from the Emory River, a crucial step in the cleanup process, since clearing the river allowed it to be reopened for the first time since the disaster. To complete the task, crews used dredger boats, equipped with underwater suction pipes, to effectively vacuum the ash from the river bottom to the shore. There, workers set out the ash to dry, then loaded it onto railcars. Trains hauled this ash three hundred and seventy miles southwest—through the soft blue hills of Tennessee; past the steel mills and suburban sprawl of Birmingham; and, finally, to the flat, quiet farm county of the Alabama Black Belt.

The journey took some eighteen hours and ended in Uniontown, a fading farming hamlet of about two thousand people, nearly all of them Black. The community is in one of the poorest counties in one of the nation's poorest states. Over a year and a half, residents watched as forty-one thousand railcars from Kingston rumbled through their little community to the Arrowhead Landfill, a thirteen-hundred-acre dump on the town's outskirts. A portion of the landfill featured a thick, almost impermeable bed of Selma chalk and clay that would prevent toxins from leaching into the groundwater. This was where much of the Kingston coal ash ended up, and locals could guess why. "You're taking that [coal ash] from a white area," one former resident said. "The white folks don't want it. Why do you think it's good enough for the Blacks?" The state of Alabama did not intervene on Uniontown's behalf to block the ash from being brought there.

Jeff Brewer would learn all this in time. In the days after his new-hire orientation, he regularly pulled twelve- to sixteen-hour shifts, driving an arctic capable of hauling forty tons or more of coal ash. Given the long hours, he could drive home to New Market only twice a week, once on Wednesdays to attend Bible study with his wife, Tammy, and three daughters, then again on Sundays for church. For the other days, Brewer rented an efficiency apartment above Mama Mia's, a pizza place, in an old tan-and-red clapboard building in Kingston. The space was smaller than the average motel room. It cost $115 a week to rent. Each morning, Brewer woke up, drank a cup of coffee, and fixed cereal or oatmeal in the kitchenette. Sometimes he might swing by Bojangles or McDonald's for a biscuit. Then he reported to work.

On the jobsite, he earned two nicknames: "Poor Boy," since his daughters kept him perpetually low on funds, and "Preacher," because of his side gig, spreading the Good Word. He didn't consider himself a "religionist," obsessed with rules, but a true believer in Christ's grace and salvation. "I'm bought by the blood," he'd tell friends. At night, after his long hours at the cleanup site, Brewer usually called Tammy and his girls to catch up, to hear their voices, to feel close. Just as often, though, he would take a shower and go straight to bed, too tired to speak. If he was lonely, at least he had a job, and at least it paid well. He pulled $22.65 an hour at Kingston and was later bumped to $25.86, a major leap from the $13 an hour he had earned at his previous company. That was a blessing.

Brewer met Ansol Clark after one of the morning safety meetings, where Jacobs's staff discussed precautions related to the day's work or changes to safety policy. Most days after lunch, Brewer drove his arctic to an area called D dike, where Ansol parked his fuel truck. As Brewer gassed up, the two talked about squirrel hunting or Teamsters business. Brewer learned to confide in Ansol. After a month or two on the job, he mentioned that something curious had happened. He didn't drink or smoke, and he'd always been healthy. But now he felt sluggish and often had to fight to catch his breath, even on the short walks from the parking lot to the jobsite. He noticed that other workers coughed up a strange black jelly. Brewer called it "the Kingston Crud," as did many others. At first, he blamed his symptoms on the long hours and the grind of the work. Then his sluggishness led to dizzy spells, then to nosebleeds, then to worse.

One afternoon in May 2011, Jim Scott drove to a little peninsula overlooking the Clinch River. Even by Roane County standards, the spring had been ruthlessly hot, with highs in the 90s and almost no rain. As the sun pounded down, Scott cruised past a few ranch-style houses until he spotted 110 Confluence Drive, a brick home perched along the river, with a four-column porch and a neat lawn. Waiting outside in a Cadillac was Walter Goolsby, a local real-estate broker.

After the Kingston disaster, more than sixty complaints, on behalf of nearly nine hundred plaintiffs, had been filed against TVA. Most concerned property damage or related matters. The plaintiffs' attorneys had convinced a federal judge that TVA shouldn't be immune from the lawsuits, as it was from most others, in part since it had ignored clear warning signs about the dike's collapse and failed to correct structural problems that could have prevented the disaster. But, with an army of attorneys entrenched in the fray, discovery—the pretrial period for requesting documents and interviewing witnesses—had dragged on for nearly a year and a half. The plaintiffs had turned over more than six hundred thousand pages of documents, and at least thirty-five people, including both Kingston locals and TVA staff, had given sworn depositions. Maybe more. Scott lost count after a while.

Together he and another attorney named John Agee represented about a hundred plaintiffs. Scott had tried to speed things along by filing a motion for summary judgment—an early ruling by a judge, based on the facts of a case. This would prevent their having to go to trial. Why bother, if TVA's negligence was so obvious? The case was straightforward, as Scott saw it. TVA had a mountain of coal ash that it knew would eventually collapse, and it ignored the problem. Then, when the mountain fell, dozens of homes were damaged. Simple as that.

But Thomas Varlan, a conservative federal district-court judge in Knoxville, denied Scott's motion, ruling that he had insufficient evidence against TVA to make his case. Now Scott needed proof that the spill had caused his clients' property values to plummet, which was why he'd hired Goolsby to survey about twenty properties. As Scott parked, Goolsby climbed from his Cadillac and ran a comb through his white, swept-back hair. He had opened a successful real-estate firm some four decades earlier and possessed a certain amount of swagger as an authority on the local housing market.

The home on Confluence Drive belonged to Gilbert Pickel, an eighty-three-year-old retiree whom Scott knew from his days in the local DA's office. As Goolsby spread out land surveys atop his Cadillac, the equally gregarious Pickel and Scott stood in the driveway and chatted about the weather and University of Tennessee sports.

As a young assistant district attorney, Scott had learned that many Roane County locals would sooner forgive someone who had stabbed them in a drunken knife fight than they would a vandal who'd damaged their property. Land was sacred, not to be messed with. Pickel seemed to share this belief, because when the conversation turned to coal ash, his genial tone darkened. The Kingston disaster hadn't destroyed his property, but, he said, fly ash blew onto his land from the cleanup site across the river. Arms folded, he explained that he and his wife were afraid to let their grandchildren swim in their backyard pool. How could they be sure it was safe? And who could they trust to tell them one way or the other? Pickel wanted to sell his home and move somewhere else, but real-estate agents had said they couldn't help him: no one wanted his property now, not after the spill. Unless TVA was held to account, "we are just stuck," Pickel later explained.

Pickel and Scott walked behind the house to the waterfront. A hundred yards in either direction, TVA had erected orange barrier fences to limit access to much of the shore, but not behind Pickel's property. From the water's edge, Scott could see the confluence of the Emory and Clinch Rivers. The Kingston Fossil Plant stood on the far bank, its thousand-foot stacks towering above the treeline and the mountainous green countryside and all creation, it seemed. White steam drifted up from the plant like campfire smoke.

In the two and a half years since the Kingston disaster, the Emory had regained much of its blue-green tint, thanks to extensive dredging. Still, Pickel said that he'd noticed far fewer people out boating or swimming than he had in the past. Scott wasn't surprised. He wouldn't readily take a dip in the rivers, either, especially considering James Crichton's story about getting chest pains and rushing to the hospital after he freed the stuck tree branch.

The men walked along the riverbank. Cenospheres—spherical, floating clumps of coal-ash particles—bobbed in the water around and under Pickel's dock. For years to come, whenever locals jumped into the river, large coal-ash plumes, disturbed by the commotion, would swell and blossom from the bottom. TVA simply couldn't dredge the entirety of both rivers. According to TVA, nearly seven hundred thousand tons of coal ash would ultimately remain in the Emory, an unalluring fact for prospective homebuyers. Walter Goolsby, in his report, would determine that, because of the coal-ash spill, home values along the waterfront had dropped by at least 26 percent. Pickel's was worse, at 55 percent. In Kingston, "you couldn't give land away," one local told *Newsweek*.

As Scott drove back to Knoxville that afternoon, he felt sure that he would have more than enough evidence once Goolsby finished his report. Scott wanted a big win for his clients, and for his own sake. He was frustrated: the longer he stayed on the cases, the less he saw of his wife and sons. Sam, in the years since his diagnoses, still ate little, a trait shared by many children with autism. But Scott had recently gotten Sam to like ribs—a major breakthrough—by watching *Man v. Food*, a show about extreme-eating challenges. Now they regularly went to Calhoun's, a barbecue joint on Kingston Pike. "Daddy, I wish the world was made of ribs," Sam said once as they ate. He'd also grown less frightened of noises. Scott felt sure that Sam would have more breakthroughs if he kept working with him, but his cases left little time for that, a point of guilt. He could get choked up thinking about it. "Daddy, is it normal to twitch?" Sam asked him one night. "Yeah," Scott said, instinctively, before stopping himself. "Sam, to be honest with you, there's no such thing as normal." He wanted that to be true.

Complicating matters further, one of Scott's four law partners, Eddie Daniel, the only non-family member, had recently gone into business for himself, complaining that he received an unfair share of the fees they'd collected. Soon after Daniel's departure, Jim and his remaining partners realized that Daniel had stolen more than $600,000 from the firm—money the firm had, in part, earned from settling the murder case of the former homecoming queen at the Knoxville Days Inn around the time of the Kingston disaster. The missing funds sparked a legal battle that, to Jim's embarrassment, had made local news. *The Knoxville News Sentinel* wrote that the dispute had "all the hallmarks of a bitter, high-profile divorce battle," with "anger and recrimination [popping] from the pages of warring legal documents."

Daniel denied that he had stolen the money, according to the newspaper's fourteen-paragraph story about the feud. He also counterattacked, claiming that Jim and his sister Dana hadn't pulled their weight, and accusing one of Scott's partners, Michael Pemberton, of infidelity. Generating more headlines, the Tennessee Bureau of Investigation announced in early May that it was investigating Daniel for fraud.* Jim worked mostly solo, but, with his firm in shambles, he feared that he might soon be truly alone.

The Howard J. Baker Jr. United States Courthouse—named after the former Tennessee lawmaker who was the vice chairman of the Senate Watergate Committee—is a neoclassical brick compound, four stories tall and two blocks long, situated roughly in the middle of downtown Knoxville. Its clock tower, slender and tall, stands over a gated, grassy courtyard. On a Wednesday morning in September 2011, Jim Scott turned briskly onto Main Street, bringing the courthouse into view. He sported a suit and toted a black overlap bag on his shoulder. He was tired but buoyed by anticipation. He had spent the past four months in a blur of meetings with witnesses and clients. He sometimes showed up to these appointments looking disheveled and bleary-eyed, clearly having slept little, and perhaps a touch woozy from enjoying some wine the night before. But he had pushed through, and now on this September morning, nearly three years after the Kingston disaster, TVA would finally have to answer for its failure to maintain the coal-ash pond.

Once through courthouse security, Scott found a seat in the gallery of courtroom 3C. The plaintiffs' attorneys had convinced Judge Thomas Varlan that TVA shouldn't be immune from suit, but he hadn't agreed to a jury trial; he alone would decide whether TVA was liable, in a bifurcated, or two-phase, trial. The first phase, which had begun with opening statements two days earlier, would center on whether TVA was responsible for the disaster; if Varlan decided that it was, a second trial phase would address damages to specific properties. One hitch was that such a large number of landowners had sued TVA that the judge had decided that the cases would be tried in two consecutive rounds, based on whenever each individual case had been filed. The round-one cases would go through both trial phases, then the round-two cases would follow.

* Daniel pleaded no contest to the theft charges brought against him. His law license was later suspended for one year by the Tennessee Supreme Court, after a panel of attorneys determined that he had misappropriated funds from his law partnership.

Scott's cases, which he'd filed later than many others, were assigned to the second round, but he had much riding on the first. If the round-one attorneys failed to prove TVA's liability, he would likely struggle to do the same and lose his negotiating leverage to secure a settlement. But if the round-one team performed well, Scott might not have to go to trial at all: the plaintiffs' attorneys could band together and negotiate a settlement for all the landowners. Millions of dollars hung in the balance. Varlan, a conservative nominated to the bench by President George W. Bush, had already demonstrated, when he denied Scott's motion for summary judgment, that the plaintiffs would need abundant proof to make their case.

At a little past nine o'clock, Tom Kilgore, TVA's chief executive, took the stand. Narrow-eyed and bony in his sixties, and dressed that day in a dark-gray suit, Kilgore was not the type to be pushed around. He had helmed TVA since 2006 and pulled nearly $4 million a year in total compensation, making him the highest-paid federal employee.

Jeff Friedman, the Birmingham lawyer who had circumvented the roadblock shortly after the disaster, had been selected lead attorney for the plaintiffs. Crisp shirt, combed hair, big smile: he knew how to present himself, and he had extensive environmental-law experience to boot. He had recently won $20 million in damages for the city of Columbus, Georgia, and other plaintiffs in a case against a company that had spewed carbon black, a dark, dusty pollutant, over homes and businesses. Friedman and Scott had met at a deposition in the land cases. In talking, they realized that they had been members of the same fraternity at the University of Tennessee, though years apart. Friedman thought that Scott, with his boat shoes and wrinkled button-downs, still resembled a frat boy. Friedman appreciated Scott's deftness with clients, but he wouldn't need his help in the trial.

Throughout the examination that morning, Kilgore refuted a claim that Friedman had made during opening statements two days earlier: that the Kingston disaster was preventable and caused by TVA's neglect. "We have a responsibility," Kilgore told Friedman, in his sturdy Alabama drawl, "to take care of our property so we don't impinge on our neighbors." He refused, however, to accept blame for the spill.

But, surely, he would concede that TVA hadn't constructed the ash pond adequately to handle the stress it was under? Friedman countered.

It had collapsed, after all. "No," said Kilgore, eyes locked on Friedman, "I'm not willing to admit that." The dike's design "was not satisfactory" for the stress it was under, Kilgore conceded, but he, and TVA, held that the dike had failed because an unstable "slimes" layer of silt beneath the sludge pile had given way without warning. It was an act of God, in other words.

Kilgore, who grew increasingly irritated as the morning dragged on, maintained that TVA was faultless even after Friedman produced a report in which a TVA employee said it had "narrowly avoided disaster" after a 2003 dike blowout. The same employee said the previous blowout should have raised more concern within TVA than it had. Kilgore also held firm after Friedman revealed that the engineer who inspected the dike shortly before its collapse, in 2008, had had no relevant experience or training. Most remarkable, when Friedman pressed Kilgore on why TVA had not reprimanded a single employee over the coal-ash disaster—a promise Kilgore had personally made to Congress—he replied that there was no need. TVA had learned its lesson and improved its policies.

Kilgore's defensiveness didn't entirely surprise Friedman. The Kingston disaster was only the latest in a series of embarrassments for TVA, and the questions that the catastrophe raised risked exposing the dangers of TVA's coal-ash dump sites and, more broadly, its reliance on coal, the rock propping up its multibillion-dollar organization. Friedman knew the history as well as anyone: that as TVA's fleet of coal-fired power plants came online after the Second World War, it had largely ignored locals' complaints about the resulting pollution. But, in the 1960s, new federal emissions standards sought to combat a litany of pollution-related afflictions caused by the nation's seven hundred or so coal-fired power plants. Acid rain was killing fish in mountain lakes and damaging forests. Smog and soot suffocated U.S. cities, contributing to tens of thousands of premature deaths each year. (One study concluded that, even after the new federal standards took effect, power-plant emissions killed some thirty thousand Americans annually.) These new federal emissions rules posed an existential threat to TVA's empire. Rather than clean up, and anxious about its production capacity, it planned to build the world's largest nuclear-power system, composed of seventeen reactors, at seven different plants. To keep these reactors fueled, TVA bought or acquired the rights to nearly a million acres of land throughout New Mexico, South Dakota, Utah, and Wyoming, from which it mined at least a billion dollars' worth of uranium. In Casper, Wyoming, it established an office, nicknamed TVA West, staffed by some forty people. But it finished only three of its seven planned nuclear plants, and it was defensive about the failure.

In March 1975, an engineering aide, using a lighted candle to find an air leak, accidentally started a fire at TVA's Browns Ferry nuclear facility, in north Alabama, the country's largest nuclear-power plant at the time. The blaze quickly spread, causing some $100 million in damages and forcing an emergency shutdown. TVA later acknowledged that the episode was, at the time, likely the most serious accident at an American commercial nuclear station. (The Three Mile Island fiasco, in Pennsylvania, overshadowed it four years later.) In 1984, TVA laid off some five hundred Browns Ferry workers, owing to safety violations; the next year, it temporarily closed all three of its nuclear plants for similar reasons. "What we are seeing at TVA now is a tragedy, the culmination of years of blunders," Representative Ronnie G. Flippo, an Alabama Democrat, told *The New York Times* in 1986. The remarks followed reports that TVA, then the nation's largest electrical-power supplier, ignored safety complaints and intimidated employees who spoke out about problems, as well as mismanaged billions of dollars of ratepayer funds. By 1989, TVA employees had filed 90 percent of all whistle-blower cases at U.S. nuclear utilities; in many instances, these employees complained that they'd been harassed or intimidated by colleagues for raising safety concerns.

Less than two months before Tom Kilgore appeared in court that September morning, he'd written a *Times* op-ed about TVA's nuclear efforts, in which he admitted, "Our program was hindered by safety concerns and a public backlash against nuclear generation." Now TVA had "a more conservative, disciplined approach" to nuclear power, Kilgore wrote. And, because of that, he argued that Bellefonte—a partially constructed TVA nuclear facility, deferred since 1988—should be approved for completion. In the meantime, TVA would remain deeply reliant on coal, which accounted for nearly two-thirds of its power production.

Kilgore's trial testimony lasted about two hours, and in that time, the most Friedman could get him to admit was that TVA had "missed opportunities in the early fifties" to correct the design and construction of the Kingston dike as the coal ash piled up. Still, Friedman would later boast that Kilgore's examination made for good, high-drama newspaper copy, and it did. Dailies across the state carried stories about Kilgore's defiant testimony.

The bench trial lasted for nearly three more weeks, but the most crucial testimony, beyond Kilgore's, came the next day, when Friedman called TVA's inspector general, Richard Moore, to the stand. Moore, as TVA's independent in-house watchdog, had conducted an inquiry into the Kingston disaster and published a one-hundred-and-ten-page report on it in July 2009. In it, Moore, a middle-aged former U.S. attorney, had lambasted TVA for ignoring "red flags" as early as 1985 that the Kingston dike might collapse. Moore's report also accused TVA of having a dysfunctional culture under Kilgore's leadership and of favoring a "litigation strategy" over transparency or accountability, to limit its exposure to lawsuits.

In the courtroom, Friedman asked Moore, on direct examination, about an engineering consultant TVA had hired to write an analysis of the disaster. That TVA would hire such a consultant "in and of itself was normal," Moore told Friedman. "The unusual part," he said, was that TVA prohibited the consultant from looking into its management practices, or commenting on its culpability, or inquiring into policy or design problems that had led to the dike's failure. The report that the consultant produced for TVA, which it in turn released to the public, called the "slimes" layer of silt beneath the coal-ash pond "a major factor in the December 2008 failure"—one that would have been extremely difficult for TVA to detect.

In the plaintiffs' opening statement days earlier, Friedman had mocked TVA's "magical layer" of slimes as an illegitimate, or at least a wildly overstated, cause for the dike's collapse. Indeed, Moore's internal review had called the consultant's focus on the slimes layer "misplaced," based on a subsequent analysis done for the inspector general's office. The slimes layer, Moore's report added, was a suspiciously "fortuitous" explanation for TVA.

Friedman asked Moore if he would use the word *convenient* to describe TVA's attributing the dike's collapse to the slimes layer.

"Yes," Moore said, "I believe it was convenient."

"Convenient because it finds a reported cause for the disaster without placing any blame [on TVA]?" Friedman asked.

"Yes," Moore said.

All told, TVA not only had failed to be transparent with the public, Moore said, but it had also broken a pledge Kilgore had made to Congress: that it would conduct a self-critical analysis of the disaster. "That was not done," Moore said.

TVA, for its part, appeared to focus its defense strategy less on rebutting Moore's claims than on discrediting him as a biased critic of the organization, one to whom Varlan, the sole juror, should give no credence. On cross-examination, Edwin Small, TVA's chief litigator and deputy general counsel, asked Moore about emails he had sent to his staff during the course of his inquiry, including one in which he wrote, "Tell me this: What do you think we can say about what they"—TVA—"have done to stop their lying ways?"

On the stand, Moore explained that TVA executives had a long history of being less than forthright with the public, and that TVA's slimes-layer theory was another "misrepresentation of the truth," based on an analysis of the dike failure done for his office.

"Okay," Small said, "but you're not an expert on geotechnical matters, are you?"

"No," Moore said.

"You're not an expert in management matters, are you?" Small said.

"No," Moore said.

"You're not an expert in risk matters, are you?"

"No," Small said.

In the defense's closing statements, Small said that the "red flags" Moore had identified about the dike's eventual collapse were "red herrings," and he argued that TVA had diligently and faithfully investigated the cause of the disaster. "The [inspector general's office] needed something to make news with so it made news with this theory that, well, we think TVA may have engaged in some kind of litigation strategy," Small said.

In the gallery, after listening to days of testimony, Jim Scott wondered what else TVA might be trying to keep out of sight, as it had so clearly, in his view, tried to obscure its role in the dike's failure. It was bad enough that it failed to prevent the Kingston disaster, but Kilgore's refusal to accept any blame astounded him, given the evidence. Why would Kilgore jeopardize his reputation with such moronic denials? Why even bring the cases to trial, rather than settle quietly?

Ansol Clark didn't improve. Colds and coughs had dogged him throughout his three and a half years at the Kingston cleanup, but, in the summer of 2012, he caught a flu that eclipsed every past ailment. He wheezed and struggled to breathe while lying down, so he slept upright, yet he still felt as if something were smothering him. Before taking a job at Kingston, he had fished in bass tournaments, hunted for deer in mountainous backcountry, and cleared the acre-and-a-half lot where he and Janie built their home. These days, though, he looked almost drained of life, at least to Janie. She hesitated to ask him to run errands or do much of anything with her on his time off. He needed to rest; he needed to regain his strength; he needed to get better.

Ansol had done fine on diltiazem so far, Janie thought, but the flu was a new setback. In September 2012, Ansol, frustrated and increasingly unwell, visited his doctor, who gave him an allergy shot. But his breathing grew more labored. Soon his stomach and feet swelled.

By this time, Jeff Brewer's shortness of breath and dizzy spells had given way to regular blackouts. The spells often hit as he waited in his dump truck for loads of ash to move. As he sat behind the wheel, he would pass out without warning. He wouldn't come to until someone walked over and knocked on his truck window or called him over the radio. At night, he washed his face with a wet washcloth, wiping away the ash. His eyes burned. He had a constant headache.

The workers were in an impossible position. Despite what Jacobs's staff had said, they felt certain that breathing fly ash had wrecked, or at least compromised, their health. The trouble was that many of the workers hailed from rural towns outside Knoxville—maybe half had finished high school—and, with the country still reeling from the Great Recession, they would be hard-pressed to land a job elsewhere, much less one that paid as well. They were family men, with children and wives and parents to care for. That was why, throughout much of the cleanup, they'd said little about their health. "Nobody would talk about nothing out there," one equipment operator explained. "Everyone was job scared." To the workers, it seemed that whoever complained, or got hurt, or caused problems, would be furloughed and never brought back. Billy Isley, the Metallica fan and truck driver, swore that a member of TVA management once told him that if anyone complained about site conditions, "There's plenty of people at the union hall that need a job."

Adding to the workers' anxieties, the number of personnel needed on-site had already shrunk from nearly a thousand to five hundred or so, and more layoffs were expected as the project neared completion. Asking for a dust mask, the workers noticed, had become a reliable way to find yourself out of a job sooner rather than later. That troubled them now more than ever, since much of the wet coal ash had dried and the jobsite had grown increasingly dusty. In the mornings, dew usually kept the ash under control and out of the air, but then the afternoon sun would burn off the moisture, freeing the ash to blow around. "It would be a complete blackout," one truck driver later explained. Sometimes the workers couldn't see trucks or other people through it. And the more fly ash that hung in the air, the more their health seemed to decline.

Most days, a group of about ten or fifteen men, usually including Ansol Clark and Jeff Brewer, ate lunch together at the Berkshire house, the home TVA bought after the dike collapsed. It had a microwave and a refrigerator and running water, making it one of the few places where the workers could wash their hands before they ate. Jacobs employees had offices upstairs, but in the basement there was a table where the workers could sit and talk as they ate. It smelled like horses for a while; the former homeowners had wintered animals down there. But what bothered the workers was the coal ash. Even if they cleaned up and washed their hands, ash clung to their boots, their clothes, their hair; it got in their sandwiches.

As the cleanup project wore on, the workers discussed their health more candidly than they had in the past. Isley had a constant cough and skin lesions, and his sex drive had plummeted to the point that his wife, Lena, asked him whether he was screwing around. He visited a doctor, he said, who told him that his testosterone levels scored in the mid-fifties, much lower than the average male range of two hundred and fifty to nine hundred, and even lower than some women's. Billy Gibson, a heavy-equipment operator, had developed asthma shortly after taking a job at Kingston, and, like Isley, he now complained of low testosterone.* He got shots every three weeks to boost his levels. One longtime TVA employee, a yard supervisor named Dwayne Rushing, mocked a worker for his low T, saying that he would service the guy's wife if he wasn't able to do it himself. (Rushing was reprimanded for the comment.)

One afternoon as the group ate, Gibson mentioned that he had stopped letting his wife wash his clothes. She kept getting sick from the ash, he explained. As soon as Gibson said that, Jeff Brewer knew. Since the cleanup began, his wife had suffered one sinus infection after the next. Their family had gone through two washing machines, which had given out for no obvious reason. Could fly ash be to blame? Had he exposed his wife and daughters?

"Something ain't right here," Ansol Clark told the others. He knew that fly ash was making him ill. Nothing else explained it. And he believed that Jacobs and TVA knew it, too, and had acted maliciously in failing to protect them.

Gibson and Ansol said there was an attorney in west Knoxville—an enthusiastic little guy that someone in Oak Ridge had recommended—who might be willing to help them. Ansol had never met an attorney before, at least not that he could recall, and, based on TV shows and movies he'd seen, he held lawyers and used-car salesmen in roughly equal regard: "They'll tell you anything to get a dollar out of your pocket." Still, he said he knew that the workers needed someone on their side if they hoped to get respiratory protection.

"I can't afford to pay no attorney," Brewer said. But he agreed that something had to change. Even in the cold, wet days of fall and winter, fly ash would whip around like snow. More troubling, over a ten-month period, Brewer's foreman had directed him and some other truck drivers to spray off some stationary air monitors with water cannons. One monitor sat near a little red barn, another on the site's north end.

To Brewer, it was obvious that hosing off the devices would manipu-

* The workers would never obtain definitive proof that fly-ash exposure had affected their testosterone, but their low levels nonetheless unnerved them.

late their readings.* But when he was asked to do the job, he didn't feel like he could push back. Brewer assumed that his foreman's orders came from Jacobs, and that Jacobs's orders came from TVA. (Other workers had similar hunches.) Still, Brewer knew he couldn't keep breathing ash all day long, and he suspected that the Jacobs staff wasn't keen to, either. Brewer had noticed that Tom Bock, the Jacobs safety officer, seldom walked around the jobsite except after a rain, when the wet fly ash didn't blow around as much. Even then, Bock seemed to stick to the main gravel road. More concerning for Brewer, Geiger counters, which monitor the air for radioactive particles, sometimes went off on-site, chirping loudly and repeatedly. Jacobs and TVA employees ignored them.

Jim Scott's office had a twelve-foot maroon sign at the far edge of the parking lot, standing a few steps from a Weigel's gas station. "Pemberton & Scott," the sign read, in white bold letters. "Accident & Injury Law." Beneath these words and the firm's phone number was the sign's most noticeable feature: a jumbo digital clock that blinked the time and temperature for passersby. As the clock neared six one autumn evening in 2012, three pickups turned off Kingston Pike, drove past the maroon sign, and parked on the freshly paved asphalt.

A few weeks earlier, as Scott worked at his desk, he had received a curious phone call from a woman named Serita Phillips. He'd met Phillips years earlier, when he worked for the DA's office and she for a sheriff's department within his district. They had struck up a friendship. Phillips, a single mother, had a knack for spotting people in need, and, in the years since Scott entered private practice, she had referred him fifteen or twenty cases, each of which had proved easy and good.

Phillips's latest call differed from past ones. "Jim," she began, concern clear in her voice, "something funny is going on out here." She'd taken a job in Oak Ridge, she explained, leading training courses for people who worked around hazardous substances, and, at the Kingston cleanup, that included virtually everyone. The EPA had declared the disaster area a federal CERCLA, or Superfund, cleanup site in 2009, and it required

* Jacobs says there is no evidence proving that the workers were instructed to spray water near the stationary air monitors.

that workers participate in forty hours of hazardous-waste training. The odd thing, Phillips told Scott, was that some Kingston workers she'd met said they had no dust masks or respiratory protection. That troubled her, since coal ash probably wasn't the safest stuff to inhale. Adding to her unease, some workers complained of feeling poorly. "You need to look into this," she said before hanging up.

At first, Scott hadn't known what to make of the call. He trusted Phillips to recommend him strong, winnable cases, but he doubted that she had the full story. There was absolutely no way, he thought, that the workers didn't have at least dust masks, a basic safety precaution at almost any jobsite, with or without coal ash. But, after speaking with Phillips, he had agreed to meet with a few Kingston workers anyway, as something of a favor. Now it was time.

After the pickups parked outside Scott's office, three men crossed the dim parking lot to the front door: Ansol Clark, Billy Gibson, and Tim Henry. Having just finished their shifts, they wore jeans and work shirts.

Scott greeted the men and led them through the office. He sported a red twill polo shirt and khakis and stood several inches shorter than the three brawny blue-collar workers. Scott, now in his mid-forties, had also grown a smidge soft around the middle, and his bird's nest of dark hair showed traces of gray. Still, he retained a buoyant, boyish quality.

The group reached a conference room, large and windowless, with a long hardwood table. Scott settled into a seat opposite the three workers. He didn't take notes, nor did he typically. He considered his memory good enough. He spoke softly and swiftly as he asked the three men about themselves, then he told them that he knew their allegations generally but he wanted specifics.

"They lied to us," Ansol said. "They told us the ash was safe—that we could eat a pound of it a day and it wouldn't hurt us." *They*, Ansol explained, were TVA and Jacobs Engineering.

Scott leaned forward and folded his hands. He knew of Jacobs, at least somewhat. The company had an office in a renovated department store in Oak Ridge, about three miles from his parents' home. He had served on local Rotary Clubs with some Jacobs employees, and he knew someone high up in Bechtel Jacobs, the Jacobs subsidiary. But he didn't have a strong opinion, either positive or negative, about the company.

There were all sorts of construction and engineering firms around Oak Ridge and Knoxville.

Ansol and the others explained that for years Jacobs staff had insisted that fly ash wouldn't hurt them, so for years they had arrived home caked in it, thinking nothing of the potential harm. Then came the nosebleeds and the blackouts and the shortness of breath. "We'd get blisters on our arms," Ansol said, lifting one of his. "And if you popped that blister, it was like lighting a torch on your arm."

As the three workers talked, they kept cutting each other off, as if they'd been holding in a secret they could finally share. TVA never talked about their needing dust masks or respirators, Henry said, leaning toward Scott, arms crossed. The agency only discussed hard hats, steel-toed boots, and safety vests. Gibson said a Jacobs safety supervisor had once told him that he'd be "run off the site" if he wore a dust mask. A Teamster sported one near a public road once, Gibson alleged, and someone made him take it off.

The three workers said it was understood that if they wore respiratory protection of any sort, they would risk their jobs. Now, they feared, something with their health was terribly wrong. Before the spill, Ansol, for one, hadn't taken any medications, and, because of his good health, he hadn't visited a doctor in perhaps thirty years beyond work physicals. And he didn't smoke. Now, "I get real tight-chested," he said, "and I can't breathe when I lie down." Gibson and Hill shared similar complaints.

You guys have been drinking too much Oliver Stone Kool-Aid, Scott thought as he listened. He knew that TVA wanted to avoid blame for the Kingston disaster, a point crystallized by Tom Kilgore's combative trial testimony a year earlier. Still, he assumed that TVA and its contractors were self-interested enough to provide workers with basic protective gear. How could two multibillion-dollar organizations *not* consider worker safety? It seemed absurd: the liability was almost limitless. He wondered, too, whether fly ash had actually caused the men's health problems. While litigating the land cases, as he now referred to the Roane County property-damage suits, he had read some TVA literature stating that fly ash was composed of "inert dust," which, though perhaps annoying, posed little threat beyond mild eye or skin irritation. Yet the three workers sitting before him had almost no energy, and their eyes and noses looked abnormally red.

Once the workers finished their stories, Scott thanked them for stopping by. "I don't want to give you great expectations," he said, "and I don't want to tell you stories about how much [money] you can get." But he said he would dig in and get back to them. That was, for now, the only promise he could keep.

Snow fell early and heavy in the high country that year. On the Appalachian Trail outside Knoxville, hikers surprised by a rare October blizzard raced to build fires and find shelter. At Mount LeConte, one of the Smokey Mountains' highest summits, three-foot drifts partially buried the primitive cabins built at the peak. Flights out of Knoxville's McGhee Tyson Airport were grounded. Mountain communities to the north lost power for weeks.

As the blizzard bore down, Janie Clark was reckoning with a storm of her own. She disliked—hated, actually—the idea that Ansol had met with an attorney. "Don't do this," she'd told him beforehand. "Don't make this about money." Like many conservative Christians in and around Knoxville—a famously puritanical town—she considered filing a lawsuit not a sin, necessarily, but in similar territory, especially if no one had died or been maimed. She questioned, too, whether fly ash explained Ansol's recent health troubles, as he insisted it had. She took TVA at its word that the fly ash was safe, as did many other Knoxvillians. Ansol had ignored her objections about meeting with Scott, telling her simply, "I'm doing it."

One November morning, a few weeks after the three workers met with Scott, Janie drove Ansol to see their family doctor. Ansol had yet to shake the flu, or whatever it was, that he'd caught over the summer. Janie hoped that the doctor could finally make sense of what was going on. Maybe Ansol needed another steroid shot? Maybe he needed to try a new allergy pill?

When they arrived, Janie waited at reception. She welcomed a chance to sit. A year and a half earlier, the focus of her life had shifted overnight after her mother, Margaret, suffered a stroke that left her partially paralyzed and in need of almost constant care. Janie had accepted the bulk of the responsibility and quit her job as a housekeeper. Now she woke up at four-thirty each morning to see Ansol off to work. After another hour's sleep, she woke again and fixed dinner for that evening, then drove across town to her mother's to spend the day. Each evening, back at home, she reheated dinner for her and Ansol. She never picked up fast food or soup and sandwiches to give herself a break, and she never took a vacation. She paid all the bills, did all the cleaning, did all the laundry, and kept track of all their appointments. She didn't mind. She loved her mother, and she certainly loved Ansol, though she did look forward to his turning sixty-six in five short years. Then he would be able to collect his full Social Security benefit and retire, and maybe they both could rest.

Janie sat in the doctor's waiting room for a long time that morning. As noon approached, the office emptied for lunch. Janie and Ansol both owned old flip phones. She seldom texted with hers, but she typed a message, asking if Ansol was okay. He responded: They want me to go to the hospital. Meet me at the car.

Janie, surprised and not sure what else to do, gathered her things and rushed outside. She started her Toyota RAV4, and Ansol soon strode outside and climbed in. "My doctor wants me to go to the hospital right away," he said. Why? Janie asked. He didn't have the flu, he explained. Something was wrong with his heart. And, according to his doctor, without immediate treatment, he was either going to have a heart attack or a stroke. But Ansol told Janie that he didn't want to take an ambulance straight to the hospital, as the doctor had urged. If he had to go, he said, he wanted Janie to drive him, and he wanted to grab a few things at home first.

Janie sped the five and a half miles back home. As she drove, her mind whirled. Why had diltiazem stopped working? Wasn't his heart mostly okay now?

Ansol said little, keeping his composure as he almost always did.

At home, she stuffed underwear and a few changes of clothes into a sack for Ansol. She later wondered why she had agreed to go home at all—why she hadn't driven him straight to the hospital as Ansol's doctor had advised. But their life had careened into strange new territory, and she had retreated home reflexively, as had he.

Ansol's doctor had alerted Parkwest Medical Center that Ansol and

Janie were en route. When they arrived, about thirty minutes after leaving the doctor's office, hospital staff were waiting. Nurses loaded Ansol onto a gurney and hurried him inside. They removed his clothes, inserted ports into his arms, checked his vitals.

Janie sat next to him in an uncomfortable chair. She knew Ansol had considered his illness temporary, a minor setback he would overcome with work and grit, as he had so many past challenges. But now as Ansol lay in bed, hooked up to a heart monitor and intravenous fluids and a urine bag, any illusions about his health melted away. And yet, to Janie, Ansol almost looked relieved. Maybe now he would get some real care, he said. Maybe now someone would take his health problems seriously and find a real fix.

Doctors performed an ultrasound of Ansol's heart. The diagnosis was congestive heart failure. Ansol's wheezing and bloating owed not to allergies or the flu but to fluid buildup in his body, a side effect of his heart failing to properly circulate blood. Doctors drained forty pounds of fluid from his body.

The news flattened Janie. She stayed at Ansol's side late into the night, bulldozed by the day's exhausting blur. She knew that her husband wasn't well, but she couldn't grasp how he had gotten so sick so quickly. Busy caring for her mother, she'd hardly researched atrial fibrillation after Ansol's 2010 diagnosis, and she had no idea that congestive heart failure was a possible effect. But she lacked the energy to dwell on this now. She needed to go home and sleep for both their sakes, she told Ansol. She promised to return first thing in the morning. Exhausted himself, he said okay.

The next day, doctors tried to shock Ansol's heart back into its proper rhythm. His heartbeat normalized for about twenty minutes before returning to its arrhythmic pattern. Subsequent attempts also failed. The damage was permanent.

After two days, Ansol was released from the hospital, and the man Janie brought home was not the one she had left with. Doctors prescribed sotalol, a medication that treats arrhythmia by slowing down the heart, but the drug drained Ansol's energy and made him feel light-headed.

Over the next few days, Ansol, having called in sick, tried to relax and recuperate at home. A few years earlier, he'd found a wild turkey egg, which he'd hatched by keeping it under a heat lamp on the dining-room table and rolling it twice a day for almost a month. He'd named the poult Junior and raised it himself. But, for whatever reason, the turkey hated Janie and wouldn't let her feed it, so, after Ansol returned home from the hospital, he continued to tend to the pet. He discovered that the short walk to Junior's backyard pen, at the bottom of a small hill, sapped what little energy he had. His skin flushed white. Once, he dropped to his knees, unable to crest the hill back to the house. Janie, watching through the kitchen window, dashed outside to help him up.

Doctors had told Ansol that his body would soon adjust to sotalol, but he couldn't afford to sit around and wait to regain his energy. He needed to work, to provide for himself and Janie, especially since she'd stopped cleaning homes to care for her mother. He took a week of sick leave, then returned to Kingston. When he did, he sometimes felt dizzy behind the wheel of his fuel truck and had to pull to the side of the road until the spell passed. For now, that seemed like his best, and only, option.

Personal-injury attorneys are gamblers, at least the ones who represent plaintiffs. That's because, under a typical contingency-fee agreement, they alone carry the burden of pursuing a case on a client's behalf, risking time and resources and mental strain in exchange for a customary third of all recovered money. If a case fails to yield a recovery, whether through a settlement or a judgment, the attorneys receive no consolation prize. Every case carries risk, and plaintiffs' attorneys who lack deep, almost cellular-level skepticism when evaluating a potential suit tend not to remain in practice long; they go broke litigating losers. Some successful attorneys decline to represent as many as 99 percent of the people who contact them for assistance. And, among the small number of cases they do take, most bring in modest fees that do little more than keep the lights on and the staff paid. Every so often, though, a potential blockbuster presents itself. These cases, usually against deep-pocketed corporations, can account for a third or a half or an even larger share of an attorney's yearly fees. They can make you not just well-off but rich. And the prospect of winning such a lucrative case can lead an attorney to suspend his or her doubts, at least temporarily, about a prospective client's claim, and to spend more time analyzing a case than one might otherwise. The Jacobs case stood to be such a blockbuster for Jim Scott.

On a chilly winter evening, pickup trucks again pulled into his office parking lot, but there were more of them this time, and motorcycles. As spaces filled up, some trucks resorted to parking at the Weigel's next door or at a nearby furniture place. About twenty Kingston workers, recruited by Ansol, Gibson, and Henry, made their way inside to the conference room. Many came straight from work, still dusted in ash.

After the first meeting, Scott remained skeptical about the workers' allegations. Ansol had called and told him about his congestive heart failure, and Scott had expressed sympathy. Privately, though, he wondered whether the fly ash had, at worse, just accelerated a preexisting condition, rather than caused the issue, as Ansol alleged. Scott also wondered whether Ansol, Gibson, and Henry had exaggerated their stories about Jacobs Engineering staff denying them respiratory protection, which still seemed outrageous. But Scott had agreed to meet with a larger group of workers in case his doubts were misplaced and the workers were telling the truth.

Scott failed to anticipate the number of men that would show up. The conference room, big and well furnished, lacked enough chairs for the crowd, so some men stood in the back. Scott, shirtsleeves rolled up and a tie loose around his neck, introduced himself and offered everyone soda or water, then he settled into a chair toward the center of the conference table. The additional workers resembled the first three—red noses, red-rimmed eyes, fatigued—and they reiterated many of the same allegations: that Jacobs staff had, with few exceptions, denied them dust masks and that their jobs were being threatened if they wore one they brought. They weren't interested in money, the men insisted, at least not primarily. They wanted protection on the jobsite, and they wanted someone to hold Jacobs and TVA to account for the harm they'd caused.

Scott explained that the workers had little chance of successfully suing TVA, since, as a federal agency, it enjoyed sovereign immunity. He promised to investigate their claims regarding Jacobs, but he tempered their expectations. The case might go nowhere, depending on what he did or, more likely, didn't find. In terms of evidence, "we're starting at zero," he said, in his soft drawl. He needed to meet with the workers individually, to gain a better understanding of their claims—and to see whether their stories had major contradictions, though he didn't say as much. Scott took down the workers' names and phone numbers and promised to be in touch.

Among the men who jotted down their contact information was Jeff Brewer, the part-time preacher. He'd decided to attend the meeting after Ansol's latest medical travail, concerned that he might meet a similar fate if nothing changed. Brewer assumed that, if either TVA or Jacobs learned that he'd met with an attorney, he would be furloughed, fired, or worse. TVA employed ten thousand people throughout the seven states in which it operated. But the Department of Energy had more than thirteen thousand employees and contractors on its payroll just in Oak Ridge, and thousands of those jobs were in construction. The workers knew from experience that if they earned reputations as troublemakers, they risked getting blackballed not only from TVA jobs but also from other government projects. They felt they had no other choice, though. They needed representation.

Scott, for his part, could see nervousness in the workers' eyes. He would come to understand why.

Over the following weeks, Scott canvassed East Tennessee in his Ford Explorer. He met the workers at gas stations and at Cracker Barrels, at barbecue shacks and at a Shoney's. They all told him the same thing: since the cleanup's start, four years earlier, Jacobs officials had denied them dust masks, not provided them with doctors, and laid off nearly everyone who pushed back. After five or six meetings, Scott thought maybe the workers were telling him the truth, because if their stories were invented or exaggerated, they would have inconsistencies, however minor, and none did.

When not visiting the workers, Scott dug into studies about coal ash. Though a lifelong Democrat, he considered himself something of a libertarian when it came to business, and he in no way viewed himself an aggressive environmentalist. As such, he sought out studies that bore no trace of what he called "tree-hugging." One of the first that he discovered was by Avner Vengosh, a Duke University professor. In early 2009, Vengosh's team had, on three separate trips, collected samples at the Kingston spill site and concluded that the coal ash contained arsenic, mercury, and radium in levels high enough to pose potential health risks if it were airborne. And, by 2010, the ash often was. In the summers, it swirled and formed dust devils forty feet tall.

Scott kept researching. In a typical civil suit, a plaintiff's attorney must prove his case not beyond a reasonable doubt, as in a criminal case, but by "a preponderance of the evidence," a lower standard which holds that an allegation must be found more likely true than not. But the lower standard of proof was still high, and Scott needed to learn as much about coal ash as he could.

He soon came across a troubling lawsuit. The case involved the AES Corporation, a Virginia-based Fortune 500 electric company that operated in twenty-seven countries. In 2003 and 2004, AES shipped eighty-two thousand tons of coal ash—at least ten barge loads—to the Dominican Republic, where it was unloaded and left uncovered near the waterfront, free to be carried by the wind. Within months, babies from local villages were born with severe birth defects: missing limbs, missing organs, internal organs outside their bodies. "When I was pregnant," a local woman told the *Miami Herald*, "I was dizzy, vomiting, and could barely walk." Her baby boy was born without arms. In 2006, the Dominican government filed a lawsuit against AES, alleging that its coal-ash dump site caused the birth defects, killed six people, and seriously sickened five others. AES settled the case for $6 million, though it maintained that it had done nothing wrong.

Scott was haunted by images he saw online of the village children. During the land cases, he had focused too narrowly on property damage, he now suspected. Why hadn't he considered the workers? He knew that TVA had failed to prevent and accept blame for the coal-ash disaster. Yet he assumed that it would clean up its billion-gallon mess responsibly—an unconscionable lapse. Also, he now felt certain that he had too readily trusted the state's and TVA's analysis of the coal ash, accepting their reports that it was a potential irritant and little more. The AES case and the Vengosh report upended this fiction.

One evening not long after he made this realization, a worker named Mike McCarthy stopped by to see Scott. Scott's office measured thirty by thirty and had wood panels that extended partly up the wall. McCarthy, who had an impressive flattop and a prominent, angular nose, sat in one of two navy-and-maroon suede chairs across from Scott's desk.

McCarthy had grown up on Long Island and still carried the accent to prove it. He told Scott that he was a member of the Operators union and one of the first men to respond to the Kingston disaster. Within two years on the job, he started to suffer chest pains, he said, and his testosterone levels had plummeted. He wheezed throughout the night and never seemed to catch his breath. But his health, though distressing, wasn't his top concern.

"I had two kids while I was out there," he said. His daughter, Angela, who was born a few months before the Kingston disaster, started to act strangely after her third birthday. She lost her appetite, he said. She sucked on ice cubes instead of eating. Her spark faded. McCarthy and his wife took her to see a pediatrician. After looking over the toddler, the doctor had her rushed across the street to the East Tennessee Children's Hospital, where she received an emergency blood transfusion for low iron and a high white-blood-cell count. The experience shook McCarthy. Then his son, who was born about a year into the cleanup project, developed lung problems. "Jimmy has a breathing machine," he told Scott, "and he's on medication daily."

McCarthy, like many of the workers, had initially believed Jacobs staff that fly ash posed no health threat. Typically, when he arrived home from work, before he even took off his ash-covered clothes, "I'd go and hug [the kids] and hold them and change their diapers," he said. "I let them down," he added, looking down at his thick, hard hands. He felt sure, though he lacked evidence, that fly ash had caused his children's health issues. What other explanation was there? If he had been warned about fly ash's dangers, he would have worn a Tyvek hazmat suit, or quit if he wasn't supplied with one.

As Scott listened, his thoughts turned to Sam, his youngest. Over the years, he had seen a seemingly endless number of specialists for his Tourette's and autism, the latter of which turned out to be mild. Still, Scott hated that Sam had to keep so many appointments and that he—a funny, brilliant kid—might view himself as different from his friends or classmates. Scott would mope if he dwelled on it too much, but he felt foolish for having such feelings now. Sam had hard days and challenges, but he was fine. McCarthy's children deserved all the empathy.

Moved by McCarthy's story, Scott asked him to bring in whatever documents or potential evidence he had.

"Well, I got photos," McCarthy replied. "I got a lot of photos." He fished his cell phone from his pocket.

Scott walked around and stood next to him. McCarthy swiped through the images. There were hundreds, some dating back years. Dump trucks kicking up clouds of fly ash. Men covered in muck. Dead geese splayed on the ground. Fish belly-up in the river. "Why are you taking all these pictures?" Scott asked, as McCarthy flicked through the collection. "You know," McCarthy said, in his heavy Long Island accent, "I want my kids to know that I helped clean up the biggest environmental disaster in the country's history." That was something to be proud of, he said.

Scott agreed. Keep taking pictures, he told McCarthy.

McCarthy said he would. Then, almost as an afterthought, he mentioned that he had some cell-phone videos that he had filmed on the jobsite. He kept his phone on a lanyard around his neck, he said, and secretly recorded sometimes. He showed one to Scott.

In the clip, a group of men stands near a large fuel truck, parked in a field of dust. The sun glints off the truck's polished tank, as a motor drones loudly. A middle-aged man, sporting sunglasses and an orange hard hat, strides past the camera. McCarthy calls to him, "Hey!" When the man—Chris Eich, a Jacobs safety supervisor—walks over, McCarthy complains that his sinuses have been acting up. Would wearing a dusk mask be signing his job's "death warrant"? McCarthy asks.

"Uhhh," Eich begins, neon vest inches from the camera. It's not the ash, he says. "The pollen this year is horrible—it's the pollen." Eich advises McCarthy to take an Allegra or two.

McCarthy, unsatisfied, repeats his question: "Do you think I would hang myself?"

"Yeah," Eich responds sharply, then he pauses for a beat before adding, "don't hang yourself with your own cock."

The conversation lasts a little over a minute.

When the video ended, McCarthy said, "I knew they'd lie. About everything."

Holy smoke, Scott thought. Make a copy, he told McCarthy, and do it right away. Now Scott had proof.

• • •

The holidays slid into view. On Gay Street, downtown Knoxville's central thoroughfare, toy elves and Christmas trees and pastries filled storefront windows. A block over, a temporary ice rink ran down the center of Market Square, a block-long concrete slab encircled by restaurants and stores. At Sequoyah Presbyterian Church, where the Scott family had long attended, a children's choir performance was coming up.

Jim Scott usually embraced the spirit of the season, for his sons' sake mostly. The year prior, he had stayed up until almost four on Christmas morning trying to put together a Ping-Pong table. He seldom triumphed at assembly-intensive projects—they took him forever, without exception—but he threw himself at them anyway. This year, however, he had neither time nor energy, so he bought his sons a forty-three-inch flatscreen TV at Best Buy instead. They would love it, he told himself.

Scott hadn't yet drafted a complaint against Jacobs Engineering, but the case already occupied an outsize place in his mind. His other work suddenly seemed trivial in comparison. In all his years in law, he had never encountered such wanton disregard for worker safety compared with Jacobs's. Mike McCarthy's "cock" video would help prove the point. A document or witness testimony might fade from a jury's memory over the course of a trial, but that video wouldn't. It illuminated Jacobs's intimidation tactics in sound and color. Still, Scott needed more evidence if he hoped to build a winnable case. And, before he tried to do that, he needed to talk with his wife.

Scott and his family still lived in the same white-painted home in Sequoyah Hills as they had in 2008, when the coal-ash dike collapsed. Jim and his wife, Mary, who was slim and had olive skin and dark black hair, had bought the place in 2003, about two years after they were married. They paid $252,000, a not-small sum for Knoxville real estate at the time. Built in the 1950s, the house wasn't monstrous, like some newer, tackier homes in the neighborhood, but it suited them fine: four bedrooms, three baths, a brick patio, a wall of hemlocks out back. The family invited neighbors over for pumpkin carving each fall. When the weather allowed, Jim liked to stand in the backyard and hurl a football over the house and into his neighbor's yard, where Jack, his oldest, would catch it. You're like Superman, Jack would say.

One of the home's most distinct, and dated, features was a wood-paneled family room. One evening after work, as Jim and Mary relaxed there on a brown sofa, he mentioned that he was interested in filing a lawsuit against a big construction firm, Jacobs Engineering, on the Kingston workers' behalf.

Mary wasn't an attorney. After graduating from UT, she had taught high-school home economics before quitting to have children. She now sat on the PTA and taught vacation Bible school. But, after a dozen years of marriage to Jim, she knew well the strain of big cases, and resented him for taking them on. Early in their relationship, Jim had spent a year or more jetting around the country to depose witnesses for a case against the restaurant chain O'Charley's, after a hepatitis A outbreak at some of its locations sickened nearly one hundred people and killed at least one man in the Knoxville area. Mary stayed at home to care for their sons. And she complained that, even when Jim was around, he did little to help her out. He'd mostly sit in the basement and drink wine and watch movies, she said. But what concerned her most about the workers' case was not the countless hours that it would surely demand of Jim but whether the case was the best use of his time. The land cases hadn't settled yet, so he hadn't earned anything from those. And didn't their house need a new roof? Mary asked. Shouldn't he be working on more fast, easy cases to generate fees?

Jim loathed such questions. He wasn't good with money and hated having to think about it. And perhaps as a result, finances had become an almost constant source of bickering between him and Mary. He had yet to recover from the Eddie Daniel debacle, after his former partner swindled a tiny fortune from his firm. Jim largely kept Mary in the dark about the whole exhausting mess. Why bother getting into it? But he couldn't hide everything.

"We're spending too much money," she told him. "It's ridiculous." They owed something like $60,000 in back taxes, and they'd racked up medical bills from Sam's treatments and doctor's appointments. (Jim eventually had to borrow $97,000 from his parents to cover bills, taxes, and the family's living expenses.) And yet, as best as Mary could tell, Jim's spending had hardly ebbed. She accused him of blowing through $1,800 a month on takeout, an "absolutely absurd" amount, she said, since he could eat dinner at home with the family.

Okay, yes, Jim conceded, he ordered a lot of takeout—especially from Calhoun's, the barbecue joint Sam liked—but he worked late and was usually starving when he left the office, and he wanted something hot and ready to eat. Jim's spending infuriated Mary nonetheless. And, given their financial predicament, she couldn't understand why he would take on another monster case on contingency right now.

Jim tried to explain that he wanted to work on cases he found interesting or important, like the workers'. He *wanted* to make money, sure, and he savored the comforts it brought. After he settled the O'Charley's suits, which generated seven figures in fees, he flew his law firm to the Caribbean for vacation. But he didn't stress out when his cash ran low. That was the nature of working largely on contingency: feast or famine, boom or bust. Yes, the workers' case would likely take years to resolve, but he stood to earn a hefty fee, and he assumed that it would help him pay off his debts. In the meantime, he still pulled in a respectable income from other cases. None of this swayed Mary.

At night, Jim, undeterred by his wife's reservations, worked at an antique wooden desk in their basement-level den after his sons fell asleep. He usually wore sweats and sipped wine. Obsession came easily for him. Once, after a friend mentioned that his pregnant wife was craving Klondike bars, he fixated on them, too. He staked out which Knoxville grocery stores had the best selection and stockpiled boxes. He couldn't help himself. But his fixation on the workers' case was of an entirely greater order of magnitude.

He'd told the workers to bring him whatever evidence they could. Mike McCarthy had come through with the damning video. But Scott couldn't wait for other such material to find him. Seated in a leather swivel chair, he pored over TVA's website, which had a section dedicated to the Kingston cleanup. On the main landing page, a slideshow rotated photos of placid rivers, springtime trees, and fishermen casting from a boat. Besides a few images of backhoes and dusty expanses of earth, the pictures in no way suggested that a billion gallons of coal sludge had swallowed the landscape.

Scott clicked around. The website contained links to hundreds, if not thousands, of documents: project plans, fact sheets, environmental-monitoring data, press releases, inspection reports. It was an ocean of PDFs. A team of lawyers could spend weeks reading it all. *Surely, there must be some sort of safety standards posted somewhere*, Scott thought as he skimmed. Past cases had taught him that big jobsites typically had documents that outlined worker-safety protocols, which he figured would prove useful.

As he read, he formed a rough outline of the cleanup project. First, during an eighteen-month sprint, TVA and its contractors raced to dredge four million tons of fly ash from the Emory River. Much of this ash ended up at the Arrowhead Landfill, in Alabama. During the cleanup's ongoing second phase, the focus shifted to clearing out some backwater sloughs, filled in by some three million tons of ash when the dike failed. For some reason, TVA had not shipped this ash to the Alabama landfill but instead dumped it on-site in a two-hundred-and-forty-acre "disposal cell"—essentially a rebuilt, reinforced version of the failed holding pond. A third, concurrent phase involved evaluating the long-term ecological risks of the nearly seven hundred thousand tons of ash that TVA had left on the bottom of the Emory River, for reasons that were, to Scott, not immediately clear.

After a week of reading, Scott happened upon a document called the "Site Wide Safety and Health Plan for the TVA Kingston Fossil Plant Ash Release Response." Prepared by Jacobs Engineering and approved by the EPA and TVA, the document ran more than three hundred pages and covered nearly every aspect of site safety: training protocols, emergency response, personal-hygiene procedures. A skimpy section detailed on-site hazards, such as slips, trips, and falls. But among the dull, innocuous pages, Scott noticed something peculiar, and alarming. One of the subsections included a table, and this table listed six toxic constituents of fly ash. Among them: arsenic, aluminum oxide, iron oxide, and silica—a Long Island iced tea of poison, he'd later call it.

He read the table again. It said that fly ash's constituents could harm the eyes, liver, lungs, kidneys, and respiratory system. Elsewhere, the document stated that the Kingston fly ash contained selenium, cadmium, boron, thallium, and other metals—several of which Scott knew to be radioactive. An updated version of the "Safety and Health Plan" disclosed that the fly ash contained at least twenty-three heavy metals and toxins.

He was stunned. The workers had mentioned not *one* of the constituents to him, much less said anything about the "Safety and Health Plan," and he felt sure they would have had they known about either.

The document seemed purposefully buried on TVA's website, and he could guess why: to him, the document not only erased almost all doubt that Jacobs and TVA knew that fly ash was more hazardous than they let on, it also spelled out how Jacobs needed to protect the workers. If the risk of inhaling fly ash grew high, for instance, Jacobs staff needed to halt operations and address the problem. That, or the workers needed personal protective equipment, like a respirator or a hazmat suit. But, insofar as Scott knew, Jacobs had taken no such precautions, at least not in any meaningful way. And, with more evidence, he bet he could prove that Jacobs had fallen short of, if not outright ignored, its and TVA's safety protocols.

From that day forward, whenever workers stopped by Scott's office, he handed out pages from the "Safety and Health Plan." They had a right to know what the fly ash contained, and about the harm that hung in the air.

Ansol Clark couldn't keep up. It was early 2013, four years into the cleanup. After his hospital stay, he had hoped that his body would adjust to the drowsy, draining effects of sotalol, his new heart-arrhythmia medication, but months had passed with little improvement. Too often, as he drove his fuel truck across the dusty jobsite, the earth beneath him seemed to bend and twist, even when he steered straight. His vision would blur, forcing him to pull over and lay his head on the wheel until the spell passed. It wasn't safe.

Since coming to Kingston, Ansol had worked alongside a few different equipment operators who rode with him to fuel other vehicles. For the past two years, his partner was Mike McCarthy, the recorder of the "cock" video. Ansol could be taciturn, while McCarthy was anything but. And yet, in time, they grew to be friends. McCarthy, originally from New York, had lived in Florida before moving to Knoxville. Ansol jokingly called him "Halfback," since living in Tennessee put him roughly halfway back home. McCarthy enjoyed hearing stories about Ansol's pet turkey, Junior, which Ansol had somehow trained to sit next to him on a patio swing.

One winter day, as they fueled a vehicle, Ansol, overcome with exhaustion, sat on the ground to take a breather. When he tried to stand again, he couldn't. His muscles just wouldn't move. He remained in the dirt, not knowing what to do, not knowing what to think. McCarthy walked over. "You okay?" he asked.

"Yeah, I'll be okay," Ansol said. "I need to sit down here just for a minute."

He regained enough strength to finish his shift, but the episode discomfited both him and McCarthy. Ansol had been a beast when they started working together, McCarthy later told a friend—like a football lineman almost, like a damn mule. That Ansol would now struggle to stand seemed impossible.

At home that evening, Ansol walked into the living room, where Janie usually read after caring for her mother all day. "Janie," he said plainly, "I'm done. I can't do this job anymore." He needed to stay on sotalol to avoid further health problems. But, if he kept driving trucks, "I'm going to hurt somebody," he said.

Ansol had mentioned the idea of quitting in the past, but he and Janie had never discussed it earnestly. Now Ansol had made up his mind, and, though the suddenness of his decision surprised Janie, she supported it. She knew as well as he did that he couldn't keep driving. What she didn't know was how they'd support themselves once he stopped. As a subcontractor, Ansol received benefits not from TVA but from his union, the Teamsters.

One day, not long after talking with Janie, Ansol drove to the local union hall, in a repurposed brick Baptist church on the north side of town. He would turn sixty-two that month, so he qualified for early retirement. The problem, a union rep told him, was that his retirement application would take a few months to process; he would need to wait until his application was approved if he wanted to retire with some benefits. He said okay, that would have to do.

The night before Ansol's last workday, on March 15, 2013, Mike McCarthy stayed up late baking a six-layer chocolate cake. The next day at the jobsite, Ansol and McCarthy and a group of guys took a long break at the Berkshire House. They ate the cake, and the group presented Ansol with a retirement present: a holster for his pistol, a Taurus Judge, engraved with the words THE TURKEY WHISPERER. On cold days during his years at Kingston, Ansol had worn the same heavy down jacket, now threadbare and full of holes. His friends auctioned off the dingy garment, which went for nearly $40. That got a laugh out of Ansol, and he got to keep the money.

Then, with no further fanfare, his working days were through. He had raised cattle, chickens, and hogs as a child; served in the Navy in his teens; and driven trucks in adulthood. Now, nothing. Knoxville had transformed as much as he had, and not necessarily for the better, in Ansol's view. His family farm had vanished during the west Knoxville housing boom of the 1980s and '90s. He could drive his Chevy through the subdivision that now occupied the land and point to where the old farmhouse, barn, and chicken coop had once stood. He didn't like to do that, though. Too many memories.

During Ansol's last year at Kingston, as overtime work tapered off, he had earned about $60,000. Once he retired, he expected to receive about $20,000 annually through a combination of Social Security and union benefits. Somehow, he and Janie would have to make that work. Health care presented another problem. Still too young to qualify for Medicare and with his union health coverage set to expire, Ansol applied for coverage with two large insurance companies. Both rejected him, owing to his preexisting conditions. The couple went uninsured for months, paying for Ansol's medications and doctor's appointments out of pocket. They finally bought coverage through the federal health-insurance marketplace, created as part of the Affordable Care Act of 2010. It was a welcome, if temporary, relief.

Jeff Friedman, the Birmingham attorney, hated the TVA Towers. The twin twelve-story structures stood at the north end of Market Square, dominating the Knoxville skyline from a hill in the middle of downtown. Built in the mid-1970s, the overlarge modern complex had an off-white facade and black slit windows, projecting an air of impenetrability and detachment from the rest of the old, mostly brick Appalachian city. Friedman had begrudgingly visited the towers to take depositions in the land cases, schlepping up the concrete steps to the plaza between the two buildings. Each time he stepped inside, TVA staff made him pass through security checkpoints and, after taking his photo, would clip an identification badge to his dark suit. He complained later that TVA stooges trailed him to the restroom whenever he went, as if he might steal something. To Friedman, the process seemed engineered to assert TVA's power; to make clear who was in control; to show him—and any other lawyer who dared to trudge up the hill—who ran East Tennessee. And it wasn't him. But the dynamic had changed recently.

In August 2012, nearly a year after Friedman sparred in court with Tom Kilgore, Judge Thomas Varlan ruled that TVA was liable for the Kingston disaster. Friedman, in other words, had won. Varlan agreed with the plaintiffs that TVA had failed to build and maintain the coal-ash dike properly, leading to its collapse, and that it had neglected to properly train its staff in coal-ash management. Still, damages needed to be decided. Rather than rush back to trial to make such determinations, Varlan ordered the two sides to try to negotiate an out-of-court settlement and to do so in good faith. The judge approved two neutral mediators to help the parties reach an agreement.

This was glorious news for Friedman. Varlan's decision had thrust TVA's legal team into a situation in which it rarely found itself: having to behave like a normal law practice, one that had to account for its client's actions, instead of hiding behind governmental immunity. And, since TVA had to participate in mediation and address the plaintiffs like equals, rather than annoyances it could ignore, Friedman decided that his days of trekking up the hill to the TVA Towers were through.

On a cold, bright morning in February 2013, Friedman and dozens of other attorneys met at the Knoxville Convention Center, a large, three-story venue, with an angular, pointed glass entrance. Both sides had agreed on the convention center, four blocks from the federal courthouse, as a neutral meeting site to begin talks before the two court-appointed mediators joined in. As Friedman tramped down the blue-carpeted corridors, dressed in a dark suit and pitched forward slightly, as was his custom, he felt satisfaction in not being on TVA turf.

In a third-story ballroom, he settled into a chair at one of several tables crowded with other lawyers and their staffs. The group comprised attorneys from at least ten different law firms who together represented about nine hundred plaintiffs. Friedman wanted to believe that TVA, humbled, surely, by the outcome of the trial, would come to the bargaining table sincerely interested in resolving the cases. No one, in his view—not him, not his clients, not the courts, not even TVA—would benefit from the two sides failing to come to terms. If negotiations failed and the cases advanced to a second trial phase, each and every plaintiff would have to have their day in court to prove their claims against TVA, and Varlan would have to award damages accordingly. This mammoth undertaking would take years, maybe even a decade. And Friedman knew that his clients, most of whom were local homeowners, wanted closure soon. The two sides had already "gone to war" for nearly four years, Friedman had explained to Varlan at a post-trial hearing, and that seemed like long enough to him. And now, as Friedman waited for negotiations to start that morning, he hoped that TVA, quickly running out of legal options, had accepted that it finally needed to do right by the plaintiffs and pony up.

Whatever hope he had of TVA's eagerness to settle dissolved the moment Edwin Small, TVA's chief litigator and deputy general counsel, strode into the beige-walled ballroom. Whereas other government agencies rely on the Department of Justice for litigation, TVA generally handles its own legal work, and its lawyers, many of them graduates of top-ranked law schools, are famously and almost proudly cocky. In some respects, "I'm not sure we weren't the best in the country," recalled Charles McCarthy, former TVA general counsel (and the father of the novelist Cormac McCarthy). Ed Small didn't subvert the stereotype.

Small, a graduate of the University of North Carolina law school, had neatly combed gray hair, wide red cheeks, and a tall frame. He had played a major role in the trial, trying to argue successfully why the mysterious slimes layer and a series of freak geological events, not TVA's negligence, caused the dike's collapse on that freezing December morning. Before the trial, Friedman had told Small that, no matter what TVA did, and no matter how long it dragged out the case, he and his team would never capitulate. "If we have to try this case for three months and only get one penny," Friedman had said, "it'll be worth it. And it will be the most painfully extracted penny in TVA history." Now, as Small stood before tables packed with plaintiffs' attorneys, he seemed bent on testing Friedman's resolve.

Small usually evoked a folksy manner, but he abandoned any hint of it that morning.* The plaintiffs, he began, didn't care about the rivers that TVA polluted. Because if they did, he said, they wouldn't have

* Edwin Small did not respond to an interview request.

thrown old refrigerators and dead cows and other garbage into the water like they had. They were polluters themselves. And now, Small said almost angrily, the plaintiffs wanted TVA to pay big dollars for putting a little fly ash in the water. Who were they to complain?

"Who in the world do you think you are?" one lawyer, seated among the plaintiffs' group, blurted out. Dead cows? Refrigerators? What was Small talking about?

Small, either ignoring or failing to hear the outburst, kept going. The plaintiffs were rednecks and felons, he said, and ungrateful ones at that. Didn't they know everything that TVA had done for East Tennessee? They should be *thanking* it, for its jobs, for its power, and for its hope, not suing it for a little coal-ash mishap. TVA hadn't really harmed the plaintiffs, Small went on. But the plaintiffs *had* harmed the people of Tennessee and the Southeast. Their lawsuits, he said, had cost TVA a lot of money, and its nine million ratepayers, spread throughout seven states, would have to cover the expense, reflected in their electricity bills. And, because of that, Small said, TVA had a responsibility, a public duty even, to keep costs low and not pay a substantial settlement.

Shock washed over the plaintiffs' attorneys. How, after the trial, after the inspector general's report, was TVA *still* in denial that it needed to take responsibility for the Kingston disaster? And was TVA really trying to argue that because the plaintiffs were rednecks—a false and derogatory statement to begin with—this somehow should preclude them from a settlement?

Small's presentation surprised Jeff Friedman, but not much. At a hearing a few months earlier, Jim Chase, a senior TVA attorney, had told Varlan that mediation was premature since the statute of limitations hadn't yet expired for property-damage claims related to the Kingston disaster. And, since it hadn't, a homeowner could theoretically, for another year and a half or so, file suit against TVA if they hadn't already. So it seemed sort of silly, Chase said, to mediate the cases until after the statute of limitations expired. Chase also tried to argue that some of the plaintiffs might not have legitimate claims in the first place, since TVA owned the riverbed and part of the shoreline near the Kingston power plant, meaning fly ash might not have washed up on their properties at all. Shouldn't an appeals court weigh in on all these concerns? he asked.

Over TVA's objections, Varlan had agreed with Friedman to move ahead with mediation. But Small's speech suggested that TVA had in no way warmed to the idea of settling the suits.

Among the lawyers in the ballroom that morning, enduring Small's castigation, was Jim Scott. He didn't shout at Small like the other attorney had, but he understood the impulse. Small's monologue struck him as fantastical nonsense, especially the part about keeping costs low for ratepayers. TVA executives zipped around on private jets and helicopters, and enjoyed multimillion-dollar salaries. (Congress had excused TVA from having to follow government salary limits about a dozen years earlier.) Two years after the Kingston disaster, TVA paid its employees $94 million in bonuses. But Scott reserved much of his ire for Tom Kilgore. He didn't take a bonus the year after the Kingston disaster—he clearly had enough sense to avoid such a public-relations land mine—but he did take one the next year, pulling in $2.7 million above his base pay. The whole thing disgusted Scott. He knew of only one plaintiff who had any sort of serious rap sheet: a former local judge, who happened to own property near the disaster site, had pleaded guilty to extortion charges a number of years earlier. Otherwise, Scott believed, you couldn't find better people than some of his clients, and now TVA was making them fight an arduous case over damage it had without question caused.

Scott had kept meeting with Ansol Clark and some other cleanup workers, and, based on their stories, he knew that TVA had treated them with equal, if not more, contempt than it now showed the landowners. Scott hadn't yet filed a suit against TVA or Jacobs Engineering on the workers' behalf. He needed more time to write a complaint, and he needed to decide whether he was able to carry the case forward alone, because he had no doubt, after Ed Small's monologue, that TVA would fight the workers' claims no less vigorously than it was fighting the landowners'. Resolving any dispute involving TVA, Scott feared, would be neither easy nor swift.

The mediation conference dragged on for three days and ended with the two sides no closer to reaching a deal than when they started. In big tort cases, like the coal-ash litigation, plaintiffs' attorneys get teamed up almost through luck of the draw, depending on whomever the claimants hire to represent them. If you're an ethical, hardworking attorney, you pray you don't get paired with crooks or incompetents, which sometimes happens. The sort of lawyer you hope to be partnered with is someone like Jeff Friedman.

Few of the other plaintiffs' attorneys knew Friedman before the Kingston disaster, but his wits and good nature had won their trust in the run-up to the trial, and his effective, eloquent dismantling of TVA's defense in court bolstered their admiration. No surprise, then, that, as the two sides planned follow-up conferences, Friedman assumed a captain's role on the negotiation team. He worked closely with an Asheville-based attorney named Gary Davis, who had a knack for the scientific aspects of environmental tort cases.

Before negotiations could get far, Friedman and the other plaintiffs' attorneys had to devise a fair, or at least a consistent, method for dividing a potential settlement, to head off any squabbling over money. To that end, Friedman and Davis and the two court-appointed mediators, Rodney Max and Pamela Reeves, created a "matrix," or a weighted system, that accounted for the value of each plaintiff's property and its proximity to the disaster site. The farther downriver you lived and the smaller your property, the smaller chunk of the recovery you'd receive, provided there was one. In the U.S., three-quarters of federal cases, or thereabouts, end with a settlement. In personal-injury suits, the rate runs closer to 90 percent. Yet a settlement was no sure thing with TVA.

Friedman and Davis met with TVA's legal team at least four times in the late winter and spring of 2013. Ed Small and Jeff Friedman remained cordial, in the mediators' opinion anyway. But they were, at their core, adversaries. Friedman thought the proposed settlement amounts that he and the other plaintiffs' lawyers devised were fair, or at least reasonable enough to warrant TVA's consideration. But when he and Davis presented Small's team with spreadsheets listing how much they thought TVA owed their clients, TVA rejected the plaintiffs' entire recovery formula. The damage estimates were high, Small insisted, outrageously high. Yet, to Friedman's frustration, Small's team didn't explain *why* they thought the plaintiffs' numbers were unreasonable, much less propose a better way to settle the cases. Rod Max, one of the two mediators, later complimented Small for his professionalism, saying his positions didn't diverge from law or fact. But, to the plaintiffs' team, TVA's mediation strategy seemed to center only on beating them down.

Jim Scott attended several of the follow-up mediation conferences, usually dressed in a blue blazer and khakis, a step up from the shorts and boat shoes he typically sported. Early in the lawsuit, he'd argued that TVA ought to pay one of his clients $10 million in damages. Shortly before the disaster, the client had listed for sale his five-bedroom mansion, perched on forty acres overlooking the Emory River. But after oily, gray coal-ash slurry flooded the waterfront, an interested buyer had backed out, and no one else had expressed serious interest since. What sane person would want to live next to such a mess? Scott contended that, on top of compensating the client for his home's loss in value, TVA should pay $20 million in punitive damages, to ensure that it wouldn't allow another disaster to occur. During mediation, TVA's legal team made clear that any such payout was wishful thinking. At one point, Small offered a settlement deal for all nine hundred or so plaintiffs that totaled less than $10 million.

"I'm tired of all this," Scott told Small, in response to the offer, as they sat across a table from each other. "When do you plan to offer substantial dollars for these people's properties?" Scott added. "Because what you're doing isn't right." After Small and the other TVA attorneys failed to supply much of an answer, Scott rose to his feet, shoved open the conference-room door, and left. He couldn't waste his time with such nonsense. He had other cases—rather, one case—that needed his attention.

PART II

2013–2017

On a bright autumn Saturday, a speck, not unlike a dot of light, appeared in the vast crystal-blue skies above central Florida. It was shortly past noon, on October 13, 1984, a warm and clear day with a gentle breeze. Eighty thousand feet above the white-sand beaches and emerald swamps, the speck moved at more than twelve hundred miles an hour, nearly twice the speed of sound. It emitted a thin trail of smoke, and then, as the speck hurtled toward Earth, two sonic booms roared across Brevard County. The space shuttle *Challenger* had safely reentered the atmosphere.

During an eight-day mission, the seven NASA astronauts aboard had deployed a research satellite and photographed Earth with a large-format camera. Now, as the *Challenger*, one-hundred-and-twenty-two-feet long and weighing a hundred tons, neared Kennedy Space Center, outside Orlando, it slowed to three hundred and forty miles per hour. Crowds watched as it closed in, falling hundreds of feet per second, transforming from a speck into a black dot and, finally, into a winged orbiter. The craft glided leaflike over a radiant lagoon. Then it touched down on a runway, rolled two miles, and stopped. A perfect landing, all the newspapers would say.

Twenty-eight years later, Jim Scott could still recall the day vividly. The *Challenger* had passed over Knoxville en route to Florida, and he'd followed its progress. About a month after the landing, Scott's rec football team had traveled to Florida to play in a tournament and stopped in Cocoa Beach, next to the space center. Scott got to see a space shuttle up close, and the futuristic, white-winged orbiter left an impression. Now, decades later, Scott wondered if he'd made a mistake regarding his career. He sometimes thought that if he had a do-over, he would have studied engineering or science and become an astronaut. Astronauts were heroes. Presidents thanked them for their courage. Cities threw ticker-tape parades in their honor. Children dressed up as them for Halloween. No one dressed up as a personal-injury attorney. People seemed to respect certain serial killers more than they did attorneys, and that bothered him. But the main reason Scott wished he'd become an astronaut was the chance to float, to feel weightless, to drift. These were sensations he wanted to experience now more than ever, because, as he pursued the workers' case, he felt as if a million pounds were weighing on him.

Initially, after meeting with Ansol Clark and the others, Scott planned to file workers' compensation claims on their behalf, to recover lost wages for work they'd missed owing to their illnesses, and he did submit a number of such claims. But his chief ambition was, or soon became, to file a civil complaint against Jacobs Engineering and TVA. That way, through litigation, he could prove that the organizations bore responsibility for the workers' health conditions and, he hoped, win them a recovery to pay for medical care. Otherwise, neither TVA nor Jacobs would be held to account for their treatment of the workers, which seemed to be growing increasingly hostile and brazen.

One summer morning, about five months after the mediation conference at the Knoxville Convention Center, Scott was walking through his law office when the receptionist beckoned him over. "Kevin Thompson is on the line," she said. "He says he's getting fired."

What? Scott thought. In the conference room, he picked up the phone. Thompson was a truck driver in his thirties who had worked at Kingston since 2010. "Jim," he began, "they're trying to send me home because I've got a prescription for a dust mask."

Thompson, like many of the workers, suffered from chest pains and breathing problems. He'd complained to his primary-care physician about both. The doctor took an X-ray and listened to Thompson's chest, then wrote him a prescription stating that he needed to wear a dust mask whenever he worked near fly ash. But, according to Thompson, after he gave the script to Tom Bock, of Jacobs, "he turned real red-faced." Bock told Thompson that the quantity of fly ash on-site didn't warrant a dust mask. And now Thompson was out of work.

As Thompson talked, Scott could hear voices in the background of the call, and he felt sure that they belonged to Jacobs and TVA staff. "Put them on the phone," Scott urged Thompson. "They can't do that."

Thompson said that the Jacobs or TVA people wouldn't speak with him. "They said they didn't have nothing for me to do," he added. His time at Kingston was over.

Scott hung up. Did Jacobs and TVA really think they could just fire workers for asking for safety gear? *You can't retaliate against people like that*, he thought. *You can't be that cruel to another person*. The situation seemed cartoonishly wicked.

A few days later, Thompson visited Scott's office. He was stocky and had close-cropped brown hair. He told Scott that he'd met with Bock at least twice about his health concerns. The first time Thompson went to Bock's office in Trailer City, a union steward, who happened to be Thompson's father, David, accompanied him—standard protocol. The meeting started fine but verged into atypical territory when Kevin handed Bock the dust-mask prescription. Bock, looking it over, demanded to know why Kevin had seen a doctor and why he thought he needed a mask. After Kevin tried to explain, Bock asked the two Thompsons to step outside for a moment. They obliged. As they waited, they heard a banging sound inside Bock's office. They looked through a window and watched as Bock, mumbling something, hit his head against the wall repeatedly.

Afterward, Bock had Kevin visit a physician provided by TVA. The doctor's examination was conspicuously brief, at least compared with the one by Kevin's doctor. "They came in and told me that I did not pass the breathing part—that my lung capacity was at 38 percent," Kevin recalled. He was fired at a subsequent meeting, ostensibly because he wasn't healthy enough to wear a dust mask and there was nowhere on-site free of fly ash for him to work without one. Kevin's father protested the decision; Kevin just stood up and left the room. He called Scott shortly thereafter.

The story was far odder than Scott first understood. What was up with Bock's head banging? And wasn't Bock, and Jacobs by extension, conceding that the fly-ash exposure did pose a potential problem if

Thompson could work nowhere at Kingston without being exposed to it? And why had neither Jacobs nor TVA honored the prescription written by Thompson's physician? Why not take the doctor's word that Thompson could safely wear a dust mask?

Thompson's termination heightened Scott's desire to file a complaint, and to do so quickly. A lawsuit, he assumed, would surely deter further retaliation against the workers.

He worked past ten most nights, drafting the workers' complaint. As he did, he pored over studies in well-regarded academic journals. The "Site Wide Safety and Health Plan" made clear that fly ash was potentially hazardous. But he needed to know precisely how much arsenic, lead, silica, and other toxins it contained, and the sort of harm fly ash could cause at different exposure levels. He'd practiced law long enough to know that hazardous substances seldom occur in concentrations high enough to cause damage. Each year, smoke alarms, for instance, expose homeowners to radiation but only in trace, inconsequential amounts. Scott hadn't forgotten about the report by the Duke professor Avner Vengosh, who warned that the Kingston fly ash could cause health problems if it dried and was inhaled, but he needed more evidence to convince Varlan and a jury of this point.

One paper quickly stood out. It was published in *The New England Journal of Medicine*, arguably the world's preeminent medical publication. In it, researchers, having analyzed decades' worth of air-pollution data from U.S. cities, drew a direct link between life expectancy and exposure to PM2.5—microscopic particulate matter that can penetrate deep into the lungs. High exposure to this tiny, nasty pollutant contributed to "significant and measurable" life-expectancy reductions, the paper concluded. And fly ash, Scott had learned, contained PM2.5.

What little time Scott had outside work he spent with his wife and sons, though his and Mary's relationship had deteriorated in recent months. She accused him of secretly obtaining new credit cards and incurring more debt, which Scott denied. Their money situation grew so dire that, for a while, Mary entertained taking a job at Hallmark stocking greeting cards, but Jim waved off the idea. The $10-an-hour pay wasn't worth her time, he told her, and it wouldn't help their situation much anyway. He suggested that they meet with a marriage counselor, but he never got around to finding one. Instead, they fought, about money but also about work, about sex, about alcohol, about everything. They both enjoyed wine and could overdo it on occasion, which amplified their bickering. Mary could also be erratic, in Jim's view, and she would later admit to screaming at him, though she said she did it only because of the stress he caused her—by falling behind on their taxes, by letting bills stack up, by not helping her around the house. He was a "frat daddy," she complained, and living with him was like living with a teenager.

Sam's therapy grew into another point of disagreement. Jim, having read widely about autism, hoped that Sam might benefit from alternative treatments—perhaps a gluten- and casein-free diet, or maybe B6 and magnesium—in conjunction with occupational therapy. He felt encouraged by Sam's progress so far and would try nearly any treatment, no matter how unorthodox, to help him make further gains, because unorthodox seemed to work. All those airport trips together and Sam's watching *Man v. Food* had proved that. But, to Jim's infinite frustration, Mary denied that Sam—high-functioning, hilarious, emotive—was on the autism spectrum at all, despite a doctor having said that he was. (Sam later said that neither parent told him he had autism, and he doubted whether he did. "Nothing was clear," he recalled.)

Sometimes at night, whenever the pressure of the case and his marriage felt extra crushing, as if someone had taken an eggbeater to his brain, Scott would walk the few blocks from his home to the greenway around his neighborhood. Seated on the banks of the Tennessee River, he would eat a bag of Skittles or peanut M&M's and watch as the black water spooled past, hissing in the dark, bending toward Kingston and cities beyond. Across the river, sheer limestone cliffs towered over the water, and the trees growing on them swayed in the wind. He wanted to be a good attorney, one who fought for justice and kept his expenses low and was liked, or at least respected, by his clients. Above all, he wanted to make his sons proud. The workers' case afforded him a rare opportunity to attempt something improbable and grand. He would carry the case as far as he was able, he decided, no matter the toll it took on his life. He had to finish the workers' complaint. He couldn't let Jacobs and TVA sicken Ansol Clark and other workers without consequence. He didn't want to live in a world where that was permissible, and he didn't want his sons to, either.

One immediate obstacle was that the EPA didn't consider coal ash hazardous waste, thanks to decades of coal-industry lobbying. In 1976, Congress had tried to regulate coal ash by passing the Resource Conservation and Recovery Act, or RCRA. But, in 1980, Alabama representative Tom Bevill introduced an amendment to the RCRA that exempted coal ash from being classified hazardous waste, thereby permitting utilities to handle and store the material nearly however they wished. Bevill, whose district depended on the coal industry, and who had earned the nickname "the King of Pork" for his skill at securing federal funds for his home state, argued that designating coal ash as hazardous would be overly burdensome to industry. Decades after his amendment passed, the EPA still didn't consider coal ash hazardous waste or require power companies, like TVA, to treat it with particular care.

After the Kingston disaster, the EPA had proposed a new rule to change coal ash's designation to hazardous. But it had yet to finalize the decision, and it was unclear whether it would. If Scott was going to make his case in court, he would need to prove that the EPA wasn't just wrong about coal ash but dangerously wrong. He wasn't only fighting Jacobs. He was taking on an industry.

Jeff Brewer had run out of options. Each morning, when he climbed into his dump truck, he could tell that night crews had tried to clean out the cab, but fly ash still covered the floorboard and the dash. Before cranking the engine and rumbling into the exclusion zone, he would rub down the interior with disinfecting wipes, though doing so accomplished almost nothing. He couldn't escape the stuff, especially not in the summertime, when the sun flared down on the bare, grassless countryside and dried the fly ash. Then the wind would stir and carry it into the air, forming great pale plumes that towered over the bulldozers and the backhoes and the trucks. Brewer didn't know if his body could endure another summer of breathing it in. But, unlike Ansol Clark, he couldn't retire or quit, especially not with job opportunities still scarce. He and the other workers had contacted Jim Scott about potentially filing a lawsuit, but Scott had told them that litigation took time, and Brewer felt that something needed to happen immediately.

One morning in the spring of 2013, he walked to Tom Bock's office in Trailer City. Bock was sitting at his computer when Brewer stepped inside. I'm concerned about my health, Brewer said, standing in front of Bock's desk. He had headaches, he explained, and his eyes burned and twitched. He coughed up a strange black jelly. Boils covered his skin. Brewer said he'd visited a family doctor, who, after giving him an exam, had written him a prescription saying that he needed to wear a respirator on the jobsite. Brewer handed the paper to Bock, who was standing now.

Brewer had heard about Kevin Thompson's asking for a dust mask, and about Bock hitting his head against the wall. With Brewer, though, Bock studied the prescription for a moment. "I'm not a pharmacist," he said, "and Jacobs isn't a pharmacy, and I don't think TVA is either."

"Tom, I'm sick," Brewer said, exasperated. "I've been telling you."

"We don't do that," Bock replied. "You can't wear a respirator."

Brewer insisted that he needed *something*. Otherwise, his health might never improve. Bock, keeping the note, sat down. He said he'd have to get back to him.

Brewer left the trailer dejected but not shocked. After all, Bock had told the workers repeatedly that they could eat a pound of coal ash a day and be fine.

Two or three days later, Brewer's immediate supervisor, a foreman named Brad Green, approached him before the morning safety meeting. You need to walk over to Trailer City and fill out some paperwork, Green said. I'll come with you.

Bock was waiting outside when they arrived. "You can't wear a respirator," Bock said. But he told Brewer that he could wear an N95 dust mask if he went to Oak Ridge and was fitted for one by the Occupational Safety and Health Administration (OSHA), a division of the Labor Department that ensures workplace safety. Brewer knew that a dust mask wouldn't protect him as well as a full-on respirator, which would have replaceable filter cartridges and a facepiece, but at least a dust mask was something. He worried, though, that the damage might already be done.

Throughout the spring of 2013, some twenty-five workers followed Brewer's and Thompson's lead and requested respiratory protection from TVA or Jacobs Engineering. Fly ash was wrecking their health, they complained. In response, most were told no, that their doctors were wrong, that they didn't have health problems and they didn't need respiratory protection. Bock claimed that TVA experts had evaluated air-monitoring data and found no link between the workers' symptoms and the fly ash.* The workers suspected another reason for the denial: that the public might see them in dust masks or respirators when they drove by the disaster site. Kingston residents were still furious with TVA over the coal-ash spill, and hundreds of workers in respirators or head-to-toe hazmat suits probably wouldn't help the situation.

In the workers' view, TVA and Jacobs staffers had little interest in discussing their health problems. But, unbeknownst to them, on May 6, as they began to ask for respirators and dust masks, Tom Bock emailed a TVA staffer explaining that Kathryn Nash, the TVA general manager of the cleanup project at the time, wanted "a plan of attack implemented by this week," in response to the workers' health allegations. In another email, Bock wrote that TVA aimed to have "a unified front . . . against the alleged exposure claims." In a flurry of messages that followed, conference calls were scheduled, attorneys looped in, reports linked to and shared. In one email, a TVA program manager encouraged Bock to gather evidence, and to do so quickly, because, with increased scrutiny surely on the horizon, they might have little time to build a defense.

The Calhoun's barbecue near Knoxville's Sequoyah Hills neighborhood sits flanked by an urgent-care clinic and a Verizon store on one side and on the other by Knoxville's defining architectural feature: a strip mall. One evening, Jim Scott took his youngest son, Sam, there for dinner. They sat at a table near the bar, flatscreens blaring sports games overhead. They ordered their usual: ribs, mac 'n' cheese, broccoli.

Jim felt good. On August 22, 2013, more than half a year after he

* Bock later said that he never personally denied any worker respiratory protection; he just processed the requests and forwarded them to TVA or other contractors on-site.

first met Ansol Clark, he had filed a civil-action lawsuit in federal court against Jacobs on behalf of thirty-two Kingston workers and seventeen of their spouses. (One worker later withdrew, dropping the total to forty-eight.) The complaint, which ran twenty-one pages, alleged that Jacobs had knowingly failed to protect the workers; lied to them about coal ash's dangers; and purposefully conducted shoddy air monitoring, in violation of federal and state laws. As a result, the complaint held, the workers had suffered, and would continue to suffer, from eye, sinus, pulmonary, and heart problems, along with undue emotional stress. The case name: *Adkisson et al. v. Jacobs Engineering Group*.

Judge Thomas Varlan had already signaled that, unlike with the land cases, TVA was immune from suits involving the Kingston cleanup, so Jacobs Engineering was, in a way, the next best thing. Based on the workers' stories, Scott suspected that TVA knew that Jacobs's staff had wrongly denied the workers respiratory protection, and that it had perhaps directed them to do so. Scott lacked evidence to support the theory but trusted it would emerge during discovery, and he was eager to find it. In 2010, the state of Tennessee had fined TVA $11.5 million for violating state water and waste-disposal laws in connection with the Kingston disaster. But that penalty amounted to a mere tsk-tsk, in Scott's mind, for an organization that made nearly $11 billion in revenue that year, as TVA had. The fine in no way represented justice.

As Sam and Jim talked, an old friend of Jim's named Greg Jones walked over and said hello. Jim invited him to join them, and Jones slid in. Their meals soon arrived. As they ate, Jones mentioned that he'd read about the workers' case in the newspaper: the day after Scott had filed the lawsuit against Jacobs, *The Knoxville News Sentinel* had published an eight-hundred-word front-page story summarizing the workers' allegations. The case sounded interesting, Jones said.

Well, Scott said, between bites, the *Sentinel* didn't know the half of it. He told Jones about the video in which the Jacobs safety supervisor obliquely threatened Mike McCarthy.

Damn, Jones replied. That sounded like a good case, especially with the recording. But, he said, "You need to be careful on this one." Jones had previously worked for the Department of Energy, which had research and production facilities outside Knoxville, in Oak Ridge. The DOE took safety and health claims seriously, Jones said. It had a health program that compensated employees, along with contractors, subcontractors, and their families, for medical conditions resulting from their involvement in nuclear-weapons manufacturing. Because of that, the DOE tended to be "non-adversarial" about health claims, Jones said. Workers, as a rule, didn't have to fight the DOE in court over medical claims. If a worker developed one of about twenty different cancers, radiation exposure was generally presumed to be the cause. Sickened workers received compensation for their exposure, along with a so-called white card, which functioned like an insurance card, except the entity covering their medical bills was the U.S. government. "No Copay / No Deductible," the front of the card read.

Jones explained to Scott that TVA had no such program, but it did have a small army of attorneys and a robust public-relations apparatus. TVA had a reputation for using both of these to fight lawsuits, and Scott could expect that it would help its contractors do the same.

The land cases had already taught Scott to be wary of TVA, and Jones's warning further heightened his unease. But Jacobs's attorneys posed a more immediate threat. The company was represented by Smith, Cashion & Orr, a Nashville-based firm that billed itself as Tennessee's largest construction-law practice, with more than a dozen attorneys on staff, plus paralegals and administrative support. Scott, meanwhile, was pursuing the case alone, with no help beyond that of a part-time secretary. And now that he'd filed the workers' complaint, he had to compile enough evidence to convince Varlan that his clients deserved their day in court. Submitting a complaint in no way guarantees that a case will reach trial. Since Scott was self-financed, there was a decent chance that he would go broke in the process, especially if Jacobs's lawyers caused repeated delays. And Jacobs's legal team, led by a middle-aged attorney by the name of Joseph Welborn, would surely try to do just that.

There's a census among Knoxville lawyers that big-city attorneys tend to be more acidic than the local talent. These out-of-towners write harsher briefs, are quicker to complain to judges about the other side, and are generally less agreeable than hometown attorneys, who by and large subscribed to the credo of "Don't be a dick," as one Knoxville lawyer put it. And to Knoxvillians, Nashville, with nearly two million people in its greater metropolitan area, qualifies as a big city, and Joe Welborn fit the associated stereotype. Before law school, he played quarterback for Rhodes College, in Memphis, where, as a six-foot-tall, one-hundred-and-ninety-pound senior, he picked up yards on quarterback sneaks and flung deep passes. He brought a hyper-competitive spirit into his legal practice. He made partner at Smith, Cashion & Orr in his mid-thirties and bought a sprawling and stately painted-brick home in Belle Meade, Nashville's lush, old-money enclave, partially built on the grounds of an antebellum thoroughbred stud farm. Former vice president Al Gore owned a mansion not far down the road from Welborn's place.

On November 12, 2013, about two and a half months after Scott filed the workers' complaint, Welborn shot back with a motion to dismiss—a quick attempt to kill the suit. The motion argued that Jacobs should share in TVA's discretionary function immunity, a form of sovereign immunity that applies to government actions not considered mandatory by law. The motion, in justifying a dismissal, pointed to two recent suits brought against TVA, both in Roane County, both about fly ash, both assigned to Varlan.

Varlan's rulings in these cases had complicated the immunity question. For starters, federal law generally shielded TVA from lawsuits over power production, since Congress had tasked it with providing electricity for the Tennessee Valley. But, in the land cases, Varlan had made an exception, because TVA had ignored its own policies by poorly constructing and maintaining the coal-ash dike. In one of the two Roane County cases, however, Varlan had decided that locals could *not* hold TVA liable for nuisance caused by the Kingston cleanup, since, in a roundabout way, the project was connected to TVA's essential, power-producing duty. Moreover, in the second Roane County case, Varlan had ruled that two engineering firms that had inspected the Kingston dike before it collapsed could share in TVA's immunity, since, in Varlan's view, they supported TVA's power-producing duties—never mind that they failed to prevent the catastrophe. Welborn's motion argued that Jacobs should share in TVA's immunity for the same reason: Jacobs was just supporting TVA.

Welborn's motion urged Varlan to throw out the workers' lawsuit, just as he had tossed out the cases against the engineering contractors. When Scott read the motion, he found the whole thing ridiculous. Discretionary function immunity didn't give Jacobs the right to endanger workers' lives, and he trusted that Varlan, thoughtful, if conservative, would agree, provided Scott submitted a strong, well-reasoned response.

A week after Welborn filed his motion, Scott asked Varlan for an extra sixty days to respond, citing a heavy caseload and the approaching holidays. Scott also needed two teeth yanked and several dental fillings. He ate candy compulsively, especially Jolly Ranchers and peanut M&M's, and his addiction had caught up with him. Varlan agreed to the request, but Scott couldn't bank on such generosity in the future.

Scott worked through the holidays, drafting his response to Jacobs while also trying to keep some smaller, less complex cases moving forward to keep his business afloat. He struggled to return phone calls about potential new work—effectively turning down cases, and money, that he needed—but his response to Welborn's motion to dismiss demanded his full attention.

That the workers' suit was already consuming an inordinate amount of his time didn't surprise him. In personal-injury cases, defense lawyers typically bill clients by the hour, creating an incentive to file an endless flurry of motions, no matter how asinine. Or that's the view of many plaintiffs' attorneys. Defense attorneys critique this characterization as cynical and unrealistic; corporate clients in particular, they say, give attorneys hell over fees. Scott, who occasionally defended clients himself, understood this dynamic but still viewed Welborn's motion as an attempt to prolong the case and generate fees, and it irritated him. Could Scott really carry the workers' case all the way to trial? Was he a moron for thinking he could tackle this case alone if this was how Jacobs intended to litigate?

On January 2, 2014, having taken no break since Thanksgiving, if not before, Scott filed a ten-page memorandum and a five-page list of undisputed facts in response to Jacobs's motion to dismiss. Scott's gifts as an attorney didn't lie in writing—grammar mistakes plagued his drafts, and his prose typically lacked flow—but his main points usually came through well enough, and other attorneys commended his knack for distilling complex ideas.

Scott's memo held that Jacobs shouldn't be immune, since the company had allegedly violated federal, state, and local regulations concerning site safety, but the crux of his argument centered on the idea that, in one key respect, Jacobs had acted independently of TVA, a fact that distinguished it from other contractors. Scott pointed out that, in the "Site Wide Safety and Health Plan," TVA had explicitly directed Jacobs to protect the workers from dangerous conditions. And, since Jacobs had failed to follow this directive, it had broken its deal with TVA and, in doing so, disqualified itself from immunity. You can't claim you're supporting the government, Scott argued in effect, if the government told you to do something and you did something entirely different—and something dangerous, at that.

He included a two-page transcript of the McCarthy video as an exhibit, along with three affidavits, in which workers swore that Jacobs staff had refused them dust masks. Scott considered the evidence convincing, and he had no question that Varlan would carefully consider it.

Judge Thomas Varlan was a gray-haired Greek American nearing sixty, with high cheekbones and a slender face. He, like Scott, had grown up in Oak Ridge, and, also like Scott, he'd earned his undergraduate degree from the University of Tennessee, before attending Vanderbilt University Law School, in Nashville. Early in his career, Varlan served as Knoxville's law director, a high-profile position in which he successfully defended the city against multimillion-dollar lawsuits. At his swearing-in ceremony for the federal judgeship, in 2003, Varlan called the job "truly my life's goal," and, in the years since, he'd earned a reputation as a careful student of the law, a fact plain in his exhaustive, meticulously written memorandums and orders, which not infrequently ran sixty pages or longer.

Varlan clearly took pride in his work and in being the first Greek American judge to serve in Tennessee's Eastern District. His grandfather's immigration papers were on display in the federal courthouse. By all accounts a kind and patient mentor, he analyzed legal problems quickly but remained open to the opinions of his clerks and interns, who worked at wooden desks outside his office. He often asked their views on legal issues, to ensure that his thinking was reasonable, and he diligently reviewed the memorandums they drafted. *You make a strong point here*, he might tell an intern, looking over her work, *but I would like more authority here. And do you think you're being as clear as possible in this paragraph?* Or he might ask what the Sixth Circuit Court of Appeals had said about an issue in question, and whether the ruling would stand up to a second pass.

Though Varlan was conservative, left-leaning attorneys commended his impartiality. Jim Scott and the other plaintiffs' attorneys had considered him an excellent juror in the TVA property-damage trial, since he always seemed more than willing to hear them out. But, during litigation, Varlan had made it clear that he insisted on the same degree of precision from attorneys as he did from his interns and clerks. For lawyers to earn their day in court, their cases had to have strong legal justification, and their arguments had to be well considered and well researched. And, unlike some other judges, once Varlan set a trial date, he expected attorneys to keep it, barring catastrophe.

By the summer of 2014, as the workers' case crossed the one-year mark, and as the sixth-year anniversary of the disaster approached, Jeff Brewer was just trying to hang on. Most mornings, he struggled to balance himself, stumbling into furniture and walls. He had regular coughing fits, and the blackouts and fatigue he'd experienced throughout his time at Kingston had grown more intense. He wanted to work somewhere else, but, as far as he knew, blue-collar jobs were still scarce in East Tennessee, and he couldn't afford to sit at home—not with three daughters and a wife depending on him. Brewer hoped that, since Jim Scott had finally filed the workers' lawsuit, Jacobs would improve the conditions at Kingston, to prevent any further complaints. Brewer's N95 dust mask was a start, even if he knew it wouldn't do much, since N95s don't protect against arsenic, a constituent of fly ash. Beyond the mask, though, disappointingly little had changed, and now that Brewer had some degree of respiratory protection, his foreman, who took orders from TVA, made him work far from any public road, so that passersby wouldn't see him in a dust mask. Or so Brewer presumed.

One humid Friday, he stood around with a group of guys before the morning meeting, preparing for a grueling day ahead. The temperature was expected to top 90 degrees. To prevent another disaster, crews had recently built a twelve-mile-long, four-foot-wide retaining wall, strong enough to withstand a 6.0 magnitude earthquake, around the rebuilt

Jeff Brewer *(left)* and Mike McCarthy

coal-ash pond. With the cleanup project approaching its final stages, the workers were now planting thousands of trees, restoring wetlands, spreading tens of thousands of pounds of grass seed, and finishing other odds-and-ends projects.

As Brewer and the other guys talked, his foreman pulled him aside and said that he needed to go to Trailer City. Brewer could guess why. He walked over to a TVA office trailer and filed inside with eight or ten other workers. A TVA field supervisor handed them each two checks: one for their hours that week and one for the week prior. It was a workforce reduction. No one explained how or why TVA had chosen that particular group for termination. Brewer signed his layoff papers, turned in his badge, and handed over his gate pass. Then he collected his things, climbed into his pickup, and drove toward home. At his past jobs, the guys who skipped shifts or ran late were typically the ones let go first whenever a project winded down. At Kingston, though, it seemed that whoever asked questions or complained ended up out the door first. Mike McCarthy, who filmed the infamous video, had lost his job nine months earlier, after he expressed concern about fly-ash exposure. Billy Isley, the Metallica fan, was terminated after he threatened to file a complaint if he wasn't allowed to view on-site air-monitoring results. Now, it was Brewer's turn.

He stopped by the union hall on the way home. He wanted to "sign the books" as soon as possible, to be the first one called for the next open job. He knew he ought to be worried because he was now out of work, yet relief washed over him. Maybe his cough would let up once he stopped working at Kingston. Maybe his life would return to normal, or something akin to it. But he worried that Ansol Clark's experience suggested otherwise.

After Jim Scott replied to Jacobs's motion to dismiss, he and the defense attorneys spent the next six months filing and responding to motions, without making much progress toward trial, and without Judge Varlan ruling on Jacobs's immunity bid. Stress radiated through Scott, blotting out every other feeling. He told himself that if he could just keep the case alive through discovery and get in front of a jury, victory would be within reach. In the meantime, he had no choice but to charge ahead, and, in doing so, he relied on Ansol for support.

They talked on the phone three or four times a week, discussing Ansol's health and how other workers were holding up. Scott learned that he could depend on Ansol, with his wide-open retirement days, to pass along updates to the other workers, few of whom regularly answered their cell phones, much less checked email, during business hours, given the nature of their jobs. Jeff Brewer joked that Ansol was Scott's secretary, and he wasn't entirely wrong. Scott would call Ansol and say, "Hey, put this out. We're going to have a meeting," and Ansol would oblige.

Scott met with the workers before and after their shifts, at his office but also at diners, at fast-food joints, in shopping-center parking lots—wherever worked best for them. He wanted to hear their stories and secure their trust, certain he would need the latter if the case ran into trouble. Few of the workers had been involved in a lawsuit before, much less dealt directly with an attorney, and, at first, many remained skeptical of Scott. But he listened. He asked about their families. He spoke like they spoke. Sometimes he called Brewer to ask how he was doing and whether he needed anything. Brewer didn't know attorneys did that. "The only thing I don't like about Jim," one worker joked, "is that he's a Democrat."

During meetings, Scott urged the workers to see doctors and to bring him documentation of their illnesses, to help build their cases against Jacobs. Ansol followed through, giving Scott a letter from a cardiologist who wrote, "It is in my opinion reasonable to assume that [Ansol's] exposure to fly ash has probably contributed or at least exacerbated his atrial fibrillation." It was a good start. More compelling, Craig Wilkinson, a heavy-equipment operator from Buffalo, New York, provided the results of a urinary analysis that had found abnormally high levels of aluminum, cadmium, lead, mercury, and uranium in his system. Wilkinson's lungs were failing, and he coughed up blood nightly. In a letter, Wilkinson's physician blamed fly-ash exposure.

Scott collected reams of similar reports, and soon binders, arranged from floor to ceiling on bookshelves, filled a large closet in his law office. He had to begin stashing some in a rented storage unit. "This [case] makes Erin Brockovich and the hexavalent chromium look like *Sesame Street*," he told a friend one morning in his office.* "There's so many more people affected." He hadn't seen such egregious behavior since his days as an assistant district attorney, when he prosecuted murders, rapists, and thieves.

He learned that some of the workers had asked for protective gear at the very start of the cleanup, almost six years earlier. Tommy Johnson, one of the few Black men on the jobsite, spent his first six months at Kingston with no safety gear beyond rubber boots. At a public meeting in the summer of 2009, Johnson's wife, Betty, had demanded to know when TVA would outfit the workers with hazmat suits, also known as coveralls. "I'm concerned," Betty had said. Anda Ray, the TVA senior vice president who'd sworn on TV that coal ash posed no health risk to the community, responded, promising Betty, "If [the workers] desire to have the coveralls, then we will have those available" within two weeks. "We will protect our workers," Ray added. Sean Healey, Jacobs's top safety manager on-site at the time, concurred.

Well, Tommy told Scott, he never received a dust mask, much less a hazmat suit, and now, he said, he had chronic obstructive pulmonary disease (COPD), asthma, and regular dizzy spells and blackouts. "I tried to save the money I made," he said. He had daughters to send to college. But his medical bills had depleted his savings. "I'm mad at TVA for letting Jacobs do what they did, for lying to us."

* In the 1990s, Brockovich, a legal assistant at the time, discovered that a utility company had contaminated groundwater in the town of Hinkley, California. A lawsuit, brought by six hundred and fifty plaintiffs, resulted in a $333 million settlement for the people of Hinkley.

As Scott heard more of the workers' stories, he realized that the site safety precautions should have likely extended beyond even hazmat suits. Jeff Brewer had a story that suggested why.

One cold evening—Brewer couldn't recall exactly when—he finished his shift at Kingston and then drove the ten minutes back to Mama Mia's Pizza, where he still rented a room. He parked behind the restaurant as always. As he headed up the stairs to his place, he passed another worker who was headed out. They stopped and talked. The other man—Brewer never caught his name—was stocky and bespeckled. He lived in the efficiency apartment next to Brewer's and worked nights on a dredger boat, sucking coal ash from the river. You work on the ballfield? the guy asked. Brewer said yeah, he did. He was driving an articulated dump truck, hauling coal ash and setting it out to dry before shipment.

"We hit some hot stuff last night," the man said, as his face filled with concern. The hot stuff, he explained, forced crews on a dredger boat to disconnect the hose that piped the wet coal ash from the river to the shore, where workers scooped it up and hauled it away. And "hot stuff," Brewer didn't need to be told, meant radioactive.

At first, he didn't know what to make of the story, and neither did Scott when Brewer relayed it to him. Was the guy screwing with Brewer? Was he nuts? In January 2009, TVA had assured the public that the Kingston coal ash was "less radioactive than low-sodium table salt." But Brewer said that, after he talked with the guy, the area where the dredger had allegedly hit the hot stuff was blocked off for several days. Brewer told Scott that neither TVA nor Jacobs had explained what happened, so he'd shrugged off the story. When his health started to decline, however, he began to wonder whether the coal ash that he trucked around all day was contaminated and whether the current was carrying the hot stuff, disturbed by extensive dredging, downriver.

Craig Wilkinson, the heavy-equipment operator from Buffalo, drove a Komatsu 600 excavator that scooped up wet coal ash that was piped to land from the dredger boats. One night early in the cleanup, a voice broke over the radio: *A dredger hit hot stuff. Stop the boats, stop the excavators, stop everything!* Wilkinson knew what "hot stuff" meant, and he wondered whether the watery slurry all around him, lit up by construction lights, would kill him. He called a buddy in a nearby excavator who'd received the same alert. "If you start glowing green, I'll let you know," Wilkinson said, trying to laugh away his nerves. Yeah, his friend replied, and "if all your hair has fallen out, I'll let you know." (The friend later corroborated Wilkinson's account.)*

After about forty-five minutes, the men received an all-clear notice, and Wilkinson resumed work. After that night, he never heard a Jacobs or TVA official mention the toxic material, so he didn't bring it up. *If you talk about it, you're gone*, he thought. Years later, when a urinary analysis found radionuclides in his system, he didn't have to guess where they came from.

Scott carried these stories, and the questions they raised, with him everywhere, a drone in his head that never yielded as he tried, fitfully, to drag the case forward.

On July 31, 2014, nearly a year after Jim Scott filed the workers' lawsuit, Judge Varlan at last scheduled a date for a jury trial: May 2015, some nine months away. The timing was fortuitous for Scott, who had already worn himself thin in responding to Jacobs's motions.

Nearly a year and a half had passed since the mediation conference at the Knoxville Convention Center. And TVA and the plaintiffs' lawyers, who represented the Roane County landowners, had finally reached a settlement agreement, thanks, in part, to Jeff Friedman, Gary Davis, and a Nashville attorney named Elizabeth Alexander, who'd haggled with TVA's legal team in a series of intense, exhausting bargaining sessions. Scott had attended some of the meetings, and, to him, TVA showed little interest in settling, and no wonder.

Though TVA had lost in court over liability, it had an edge in mediation, in that it could refuse to settle and force the cases back to trial, which the plaintiffs' lawyers wanted to avoid—had to avoid, even. Despite the Kingston disaster's magnitude, some of the landowners would likely struggle to prove that TVA had hurt their property values, since the spill had coincided with a nationwide real-estate meltdown following the 2008 financial crisis. Returning to trial would also mean

* Jacobs says its staff had no role in testing river sediment for radionuclides, but it called the workers' claims about potentially being exposed to contaminated sediment "false."

fighting over damages for every plaintiff individually, since the cases weren't a class-action suit. That would demand tremendous time from all the attorneys. But, while TVA could throw salaried lawyers at the cases with minimal concern over cost, the plaintiffs' team, working on contingency and self-financed, lacked the resources for a protracted battle. The steep expense of getting experts to testify on the landowners' behalf, a necessity in proving damages, alone made returning to trial an almost unfeasible option.

But, after four unsuccessful mediation conferences, fate had unexpectedly shifted in the plaintiffs' favor: President Barack Obama tapped Pamela Reeves, one of the two mediators in the cases, to serve as a federal judge in the Eastern District of Tennessee, seated alongside Varlan. Federal judges wield tremendous power over the cases they hear, and Reeves, a fifty-eight-year-old Democrat, raised in the mountains of Virginia and Tennessee, would no doubt have a pro-worker bent. She had represented individuals pro bono in employment disputes against companies, and, in a monthly column she wrote for *The Knoxville News Sentinel*, she drew attention to the poor treatment of women in many workplaces and alerted the public to retaliation protections afforded to them under the law.

After Reeves's nomination, TVA's stance in mediation swiftly and uncharacteristically softened, and the plaintiffs' attorneys felt sure they knew why: odds were that, sooner or later, TVA would have to appear before Reeves, never mind that it wiggled out of most lawsuits with governmental immunity, and that possibility meant that TVA couldn't risk falling out of her favor by openly resenting having to pay the landowners a settlement. Reeves's pro-worker positions threatened to complicate TVA's legal defenses enough as it was. To be sure, Ed Small and the other TVA lawyers never communicated any of this to the plaintiffs' team, but their abrupt about-face said enough. TVA tentatively agreed to pay just shy of $28 million to resolve sixty-three suits filed against it over property damages. One catch was that TVA insisted that all nine hundred or so plaintiffs agree to the settlement terms and drop their complaints.

Jeff Friedman and the other plaintiffs' attorneys spent weeks calling and meeting with their clients to see if they were willing to agree to the terms. Jim Scott was among those who made calls. In his opinion, all the conjecture about TVA's not wanting to tick off Pam Reeves was bunk. God didn't even scare TVA, he believed, so Reeves didn't either. Plus, TVA's settlement offer was far from fair, in his view. Under TVA's proposed offer, each plaintiff would receive, on average, less than $30,000 once the attorneys deducted their fees. Scott thought that if TVA really cared about not irking Reeves, it would have offered a much more equitable sum.

Scott called James Crichton, the statistician who had waded into the ash-clogged river after the disaster. "Look," Scott told him, "they're willing to settle." He explained that, based on the matrix devised by the plaintiffs' attorneys, Crichton would get about $25,000, minus Scott's fee and expenses, leaving him with about $17,000. "You can take the money," Scott told him, "or you can keep fighting for the original amount we asked for." But Scott warned him that proceeding would be difficult, since other cases were settling, which would weaken their leverage. Either way, Scott said, Crichton needed to decide quickly.

Crichton told Scott it would have been nice to get at least $100,000 for his property—roughly the amount of equity he had in the place. But he also wanted to move on with his life, to stop thinking about TVA every day. Well, Scott told him, he should probably take the settlement offer, then. "Yeah," Crichton said. "Forget it. Let's end it."

Most of the plaintiffs responded in a similar fashion. On the afternoon of August 1, 2014—the day after Varlan set a trial date for the workers' case against Jacobs Engineering—*The Tennessean*, Nashville's daily paper, broke the news that the two sides had reached an agreement, ending six years of litigation. A TVA spokesman, Scott Brooks, told reporters that TVA and the plaintiffs agreed that settling the suits presented the best resolution. "For us," Brooks explained, "it's another step toward finishing what we said [we] were going to do, which is to make the community as good or better than it was before the spill."

Though Scott had hoped for a larger recovery, the settlement did afford him and his clients relief. He was now able to focus solely on the workers' case. And he thought he now had an opportunity to recruit some assistance.

A day after the land settlement was announced, Scott called Jeff Friedman and laid out the workers' suit. It would be a perfect case for them to tackle together, Scott told him. He needed help, ideally from an attorney who knew all about the Kingston disaster. "Jim," Friedman replied, "it's one thing to prove that millions and millions of tons of coal ash got dumped into the river. When you start trying to prove that exposure to ash is the cause of diseases and injuries, that's a different matter." Losing such a case could bankrupt a firm, with all the costly experts and reports required, to say nothing of the time commitment. Friedman said he wouldn't join—he already had too many cases—but he told Scott to keep him updated.

Scott's problems compounded. He had pushed the immunity question out of his mind after Varlan set a trial date, assuming the judge wouldn't side with Jacobs's motion to dismiss, given the evidence Scott had gathered. But, a little over a month after Varlan scheduled a trial date, he reversed course, ruling that Jacobs could share in TVA's immunity—killing the workers' suit. Scott received the opinion by email. Reading it flooded him with embarrassment. Had he not taken his response to Jacobs's motion seriously enough? Was his argument weak or poorly argued?

He had only one move that could possibly save the case, and he knew it was unlikely to succeed. When he called and told Janie and Ansol Clark about the judge's decision, they demanded to know how Varlan could do such an awful thing. Had TVA gotten to him? No, Scott told them. Varlan was a careful, conservative judge, and this was what careful, conservative judges did sometimes. "So, what now?" Janie asked.

"I'm not going to quit," Scott told her. "I'm taking the case to the Sixth Circuit."

The U.S. Federal Court System comprises three tiers. Ninety-four district courts, where jury trials are held, compose the lowest. Thirteen circuit courts, one level above, hear appeals from the district courts. And at the top sits the U.S. Supreme Court, the final say.

Jim Scott kept his word to Ansol and Janie. After Varlan dismissed the workers' case, on the grounds that Jacobs could share in TVA's immunity, Scott quickly appealed to the U.S. Court of Appeals for the Sixth Circuit, which has jurisdiction over nine district courts scattered throughout Kentucky, Michigan, Ohio, and Tennessee. For many lawyers, arguing a case before a federal appeals court carries much prestige, given the possibility of setting precedent that affects hundreds of thousands, if not millions, of people. That graduates of the nation's elite colleges, particularly Harvard and Yale, have an outsize presence on appellate benches and among appellate attorneys amplifies the esteem. But Scott was not an appellate lawyer, nor did he aspire to be.

He had never argued a case before the Sixth Circuit but had appeared before the Tennessee Court of Appeals, the state's appellate equivalent, and he found jury trials far easier in comparison. He liked the human element of trying to convince members of the public that his side was right, both factually and according to the law but also morally, since that often mattered most to a jury. In doing so, Scott often presented himself as a simple country lawyer. He purposefully wore cheap suits. He played up his East Tennessee accent. He used the pronoun *y'all* freely. If he thought a jury's attention was flagging during an examination, he moved his arms to catch their attention, and he made as few objections as possible, to prevent a trial from dragging. These tactics, Scott believed, helped him to curry favor with Tennessee juries, by signaling that he was no different from them. Which he basically believed to be true. In the Sixth Circuit, though, he would have to make his case to a three-judge panel, a Harvard Law graduate among them, using documents already in the record and his legal argument. Homespun charm would not carry the day.

At two o'clock on a crisp November afternoon in 2014, Scott huddled around a speakerphone in his office conference room. Ansol Clark, Tim Henry, and one or two other workers joined him. Scott had appealed Varlan's decision, but, before the Sixth Circuit decided whether to hear oral arguments in the case, it required both sides to meet with a mediator to try to reach a settlement and avoid further litigation. Ansol and Henry and the others had shown up to listen in.

To keep the negotiation civil, the mediator switched between Jacobs's attorneys on one phone line and Scott on another. When Scott's time came, the mediator warned that the Sixth Circuit reversed or remanded about 16 percent of the cases it reviewed—slim odds that Scott and his clients should carefully consider when weighing whether to accept Jacobs's offer. Scott had no idea he faced such an outside shot. Then the mediator shared Jacobs's offer: $100,000. Scott's face reddened. "There's no way my clients will take that," he said into the phone.

If the forty-eight plaintiffs split the proposed settlement amount evenly, they would end up with *maybe* a thousand dollars each after Scott subtracted his fee, a ludicrously low recovery, in his view, given the credibility of their claims. Still, Scott, trying to keep his composure, agreed to discuss the offer with his clients.

He put the mediator on hold. Ansol and Henry, seated across from Scott, had remained silent throughout the call. Now anger stamped their faces. "I can't take the settlement unless you tell me to," Scott said, trying to put them at ease. The offer was lousy, he said, and he wouldn't pressure them to accept it.

Ansol, brow furrowed and eyes hard, said he appreciated that. "They don't want to take responsibility for what they done," he said of Jacobs. Scott had to try his luck in the Sixth, Ansol added, to hell with the long odds. Scott agreed. He couldn't articulate why, but he felt certain, less because of chutzpah than because of a sense of almost divine assurance, that there was no way he would lose this case. The appeal would be in the 16 percent that the Sixth Circuit reversed or remanded. It *had* to be, he told himself.

When the mediator came back on the line, Scott said that his clients had declined Jacobs's offer. He said he appreciated the mediator's time, but, he added, "I believe I'll carry the case on a little further."

One relief for Scott amid mediation was that his money concerns had abated somewhat in recent months, albeit at a professional cost. He liked running his own law practice, but the debacle caused by his former partner who'd defected had strained his relationship with his sisters and his brother-in-law Michael Pemberton. They bickered about partnership voting and about the direction of the firm. Then, in August 2014, Pemberton won a judicial seat in Tennessee's Ninth Circuit and decided to leave private practice, which made it a good time to dissolve the firm, as much as it pained Scott.

With suddenly no firm to lean on for administrative, much less financial, support, Scott contacted Ellis "Sandy" Sharp, a mustachioed former assistant city attorney with a fondness for sports cars. Sharp ran a local insurance-focused practice, and Scott had known him for years. After trading a few messages, Sharp showed up at Scott's office to discuss a potential arrangement to bring Scott to his firm. Sharp offered Scott what he wanted: a regular paycheck and money to help cover the cost of pushing the workers' suit forward. The catch was that Sharp's firm would take a cut of the recovery from each of Scott's cases, including the one he hoped to secure for the Kingston workers. Scott didn't like splitting fees for work he did alone, but he needed money, likely a lot of it, to keep the case alive, so he accepted the arrangement. He couldn't carry all the expenses by himself, provided he wanted to pay his mortgage and keep his boys fed.

He moved to Sharp's law office, in a tan, two-story riverfront building next to a Ruth's Chris steakhouse. He took Sam and Jack to eat there often; they'd sit at the bar and order burgers and fries. Light poured in through a wall of glass facing the river. Maybe the new office wasn't so bad, Scott thought, and maybe carrying the case forward would get easier. Besides, what other option did he have? He knew that if he didn't advocate for the workers, likely no one else would, and he couldn't stomach the idea of forsaking them, with their health problems growing increasingly dire.

Early in Ansol's career, when he still drove trucks cross-country, he grew accustomed to occasional layoffs. It came with the job. Naturally, he and Janie fretted about money whenever he was out of work, but nonetheless he enjoyed his short breaks at home. He spent hours on the floor with their son, Bergan, a toddler then, playing with alphabet blocks and teaching him how to read. At the grocery store, Ansol would push Bergan down the aisles in a cart and let him pick items off the shelves, then Ansol would tell him the name of each. Now that Ansol had retired, though, his poor health largely robbed homelife of its pleasures. Bergan, now grown, was still around, as was Janie, of course, but Ansol had little energy for projects or walks or camping trips or much of anything that he loved. He worried that if he were fishing and fell out of the boat, he would sink to the bottom of the lake, lacking the strength to swim. And there was no way he could grow a big backyard tomato garden like he had in years past. At least he was still able to take care of Junior, his pet turkey. Walking down to the bird's backyard pen lent structure and purpose to Ansol's days as he waited for updates about the case, the slow pace of which surprised both him and Janie.

On March 5, 2015, three and a half months after the infuriating mediation call with Jacobs's attorneys, Ansol was in his bedroom, getting dressed to feed Junior. As he pulled on his clothes, his vision blurred. He grabbed hold of his bed. Blackness.

He woke up at Parkwest Medical Center, in Knoxville, as an emergency crew worked to keep him alive. He couldn't recall leaving the house or reaching the hospital, but he'd made it, thanks to Janie, who'd called an ambulance. He was given a room and examined by doctors. He'd suffered a stroke, resulting from a tear in an artery that supplied blood to his brain. He was lucky—very lucky—to be alive, doctors told him, but the stroke stole his peripheral vision and forced him to wear glasses. More distressing was the brain damage. "When I was younger," Ansol recalled one morning, "I could remember numbers like crazy," especially phone numbers. Now he drew great, gray blanks whenever he tried to recall such details, as if his mind were made of snow. He was concerned for himself but more so for Janie. What would happen to her if he wasn't around?

When he returned home from the hospital, he had to wait a month before a neurologist was available to see him. When his appointment finally came, the neurologist said the stroke could have easily killed him or left him in a vegetative state. The doctor prescribed blood thinners to prevent a repeat incident, because if Ansol had another stroke, "he will not make it," the doctor warned Janie. Those doomful words rolled around in her mind for weeks.

She knew that the world had changed a lot since the day she and Ansol had driven to the Maryville courthouse and eloped, and for the better in many ways. Now, even in a small city like Knoxville, women could have high-powered, lucrative careers. They didn't have to carry the full burden of cooking, cleaning, and child-rearing like she had, on top of her housekeeping job. And good for those women, Janie thought. She knew that she might seem old-fashioned in comparison, but her chief ambition had always been to be a good wife and a good mother, and living this dream had given her joy and purpose. She had no complaints, in a world full of them. She and Ansol had planned, after years of saving, to vacation in coastal North Carolina after he retired. She had never visited or seen the ocean, and he promised to take her. They would drive over the mountains to the coast and find a quiet spot among the dunes and walk to the water's edge together, a reward for their decades of hard work. On the way, Janie wanted to stop in Mount Airy, the hometown of the actor Andy Griffith and the inspiration for the fictional hamlet of Mayberry. She had lived her own version of a picturesque Mayberry life, and she wanted to see the real thing. But, after Ansol's stroke, she worried about venturing far from his doctors. Was it safe to leave Knoxville? What if he had a stroke while they drove?

After Ansol's neurologist appointment, Janie insisted that he visit his primary-care doctor for a checkup. "You got to go," she told him. He did, and tests revealed more problems: elevated testosterone levels; an enlarged prostate; and, most alarming, a blood abnormality. The doctor sent blood samples to a lab for further analysis.

Two weeks later, Janie walked outside to check the mail and found a letter addressed to Ansol from something called Tennessee Cancer Specialists. She didn't recognize the name. In the kitchen, she tore open the envelope and read the contents carefully. A letter stated that, based on Ansol's blood samples, he needed to come in and see an oncologist. Janie, drowning in the implication of what that meant, stood motionless holding the phone. *I've got to call these doctors*, she thought. *Ansol doesn't have cancer. There's been a mix-up*. There was no mix-up.

At an appointment, doctors informed Ansol that he had polycythemia vera, a rare form of blood cancer that causes bone marrow to overproduce red blood cells, thickening the blood. From then on, he would have to be checked once a month. If his blood was too thick—as it often would be—nurses would need to drain pints of it from his arm. Otherwise, he might have a heart attack or stroke, a suffocating possibility for Janie.

She had suffered through hard, almost impossible days in her life—the day her father died, the day of her mother's stroke, the day her young aunts drowned in the flood—but none compared to this one. She had devoted herself to Ansol in full. She knew no other life and didn't want to. She almost couldn't remember a time before they were married. There would be no beach vacation, no Mount Airy, no retirement trip anywhere. She and Ansol had hopes for a future together, to live out their golden years. Jacobs had stolen that, she believed.

It felt as if an abyss had opened beneath them, sucking them down, slowly smothering them alive. One night, while lying beside Ansol in bed, she took his hand and laid it over her heart. She wanted to share her life force with him, to let her love flow in and overtake the poison in his body. But she knew that, short of divine intervention, Ansol would never be the same. Win or lose the case, he would largely be confined to their home for the rest of his life. The disease would win. She had to accept that. And, she decided, she had to ensure that other families weren't hurt like theirs was. That was why the case mattered; the money was almost beside the point. She had to fight for those other families, for those other men and those other women. Whenever she went to Holy Mass, she would add names to a prayer list, and Jim Scott's was never left off. He would need all the help he could get. "They have million-dollar law firms," she later told a friend, "and we've got Jimmy."

One April night about two months after Ansol's stroke, two police officers drove through the dark, sleepy streets of Sequoyah Hills. It was nearly ten-thirty. The air was cool. The deep springtime lawns were quiet and green. The officers turned onto Talahi Drive, a narrow, tree-lined street, and passed three or four houses before stopping in front of number 3639, the home of the Scott family.

A fight had broken out. The officers parked and crossed the yard to the front stoop of the white-painted home. Jim answered the door and tried to explain what had happened, but it didn't come easily. He said that, while in another room, he'd heard his wife arguing with their oldest son, Jack, almost thirteen now. When he walked into Jack's bedroom to investigate, Jack's iPad and Nintendo 3DS gaming system lay smashed on the floor. Apparently, Jack had gotten "snippy" with Mary as she put him to bed and cursed at her. She had reacted by grabbing and hurling the objects. When Jim intervened, Mary, fuming, accused him of taking Jack's side and smacked him three times in the ear. Or, as Jack put it, "She punched the shit out of Dad."

Mary, crying and upset, left the house on foot after Jim called the police. Their son Sam told the officers that she had probably walked to his grandmother's condo a few blocks away. The two officers drove to a three-story apartment complex a quarter of a mile down the road, and, as Sam correctly guessed, Mary was there. Her version of events aligned with Jim's, though she insisted that she hadn't left the house to flee from the police, as he'd suggested, but to calm down. She and Jim were about to divorce, she explained, and his 911 call was "bogus." She accused him of trying to make her look bad to help him win custody of their sons. He was a "non-husband," she said, who was never around.

The police left without making an arrest, since Jim's face showed no sign of injury; Jack also begged his dad not to press charges. Mary denied that she hit Jim that night. Still, "I told [the boys] I was very sorry," she later said. She wasn't accustomed to having one of her children curse at her, she explained.

For a time, Jim had hoped that they could avoid a divorce, knowing the pain it would cause their sons. But the fight washed away all doubt that, after seventeen years of marriage, his and Mary's relationship was over. They hadn't had a perfect life together, but they had been happy sometimes, then seldom at all. The threads that held them together frayed around the time he filed the workers' lawsuit against Jacobs. He worked too much and was out too often, while Mary fumed, drank, and fretted.* How would they ever dig themselves out of their financial hole? she asked. How could they keep paying their bills with Jim's full focus on the workers' case? These concerns were the gasoline that Jim ignited when he intervened about Jack's smashed gadgets.

The fight left Jim in a panic. Not only had his marriage collapsed, but, a month and a half earlier, the Sixth Circuit had notified him that it would hear oral arguments in the workers' case in Cincinnati, Ohio, on April 29, 2015—now three short days away. Scott had requested oral arguments, given the "very serious, complex legal issues and facts," as he wrote in a brief. Now that the Sixth Circuit had added the workers' case to its docket, he had to show up. Ansol Clark and the other plaintiffs had chipped in for his airfare. He couldn't disappoint them.

Joe Welborn had filed a seventy-three-page brief arguing why the Sixth Circuit should uphold Varlan's decision to toss out the case, which Scott had to prepare to attack. If Scott lost, the workers stood no chance of recovering damages to cover their mounting medical bills, and he wouldn't be able to live with himself if that happened. When he learned of Ansol's cancer diagnosis, he researched polycythemia vera. Among the causes: exposure to radium, a constituent of coal ash. After the fight

* "I didn't have a drinking problem," Mary Scott later said. "I had a Jim Scott problem."

that April evening, Jim didn't want his boys—his chief concern, always—to stay with their mother while he traveled, so he put aside his trial prep and searched for a babysitter. He had to trust that the law was on the workers' side.

The Sixth Circuit Court of Appeals was, and remains, a conservative institution composed of sixteen active judges, ten of them Republican appointees. Not six months before Jim Scott was set to argue the workers' case, the court had upheld bans on same-sex marriage in Kentucky, Michigan, Ohio, and Tennessee. It would later uphold an Ohio law defunding Planned Parenthood, allowing, in the view of one dissenting judge, for targeted attacks on abortion providers. Still, on the whole, "they typically get it right," one Knoxville attorney said of the court. Scott hoped that was true.

He flew to Cincinnati a day before he was to appear in court. He watched the Reds play the Brewers that evening with an attorney he knew, but he left before the game was over to finish some last-minute prep. The next morning, on perhaps the most important day of his career, he dressed in his smartest suit—dark navy and custom-tailored—left his hotel, and walked to the courthouse, a few blocks away.

As he strode down the sidewalk, his sons filled his thoughts. He teared up and stopped to collect himself. He knew, and dreaded the fact, that his divorce would, in a way, also be their divorce. He and his wife were bound to have a contentious custody fight. But he had to carry on. Janie and Ansol Clark were becoming family. The case had to move forward for them. His problems couldn't, must not, affect his courtroom performance.

The Potter Stewart U.S. Courthouse sits at a busy intersection in downtown Cincinnati's business district. Scott reported to the clerk's office, on the fifth floor, at eight-thirty, then proceeded to a sixth-floor courtroom. It was a dim, wood-paneled space, filled with fifteen or so people, nearly all of them lawyers. As Scott waited in the gallery, he felt as if he were a kid again, afraid to cause a disturbance in church.

Unlike in a jury trial, in an appellate court a panel of judges can, and typically will, interrupt an attorney with questions. Scott would make his argument to an especially "hot bench," in that the panel of three judges—Ronald Lee Gilman, John M. Rogers, and Jeffrey S. Sutton—customarily had animated exchanges in the fifteen minutes allotted to each lawyer. The most well known of the judges was Sutton, a George W. Bush appointee and a former clerk for ultraconservative Supreme Court Justice Antonin Scalia. It was Sutton who had penned the Sixth Circuit's decision that upheld discriminatory same-sex marriage bans. (The Supreme Court would overturn the decision in June 2015 and, in doing so, legalize same-sex marriage across the U.S.) Scott assumed that, if any of the three judges were to hold pro-business views that might benefit Jacobs Engineering, it would be him.

The panel had five cases on its docket that day, including the Kingston workers', which was scheduled to be heard second. The three judges sat side by side on an elevated bench. When Scott's time came, he stepped to the lectern, positioned squarely in front of them. He carried a notepad but only for appearances; he knew what he planned to say. He flipped open the pad and set it down, then took a long, heavy breath. Whereas other attorneys tended to recite memorized remarks dryly, Scott seemed to have no script at all. Instead, "it was like he had a lot of coffee," recalled another lawyer present in the gallery.

"Good morning, Your Honors," Scott began, hands on the lectern. He represented the cleanup workers, he said. But "I feel somewhat that I'm put in a unique position," he added, "because I feel like I'm here in the interest of the Tennessee Valley Authority as well."

Jacobs Engineering had complete control over worksite safety, Scott explained, voice sharpening, eyes locked on the judges. And, he said, in refusing—absolutely refusing—to supply the workers with respiratory gear, Jacobs's staff not only violated the workers' rights and broke state and federal laws, but it also breached the terms of its multimillion-dollar contract with TVA, which had directed Jacobs to protect the workers from unnecessarily dangerous situations.

This was a crucial point. Scott knew that, if the judges were to strip Jacobs's immunity, they had to believe that the company had acted outside TVA's authority and done so purposefully. By claiming to represent TVA's interests, Scott was trying to isolate Jacobs in the judges' minds and suggest that TVA, and the federal government by extension, had been wronged.

Scott moved his hands as he talked. His dark curly hair, as wild and unkempt as ever, bounced around. "We're not dealing, truly, with negligent conduct," he said. "We're dealing with *intentional* conduct." Jacobs had willfully and repeatedly ignored TVA's safety directives, he said, which were outlined in the "Site Wide Safety and Health Plan"—the bible of the cleanup project. And, since Jacobs's conduct ran counter to that plan, Scott said, the company had disqualified itself from immunity. This was essentially the same point he'd made to Judge Varlan: that Jacobs couldn't claim that it acted on the government's behalf when it hadn't followed its directives.

No less crucially, Scott added, his clients credibly alleged that Jacobs had manipulated air-monitoring data, in a scheme to misrepresent coal ash's dangers to the workers and to TVA.

"Just to make sure I'm grasping this first argument," Jeffrey Sutton interrupted. Hypothetically, had TVA overseen site safety instead of Jacobs and acted the same way, could TVA be sued, or would it be immune?

Scott had skated over TVA's immunity in his brief to the Sixth Circuit; it didn't serve his interests to dwell on TVA's legal shield and what conduct *should* be immune, since doing so risked the judges' conflating TVA and Jacobs as one and the same, or at least operating as such. "I'll give you an answer in regards to that," Scott replied, wavering. "In doing so, I want to go back to the *Mays* case . . ."

"Is the answer yes or no?" Sutton interrupted.

"Yes, yes sir!" Scott sputtered. TVA could be held liable and sued, he said, had it behaved like Jacobs. The Kingston disaster area was a Superfund cleanup site, Scott explained, regaining his composure, and Superfund law barred any firm or government agency from violating jobsite safety protocols or from threatening workers by saying, for example, "They're going to be hanging themselves with their own genitalia if they were to wear a dust mask."

Sutton seemed reasonably satisfied with the response, and Scott's allotted time finished without his having to opine about any more hypotheticals.

Joe Welborn, the hulking, blond-haired former Rhodes quarterback, then appeared on Jacobs's behalf. In a brief submitted to the court, he'd defended Jacobs's conduct and maintained that, according to air-monitoring data, respirators were not needed on-site, contrary to whatever the workers alleged. More pertinent to the immunity question, Welborn's brief argued that Jacobs had, in fact, followed TVA's directives in the "Site Wide Safety and Health Plan" and, because of that, Jacobs enjoyed broad immunity as a government contractor.

John Rogers, a gray-haired George W. Bush appointee, interrupted Welborn almost immediately and cut to the core of the issue: "You wouldn't argue that everything done pursuant to [the 'Site Wide Safety and Health Plan'] is immune from suit, do you?"

Welborn's brief had suggested as much: that, since Jacobs was under contract with TVA, a quasi-governmental entity, more or less anything it did at the jobsite served the government's interests and was shielded from suit.

"Well, I do," Welborn said, meekly.

Mild shock flashed across Rogers's face, to the satisfaction of Jim Scott, seated in the gallery. "Then let's say," Rogers said, "that pursuant to that plan, you drive down the street to pick up some gas masks and you drive too fast and you hurt someone—that's pursuant to the plan, isn't it?"

Rogers's point was clear: Jacobs's interpretation of the law was too broad. Not every action loosely connected to the cleanup was immune from suit.

Welborn conceded that reckless driving wouldn't be immune, nor would other similarly negligent behavior.

Then why, Rogers asked, should Jacobs be immune if some of the workers' allegations concerned negligence?

Well, Welborn said, Jacobs had already shown in court filings that every action that the workers claimed was negligent or misconduct, like denying them respirators, was, in fact, carried out in accordance with the "Safety and Health Plan." Jacobs hadn't violated TVA's safety guidelines at all, Welborn said: it had followed the rules and found that some workers weren't healthy enough to wear respirators. "[They're] doing work out in a dust field that's 95 degrees in East Tennessee," Welborn explained. Wearing a hot, hard-to-breathe-in respirator could cause them to overheat. So Jacobs, Welborn said, would have acted contrary to safety guidelines had it done anything *but* forbidden some workers from wearing a respirator or dust mask.

The panel's third judge, and its sole liberal, Ronald Lee Gilman, brought up the workers' allegations that Jacobs staff had altered air-monitoring results by having the workers spray water around the stationary air monitors. The "Safety and Health Plan" surely didn't encourage such conduct?

"I'd like to address that," said Welborn, clearly ready for the question. Federal appellate courts only allow attorneys to reference allegations and documents already in the official record—you can't present new evidence or make further claims. And the workers' original complaint against Jacobs, filed by Jim Scott in 2013, said nothing about "altering air-monitoring results," Welborn said. "I've never seen this allegation . . . until this appeal was filed."

Wait, Sutton asked, that allegation isn't in the workers' original complaint?

"I don't believe it is, Your Honor," replied Welborn. The workers' complaint vaguely alleged that Jacobs had engaged in "improper air monitoring," Welborn said. Well, what does that mean? he asked rhetorically. The plaintiffs, Welborn said, had brought forward no evidence to support or clarify any such claim, or any claim involving altered air-monitoring results. "There's a lot of allegations," Welborn added, shortly before his allotted time expired, "but there's no basis for those allegations. There's no proof in the pudding. They keep alleging that you violated this, you violated that." But, he said, their allegations had no basis in reality or fact.

Scott made for the doors after Welborn finished his argument. As he left the courtroom, other lawyers told him that he stood a good chance of winning. He knew the odds suggested otherwise.

The Sixth Circuit Court of Appeals could take weeks, if not longer, to issue a decision, so when Jim Scott returned home his attention immediately shifted back to his marriage, and how to get out of it. The day after he appeared before the Sixth Circuit he met with a family-law attorney in Knoxville to sign some paperwork, and he filed for divorce by the end of the following week. "Irreconcilable differences exist between us," he stated in an affidavit. "Our marriage is irretrievably broken." The affidavit listed specific grievances, chief among them Mary's striking him during the argument over the smashed iPad and

Nintendo. His divorce complaint stated that he wished to sell their home on Talahi Drive and split the money; Mary could keep their 2006 Lincoln Navigator and 2002 Mercedes Wagon, and he would stick with his Ford Explorer. And he wanted full custody of his sons.

The local paper probably wasn't going to publish a puff piece about what a terrific dad he was anytime soon—*The Knoxville News Sentinel*, like all respectable small-town papers, occasionally did that sort of thing—but he had tried to be a decent father. He coached Jack's rec sports teams, and they went on night walks together, flashlights guiding the way. One Halloween, Jim made Sam a Heisman Trophy costume, painting his face gold and outfitting him with a leather helmet and an overstuffed sweatshirt. Another time, at the beach, Jim came down with the flu but spent an entire day in the sun building the boys an elaborate sand fort, using painters' buckets to make Romanesque columns. He nearly passed out and had to recover on the couch. Nowadays, the workers' lawsuit absorbed nearly all his attention, but, even with the case's Everest-sized demands, he believed that, for his sons' safety and well-being, they needed to spend most of their time in his care. His boys said they would prefer that arrangement, too.

Scott's divorce, for all its unpleasantness, had one minor benefit in that it prevented him from dwelling on, and fretting over, and dreading, the Sixth Circuit's impending decision. Ansol and Janie Clark, who had no such life-upturning diversion, listened over and over to Scott's oral argument, an audio recording of which the court had posted online. They had a desktop computer in a sunroom off their kitchen, next to their cat's scratching tree. They called other plaintiffs and put the phone up to the speaker, to let them listen to parts. Janie had no idea whether they would win.

At around ten one June morning, a little over a month after oral arguments, Scott was at his desk when his secretary walked into his office. Had he checked his email lately? she asked. He hadn't. The court had filed its decision, she said. *Please, God*, he thought, *tell me that I won.*

The Sixth Circuit had ruled in the workers' favor, she said, a smile widening across her face. The panel had sent the case back to Judge Varlan in the district court.

Scott launched to his feet. "Oh, my God, I did it!" he yelled, startling the woman. He paced around his office, fists clenched. The case was still alive. Jacobs would likely have to stand trial in Knoxville. The workers still had a shot.

Janie Clark was in her kitchen when the phone rang. Scott, overworked and overstressed, didn't always seem terribly happy when he called. This time he shouted, "We won! We won! We won!" Janie jumped up and down and yelled for Ansol to pick up the phone in the other room. Scott thanked the Clarks for their support and apologized for everything they'd endured. Still, with a jury trial yet to come, he knew more difficulties lay ahead.

On Sunday, December 28, 2008, six days after a billion gallons of coal sludge cascaded over three hundred acres in Roane County, Tom Kilgore, the bony, Alabama-born chief executive of TVA, strode into the gymnasium of Roane County High School, an aged brick structure on the banks of the Clinch River. Kilgore wore a white dress shirt and a black suit jacket with no tie, which lent him a weary, embattled look. More than three hundred anxious residents were crammed together on the bleachers. Kilgore, microphone in hand, told the crowd that he couldn't say when the avalanche of coal ash would be removed, but, he insisted, "we're going to clean it up, we're going to clean it up right." He added, "This is not a time that TVA holds its head high." Six years, five months, one week, and a billion-plus dollars later, Craig Zeller, an EPA project manager in his forties, appeared in the auditorium of the same high school to report that the cleanup was at last complete.

It was a little past six o'clock on June 4, 2015, a dry, oven-hot day. Members of a Roane County environmental review board were present, along with at least one reporter. Otherwise, the meeting occasioned little fanfare. Zeller, the EPA's top staffer at Kingston since 2010, stood at a lectern and clicked through a presentation. He wore a white short-sleeve button-down shirt. On a screen, aerial photographs showed the collapsed holding pond; the sea of gray sludge that it unleashed; and the soft, green expanse as it now appeared. The disaster was "an unfortunate tragedy," Zeller said, one caused by a "perfect storm" of factors. He repeated one of TVA's pet theories, which Richard Moore, the inspector general, had rebuked in the 2011 trial: that an unstable "slimes" layer of silt beneath the coal-ash pond had led to its collapse, not management failures or incompetence.

Zeller had echoed other TVA talking points at past public meetings, including that fly ash didn't pose "an unacceptable risk" to the community or to on-site personnel. "Adequately protecting the workers," he explained at another meeting, was the EPA's chief concern—which was why, he said, the workers wore portable air-monitoring devices on the job, "to make sure we're not exposing them." In the auditorium that June evening, he offered further assurances, saying that regular monitoring would continue until 2017, and to a lesser extent after that.

Zeller's presentation marked the end of one of the most embarrassing periods in TVA's history, one that forced it to reconsider its energy mix and move away from coal. In the years since the disaster, TVA had decommissioned two of its eleven coal-fired power plants, and it would shutter four more over the next five years. These facilities were among the nearly two hundred coal-fired power stations that closed in the U.S. between 2008 and 2015, as environmental nonprofits ratcheted up lobbying and litigation efforts to curb coal pollution, the single largest source globally of planet-warming carbon emissions since the Industrial Revolution. The U.S. had begun to wean itself off coal, but it remained the top source of emissions worldwide, surpassing both oil and natural gas.

TVA anticipated that, with public concern growing over climate change, it would soon face increasingly stringent federal regulations regarding coal and that it would need to implement "exceptional environmental controls," as one TVA presentation slide put it. To offset the inevitable decline of coal, Tom Kilgore had pushed forward a plan to complete Watts Bar Unit 2, a nuclear reactor halfway between Knoxville and Chattanooga, construction of which had been halted since 1988.* (Bellefonte, another deferred plant, which Kilgore, in a *New York Times* op-ed, had argued should be completed, remained mothballed.) TVA would also begin transitioning some of its power stations from coal to natural gas.

Despite TVA's carbon-cutting gestures, coal still accounted for 36 percent of its energy generation at the time of Zeller's presentation,

* Watts Bar Unit 2 would generate power for the first time in 2016, forty-three years after federal regulators greenlit the project.

down from 60 percent when the coal-ash dike failed but well above the national average of 20 percent among major power providers. And TVA seemed ambivalent about curbing its coal consumption further than necessary. It contributed millions of dollars to an industry group that battled the EPA over regulations. It fought Tennessee regulators over whether it had let unlined, leaking coal-ash dump sites pollute groundwater and rivers around Nashville.* And, perhaps most significant, when Kilgore retired in 2012, TVA replaced him not with a renewable-energy guru or a forward-thinking executive but with Bill Johnson, a six-foot-five former CEO for Progress Energy, a North Carolina power company that burned almost as much coal as TVA did.

Johnson had led TVA through the end stages of the Kingston cleanup. In the high-school auditorium that summer evening in 2015, residents expressed dissatisfaction with TVA's efforts under Johnson's leadership. TVA had spent tens of millions of dollars to improve local recreation areas and trails, which folks appreciated, but the years-long cleanup had compounded the distrust that many locals already felt for TVA, mostly for failing to curb its pollution.

On June 5, 2015, *The Knoxville News Sentinel* carried a story about Craig Zeller's presentation, noting that, if lined up end to end, the forty-one thousand railcars that hauled the Kingston ash to the landfill in Uniontown, Alabama, "would stretch from Knoxville to Nashville"—a distance of one hundred and eighty miles. The paper also reported that TVA ratepayers, some nine million in all now, would each pay a fifty-nine-cent surcharge on their monthly power bills for the next nine years, to help cover the cleanup's $1.134 billion price tag.

The story ran on page thirteen, next to an item about Knoxville building-preservation grants. The same edition of the *Sentinel* carried another story related to the Kingston disaster, with much more prominent placement. "Ash spill workers get 2nd crack," the front-page headline read.

• • •

* In 2019, a judge, ruling in favor of the state and several nonprofits, ordered TVA to dig up and remove millions of tons of coal ash from a dump site near Nashville.

Janie Clark was elated as she read the *Sentinel*'s story about the Sixth Circuit's ruling. She did so carefully, taking care not to fold or crease the newsprint. The paper had not only covered the workers' victory, but it had also tasked its star reporter, Jamie Satterfield, to write the piece. *Jamie Satterfield!* Janie thought. *She's an icon!* Every five years or so, a murder of a true horror-movie quality tends to rock Knoxville—like the twenty-eight-year-old man who, a few years later, would stab and dismember his parents and then stew his mother's head on the family's kitchen stove. Satterfield, a wheat stalk of a woman in her forties, with narrow, blue eyes and a Virginia Slims habit, had covered many of the city's nightmarish crimes over the previous two decades. Most famous among them was the 2007 carjacking, kidnapping, torture, and murder of a young Knoxville couple. Satterfield recorded video dispatches outside the courtroom during breaks in the killers' trials, and, on a not-infrequent basis, she appeared on national newsmagazine shows, like *Dateline NBC*, to discuss grisly stories she'd covered.

Janie Clark had saved a copy of the *Sentinel*'s first story about the workers' lawsuit, which the paper had published shortly after Jim Scott filed the complaint against Jacobs. She would have hated it if that story or Satterfield's update got ripped or lost in a drawer, so she and Ansol spent the better part of a day motoring around Knoxville searching for the perfect newspaper-sized frames.

Ansol's stroke, three months earlier, had upturned their worlds, but Scott's Sixth Circuit victory boosted their spirits considerably. Their little frame-hunting mission was the most fun Janie had had in weeks. She felt blessed that Ansol hadn't been paralyzed or worse and that they could still ride around together. They tried Hobby Lobby and Old Time Pottery first before ending up at the Turkey Creek Walmart, in the west Knoxville suburbs. The frame selection was impressive. She and Ansol stood in the aisle looking around until she spied a promising option. Ansol had a copy of the *Sentinel* with him. "Ansol," Janie said, "lay that on there." The newspaper fit perfectly. Janie grabbed four or five frames.

Satterfield's latest story, ten short paragraphs in all, barely mentioned why the workers had sued Jacobs, and it included no original quotes from the plaintiffs or from Jacobs's lawyers. Still, Janie was optimistic that now that Satterfield had filed one story, more reporting would follow. Jacobs and TVA would be held responsible, she felt sure, not just in the courts but in the city's largest, and only true, newspaper. She would have her frames ready.

Jim Scott was as invigorated as the Clarks. The Sixth Circuit hadn't ruled on the veracity of the workers' allegations or whether Jacobs was liable for their health problems, but it did give the case a tentative green light to proceed, on the basis that Jacobs wasn't necessarily entitled to the same immunity as the government. Thanks to this decision, nearly two years after Scott filed the workers' lawsuit, the case could finally begin in earnest—at least whenever Judge Thomas Varlan ordered discovery to begin. And yet, just as Scott cleared this hurdle, others appeared in his path.

After the Kingston spill, Congress's threats to hold TVA to account had proved empty. For a time, Scott had hoped that, at the very least, the EPA would bring the hammer down on TVA, especially with a Democrat, Barack Obama, occupying the White House. But, on April 17, 2015—days before Scott flew to Cincinnati—the EPA had finalized the first national coal-ash disposal rules, which it had created largely in response to the Kingston disaster and to another coal-ash catastrophe, in 2014, in which a power plant, owned by Duke Energy, spewed thirty-nine thousand tons of coal ash into North Carolina's Dan River. In a report accompanying the new regulations, the EPA identified one hundred and fifty-seven cases in which leaky coal-ash dump sites had harmed or potentially harmed human health. Each year coal-ash ponds—there were some seven hundred and fifty scattered throughout the U.S.—contaminated four thousand miles of American rivers, compromising the drinking water of nearly three million people, according to a study by environmental groups and the former head of the EPA's Office of Water. To curb such pollution, the EPA would require utilities and power plants to monitor whether their active coal-ash pits contaminated groundwater, and to stop receiving further coal-ash shipments and to clean up the site if they had; new pits would also need liners. And yet, to Scott's disbelief, the EPA *declined* to impose its rules on "legacy," or inactive, dumpsites, or to designate coal ash hazardous waste. The regulations made little sense: the EPA acknowledged that coal ash's constituents—arsenic, beryllium, lead, mercury—were toxic. Yet somehow, when mixed together, these materials transformed into a "special waste" that power plants didn't need to handle or transport with extra care. Remarkably, these decisions came *after* the EPA had concluded that people who drank water contaminated from leaking coal-ash ponds increased their risk of cancer several hundredfold, owing to arsenic poisoning. A report that contained this information was long withheld from the public by the George W. Bush administration, which had been friendly to both the oil and coal industries.

The coal lobby had undoubtedly influenced the EPA's latest decision. Fly ash was big business. Each year, power companies generated about one hundred million tons of it and other coal wastes, more than half of which ended up not in holding ponds but in concrete, drywall, roof tiles, road base, and structural fill. Power companies made billions of dollars annually selling fly ash for such purposes. The EPA's weak new rules not only protected this lucrative revenue stream at the public's expense, but, Scott felt, also afforded Jacobs a chance to undercut the workers' allegations that fly ash had caused their health problems, since it could argue that, according to the federal government, the ash wasn't truly hazardous.

Scott was still effectively working alone, despite his arrangement with Sandy Sharp. Proving that exposure to fly ash had harmed the workers would be a gigantic task. He needed strong epidemiological evidence to build a winning case, and Scott had very little of it, something Jeff Friedman would be able to help him with. He reached out by email, attaching a copy of the Sixth Circuit's decision and including a link to the recent *Sentinel* story by Jamie Satterfield. His message was brief: *Are you interested yet?*

After Friedman read Scott's email and the Sixth Circuit's ruling, he agreed that Scott had won a major victory. Still, he doubted Scott's ability to prevail in the case, owing to the high burden of proof in toxic-exposure suits. He also worried that Scott might go broke. Scott's team would have to pay for every expert, every deposition, every travel expense. That meant Friedman would need to be willing to risk every dollar he had if he agreed to help, and he wasn't willing to take that gamble. During the land cases, Friedman had admired Scott's energy and his rapport with clients, but Scott clearly wasn't the world's most organized attorney or its best at meeting deadlines. And a multibillion-dollar company like Jacobs Engineering would take advantage of such missteps without mercy.

Keep me in the loop, Friedman replied to Scott, and call if you have any questions or want to talk. But, Friedman added, it wasn't a good time for him to dive into another big lawsuit up in Tennessee.

Scott, irritated but undeterred, pressed on. Before he flew to Cincinnati for oral arguments, a few additional Kingston workers beyond the forty-eight plaintiffs had contacted him about suing Jacobs. In the weeks following the Sixth Circuit's decision, dozens more called seeking representation, encouraged by the win. Scott scheduled time to meet with them and quickly filed another lawsuit against Jacobs on behalf of eleven additional Kingston workers. The court, in turn, consolidated this new case with the original one, since the complaints were substantially similar. *Adkisson et al. v. Jacobs Engineering*, the first suit, was made the lead case that would represent the group. Jacobs would eventually face a total of ten lawsuits filed on behalf of almost two hundred and fifty former Kingston workers and their family members, which the court would also consolidate.

Scott needed to act fast to advance the cases. With the cleanup project over, the workers had taken jobs elsewhere, most of which had nothing to do with coal ash. But, whenever the workers visited his office, he was struck by how severely their health had continued to decline. Billy Isley, the Metallica fan, explained to Scott that, while driving a tractor trailer in Colorado, he'd noticed a lesion on his face that quickly tripled in size. He regularly coughed up blood, too, he said. Meanwhile, his wife, Lena, had suffered three strokes, which she blamed on having washed Billy's ash-covered clothes.

In July 2015, about a month after Scott's Sixth Circuit win, another former Kingston worker, a fifty-one-year-old truck driver by the name of Mike Shelton, visited a health clinic at his wife's urging. An X-ray revealed a spot on his lungs—cancer. Later that month, he underwent surgery, in Chattanooga, to have the tumor and part of a lung removed. Before doctors sedated him, he hugged and kissed Angie, his wife of nearly twenty-five years. "You be strong," he told her. He died of complications days later.

When Scott received the call at his office, the news rocked him. He knew that Shelton, a former smoker, was in particularly poor health. During a visit to Scott's office shortly after receiving his cancer diagnosis, Shelton had coughed up a gray, bloody, jellylike substance. "I can't lose Mike," Shelton's wife had told Scott during a separate meeting. "He's my rock." She was a homemaker, with no children and no close family. With Mike gone now, she would have to provide for herself for the first time in her adult life, no easy task in the speck of a town where she lived, which had little besides fast-food places and a Piggly Wiggly grocery store. She eventually found a cleaning job at a funeral home, but she still struggled to pay her electric bill and to afford dog and cat food. Each night, she texted Scott prayers, blessing him for his work.

Jeff Brewer, upset about losing a friend and anxious that he might meet a similar fate, thought about Shelton's death perhaps even more than Scott did. To Brewer's relief, after his layoff from Kingston, he quickly found a new trucking job, and he felt grateful for that. But whatever toxins he'd inhaled at Kingston seemed to wear him down little by little. He lacked the stamina to coach his daughters' soccer and basketball teams, and he broke into a heavy sweat and fell short of breath while doing minor household chores. He tried to hide his condition from his three daughters, to avoid upsetting them, but it was no use. He comforted himself by trusting that he would leave this Earth only in God's due time, but he prayed that he first got to see his daughters grow up and have children of their own. He wanted to hold one of his grandchildren at least once.

As Brewer's health slipped, he still attended church, but he couldn't bring himself to forgive Jacobs or TVA, as his faith instructed he ought. He often thought about Christ's persecution—how, while hanging on the cross, the Lord had said, "Father, forgive them. They know not what they do." That, Brewer thought, was the problem with TVA and Jacobs: they knew what they were doing.

Mass tort cases, like the workers' against Jacobs, seldom reach speedy resolutions. After filing suit in 1984, four thousand residents of Glen Avon, California, waited eleven years for a settlement after they sued scores of companies for dumping thirty-four million gallons of hazardous waste in an area pit, contaminating their groundwater. The duration of the case owed partly to the large number of plaintiffs but more to the resources of the companies who fought their claims. The ordeal took more than three decades to be fully resolved.

During the winter of 2015, Jim Scott worried that the workers' case was following a similarly glacial pace. A few months after his victory in the Sixth Circuit, Jacobs's attorney Joe Welborn appealed the decision to the U.S. Supreme Court, and neither *Adkisson* nor any of the other suits could proceed until the Court decided whether to take up the case. Scott felt sure, based on the Sixth Circuit's strong ruling in the workers' favor, that the Supreme Court would reject Jacobs's appeal. Then again, he'd believed that Judge Varlan wouldn't throw out the workers' case in the first place.

Frustrated and fatigued, Scott drove his Ford Explorer to Janie and Ansol's home once every week or so, ostensibly to discuss the case. He and the Clarks usually talked at the dining-room table, while eating cookies Janie had baked. Gray winter light poured into the room from a bay window as traffic floated by soundlessly down the hill. Sometimes other workers joined them. Scott's objective was always the same. By his count, more than thirty of his clients now had respiratory or pulmonary problems, and another ten had cancer. He wanted them to know that he took their health problems seriously and that he hadn't quit working for them. Perhaps most of all, he wanted them to feel heard, as they had seldom been on the jobsite.

"They never thought they'd be caught!" Janie said of Jacobs at one of their get-togethers. She believed that the company assumed the workers would get sick decades after working at Kingston, then, she said, "we'd die, and we wouldn't connect the dots!" But the workers fell ill faster than Jacobs had anticipated, she said, and that was the only reason they had a lawsuit at all. Well, that and because Scott was the only person who took them seriously. Janie adored him for that.

As Scott sat at the table, listening to Janie and Ansol tell stories, he often thought, *This is a married couple that truly loves each other.* Throughout that fall, he and his ex had been in a custody fight over their sons and bickering over a condo they rented out. The Clarks' home afforded Scott a rare bit of peace. He told them little about his divorce, and yet Janie still worried about him. She came to view him as something of a kid brother. His commitment to the case, despite his personal turmoil, despite the long odds, restored her faith that there was still some decency in the world, a feeling she'd lost after learning about TVA's and Jacobs's deceptions. "Jim could be working privately and making millions, but he chose to do this," she explained to a friend. They hadn't paid him one dime, either, and wouldn't unless they won. "He *wants* to do this case," she said.

For all the Clarks' concern and kindness, Scott knew he could wait no longer for help, because if the Supreme Court rejected Jacobs's appeal, Varlan would probably thrust the case right into discovery. Scott would then need a partner to help him pore over documents, take depositions, and respond to Jacobs's motions. He needed another attorney, and only one other person came to mind.

John Dupree was a forty-seven-year-old personal-injury lawyer, with shaggy blond hair, a wife and three children, and a deep appreciation for smokeless tobacco. He liked to hunt and fish and search for arrowheads and collect old Coleman camping equipment. He enjoyed woodworking, too, and whiskey. Around the office, he wore jeans, short-sleeve button-downs, and scuffed leather boots with American flag shoelace charms. "I'm going to take me a chew of tobacco," he would say softly, pausing a conversation with a visitor to retrieve a tin from his desk.

Dupree grew up in Chattanooga, Tennessee, a fading Appalachian steel town in those days, one hundred miles south of Knoxville near the Georgia border. His dad sold sawmill equipment. His parents divorced when he was eight, and he and his mother and three siblings lived in a hillside stone house in partial disrepair. He was voted the wittiest boy in his high-school graduating class. After earning his undergraduate degree from the College of Charleston, he applied to become a police officer in Franklin, Tennessee, a Nashville suburb, but then attended the University of Tennessee College of Law, in Knoxville, when he was accepted. His mother had carried the brunt of raising Dupree and his siblings while also holding down a job as a probation officer. He was *going* to law school, she told him.

After earning his degree, Dupree spent a largely unsuccessful year as a solo practitioner in Nashville before returning to Knoxville to defend insurance companies at one of the city's biggest law firms, Frantz McConnell. His first jury trial involved an uninsured elderly woman who'd bumped into another motorist at a drive-through ATM. Dupree flubbed so badly and the woman was so ancient and helpless that the judge dismissed the case halfway through the trial—an act of mercy. As a lowly associate, he tried a car-wreck case almost every week. Grunt work, but a good education.

After two-odd years at Frantz McConnell, Dupree left for another local firm, where he defended insurance companies in black-lung suits brought by sick coal miners. The scales of justice tilted heavily in his clients' favor, he quickly realized. Nearly all the coal miners smoked cigarettes, and had done so for years, if not decades, which made proving that coal dust, not tobacco, had wrecked their lungs nearly impossible. If the miners did somehow overcome this legal hurdle, the federal government capped the amount of money they could recover, which disincentivized many good lawyers from taking their cases—why try with no hope of a big payday? Dupree could recall losing only one black-lung case out of the hundreds he litigated. He would later tell an acquaintance that he didn't feel morally conflicted about fighting black-lung cases. Insurance companies hired him, and it was his job to defend them. Still, he had something of a renegade spirit, and, after four years, he grew restless and decided to start representing people who wanted to sue insurance companies.

He worked for himself, but for several years he rented office space from Jim Scott's old law firm on Kingston Pike. Dupree and Scott had known each other for years, having both launched their law careers in Knoxville around the same time. Within a few months of sharing an office, they became close friends.

Scott would bounce from room to room, rambling about ideas for cases, University of Tennessee basketball, two-headed snakes, or whatever else popped into his mind. Dupree realized that Scott's boundless energy, though occasionally grating, had a magnetic quality. Scott would walk into a party—any party—and by happenstance already know most of the people there, and he would befriend everyone else by the end of the night. People couldn't help but like Scott, which, for Dupree, helped to explain his effectiveness with juries.

Scott, for his part, appreciated Dupree's diligent, must-make-money attitude, and was endlessly amused by his thriftiness. For lunch, Dupree often walked to a gas station and bought a jar of pickles or a can of tuna. Half of his suits came from Goodwill, Scott once joked, and, even if they weren't secondhand, they looked like it.

After Scott's law firm disbanded in 2014, Dupree had relocated to 713 Market Street, a three-story, redbrick building in downtown Knoxville. The handsome, century-old structure stood fifty paces from the rear of the federal courthouse on a narrow, tree-lined street, among a row of other turn-of-the-century buildings. Dupree shared the second floor with two other attorneys. His office was in the back corner of the building. A painting of two hunters and their bluetick hounds hung on the wall, along with dozens of family photos and a framed copy of *Field & Stream*, with a cover illustration of a rabbit darting through snow.

Dupree and Scott had stayed in contact after they moved offices, and Scott had mentioned the Kingston workers' case, so Dupree wasn't surprised when his friend appeared at his office one day shortly after the Sixth Circuit handed down its ruling. "Hey, John," Scott said, as he took a seat across from his desk, "will you help me tackle this case?" They would make a good team, Scott said. Dupree, a strong writer, could draft the pleadings and the motions, while Scott dealt with the clients and prepared for discovery.

Dupree had thought about the workers' suit off and on ever since Scott had mentioned it months earlier, and he had reservations. The main problem was money, he told Scott. Dupree made a good living—like Scott, he owned a nice home in Sequoyah Hills—and *Adkisson* was the kind of case, Dupree said, that could ruin a small firm. If a plaintiff had cancer, say, it might cost $2,000 to print all their medical records, and Scott had nearly fifty plaintiffs on the lead case alone, to say nothing of the hundreds of others. And, if the case reached discovery, the attorneys would need to pay court-reporter fees, filing fees, and expert witnesses with steep hourly rates.

Listen, Scott told Dupree. The case would cost money, yes. Perhaps a great deal of money. But nothing about it spooked him or gave him pause. Jacobs's attorneys had a larger war chest than he did, but the case was winnable, Scott said, in part because the workers' stories were simple enough for any jury to understand. "The way I look at it," Scott said, leaning forward in his chair, voice low, eyes steady, "is that they had a toxic tub of goop, and it blew up." Then, he continued, TVA hired Jacobs to clean up the goop and to protect the community and the workers in the process. "And they just lied to them and didn't do it," he said, and now people were sick.

Dupree never took a case unless he felt certain that he could win—it wasn't good business otherwise. He didn't disagree with Scott that the workers' stories would resonate with a jury, and the Sixth Circuit's ruling vouched for the case's potential. But perhaps the main thing on Dupree's mind was Scott's divorce, which had imploded his life. "I'm not entirely sure you can prove this case," Dupree told Scott. "But I'll help you."

The Peninsula Club, a private swim-and-tennis complex, occupied a small, semi-forested tract of land on a bend in the Tennessee River, about ten miles south of downtown Knoxville. A stand of mature, leafy hardwoods towered over six cool blue swim lanes that glinted in the sunlight. During the summer of 2016, from nine in the morning until eleven, Monday through Thursday, Jim Scott tried, and usually failed, to work comfortably on the pool deck. As his sons practiced their strokes, he parked himself under a covered wooden awning and spread documents on a picnic table. As the morning wore on and the temperature climbed to a sticky, suffocating 90 degrees, sweat drenched his khakis and button-downs and dripped onto his notebooks and case files as he scribbled.

Scott had kept atypical office hours ever since he entered private practice, but, after he filed for divorce, he stopped working normal hours, or in normal locations, almost entirely. A Knox County judge had recently ordered his ex to move out of the family home on Talahi Drive and had given Jim sole custody of his two sons. That meant Jim was no longer merely their dad, the harried breadwinner, the preoccupied attorney; they now depended on him for rides, meals, homework help, safety, and general amusement. Scott had pushed for this custody arrangement, and was glad that the judge had agreed to it, but a career in a courtroom hadn't prepared him for the rigors of single parenting. And now, with school out for summer, the three Scotts had a lot of hours, too many hours, to fill. Swimming helped to occupy Jack and Sam, for part of the morning anyway, as Jim tried to work. He had much to do.

To Scott's relief, in January 2016, the Supreme Court had declined Jacobs's appeal, for reasons it didn't specify, clearing the way for the workers' case to advance in the district court. Nearly three years after

Scott filed the workers' complaint, a federal magistrate judge who worked under Judge Varlan had ordered discovery to begin. Scott, therefore, was preparing for depositions—sworn, out-of-court testimonies that would provide elemental material for building a convincing case against Jacobs. Scott had to make the most of his time with each witness. Under the rules governing depositions, the witnesses would have to answer his questions under oath, with no judge present. Scott had already emailed Jacobs's attorney Joe Welborn the names of a dozen Jacobs or TVA staff members he wanted to depose, and he had spent weeks poring over affidavits, medical literature, and TVA safety manuals to prepare his questions.

Scott leaned on his parents for child-care help. When school was still in session, Buddy, the old judge, often dropped off the boys in the morning and picked them up in the afternoon and watched them until Jim came home for a brief nap and dinner. Jim intended to follow through with his plan, as he stated in his divorce complaint, to sell the family home on Talahi Drive. Buddy assigned Jack, now thirteen, what he called "Mr. Miyagi projects" to fix up the place for listing. Jack caulked tile, painted doors, and replaced old knobs, loving it all.

As the summer dragged on, Jim's mother, Mildred, and Buddy pitched in with morning swim-practice duty. Once, Jim showed up unannounced to watch his sons. "What are you doing here?" Buddy asked. "You've got stuff to do! The law is a jealous mistress." Jim knew his dad was right; he had no time for diversions. Judge Varlan had scheduled the trial to begin the second week of January 2017, a quick six months away.

At the little brick office building near the federal courthouse, Scott and John Dupree discussed how to maximize their time with each witness during the depositions. Scott would handle most of the questions. First, he said, he needed a TVA staffer to establish what TVA considered acceptable safety procedures on-site; then he needed a Jacobs staffer to admit to the ways he or his colleagues had deviated from TVA's safety protocols—likely the far tougher of the two objectives. Dupree, for his part, needed to keep Scott from wandering off in tangential thickets, for which he had a gift.

During one midsummer meeting, Dupree told Scott they needed more manpower and more money, a point of anxiety for him from the start. The *Adkisson* case had just begun in earnest, and it was clear that they would need to spend hundreds of thousands of dollars to bring it to trial. Each deposition would be a thousand dollars out the door in transcript and court-reporter fees, and they might need to take dozens of depositions over the next few months.

Scott agreed. Beyond paying court reporters, he and Dupree would need to hire subject-matter experts to testify about coal ash's dangers. And he knew from experience that experts tended to devote minimal time to a case and perform poorly in a trial when not properly compensated, even if they volunteered to help and meant well. The trouble for Scott was that Sandy Sharp, the sportscar-loving insurance attorney, had proved disappointingly frugal in backing the workers' lawsuit, so much so that Scott and Sharp had decided to part ways.

What about Keith Stewart? Dupree asked Scott.

Scott knew Stewart, a successful local personal-injury attorney. He owned the second floor of the brick building where Scott was sitting at that very moment. A conference room separated Stewart's office from Dupree's.

"You come over here," Dupree told Scott, "and [we'll] handle Jacobs, and Keith will bankroll us." Scott could use an open office on the first floor, right below his and Stewart's.

"Keith has that much money?" Scott asked.

"Yeah, Keith can bankroll the whole thing," Dupree said. Stewart could manage document requests in discovery, too, Dupree added, which would afford him time to address Jacobs's flurry of motions and free up Scott to throw himself at depositions.

Dupree had overstated Stewart's financial resources—Stewart made a good living but only that—but kept talking. "Keith is a bulldog," he said. He wouldn't let Jacobs's attorneys push him around.

Scott didn't doubt that.

Of all the attorneys Scott knew, Keith Stewart was the only one who had been shocked by a livestock prod. He was the son of a contractor who had a sideline running beef cattle. He stood six foot three in cowboy boots, sported a black goatee, and spat chewing tobacco into a wastebasket under his desk during meetings. When discussing cases, he said things about other attorneys like, "I'm going to knock their dicks in the dirt," or he might call them "fucktards."

Stewart grew up in Rogersville, Tennessee, a quaint town sixty-five miles northeast of Knoxville. He lived a couple of miles from a patch of land where his dad grazed cattle—the site of the stock-prod mishap, which involved a corral-resistant bull and a prod-happy cousin with poor aim. Stewart's father, who was a church deacon and a Gideon, handed out pocket-size New Testaments on the University of Tennessee campus, and he helped to build churches in developing countries. Stewart's mother ran a beauty parlor out of a shop, custom built by his father, just across the carport from the family home. She refused to keep sodas, much less alcohol, in the house and cooked every meal the family ate. She grew corn and beans and tomatoes and canned it all. Stewart bucked his parents' pious example. At age sixteen, while hanging out by a movie theater, he drank half of a fifth of vodka to impress a girl and ended up in the Kingsport, Tennessee, jail for a night. Late in Stewart's senior year of high school, his father urged him to attend the Citadel, a military college in South Carolina, to help him straighten up. Keith lasted three weeks in the lowcountry heat before hitchhiking home, never to return.

He developed a taste for cocaine while enrolled at Centre College, in Danville, Kentucky. In the September of his sophomore year, his mother died of cancer, after a long illness. He withdrew from classes at Christmas and returned to Rogersville. One night, in October 1987, he and two friends sold ten thousand dollars' worth of coke to an undercover cop at a roadhouse called the Starburst Club, eleven miles outside Greenville, Tennessee. After the drugs and money traded hands, Stewart pulled his '78 Toyota Celica onto the highway and sped toward town. He didn't get far. The officer who pulled him over pointed a .357 Magnum at his skull and told him to put up his goddamn hands. "I was the worst drug dealer in history," Stewart explained to an acquaintance one morning years later, reclining in his office chair. "I got caught up in a sting and there was no good way out of it."

He accepted a plea deal in exchange for a seven-year sentence. He turned twenty-one in prison, just like in the Merle Haggard song "Mamma Tried." For years to come, he would be haunted by the chorus, with its lyrics about a son rejecting his mother's efforts to steer him right. He killed time behind bars in the law library, reading newspapers and magazines. After a while, he picked up the law books. After eighteen months, he was paroled. He finished his undergraduate degree, took the

LSAT, and was accepted to the University of Tennessee College of Law. He met John Dupree after graduation during bar-review classes. They became golf pals and rented an office together for a few years early in their careers. They shot crossbows outside into the weeds and threw baseballs in the hallway. A clock, hung low and off-center, covered a hole in the drywall from a missed catch. Respectable law firms tend not to hire convicted felons, so Stewart had always worked for himself. He handled a bit of everything: criminal cases, DUIs, car wrecks. "I love a good assault case," he once said. "They're so much fun. Because it's always he said, she said."

The Lord never found Stewart, as He had his parents, but he couldn't shake a sense of deep Baptist guilt from his upbringing, and his personal reformation continued as he aged. He stopped drinking almost entirely in his early thirties, following a long, painful flight home from a weekend in Las Vegas. After a divorce around the same time, he remarried well. His second wife was an assistant district attorney in Knox County. Later, he would become the only attorney in memory to win the Knoxville Bar Association's ethics quiz competition two consecutive years. "Say what you want to about Keith Stewart, and a lot has been said," another attorney wrote in the bar's monthly magazine following Stewart's second win, "but the guy has panache and apparently he knows the Rules of Professional Conduct."

After years working apart, Stewart had been glad to reunite with John Dupree at the Market Street office. They formed a legal association: they didn't share cases or profits, as partners do at traditional law firms; instead, they operated independently but pitched in for rent and utilities and some shared services, and they relied on each other for legal muscle on an ad-hoc basis.

The conference room between their offices had pocket doors they usually left open, so they could shout at each other from their desks. In the summer of 2016, Dupree yelled for Stewart to swing by real quick. Stewart walked through the conference room and stood in the doorway. What's up? he asked.

Dupree, leaning back in his chair, feet propped up, laced his fingers behind his head. "Jim has this case," he said, "and he needs my help with it. And if I'm getting into it, I need your help."

"What is it?" Stewart asked. He didn't know Scott well, but he had a favorable opinion of him, and he knew that he'd made "a good lick," as Stewart put it, a few years earlier representing folks who got ill eating at O'Charley's.

"There's a bunch of workers," Dupree explained, "and they're all sick." The plaintiffs had worked at the big Kingston cleanup site a few years back, Dupree said, and his and Scott's theory was that TVA and one of its contractors had failed to control fly ash or provide personal protective equipment to the workers out there. He'd signed on to help Scott, but they needed to bring in a third attorney.

"Jim is a spider monkey," Dupree told Stewart—a creature they could unleash to irritate and exhaust Jacobs's attorneys. But "Jim can't write for shit." So Dupree would draft and respond to motions. What their team needed now, he said, was someone to respond to Jacobs's requests for documents, manage the litigation, and keep him and Scott organized—no small task.

Something in Dupree's eyes betrayed that he had more than he could handle. "Well, fuck it," Stewart said. "I'll help out."

Scott and Dupree didn't reveal the size or complexity of the workers' case to Stewart until a follow-up meeting on July 12, just nine days before the first deposition. In the conference room between their offices, Stewart and Dupree reclined in two black swivel chairs around a six-foot hardwood table, which Stewart had refurbished himself and stained cherry red.

Scott tried to paint Stewart a fuller picture of the case. On a whiteboard hanging on the wall, he drew two large circles, one inside the other, representing the cleanup site. "This is what I'm calling the 'donut of death,'" Scott said, motioning his hand in a circle. He drew four or five sprinklelike asterisks on the donut. And here, he said, were the stationary air monitors, set up to detect hazards. Most of these monitors had stood across the river or across a narrow bay from the heart of the jobsite, Scott said, and water trucks had made sure to keep the ground around these monitors moist. That way, the fly ash wouldn't dry out, flare up, and cause high readings. But, Scott said, in the donut's center—in the hole—the fleet of water trucks hadn't been able to keep all the fly ash wet. There was just too much of it. Plus, the ash had to be dry before crews could load it onto the Alabama-bound trains. So, at times, the workers had been instructed *not* to water down the ash at all—at least according to some workers—thereby creating a giant dust bowl. "And that's where the workers were," Scott said, and almost all of them had gone without respiratory protection.

Scott had learned much of this from a deposition he took a year earlier with a truck driver and foreman named Brad Green, who oversaw more than fifty people at the Kingston cleanup, including Jeff Brewer. Scott had deposed Green as part of a workers' compensation case he'd filed against GUBMK, the construction contractor closely associated with TVA. Green's question-and-answer session was something of a warm-up for the Jacobs depositions, and a revealing one. Green worked for GUBMK but had taken orders from "TVA people," he said. Both Jacobs and TVA had a financial interest in watering heavily around the air monitors, he explained, because "if them monitors spiked, [the EPA] would shut us down." That would have cost both organizations time and, as a result, money.

"Holy shit," said Stewart, as Scott recounted Green's testimony. "It's all about power and greed."

Exactly, Scott said. "It's truly the greatest injustice I've seen in my career, by a long shot."

Scott grew more animated. Flaggers, he said, had probably inhaled the most fly ash, since they worked in the open, directing vehicles around the jobsite. They were among the first to get sick, Scott said, probably since they hadn't work in enclosed vehicles, which afforded guys like Brewer some mild protection. Scott went on, explaining that fuel-truck drivers and operators, like Ansol Clark and Mike McCarthy, had also likely inhaled a lot of fly ash, since they climbed in and out of their vehicles to pump diesel throughout their shifts.

So, Stewart said, summarizing the workers' plight, "you worked your ass off, you got exposed to toxic shit, and now you're going to die."

That's right, Scott said. Many of the workers didn't have health insurance and couldn't afford to see doctors regularly, and most who were insured had lousy policies. Workers had begun calling him "because they had thirty days to live" in some cases, Scott said. As time wore on, more workers would surely fall ill, since the latency period—the time between exposure and developing a disease—for fly ash could be a decade or more. And the tenth anniversary of the Kingston disaster was only two and a half years away. If they didn't need medical care now, they would soon.

Stewart said that Jacobs's wrongdoing seemed clear and provable. It was clear, too, that the three lawyers each stood to earn a sizable fee for their efforts if the case yielded a recovery. He agreed to help finance and push ahead the lawsuit, in exchange for a third of the contingency fee. That arrangement suited Scott and Dupree.

They all agreed to appear in court when needed, to help one another meet deadlines, and to deal with opposing counsel. Beyond that, Dupree would focus on writing briefs and pleadings, while Scott tracked down experts to testify on the workers' behalf. Scott would also lead client relations. As for Stewart, he would oversee the business end of things, and collect and organize client documents.

Stewart stressed the importance of the latter task. "I need medical records and medical bills," he said. "I need to start putting together a medical profile for each of these guys, because everyone's damages are going to be different," based on their exposures. The attorneys needed to make sure they scanned and digitized each bill or record the workers handed over, Stewart added. Their office building had storage in the basement, but it would fill up quickly. Basements can also flood.

The trickiest part of the discussion involved next steps. The three lawyers understood the basic shape of a car-crash case or a medical-malpractice suit, say. But their hastily assembled team didn't specialize in environmental law; none of them had navigated a sprawling toxic-tort suit anything like *Adkisson*. They scribbled ideas on a small white-board next to the one with the death donut. They decided that first they would get the facts of the case through depositions. Then they would obtain the opinions of epidemiological experts, who could review studies or data and conclude whether the fly ash at Kingston occurred at high enough concentrations to cause injury. Last, the attorneys would hire medical experts who could address whether fly ash caused the workers' specific illnesses.

On the attorneys' immediate to-do list: address Jacobs's requests for documentation production and schedule depositions with more Jacobs and TVA staff members.

Scott, who'd moved out of Sandy Sharp's riverfront law office, had followed Dupree's suggestion to rent space on the first floor of the Market Street building, to be near the rest of their little team. After the meeting, he went downstairs and returned with a transcript of the Brad Green deposition. The transcript, dog-eared, coffee-stained, and highlighted, ran one hundred and seventy-one pages. "Read this," Scott said, handing the sheaf to Stewart. "It's really good."

Stewart flipped through the transcript a few days later and, in doing so, realized that Green had corroborated many of the Kingston workers' allegations, including that fly ash blew around the site constantly and that Tom Bock and other Jacobs staffers had threatened to fire whoever asked to wear a dust mask. What's more, according to Green, workers had periodically worn personal monitoring devices to detect airborne hazards, like those in fly ash. But, Green said, these devices were usually distributed while it was raining or soon after it stopped.* No TVA or Jacobs higher-up explained to Green the reasoning for this unofficial policy, but they didn't need to: wet days were nearly the only time when fly ash stuck to the ground and wouldn't cause the monitors to record high readings.

Stewart threw down the transcript. "What the fuck!" So, Jacobs's safety protocols were all a sham? Was there any other way to read Green's testimony?

After a moment, Stewart picked up the transcript and read three or four more pages. He knew that Scott suspected, without much evidence yet, that TVA had either encouraged or tacitly permitted Jacobs staffers, like Bock, to deny the workers respiratory protection. Green lent plausibility to the hunch. TVA safety managers, he explained, "would pretty much do whatever they had to do to keep [an injury] from being recorded," since "it affected their bonus." The Kingston land cases, led by Jeff Friedman, also seemed to have influenced site safety, for the worse. Green claimed that Dwayne Rushing, the TVA supervisor who had mocked a worker's low testosterone and poor bedroom performance, had once told him that TVA didn't want the public to drive by and see workers wearing respirators, since TVA had "a big lawsuit going over the fly ash, and they didn't want to add fuel to the fire."

* Jacobs disputes this allegation and many others. See Notes for details.

"Jesus Christ, this is miserable," Stewart said to himself as he flipped pages.

Stewart already admired Jim Scott for single-handedly bringing the workers' case as far as he had, and all the information he had gleaned from a single deposition was a feat. Still, when Stewart saw Scott a day or two later in the office, he mocked the way his questions had bounced around. "It's like a monkey fucking a rusty tricycle!" Stewart said.

"I try to be all over the place!" Scott replied. "I don't want the witness to get in a rhythm, so I don't go subject by subject."

Well, Stewart said, the strategy seemed to work, and he hoped that it would continue to, so they could build a convincing case for trial. Because trial, Stewart believed, was where Scott would truly shine. "Look at him," Stewart explained to a visitor one morning later, pointing toward Scott, seated on the far side of his office. "He's adorable. He's relatable. He's honest. He clearly cares about his clients. He's not there for the money. He's there for justice." No Tennessee jury would turn against Scott, Stewart believed, provided their three-man team could get the workers' case in front of one.

There's a life-size bronze statue of a woman outside the old redbrick courthouse in Sevierville, Tennessee, a mountain town twenty-five miles east of Knoxville. The woman—young, smiling, full-faced, full-figured—sits cross-legged on a boulder, jeans cuffed at the ankle, an acoustic guitar resting on a knee. She gazes out over the little Appalachian village as if it were Eden, as if she would rather be nowhere else in the world. A plaque on the boulder beneath her reads, simply, DOLLY.

On the morning of July 21, 2016, Jim Scott drove to Sevierville, the hometown of the country-music superstar Dolly Parton. He met John Dupree and Keith Stewart at an attorney's office in a squat, renovated former hosiery mill a few blocks from the bronze Dolly effigy. He paid it no attention. The first deposition was set to begin that morning, and Scott suspected that it would be among the most significant. The attorneys were scheduled to depose Tom Heffernan, TVA's former head of safety at the Kingston cleanup. Scott had heard that Heffernan, who lived in Sevierville, hence the site of the deposition, had a reputation for being generally upright and honest. Scott believed that to build a winnable case he needed a TVA staffer, preferably a high-ranking one like Heffernan, to state on the record what TVA considered acceptable safety practices. That way, Scott could have other witnesses testify about how Jacobs's actions had violated these protocols.

Inside, Scott, Stewart, and Dupree walked down a long narrow hallway, shoes clopping on the polished concrete floor. They turned right at a reception desk and filed into a conference room they'd reserved for the day. A window offered a view of a high school and a few low-slung government buildings across the street. Scott walked around a long conference table and took an empty chair facing the door. Dupree and Stewart flanked him. Scott took depositions regularly, and he felt well prepared for this one.

A court stenographer and three defense attorneys arrived. Notably, Joe Welborn, the former quarterback, wasn't among them. To support its defense team, Jacobs had recently hired Covington & Burling, a premier white-shoe firm with a staff of more than eight hundred and fifty lawyers around the world; its clients included the National Football League, the Union Bank of Switzerland, and several Guantánamo Bay detainees. Eric Holder had been a partner before becoming the U.S. attorney general under Barack Obama in 2009. A D.C.-based Covington attorney by the name of Kurt Hamrock had flown in specially for the deposition that day. He wore an expensive-looking watch and a dark, well-tailored suit with no tie. That he'd traveled all the way to tiny Sevierville sent a clear message to Scott: Jacobs was ready to throw bodies and money at the case.

Tom Heffernan arrived that morning wearing a blue button-down shirt, with a TVA emblem emblazoned above the breast pocket, which left no doubt in Scott's mind where Heffernan's allegiances lay. He sat across the table from Scott facing the window, with a defense attorney on either side of him. He had a wide, sincere face and a fair complexion. The stenographer, seated nearby with a little typing machine, swore him in.

"I'm the master at asking cryptic questions," Scott began, "so if I ask you something that is confusing . . . ask me to rephrase it. I don't want to ask anything that's confusing. Okay?"

"Yes, sir," Heffernan said, in a syrupy Appalachian drawl.

Scott asked about Heffernan's educational and work histories. Heffernan explained that he had spent thirty-one years at TVA. "When I retired," he said, "I was the senior manager of safety for fossil, hydro, and power."

And what year did you retire? Scott asked.

"In 2009, I retired," Heffernan said, adding, "I came back at the request of TVA to work at the Kingston ash recovery."

Scott could understand why TVA had asked Heffernan to return. He seemed kind and cooperative, a good company man. (Indeed, he took his job seriously, according to one TVA employee who worked with him.) Scott moved on to Heffernan's time at the coal-ash cleanup: "How many hours would you travel on foot per week versus that of being in a vehicle?"

"I couldn't tell you that," Heffernan said.

Well, Scott said, did he know of any documents that might indicate how much time he spent in the exclusion zone—the cleanup's gated-off ground zero—as opposed to, say, near the river?

"The only thing I can think of, sir," Heffernan said, "would be when I exited the exclusion zone, they would typically write down the license plate of the car that went through . . . because it had to be [decontaminated]." That process involved a multistep car wash, with automatic sprayers and a pressure-washing crew. Heffernan added that, under federal Superfund requirements, anyone who left the exclusion zone had to wash off their boots.

Because if you left without decontaminating your boots, that would be dangerous, right? Scott asked.

"Object to the form," said one of Welborn's associates, Josh Chesser.

The objection in itself didn't surprise Scott—attorneys often object during depositions—but the lawyer who spoke up did. Scott turned to the three defense attorneys across the table. "How many lawyers have we got here?" he asked, eyes wide. His meaning was clear: under the rules governing depositions, only one attorney is generally permitted to speak for each party, and Scott had assumed that Jacobs's new D.C. lawyer, Hamrock, would fill the role for the defense, not one of Welborn's lackeys. So who was it?

"I'm representing him," Hamrock said, referring to Heffernan. Chesser was there on Jacobs's behalf.

Before Scott had a chance to say more, Heffernan kept talking: "I can't say that [coal ash] is dangerous. I would say that it's—that we didn't want to spread it outside the decontamination area."

As Scott listened, he processed Hamrock's remark about representing Heffernan. Heffernan was an independent, third-party witness. He had worked not for Jacobs but for TVA, which wasn't a defendant in the case. Could Hamrock ethically represent both Heffernan *and* Jacobs? Wouldn't that inevitably result in witness tampering, or at least create a conflict of interest?

Scott asked follow-up questions about the exclusion zone as he considered his next move. Heffernan conceded that vehicles leaving the gated-off area were "absolutely" decontaminated because of safety concerns. When Scott pressed him further about safety, Heffernan gave mostly pat answers. Of course, he would have reported anything improper to TVA higher-ups, he said, and, of course, rule breakers would have been dealt with according to TVA policy. Heffernan also agreed that no worker should have been told that fly ash was safe to eat (something Tom Bock, of Jacobs, had said repeatedly).

Scott sensed that Heffernan didn't appreciate any suggestion that he had acted negligently or put people at risk. So, about thirty minutes into the deposition, Scott asked a bold question: "If you would have seen somebody destroying dust masks to help protect people that had breathing problems . . . I'm just going to ask it quite bluntly—you would have raised hell, would you not?"

"Yes, sir," Heffernan said decisively.

"Because that kind of safety violation is intolerable?" Scott asked.

Hamrock objected, as he had nearly ten times already, but in depositions, witnesses generally must answer all questions posed by opposing counsel; judges rule on the objections later.

"In my mind, that's a zero tolerance," Heffernan said.

So, Scott asked, if a Jacobs staff member threatened to fire a worker for requesting respiratory protection, "that would have been something that you raised hell over?"

"It's something that I would have corrected, yes," Heffernan said. But he claimed that he had no knowledge of such threats. These were exactly the sort of responses that Scott needed on the record. Here was

TVA's lead safety guy testifying, in effect, that Jacobs staff had broken TVA rules. Or so it seemed to Scott.

After a short break, Scott asked Heffernan whether Jacobs employees should have complied with TVA safety protocols, like those outlined in the "Site Wide Safety and Health Plan," along with state and federal safety rules. Heffernan said yes, that was true. Jacobs staff should have followed them all.

"And if you intentionally deviate from those rules and regulations," Scott asked, "based upon your knowledge, training, and experience, can you tell me whether or not that is criminal?"

Hamrock had objected to nearly thirty of Scott's questions by now, and he objected to this one, too.

Scott's patience had evaporated. "Off the record," he told the stenographer. He fixed his eyes on Hamrock, seated across the table. Do we need to get the judge on the phone? Scott asked. Or do you want to keep digging your hole? Because this sort of thing, he said, isn't supposed to happen. Scott made clear that, in his view, it was highly unethical for Hamrock to represent both Jacobs and Heffernan, an independent lay witness, since Hamrock sure seemed to have Jacobs's well-being in mind more than Heffernan's, suggesting a potential conflict of interest.

Hamrock, stern-faced, said nothing.

After a few uncomfortable moments, Scott went back on the record. He asked a few questions about training and safety procedures, then he brought up Jacobs's Tom Bock, who had worked closely with Heffernan on the safety team. "If someone went to Tom Bock with a prescription from their doctor for a dust mask, it should have been honored by Mr. Bock, should it not?" Scott asked.

Hamrock objected.

"Yes," Heffernan said.

"The same thing with a respirator, correct?" Scott asked.

Hamrock and Welborn's associate both objected. But Heffernan answered Scott's question with no qualifiers or caveats. "The answer is yes," Heffernan said. Those prescriptions should have been honored whether they were written by a worker's doctor or by a physician provided by TVA.

"And Mr. Bock," Scott went on, "shouldn't have said to an individual, let's say hypothetically—I don't know if you know him or not, Kevin Thompson—shouldn't have said, 'Well, you're not going to be able to work here anymore'?"

"I have no knowledge of that," Heffernan said, adding, "I can't imagine any safety professional saying such." Heffernan explained that he would have expected Jacobs staff to share with him whatever health complaints they received. But, he said, "I never recall being told about health concerns about fly ash." In fact, Heffernan said, he hadn't known the workers were sick until he read about their case in the newspaper.

How is that possible? Scott thought. Heffernan had testified that he often worked fifty-hour weeks and spent most of his time not in an office but out on the jobsite. Surely someone would have said something to him, as TVA's head of safety, about the workers' health complaints.

"Counsel, we're going to have to shut down the deposition in the next couple of minutes," Hamrock said, after several hours of back-and-forth. He had to catch a flight.

After a few final questions, Scott said, "Nothing else, sir. Thank you, Mr. Heffernan. I appreciate your time."

Afterward, Scott, Dupree, and Stewart met outside near reception. "Guys, he set the standard," Scott said of Heffernan. "We're going to be good." Scott hadn't expected Heffernan to be as cooperative as he had been, especially after he showed up wearing that TVA shirt. But he had given clear, plain answers, seemingly without trying to cover for Jacobs, or at least not much. Scott suspected that people within TVA were well aware of fly ash's dangers, but Heffernan's testimony gave him ammunition to argue that Jacobs had gone rogue and violated all sorts of TVA, state, and federal safety rules, and at the moment that mattered more than implicating TVA.

Dupree said that Scott's questions had seemed to irk Hamrock, who had, by his count, objected at least ninety-five times, an outrageous number for a deposition of a third-party witness. Scott, Dupree, and Stewart agreed that Hamrock's stunt of claiming to represent Heffernan and Jacobs was odd. "He didn't know who he was working for," Stewart said. Still, Heffernan had provided what they needed, and the three attorneys had larger concerns than Hamrock: eight more key depositions, nearly all back to back in the coming weeks.

• • •

The next four depositions proved nearly as fruitful as Heffernan's. In one, a TVA supervisor testified that telling the public that fly ash was safe, as the workers alleged that TVA and the EPA and Jacobs had all done at various points, ran counter to federal hazardous-waste safety training. In another deposition, a contractor who dealt with budgets explained that a large number of injuries would have caused costly project delays, perhaps incentivizing TVA and Jacobs to downplay fly ash's hazards. The contractor also said that, in the event of an injury, TVA would have had to pay for the workers' compensation claims that resulted from the incident. And he said that the sickened Kingston workers should have been provided a doctor if they requested one, which Scott knew hadn't always happened.

The next deposition, on August 9, would have been less consequential compared with the first several if not for a few comments. The deposition was in Troy, Alabama, with a member of the U.S. Coast Guard named John Parker, who'd worked at the Kingston disaster site beginning in 2009. Dupree drove down from Knoxville to represent the plaintiffs, and, throughout Parker's deposition, Hamrock objected to Dupree's questions at least two dozen times. Annoyed, Dupree eventually asked Parker, "How did you find Kurt?"

"He found me," Parker said. But he added, "I don't have anybody retained as an attorney."

"So he's not representing you?" Dupree asked, referring to Hamrock.

"He is not representing me, no," Parker said. But he explained that Hamrock and another attorney had reviewed and made changes to a sworn declaration he'd written, which the defense had used as an exhibit.

"Let me make a statement on the record," Hamrock jumped in. "At some point we offered to represent Mr. Parker for purposes of this deposition. And I will allow him to say how he responded."

"I mean, that's basically how it went down," Parker said. "I mean, I'm not paying him to be my attorney."

"No representation agreement and no pay?" Dupree asked.

"No, uh-uh," Parker said.

This is a problem, Dupree thought.

He called Scott on his way back to Knoxville. Dupree said he had never encountered such audacious behavior in his decades of practicing law. Hamrock wasn't representing Parker; he was trying to influence him. How was this anything but witness tampering? Did Jacobs's legal team really think it could pull this stunt on them?

Scott said he had never encountered anything like this either, and he thought about delaying or rescheduling the upcoming depositions until Judge Varlan could weigh in. Then again, despite Covington's shenanigans, their little three-man team was getting good material from the witnesses, and they had momentum. After some debate, Scott and Dupree decided to move ahead with the depositions already scheduled and then decide what to do about Covington. "Let's let them hang themselves," Scott said.

There was another deposition the following day, this one with a seventy-one-year-old TVA staffer named Jamie Keith, whose job centered on contracts and procurement. She too testified that a Covington lawyer had revised a sworn declaration she'd provided for the case and that she hadn't paid for legal representation. A Covington lawyer had typed her declaration, but she added, "I'm a contracts person, so I looked over it several times, and pretty carefully."

She explained that she'd met with one of Hamrock's colleagues for several hours to prepare for her testimony that day. As a result, she struggled to answer even simple yes-or-no questions, or at least so it seemed to Scott and Dupree. When Scott asked about the ethics of Jacobs's paying a lawyer to prepare her declaration, she didn't have a chance before Hamrock's colleague objected. Do not answer that, he told her.

Back at the office, Scott, Dupree, and Stewart seethed. "I want to embarrass the shit out of them," Dupree said. He insisted that they file a motion to disqualify Kurt Hamrock and the other Covington attorneys. Their conflicts of interest violated all sorts of rules of professional conduct, Dupree said; Varlan should throw them out of court. "This is discovery abuse," Stewart agreed. "This is bullshit." He suggested that they alert the U.S. Attorney's Office, because if Covington's antics weren't illegal, they should be.

"Damn it," Scott said, "do not file a motion to disqualify." He agreed that the Covington attorneys had probably run afoul of one rule or another, but "just ask for sanctions and some sort of special jury instruction," he said. "We want them in this. Let's get these assholes in front of a jury."

In Scott's view, the Covington attorneys, with their pricey suits and sharp haircuts, stood zero chance of winning over an East Tennessee jury. "These guys are going to keep fucking up," Scott went on. "We can own them." Plus, he said, if Varlan booted the Covington lawyers, Jacobs might hire talented replacements, and "then we're going to be in trouble," he said. Covington was also known to settle, Scott added.

Jacobs wasn't going to settle this case, Dupree said, and no Covington attorney would ever step foot in front of a Knoxville jury. Jacobs wasn't dumb enough to try that. Dupree guessed that Welborn, a football-loving Southern boy, would likely cross-examine most of the witnesses in the trial, so Covington's involvement only stood to hurt them.

Maybe Dupree had a point, Scott thought. But one of the upcoming depositions promised to be among the case's most critical, and Scott had to focus on it before figuring out what to do about Covington. The witness was Tom Bock.

Bock's deposition took place on a scorching late-August morning on the top floor of a nine-story glass office tower in downtown Knoxville, a block from the federal courthouse. Scott had named GUBMK, TVA's construction contractor, as a defendant in one of the several cases he'd filed against Jacobs, and its law firm had agreed to host Bock's deposition at its office. Scott, Dupree, and Stewart walked over together from their office a few blocks away and rode the elevator up.

Once inside, the three attorneys were led to a conference room and took seats at a long table. Large windows offered views of the Tennessee River and the gray, arching Henley Street Bridge, which led from downtown to south Knoxville to the green high country of the Smoky Mountains miles beyond. Settling in, Scott set an outline and a notepad and some documents on the table; he usually forgot about his outline once a deposition was underway, but he still liked to keep one handy. A trio of defense attorneys soon filed in and took seats across the table from the three plaintiffs' lawyers. Welborn was among them, but not Hamrock.

Then Bock stepped through the door, walked across the room, and took a seat across from Scott at the far end of the table—a stenographer at the head of the table next to him and Welborn on his other side. Scott had anticipated this day for years, and, finally, here was Bock, the subject of so many stories, the focus of so many of the workers' claims. Bock, fortysomething now, had short brown hair and wide cheeks. He wore a button-down shirt and khakis. Scott didn't know much about him other than that many of the Kingston workers hated him for failing to protect them, for dismissing their illnesses, for his snide remarks, for his arrogance. "Tom Bock has a gift to know how to push your buttons," Brad Green, the truck driver, had testified. Green even alleged that he had to restrain a few guys from "beating the crap out of Tom Bock." Even workers who got along with Bock, and there were a few, said they loathed the thought that he might have failed to protect them.

To build a strong case for trial, Scott needed to get Bock to admit to ways in which he or other Jacobs staff had violated TVA safety rules. Scott also wanted to set up Bock for cross-examination, so he needed to save his hardest blows for the trial.

Bock, sitting stiff and straight in his chair, betrayed no hint of nervousness as the stenographer swore him in and as Scott ran through some simple biographical questions. Bock attended high school in West Virginia, he said. In 1997, he earned a degree in safety technology from Marshall University, also in West Virginia. Over the next decade, he held safety-manager positions at various industrial or construction companies, including a nuclear-energy firm called British Nuclear Fuels Limited (BNFL). As Bock detailed his professional history, he seemed pleased with his responses. He explained that he'd learned about radiological material as part of his training at BNFL. When Scott asked about the potential hazards of such material, Bock said, "You don't want to get it in you or on you. That was the big takeaway." Then again, Bock said, "everything has to do with dose," adding that even bottled water could be hazardous in high quantities, which explained why athletes "all the time are dying" from drinking too much of it.

Scott's eyes widened. *Is he seriously comparing radioactive material with water?* he thought. "I've never heard of that happening," Scott said.

Google it, Bock said.

Okay, Scott said, even if he was right, "you need to be a heck of a lot more careful around radiological material than you do most bottled waters, do you not?"

"If the concentration is at a level that is hazardous to you, yes, sir," Bock said.

"What target organs do purified water attack?" Scott shot back.

"Sir," Bock replied, "I'm not a medical expert; I can't answer that question."

(Bock later said that, in retrospect, his water comparison was "probably not the greatest example.")

Scott rattled off questions about Bock's safety training (extensive) and about whether he was warned about the hazards of fly ash when he came to Kingston (yes). As the morning wore on, Bock's mood hovered somewhere between irritable and arrogant. When Scott pushed for more detail about his safety responsibilities at BNFL, Bock replied, "Do you want me to attempt to repeat what I already said?" And when Scott asked another question about his training, Bock flatly responded, "I answered that."

These remarks aligned with Scott's understanding of Bock. After the Kingston disaster, TVA had recruited recent retirees, including Tom Heffernan, to help run the cleanup project. Many of these retirees worked in Trailer City, the portable offices on-site, and among this older crowd, Bock—energetic, enterprising, young—stood out. He wasn't necessarily a bad guy, one TVA employee later explained, but he could be overeager and hubristic. Neither trait slowed his ascent. Initially, Bock reported to another Jacobs safety officer, but, as other staff eventually moved on or re-retired, TVA elevated him to lead safety officer over the cleanup project.

When Scott moved his questions to the Kingston project, Bock conceded that sometimes frustrated workers had cursed at or threatened him. Once, Bock said, a worker had accused him of purposefully hurting workers. When Scott asked for specifics, Bock said he couldn't recall any, and his memory seemed to grow increasingly fuzzy the longer he talked. Feigning memory lapse, a classic defense tactic, usually annoyed Scott, though in this instance he thought Bock's poor recollection reeked of incompetence, so he didn't challenge him on it.

Many of Scott's questions concerned the group of workers who'd requested respiratory protection and complained about their health problems in 2013, as he began to investigate their claims. That was when Kevin Thompson had given Bock a dust-mask prescription from his doctor, only for TVA to lay him off shortly thereafter. Another worker, Greg Adkisson, alleged that he'd asked for a dust mask daily and never received one. Ansol Clark claimed that when he asked for respiratory protection, Bock had told him, "I'll check into it," and never followed up. Billy Isley claimed that Bock once told him, "There's nothing out there [on the jobsite] that'll hurt you, Billy."

Scott didn't bring up these specific stories, intending to save them for the trial, but he did ask Bock whether it struck him as odd, as a safety professional, that twenty-five or twenty-six workers would claim to have breathing problems at a CERCLA, or Superfund, site?

"Not at that time, sir," Bock answered. Still, he said that he did inform TVA and GUBMK about the workers' requests for respiratory protection and about their health complaints. Some TVA experts had visited the site to investigate their claims, Bock told Scott, and these experts had evaluated air-monitoring data. "And their conclusion was that there was no connection to the symptoms that the individuals were expressing." That was ostensibly why TVA, and Jacobs in turn, had largely denied the workers' respirator requests.

But twenty-five workers is a lot, correct? Scott asked.

Yes, Bock said. "Twenty-five to twenty-six people out of the site numbers I would say is a representative number."

Scott suspected that the air-monitoring data Bock had referred to was mostly, if not totally, junk. Brad Green had testified that Jacobs had outfitted workers with wearable, personal air monitors primarily after it rained, and Scott had reason to believe that the data could be compromised in other ways, too. But, rather than challenge Bock on this, he decided he would focus on the air-monitoring data in the trial.

During a break for lunch, Scott talked with Dupree and Stewart. "This is the guy they chose to run the safety program at this site?" Dupree said of Bock. Not only did Bock seem to know little about fly ash, but he also seemed unconcerned about its potential dangers. Dupree swore he saw Bock almost smile at some of his responses.

To Stewart, Bock's answers seemed "condescending as fuck." Stewart said he hadn't seen Bock glance at Welborn once for assurance about his responses, as witnesses typically do. It was as if Bock felt absolutely confident in his testimony, as if Scott's questions created no doubts in his mind about his behavior.

Scott expected Bock to perform better after strategizing with Welborn and the other defense attorneys during lunch, but when Bock resumed his place across the table from Scott, he looked rattled and wide-eyed, as if he had been scolded.

Once back on the record, Scott said, "I want to go back to the twenty-five, twenty-six employees . . . that came to you with regard to breathing issues," Scott said. "Based upon your knowledge and experience of working that site, they came to you because you [were] the head safety officer, correct?"

Typically, Bock said, the workers had approached their immediate supervisors before coming to him. When Scott asked Bock how he first learned about the workers' complaints, then, his recollection grew fuzzy. "Remember what?" Bock asked, as if confused by the entire premise of the question.

To Scott, Bock's memory lapses bordered on obstruction. "You have not recalled a lot today," Scott said. "Just for the record, as an exhibit to this deposition today, I would like madam court reporter to submit as an exhibit the number of times Mr. Bock has said, 'I do not recall,' 'I do not remember,' or 'I do not know.'" The number would total one hundred and five by the day's end.

Scott, leaping between topics to keep Bock on edge, brought up the "Site Wide Safety and Health Plan." It was the most important document on-site, right? Scott asked. He didn't design the question to be difficult. Heffernan had readily admitted to the document's importance. Bock, in contrast, allowed that the plan needed to be followed, but, he said with a simper, "I would say my employment with Jacobs was my most important document, because that's what paid me at the end of the day."

"I understand completely," Scott said. Bock had, amazingly, waltzed into a trap that Scott hadn't even set. Entirely unprompted, he had uttered a damning comment that Scott would, without question, bring up in the trial. Even if Bock were attempting humor, in what universe did he, as a safety professional, think it appropriate to suggest that his paycheck, in effect, trumped EPA-approved safety rules? Was he oblivious?

Scott, knowing he had gold, moved on. The "Safety and Health Plan" included a fifty-five-page appendix about respiratory protection. Scott asked Bock to tell him about it. "If respiratory protection was needed," Bock began, processes dictated how to provide it to the workers. But respirators were "the last protection," he said, and used only "if we could not control the hazards other ways."

"So," Scott said, "respiratory protection should be the last resort?"

"In most cases," Bock said, "the goal was—" He stopped himself. "The last thing you want to do," he said, "is have ten other things that this worker has to wear on a day-to-day basis." You could overheat in a respirator or a dust mask during the punishing Tennessee summers, so workers needed to prove that they were fit enough to wear one.

Scott was sharpening his knives. He had copies of the safety plan with him, and he handed Bock the fifty-five-page appendix regarding respirators. He asked him to read a sentence in the first paragraph. "Sure," Bock said, studying the document. The sentence read: "Respiratory use is encouraged, even when exposures are below the exposure limit, to provide an additional level of comfort and protection for workers."

Scott, trying to draw blood now, asked Bock why, considering this sentence, the twenty-five workers were denied respiratory protection.

"Object to the form," Welborn said.

"Sir," Bock said, "I never denied anybody respiratory protection."

"I didn't ask about you," Scott said. "I said why were *they*?"

"I don't know why people were, sir," Bock responded. They weren't his employees.

Scott quickly shifted course: "Do you know why Chris Ike would have threatened an individual asking for respiratory protection?" Scott was referring to the "cock" video, in which Ike, a Jacobs safety officer, had obliquely threatened Mike McCarthy's job. Bock, in response, said that he didn't know that Ike had threatened anyone and that Jacobs's policy certainly prohibited such behavior.

Scott assumed that Jacobs policy also surely forbade telling two hundred workers that wearing a dust mask was a good way to get "run off," as Bock had allegedly done, but he didn't bring it up. Another topic for trial. Instead, he zagged back to the "Safety and Health Plan": "So, respiratory protection—if an employee felt they needed it for their health or comfort, [it] should have been provided, correct?"

Well, Bock said, guidelines stipulated whether a worker could wear a respirator voluntarily or not.

Wait, Scott said, the safety plan was clear, was it not? Didn't the excerpt Bock just read state that respirators were encouraged?

"Yes, sir," Bock said, "but this is only one page of a document, sir." Elsewhere, it stated that a worker had to meet certain health criteria to wear a respirator, and that required a medical evaluation—which many of the workers had received from their health-care providers. Bock was not wrong about this: the safety plan did stipulate that workers needed a physician's written opinion in order to wear a respirator, but it did not specify that the physician had to be one of Jacobs's or TVA's choosing. Bock maintained, though, that such precautions were unnecessary anyway: no data suggested that fly ash posed a legitimate threat to the workers. He said he had reported the workers' health complaints to TVA, to GUBMK, and to his supervisor at the time, a Jacobs staffer named Sean Healey, not out of concern but as a matter of protocol.

"What did Mr. Healey do?" Scott asked.

"I can't tell you what he did," Bock said.

Scott pounced: "Weren't you concerned enough, as a human being, when you get twenty-six, twenty-five complaints of people having breathing problems in a [Superfund] remediation zone that you follow up?"

"Sir," Bock began, "if I had twenty-five people tell me they just got back from the moon, it doesn't necessarily mean that I'm going to believe them . . . I have to have some evidence, some results, some science to back that up." He insisted, though, that he never told anybody that fly ash was safe, and neither had Jacobs, the EPA, nor TVA—a claim that seemed to contradict his insistence that fly ash posed no risk to the workers.

As Bock talked, Dupree, seated next to Scott, whirled his finger in a slow, discrete circle, as if to say, *Keep him talking*. Scott did.

Bock went on: "Does [fly ash] have hazardous constituents in it?

Sure, it does." But, he said, what mattered was the concentration—the dose—of the hazards, which was low. Bock told Scott that, even when dust devils or whirlwinds of ash spun around the jobsite—which happened not infrequently, according to the workers—exposure levels didn't exceed permissible limits.

Okay, Scott said, even if that were somehow true, if a worker brought in a respirator prescription, they shouldn't be fired, right?

"I'm not a pharmacist," Bock shot back, repeating a line that he had told Jeff Brewer years earlier, "and Jacobs isn't a pharmacy, and I don't think TVA is either, so I don't think they really care whether somebody has a prescription or not."

This answer jolted Scott. Heffernan had said, unequivocally, that if a worker had a prescription, it should be honored. And yet here was Bock, seeming to undercut the entire idea—or maybe the entire illusion—that Jacobs or TVA should care about such things. Still, as telling as Bock's response was, he hadn't answered Scott's question, so he restated it: Should a worker be fired for being prescribed a respirator?

"I wouldn't see that in a list of fireable offenses that I'm aware of," Bock replied. But he claimed that it wasn't his job to make such determinations; a worker should have given the prescription to his or her contractor, like GUBMK, not to Jacobs.

As the deposition dragged on, Bock downplayed Jacobs's role further, insisting that the company had minimal influence over whether workers had proper respiratory protection. Scott didn't buy it: Heffernan had testified that TVA relied on Jacobs to manage day-to-day site safety, and a GUBMK employee had testified that it was Jacobs's decision alone whether the workers were allowed to wear dust masks or respirators.

"Mr. Bock, I promise you there's an end in sight," Scott said, toward the end of the long afternoon. "And I'm not going to go back to it very much, but I just want to make sure I understand your testimony." Scott mentioned, yet again, the twenty-five or so workers who had complained about their breathing problems. He asked Bock, "It sounded like you based your decision-making in part, if not in whole, upon the underlying air-monitoring data in determining whether or not there is a relationship between their breathing problems and the fly ash?"

Bock agreed that that was his testimony: the personal air-monitoring data, which Jacobs oversaw the collection of, suggested that fly ash hadn't harmed the workers.

But, Scott asked, what if the air-monitoring data was wrong? Could his conclusion about the hazards also be wrong?

"Yes," Bock said.

After the deposition, the three plaintiffs' attorneys took the elevator to the street. The deposition had gone exceptionally well, they agreed. But, as the attorneys walked through the late-afternoon heat back to their office, they exchanged no high fives or pats on the back. Stewart said that he felt disappointed, in a way. Before the deposition, he was convinced that "this motherfucker was the devil," he said of Bock. Instead, Bock struck him as a pathetic, small man, someone who was willing to follow his lawyers' script to dodge legal trouble. He wasn't a criminal mastermind. He was a yes-man, a fall guy, a sucker—though, to be sure, his comments were cruel. "He didn't give a second thought to any worker," Stewart said. "They were expendable."

Scott mostly agreed. "You know," he said, "it's kind of scary that he gave the answers he did." Scott expected a more effective level of dishonesty from Bock. And yet, in a way, thanks to Bock's botched testimony, Scott felt something like relief. If Bock came off as arrogant and annoyed during the trial as he did in the deposition, his clients were going to be all right, Scott figured. No jury would side with Bock. What's more, Scott guessed that he could easily undercut Bock's credibility during cross-examination, whether by questioning Jacobs's respirator policy, or the air-monitoring data that it oversaw, or half a dozen other things.

Whatever relief Scott felt dimmed by the time he and Stewart and Dupree reached their office building at 713 Market Street. Days after the depositions began, the court had pushed back the start of trial from January 9, 2017, to May 1, 2017, to give the plaintiffs more time to respond to some of Jacobs's motions. That meant the plaintiffs' team had eight months to prepare their case for a jury, but Varlan had given them tight deadlines for their motion responses, and the defense was demanding that they produce documents more quickly than they could gather and turn them over. The defense had also insisted that Scott's team produce more evidence to support the workers' claims against Jacobs, including the specific date, time, and location of the workers' fly-ash exposure—as if it hadn't been constant. Discovery had hardly begun, and already Scott's little team was overwhelmed.

PART III

2017–2023

The lawyers' redbrick office building was filling up with documents. Couriers delivered them in heavy banker boxes and stacked them in the conference room, in John Dupree's and Keith Stewart's offices, in a hallway—wherever there was space. In a civil-action lawsuit, witness depositions tend to produce valuable information for lawyers building a case, but another crucial part of discovery involves the exchange of internal documents between the parties. Jim Scott and the plaintiffs' team had asked the defense to produce nearly any document they had that involved site safety, fly-ash monitoring, or site hazards, along with emails between TVA and Jacobs staff. Jacobs obliged, in a big way, turning over more than sixty-six thousand individual documents, plus thumb drives loaded with material. Stewart guessed that the total number of pages easily topped a million, but neither he nor anyone else had time to count.

When Scott looked at the boxes piled around the office, one thought flashed to mind: *There's some damning stuff in here, and they don't want us to find it.* It was clearly a document dump—an attempt to overwhelm his team and bury evidence among a deluge of useless paper. Worse, as Scott, Stewart, and Dupree rummaged through the boxes, they found redacted and unreadable pages. (When Jacobs's lawyers asked Scott's team for, among other things, medical records and life-insurance applications, the plaintiffs dumped documents right back, turning over twenty-four banker boxes containing some eighty thousand pages.)

Stewart hired a company to scan Jacobs's documents so they could search them by keyword. Then the lawyers began to read. Scott threw himself at the task. He word-searched the documents for "dredge" and "safety plan" and "air monitoring." He skimmed the results on a computer, then printed out promising documents for closer inspection. He read at a library near the office; he read at his house while keeping an eye on Sam and Jack; he read at restaurants while they grabbed dinner. The pages absorbed him, gnawed at him, almost drowned him. He wanted to find, in some obscure footnote, in some tossed-off spreadsheet, in some hastily sent email, evidence to support the most grievous allegations against Jacobs, and he wanted to prove that Jacobs knew, or at least should have known, the dangers posed by fly ash. He had a constant, nauseous fear that he might miss something—a document, a deadline, drawing a connection between two discrete details. He would often wake up in the middle of the night in a panic. He felt this way during the land cases to a degree, but now the feeling never left him and never softened.

During this frantic period, he typically stayed at the office well into the evening, then he would return home to relieve his dad from watching his sons, eat dinner, and then work until the small hours of the morning. He hated living this way, barely having time to fix his sons' breakfast before rushing to the office, barely having time to watch movies or TV with them at night. "I wish you would've never taken those cases," Jack, his oldest, told him at one point. "It was the worst thing you ever did." On weekends, the boys begged him to log off his computer and spend time with them. "Look," Scott finally told them, "these people are really hurt, and they need help." He had to trust that one day his sons would understand.

Dupree and Stewart worked equally punishing hours. Throughout the day, Dupree would walk into Stewart's office and ask if he'd come across any document about, say, coal slag. Stewart would hand over whatever he had or make a note to look out for anything on the subject. As the attorneys plowed through the documents, one thing that struck them was the cleanup effort's official name: the Kingston Recovery Project. And what TVA and Jacobs had recovered was cenospheres, the spherical, floating clumps of ash Scott had seen around Gilbert Pickel's dock years earlier. The dike failure had scattered cenospheres up and down the frigid Emory River. Then, as now, cenospheres were used in cosmetics and as a filler material in bowling balls, concrete, and other goods. And, since cenospheres had value, TVA had made "recovering" them a priority.

The documents that Jacobs produced included more than three hundred pages of daily safety logs that Tom Bock and various Jacobs and TVA staff members had updated throughout the cleanup. Bock had insisted in his deposition that the quantity of fly ash at Kingston wasn't capable of harming the workers. And yet one day, as Scott read at home, he came upon a curious entry in the logs from 2010. "Large quantities of dust in Jacobs trailer," a Jacobs staffer had written. "Need to look into ventilation filters (if any exist) and possibly station air monitors in the office. Dust is fine particulate and could be ash particle which are unsafe to breath [sic]." Scott almost jumped out of his chair when his eyes scanned those words. Jacobs staff had insisted that the fly ash posed no legitimate threat to the workers, yet they'd worried among themselves that the stuff had inundated their office trailer. Another entry, from 2011, noted that dust had forced a work stoppage at part of the site, something Bock testified had "never happened."

Just as interesting, in one email from 2010, a Jacobs manager had warned several contractors and TVA staffers, including the general manager over the entire project, Stephen McCracken, that vehicles were driving too fast and kicking up too much fly ash, potentially resulting "in unacceptably high levels of ash dust migrating to on- and off-site locations." The Jacobs staffer added that this dust challenged Jacobs's ability "to protect our health and comply with applicable Federal, State, and TVA environmental protection requirements."

Then the attorneys uncovered a trove of true riches. Several days each month, Jacobs had distributed personal air-monitoring devices to groups of five to ten workers. These monitors, which were clear and small and clipped to the workers' clothing, sucked in air through a little hose, sampling it for hazards. "Reminded me of a fish-aquarium vacuum," Jeff Brewer, the part-time pastor, later said of the devices. The data from the monitors was intended to supplement that from the larger stationary air monitors around the donut of death.

The attorneys found calendars among Jacobs's documents on which Bock had marked in green the days the air monitors were distributed to the workers. Tellingly, the calendars also noted rainy days, marked in blue, and the corresponding precipitation levels. According to the calendars, Jacobs and another contractor, EnSafe, which oversaw the air-monitoring process for a time, had not given the workers the devices on the same day each week or each month but in a scattershot fashion. The reason why seemed clear. The workers had told the attorneys that the fly ash had typically stayed damp and clung to the ground for about twenty-four hours after a rainfall. According to the calendars, EnSafe had handed out the air monitors to workers on nineteen different days between June 1 and September 1, 2009, spanning the peak of East Tennessee's inferno summer. All but two of these sampling, or testing, days fell on a rainy day or the day immediately after one. Jacobs took over the air-monitoring duties in the summer of 2010, but the calendars still showed a significant overlap between rainy days and sampling days. Not only that, but the attorneys also noticed that the number of sampling days plummeted in 2012, the same year many of the workers began to complain about their declining health. In August 2011, for instance, Jacobs had given the workers air-monitoring devices to wear on ten different days; the following August, it did so on only five days, three of which were rainy.

The calendars stunned the three attorneys, and certainly seemed to illustrate that Jacobs had manipulated the site's air-monitoring data.* "These are unsophisticated guys," Stewart said of the workers, while rifling through papers on his desk, "but I haven't caught *any* of them lying to me. Not once! About anything. Which is shocking." Because, in his experience, everyone lies to their lawyer, even just a little. Yet the lawyers were finding evidence—good, solid evidence—to shore up even the workers' most severe allegations. Scott, seated at a table across from Stewart's desk, agreed that it was shocking but said the workers were right: "The cleanup didn't have anything to do with safety. It had to do with time and money, and that was it."

Stewart had figured that out himself by poring over Jacobs's contract with TVA. The EPA, which had jurisdiction over the cleanup, had given TVA tight deadlines to complete various phases of the project, and it

* Jacobs Engineering denies that its staff conducted air monitoring on rainy days to limit the concentration of airborne particulates that would be detected, and it denies that its air-monitoring procedures were in any way inadequate.

threatened to fine TVA thousands of dollars each day it fell behind. TVA, in turn, had packed Jacobs's contract with incentives to avoid safety-related work stoppages. Altogether, the incentives in Jacobs's contract between July 2009 and July 2010 totaled $1.5 million, but it earned far more than that when TVA extended its contract and raised its total compensation from $28 million to almost $64 million. TVA received one important thing from Jacobs in return: a diffusion of responsibility. "TVA didn't want to be in charge of the site, because of possible lawsuits and safety issues," one TVA employee later explained.* In time, Scott would obtain documents that suggested why it had good reason to prefer such an arrangement.

In the summer of 1964, Bob Steber, a veteran reporter for *The Nashville Tennessean*, took a boat onto Old Hickory Lake, outside Nashville. He wanted to investigate a tip. Steber wrote a Sunday outdoors column for the newspaper called "Headwaters 'N Tailfeathers," which he usually filled with light stories on dove shoots, trophy bass, skeet trials, or whatever game was in season. His outing on Old Hickory concerned more serious matters. Anglers had complained to him that a gritty substance—no one could say what it was—had saturated parts of the river, ruining the bass fishing and, in some cases, killing catches tied to their stringers. A deposit of the stuff three to five inches thick had washed up along miles of shoreline. As Steber's boat motored up a channel, he discovered the source of the material: three large metal drainage pipes, surrounded by a plume of floating residue. The pipes, which ran from the shore and dove deep into the water, came from TVA's Gallatin Steam Plant, on the lake's north bank, and the substance was fly ash.

Steber, in his column, accused TVA of polluting Old Hickory and of trying to hide the fly ash. TVA responded to Steber's piece by swiftly removing the pipes, and its general manager at the time, L. J. Van Mol, told Steber for a follow-up story that "avoiding stream pollution from the operation of our plants [was] paramount."

What Van Mol presumably didn't tell Steber was that months earlier

* In 2019, TVA said in a statement that it hired Jacobs in part because it had worked "on complex, environmental recovery projects."

he'd received a memo from TVA's director of health about fly ash: it was raining over the village of Paradise, Kentucky, ninety miles north of Nashville. TVA had built a coal-fired power plant in Paradise recently, and the health director warned Van Mol that fly ash it emitted was having "detrimental effects" on the paint of employees' cars. Tests had confirmed the "definitive corrosive tendencies of the dampened fly ash," the health director added. This corrosive tendency helped to explain why Paradise residents had complained that fly ash ate away at corncobs and heads of cabbage whenever it fell over their gardens.

No mention of the Paradise fly-ash tests appeared in any newspaper, however. What TVA did tell Bob Steber and other members of the press, in September 1964, was that it had sold twenty-five thousand tons of fly ash, used as a popular concrete substitute, for $30,000 (the equivalent of $294,000 today). TVA explained in a press release that it hoped to earn $240,000 ($2.3 million today) annually from future fly-ash sales. To Jim Scott, it was obvious why TVA hadn't publicized everything it knew about fly ash: then, as now, fly ash was marketable, and acknowledging its hazards might hurt TVA's ability to sell it.

Perhaps more incredible to Scott was that the EPA, the American people's supposed protector, which had staff on-site throughout the Kingston cleanup, seemed to know just as well as TVA that fly ash posed grave health risks, and yet it had failed to ensure the workers' safety. The day after the Kingston disaster, the EPA had collected water samples from the Emory River and found arsenic at concentrations one hundred and forty-nine times higher than what it considered permissible. But the EPA assured the public that the local drinking water was safe and claimed that fly-ash samples taken near public roads hadn't detected high arsenic levels. The EPA made these statements even though, two years before the Kingston disaster, it had determined that as many as one in fifty people who lived near an unlined coal-ash pond, like TVA's in Kingston, would likely get cancer as a result of ingesting arsenic that had leached into the drinking-water supply.* This risk of exposure

* In 2014, ProPublica revealed that lobbyists and the George W. Bush administration had had a hand in shaping the EPA's coal-ash policies to the benefit of power companies, which might explain some of the EPA's actions at Kingston.

exceeded the National Institute for Occupational Safety and Health's recommended limit by two hundredfold. Then there were fly ash's airborne hazards. Remarkably to Scott, in a 2009 *60 Minutes* segment, Leo Francendese, the EPA's on-site coordinator at Kingston at the time, had told the journalist Lesley Stahl that coal ash could cause harm. "Breathing it, that's dangerous," he said. (At public meetings, Francendese downplayed fly ash's hazards, comparing it to sand.)

When Ansol Clark and the others first approached Scott almost five years earlier, he hadn't considered himself an environmentalist, and he still didn't embrace the term. But the case had without a doubt upturned his view of the world. In his opinion, major American institutions—TVA, the EPA, Jacobs Engineering—hadn't just acted negligently but had deliberately sent the workers into a hellscape, knowing the dangers that awaited them. One of TVA's own employees, Jean Nance, had died of leukemia in 2015 after spending four years in an unventilated trailer at Kingston. Nance had worked in the safety department. Even so, according to her family, she had no idea that fly ash posed a serious health risk. Scott considered it unforgivable that the system—the courts, the law, the powers that be—was now dragging her family and the surviving workers through years of legal hurdles for a slim shot at justice. But perhaps what bothered him most were the sick children, like Mike McCarthy's two young ones. Over a rare Friday afternoon beer, Scott told a friend to be thankful that he had a healthy newborn daughter. There was no greater blessing, he said.

On a cloudy late-September afternoon in the middle of discovery, and in the middle of all the reading, Scott, Dupree, and Stewart took the elevator to the third floor of the federal courthouse in Knoxville. They walked down the wide corridor, overlooking a green, well-watered lawn, and pushed open the doors to courtroom 3A. Seven defense attorneys, including Kurt Hamrock and Joe Welborn, joined them in the wood-paneled room, as did a few older gentlemen. The latter group sat toward the back of the gallery. Among them was a senior partner at Covington & Burling, the elite East Coast law firm that employed Hamrock. This particular partner wore what looked to Scott and Stewart like a $10,000 suit. This power lawyer had almost certainly trekked all the way to Knoxville in the event that the firm landed in trouble—as it very well might during the day's hearing.

After Tom Bock's deposition, Dupree had filed a motion to disqualify Covington. He accused the firm of unlawfully creating a conflict of interest by representing former TVA staff and of soliciting potential clients—a major no-no. He also accused the Covington lawyers of obstructing the plaintiffs' access to evidence by constantly objecting to Scott's deposition questions and by instructing witnesses not to answer some of Scott's queries altogether.

The judge who would preside over the hearing was not Thomas Varlan but a magistrate judge who worked under him by the name of Bruce Guyton. At two o'clock, Guyton—round-faced, bespectacled, a few years from retirement—strode into the courtroom and took his place beneath the golden seal of the United States, mounted on the wall behind the bench. Scott's team sat at the counsel table on the right side of the room, next to the empty jury box; the defense took the table across the aisle. Before Dupree filed the motion against Covington, Scott had called a few lawyer friends, who all told him, in effect, that Covington's tactics were "unethical as shit," which convinced him to go along with Dupree's plan to try to disqualify the firm. Still, asking a judge to boot attorneys from a case was an extreme move, and Scott couldn't guess how Guyton would respond.

In a typical hearing, whichever side files the motion up for debate gives its argument first. But, as Scott and Dupree prepared to speak, Guyton said, "Mr. Hamrock, would you come to the podium?"

Hamrock obliged.

Scott was on friendly terms with Guyton, who, like many members of Knoxville's legal community, lived in Sequoyah Hills; Scott had crossed paths with him on at least one Halloween as he walked the neighborhood with his sons. Scott thought Guyton probably liked him well enough, but he had never seen a judge break procedure like this, and it didn't strike him as a positive sign.

Guyton's gaze fell on Hamrock. "I told my law clerk this situation reminds me of my pair of old running shoes," he began. "Looks bad, smells bad."

Hamrock, positioned at the lectern, tried to explain that, as Covington began investigating the workers' case against Jacobs, he and his colleagues had asked TVA for its okay before they contacted some of its former employees, and TVA had agreed. Then, Hamrock stammered, "when we sat down with the [TVA] witnesses, they asked us, 'Well, do I need a lawyer?' And we informed them, 'Well, you can proceed without a lawyer if you like . . . or we'd be happy to represent you, and TVA has authorized us to do that.' "

Guyton, incredulous, interrupted: "You told them TVA authorized you to represent them?"

"Yes, Your Honor," Hamrock said.

Okay, Guyton said. But did the TVA employees sign a form consenting to let Covington represent them in the depositions? That would have made the arrangement official.

"No, Your Honor," Hamrock said, "we did not believe that was necessary."

The hearing did not improve for Covington the longer it went on.

In Guyton's ruling, issued a month later, he admonished the Covington lawyers for their "troubling" actions, because they certainly appeared to be trying to influence the testimonies of former TVA staff. Then again, the magistrate added, several testimonies did reflect poorly on Jacobs, and, since these testimonies made it impossible to conclude definitively whether Covington's shenanigans created a conflict of interest, Guyton declined to throw out the firm. But he warned, and warned sternly, that if Covington didn't behave itself—that if it didn't cut the shit, in other words—he would haul their lawyers straight into a conference, which would not be a pleasant experience for them.

Guyton's ruling didn't upset Scott; the motion to disqualify was, in retrospect, a long shot. But he worried about what Jacobs would try next.

The next significant hearing came about four months later, and it came with almost no notice. On May 16, 2017, Guyton gave both parties two days' warning that he wanted to see them in court to discuss discovery. When the afternoon came, Scott, Dupree, and Stewart trudged over to the courthouse. They all knew why they'd been summoned.

Judge Varlan had recently decided to move forward with a bifurcated, or two-part, trial plan. In the first phase, a jury would determine whether Jacobs had failed to protect the workers and whether fly ash was conceivably capable of causing their injuries. If Scott's team prevailed, a jury in a second trial phase, at a later date, would award damages to each worker based on their specific exposures and injuries. Varlan had scheduled the phase one trial to begin on January 29, 2018, some eight months away. Now that he had set a new trial date, the two sides could commence arguing over one of the most contentious issues in almost any toxic-exposure suit: expert witnesses. Weeks earlier, Scott's team had disclosed to Jacobs the names of nine doctors or academics it might want to testify in the trial. Unsurprisingly, the defense team had issues with some of them—hence Guyton's notice to meet.

The hearing began at two o'clock, and one thing that immediately distinguished it from past proceedings was the diminutive, sharply dressed attorney who strutted into the courtroom with Joe Welborn. "May it please the Court, I'm Jim Sanders," the lawyer said after Guyton took the bench.

One of Scott's greatest concerns had just been realized: Jacobs had sidelined Covington & Burling—and it would soon do the same to Welborn—and brought in James F. Sanders, an elite corporate trial lawyer and a partner at the Nashville firm Neal & Harwell.*

"I know you, Mr. Sanders," said Guyton, clearly amused. "I remember meeting you the first month I was licensed as an attorney in one of the old Butcher cases"—a reference to Jake Butcher, an East Tennessee financier who, in 1985, had pleaded guilty to bank fraud and tax evasion. Sanders's firm had represented him.

"I didn't do anything wrong there, did I?" Sanders asked Guyton, in a bright Southern drawl.

"I don't remember," Guyton said.

Sanders laughed. "Good!"

No matter the case, it would have been hard for anyone to forget Sanders. He had flowing white hair and a long white mustache, in the style of an old-time riverboat captain. Lending him further flair, he often wore showy three-piece suits, which he tended to complete with colorful geometric ties and cowboy boots that boosted his height by several critical inches.

* Sanders declined multiple interview requests for this book. See the Notes for information on sourcing.

After the *Exxon Valdez* supertanker ran aground on March 24, 1989, and spewed eleven million gallons of oil into Alaska's Prince William Sound, Exxon had called Jimmy Sanders for help. The energy giant relied on him for "its most risky, sensitive jury cases," the journalist Steve Coll wrote in his definitive history of the company. General Motors had put equal trust in Sanders when it tasked him to defend it after faulty ignition switches in its vehicles resulted in the deaths of more than one hundred people and forced it to recall 2.7 million cars in 2014.

Sanders grew up in the mountain town of Johnson City, Tennessee, where he gained fame in high school as the go-to receiver for the team's star quarterback, the future Heisman Trophy winner Steve Spurrier. Sanders attended Vanderbilt University on an athletic scholarship, and after completing undergrad, he stuck around for law school. He considered himself a yellow-dog Democrat. He once told an interviewer that the war in Vietnam had turned him "very anti-establishment," and that, while at Vandy, he had been "very interested in the role of law improving society." Yet he had spent his career defending not only Exxon but also such unsavory corporations as Purdue Pharma, maker of the addictive opioid OxyContin, and CoreCivic, one of the nation's largest private-prison companies. "I don't have moments in the middle of the night where I anguish over these things," Sanders explained, when asked about the apparent contradiction in his political views and the clients he represented. He was a mercenary whose mantra seemed to be "Have gun—will travel," according to one former colleague.

During trials, Sanders would often stand close to the jury box, right next to the rail, so he could speak to the jurors softly, as if he were an old friend. "Niceness is his weapon," recalled one plaintiffs' attorney. Adding to the effect, Sanders often apologized for his clients' actions, at least some of them, and he never badgered a witness for sport or for pride. And no matter how high the stakes of a trial, his composure never seemed to waver, a trait his colleagues guessed partly owed to the vast quantities of Nicorette gum he chewed.

Sanders, for all his charm, didn't always win cases in the sense that a jury ruled in his favor, but he tended to prevail by the metric that mattered most to his clients—money. After the *Valdez* oil spill, some thirty-two thousand fishermen, Alaska Natives, and other locals brought suits against Exxon for wrecking the Prince William Sound fishery. In a twenty-week trial that began in May 1994, Sanders and his co-counsel tried to convince a jury that careless individuals, not Exxon, bore responsibility for the disaster. The jury, despite Sanders's efforts, ordered the company to pay $287 million in compensatory damages to some ten thousand commercial fishermen, to make up for their lost harvests. (Exxon also paid a settlement of $20 million to thirty-five hundred Alaska Natives.) Most significant, though, was the jury's decision to punish Exxon for its bad behavior by awarding the plaintiffs $5 billion in punitive damages—"the largest ever [judgment] in a pollution case," the *Chicago Tribune* reported at the time.

Exxon's legal counsel, led in part by Jimmy Sanders, appealed the jury's decision and, in 2006, successfully petitioned an appeals court to halve the $5 billion punitive award. Exxon appealed further, taking the case to the U.S. Supreme Court. During oral arguments, one of Sanders's co-counsel argued that $2.5 billion in punitive damages was excessive and served no additional "public purpose" to deter negligence. Exxon, in other words, had learned its lesson. The Court agreed and ruled that in maritime cases, and maritime cases alone, punitive damages shouldn't exceed compensatory damages—that is, money paid to plaintiffs to cover lost wages, medical bills, or other such expenses. The Court cut the punitive damages against Exxon to a little over $500 million, which amounted to less than a week of lost profit for Exxon and was a tenth of the jury's original award.

Sanders didn't sit around and think, *How can I fuck over these poor people?*, according to one attorney who knew him well, but Sanders's work often had that effect. The *Valdez* plaintiffs waited nearly twenty years for punitive damages, and each received, on average, about $30,000. Moreover, the Supreme Court's decision that punitive damages should not exceed compensatory damages in maritime cases created a "completely arbitrary" benchmark, two law professors at Vanderbilt later wrote. In a dissenting opinion, Justice Ruth Bader Ginsburg worried that this new standard would influence cases that had nothing to do with maritime issues. Indeed, lawyers soon began to cite the *Valdez* decision as precedent for capping punitive damages in all manner of cases, and the Supreme Court began striking down punitive awards it considered excessive. "Judges have taken power from juries," said Peter Ehrhardt, one of the plaintiffs' lawyers in the *Valdez* case. And, as a result, corporations no longer needed to fear punitive damages. "Against these big institutions," Ehrhardt added, "the little guys are just fucked." And that, Jim Scott presumed during the status conference that May afternoon, was why Jacobs Engineering had hired Jimmy Sanders.

The federal rules that govern civil-action lawsuits aim to prevent what lawyers call trial by ambush, where one side learns of the other side's evidence only when they meet in court. To prevent such sneakiness, federal rules require that expert witnesses retained by either party submit a detailed report of his or her findings well before trial. That way, a judge can decide whether to let the expert testify based on the strength of their research, while opposing counsel, who are able to review the expert's work, can prepare a rebuttal or try to convince the judge to block the witness. In the hearing that afternoon, Sanders wasted no time laying the groundwork for the latter approach.

He first attacked a Dallas-based surgeon by the name of William Rea. Scott's team had recently paid to fly Jeff Brewer, Ansol Clark, and one other worker to see Rea for testing. Afterward, Rea had written a three-page memo, in which he stated that, based on his analysis, only fly-ash exposure explained the workers' health issues. That didn't satisfy Sanders. He told Magistrate Guyton that, before the court agreed to let Rea testify, "we'd like to see the data" underlying his report.

For the plaintiffs, Keith Stewart argued that the defense had no right to demand Rea's underlying data before he finished a full report, which he was working on. Stewart told Guyton that he understood why Sanders was requesting Rea's data. "It's a tactical move, and it's a pretty good one," he said. "I just don't think they're entitled to it yet." He promised Guyton that the plaintiffs' team would, without a doubt, turn over the data whenever Rea finished his full report, but until then, Stewart said, "I think it's premature."

"When is that going to happen?" Guyton asked.

"I can't answer that as we stand here today, judge," Stewart said.

Guyton warned him to figure it out, fast, because at some point the plaintiffs would need to disclose full, complete reports for whichever experts they wanted to call to testify, otherwise Judge Varlan might block them.

Next, Sanders targeted Paul Terry, an epidemiologist at the University of Tennessee. Scott had contacted Terry, who had a PhD from

Columbia University, a year or two earlier to ask some questions about the workers' health. Terry, intrigued by the conversation, had decided to investigate the workers' medical issues, independent of Scott. Stewart explained to Guyton that Terry and a colleague planned to produce a detailed report of their findings, though he said he had no idea when they might finish. Terry and his colleague weren't "our guys," Stewart told Guyton. "Did we recruit them? Did we go seek out their opinion? No." That was a critical distinction between Terry and Rea, because, whereas the plaintiffs had retained, or paid, Rea for his services, Terry was a disinterested university researcher with no financial stake in the case. Stewart said that, since their side hadn't retained Terry, under federal rules he didn't need to produce a report in order to testify.

Sanders balked. "It doesn't matter whether the person is a volunteer," he told Guyton. "It doesn't matter if the person is an official interloper—if they're going to give expert testimony to a jury, then we're going to have to have some sort of report and basis before that testimony can even come in."

Guyton said he understood both sides' arguments and promised to look into the issue further.

On a cloudy spring night, Jim Scott drove his son Sam to Calhoun's, the barbecue place, to play trivia. Jim had an almost photographic memory, but Sam had a special gift for retaining obscure facts, especially about sports and movies, and trivia had become a favorite pastime. He started to beat Jim around the time he turned ten, and, now almost thirteen, he regularly trounced a group of seniors who competed at Calhoun's.

Jim and Sam sat near the bar. As the game host asked questions, Sam, who had dark curly hair just like his father, jotted down answers and playfully jeered at the geriatrics whenever he correctly guessed a question they missed. As Jim sat next to him, a friend sent over a drink, a Long Island iced tea or something of that variety, to the table—a nice, well-timed gesture.

The first hearing with Jimmy Sanders, six days earlier, had marked a new, more difficult phase in the case. Scott had done his research and realized that it would have been difficult for Jacobs to find a more perfect lawyer. Not only did Sanders have decades of environmental litigation experience, but he could also, unlike the Covington & Burling attorneys or even Joe Welborn, speak to a jury as a fellow born and reared East Tennessean, negating what would have been one of Scott's clear advantages. Sanders's Tennessee bona fides were impeachable. One of his great-grandfathers had served as governor from 1921 to 1923.

More disconcerting, during the hearing, Sanders had telegraphed that he would try to exploit the plaintiffs' most glaring weakness: expert witnesses. Magistrate Guyton had decided that Terry did, in fact, need to submit a lengthy epidemiological study in order to testify, and he'd given Scott's team just shy of two months to produce one and to supplement reports by their other expert witnesses. Once Scott filed these reports, Sanders would surely try to block all the plaintiffs' experts. If he succeeded, the workers' case stood almost no chance of success; Scott's team would need experts to convince a jury that fly ash had caused their illnesses.

At around eight-thirty, Jim and Sam left Calhoun's and climbed into Jim's SUV. Jim cranked the engine and turned out of the parking lot onto busy Kingston Pike and headed home. He cruised in the left lane for about a mile. As he drove, a car gained on him quickly. He glanced in the rearview mirror. *Why the rush?* He clicked on the direction signal and merged into the right lane. But he failed to see another vehicle beside him. It swerved off the road and bounced onto the sidewalk. After a few long moments, it pulled back onto Kingston Pike and sped away. But, as it did, flashing blue lights suddenly filled Jim's rearview mirror: a police cruiser.

Scott turned in to a strip-mall parking lot and pulled into a spot. The cruiser stopped behind him. *Shit.* How had he not seen that other car? He didn't feel drunk, but he had alcohol in his system. He told Sam to text or call his grandfather Buddy.

An officer walked over and asked for Jim's license and registration, then returned to her cruiser. More officers soon arrived. An hour or more passed before Buddy and Jim's mother, Mildred, rolled into the parking lot, too. The old judge, white-haired and ruby-faced, parked, then plodded over to Jim's SUV. "Let me smell your breath, son," Buddy said through an open window. Jim exhaled. "You're sober," Buddy said.

"I know, I know," Jim said. He said he doubted the officer would give him any trouble—his speech wasn't slurred, and he felt fine, and anyone might have failed to see the car he almost sideswiped. But he'd also been a lawyer long enough to know the value of having a reliable witness, like a retired judge, just in case.

The officer asked Jim if he would walk in a straight line to test his sobriety. He agreed, but his performance wasn't convincing. "The defendant could not complete the field sobriety test as instructed," the officer later wrote in an affidavit. Jim asked for a blood test, to determine the precise amount of alcohol in his system. The officer said she would drive him to a hospital to have a test done, but not before she placed him under arrest.

Scott, charged with driving under the influence, spent the night in a jail cell full of drunks. Did he have a drinking problem? And whether he did or not, how would he ever get expert reports in order if he also had to fight a DUI charge and deal with his divorce? He had hoped, prayed even, that he might do some good with the workers' case. What had his noble intentions gotten him? Divorced, low on cash, crushed by stress. But he couldn't back out now.

The next time Scott showed up at the office, he asked Keith Stewart if he would help him fight his DUI charge. Of course, Stewart said. He had handled plenty of DUIs. At the Knoxville City County Building downtown, Stewart met with prosecutors and insisted that Jim would not have driven drunk. He gave prosecutors an affidavit by Buddy Scott, in which the retired judge stated that, based on his observations that night, Jim hadn't smelled of alcohol, nor had he talked with slurred speech, nor had his eyes looked bloodshot or glassy. Stewart harped on the most important fact: that Jim's blood test left room to doubt whether he was impaired. After at least six hearings, prosecutors agreed to reduce Scott's charge to reckless driving, so long as he paid a $50 fine and submitted a monthly urine test, to prove he was sober.

Throughout 2017, as the two sides went back and forth filing and responding to motions and briefs and preparing for trial, Scott, Stewart, and Dupree took depositions at a near-frantic pace, focusing not on TVA or Jacobs staff now but on the workers. Billy Isley was among the sickest. When Scott first met Isley, in late 2012, he thought he resembled a professional wrestler, with his thick arms and hulking frame and bald head. But by the time the attorneys deposed Isley at their offices on Market Street one hot summer morning not five years later, he looked weak and sickly, and he struggled to stop coughing.

The Kingston workers had something of a day-off uniform: jeans; a wide leather belt; new work boots they were breaking in; and a clean T-shirt with or without a Carhartt coat, depending on the weather. Isley didn't deviate from the look. Sitting across a table from the attorneys, he explained that, after leaving Kingston, "I had some heavy-metal tests run on me. It come back arsenic in my blood." Tests had also found traces of lead and mercury. He had medical records on hand to prove it. Of the arsenic, Isley said, "I don't know what that's done to my system." He told the attorneys about the lesion on his face that had rapidly grown, about his unbearable headaches, about how sluggish he felt, and about his wife's three strokes. He had returned to driving tractor trailers professionally, he said. Despite his deteriorating health, he pulled long hours to sock away money, because his family might need it, because he might not be around.

During the deposition, one of the defense attorneys asked Isley about a form he had signed in 2010 indicating that he'd been given a copy of the "Site Wide Safety and Health Plan." As Scott had learned, the safety plan listed twenty-three constituents of coal ash, many of them highly toxic, and Isley's signature on the form seemed to undercut his claim that Jacobs staff had deceived him about coal ash's dangers. Isley said he couldn't recall whether Tom Bock—"a collegiately educated moron," in his words—had actually given him a copy of the plan, despite whatever the form suggested, but he said he could recall Bock assuring him that the site was safe, that nothing would hurt him there, so long as he didn't inhale the fly ash. But Isley had discovered that you couldn't help but breathe it in. He had worn a personal air monitor at one point, he said. When he wasn't given the results, he threatened to file a complaint. He then received a piece of paper with the readings. "They were above the limits," he told the table of attorneys. He felt certain the fly ash had harmed him. "I don't even want to cut my own grass anymore," he said at the end of the deposition. "I don't care if the world quits turning anymore," he added. "I have no energy—no ambition."

Isley and his wife, Lena, and their fourteen-year-old daughter lived in LaFollette, Tennessee, forty miles north of Knoxville. They owned a mobile home on the side of a large grassy hill that overlooked miles upon miles of forested countryside. One January night, less than a year and a half after Isley's deposition, Lena was in the laundry room when she heard a thump in the master bedroom. A few days earlier, Billy had returned home to enjoy some time off after two months on the road. Lena had bought them tickets to see Metallica, his favorite band, in Nashville, but, leading up to the concert, she'd noticed him staggering around and bumping into walls, and he gasped for breath while he slept. She'd begged him to see a doctor. "I'm just tired," he said.

But Lena knew better, and when she heard the thump, she rushed to the bedroom. Billy, shirtless on the floor, was trying to stand.

"What are you doing?" she asked.

"I don't know," he said, lifting himself up. He'd fallen and bitten his tongue. "No big deal," he said. "Go back to doing what you was doing."

Lena, concerned and weighing her next move, walked back toward the laundry room but made it only to the kitchen—another thump, louder this time. Go to your room, she told her teenage daughter.

This time she found Billy in the master bathroom, slumped over the tub. Blood on the floor, blood on the toilet, blood on the walls.

"Billy, hang on," Lena said, grabbing him. "Billy, can you breathe?"

He shook his head no. He coughed, spraying red droplets.

She laid him on the floor and turned him on his back. He kept coughing and the blood kept coming. His tongue bite didn't seem to account for all of it. She turned his head, trying to clear his airway, but when she did, "he had blood just gushing out of his mouth," she later said. She tried to sit him upright. When she did, he spat red all over her. She ran to find her cell phone and dialed 911. Lena had previously worked as a hospital surgical tech and was CPR certified, so she performed chest compressions. Billy turned blue all the same. He smiled at Lena a final time before closing his eyes and foaming at the mouth. By the time emergency personnel arrived, William Franklin Isley was dead. He was forty-five years old.

Ansol and Janie Clark called Scott with the news. He hung up and dialed Lena. "It's not fair," she said, with tears in her voice. "TVA killed my husband, and I truly believe that. I truly believe that TVA just killed my husband." She would never get him back, and neither would their daughter. None of this would have happened, Lena said, had TVA and Jacobs done the right thing. "Billy was always afraid that he wasn't going to be here for the outcome of the trial," she said, "and he was right."

A county medical examiner conducted an autopsy and determined that Billy had died from a heart blockage. The examiner blamed the block on severe hypertensive cardiovascular disease, a heart condition that fly-ash exposure is known to exacerbate. Isley also suffered from pulmonary emphysema, a chronic lung condition caused by, among other things, exposure to fly ash and toxic particles.

The night of Billy's death, Lena, frantic and covered in blood, had told a sheriff's deputy that a friend had mentioned to her that, as Billy grew weaker, he'd resorted to amphetamines to stay awake while driving his semi-truck, but she insisted that he hadn't used any that day. With Lena's consent, the deputy searched the room where Isley had collapsed. In Isley's travel backpack, he found an empty bottle of OxyContin and a small bag of methamphetamines.

When Scott learned about the deputy's discovery, it pained him that Isley had been in such agony, had had such little energy, and had so few options that he'd turned to drugs, and Scott knew that the drugs would complicate Isley's case against Jacobs. But a toxicological report found that, though Isley had both OxyContin and methamphetamines in his system at the time of his death, he hadn't overdosed on either; the concentration of drugs in his blood was far below the typical fatal levels. That left no question in Scott's mind about the primary cause of Isley's death: fly-ash exposure.

Billy Isley's funeral service was held at a Baptist church in LaFollette. Keith Stewart and John Dupree drove out to pay their respects. (Scott had to stay home with his sons.) As Dupree and Stewart stepped inside the church vestibule, they could hear Lena wailing through the closed sanctuary doors.

Jim Scott knew that the surviving workers felt as if they were in a pressure cooker. Many now gravely sick hadn't anticipated that the case would take five years or more to reach trial, and they fretted that they would die before Jacobs agreed to cover their medical bills. Scott carried their concerns with him everywhere. It wore on him. He felt older. His hair was turning gray. He sometimes wondered if his heart might explode, or if he might have a stroke.

One autumn afternoon, he strode into John Dupree's office and took a seat. "We need more time," Scott said. They had an expert problem, and a not-small one at that.

Magistrate Guyton had given their team two quick months to produce a proper, lengthy report by Paul Terry, the UT epidemiologist, who would be their star expert witness. But Terry hadn't submitted a study yet, and, amid the crush of taking depositions and dealing with the DUI, neither Scott, Dupree, nor Stewart had asked the court for a deadline extension. Terry's report was due in July. Now it was October. They had missed the deadline, extravagantly so.

Dupree, already aware of this, told Scott that he had begun drafting a motion to urge Judge Varlan to push back the trial and allow them more time to sort out their expert issues. Jacobs bore the blame for their delay, Dupree believed, since the defense had been slow to turn over documents that Terry needed to finish his study.

Scott said their problems went beyond Terry's report. They'd recently agreed to add another attorney to their team by the name of Tyler Roper. Roper rented an office on the first floor of their building, where he ran a small collections practice. Scott, Dupree, and Stewart had mostly brought him on to sit in depositions with the workers as the defense lawyers hammered them with questions, and Roper, a former mountain-climbing guide in his forties, had helped in this regard. But he had neither significant trial experience nor vast financial resources, and their team needed both.

"I need to call Jeff Friedman," Scott told Dupree. "We're running out of money." Their expenses were approaching $250,000 and could quickly double or triple. If they prevailed in the first trial phase, Scott said, they would have to return to court and fight for damages for each plaintiff—no cheap task now that they represented almost two hundred and fifty workers. "I'm trying to avoid a financial hemorrhage," he said.

Dupree said he didn't know Friedman.

"He did a good job in the land cases," Scott said. And, because of those suits, Friedman already knew all about the Kingston disaster and would need only minimal briefing on the workers' case.

Dupree said he wanted a second opinion. The pocket doors between his and Stewart's offices stood open. He leaned back in his chair and turned his head. "Hey, Keith," he yelled, "what about Jeff Friedman?"

"I don't know who the fuck that is," Stewart yelled back. But, he said, if Scott thought he could help, they should meet with him.

Scott phoned Friedman while driving home from work that evening. "Just come up here and meet with me and with my partners," Scott told him. They needed an ace trial lawyer to square off against Jimmy Sanders, and Jacobs deserved to be held to account, just as Friedman had done with TVA in the land trials.

Somewhat to Scott's surprise, Friedman said he was open to the idea. He didn't know Sanders personally, he said, but he had practiced law with attorneys like him—arrogant, priggish corporate puppets—throughout his career. And it bothered him a great deal when they won.

During football season, game-day partying in Knoxville starts not on Saturdays before kickoff but on Thirsty Thursdays, with throngs of coeds crowding the bars along the Strip, a debauched stretch of dives and fast-food places on Kingston Pike, or Cumberland Avenue, alongside the University of Tennessee campus. Late in the night, the most misguided among these students stumble to Cookout to eat chicken strips or corn dogs or cheeseburgers in the dining room, where Christian music blares from speakers overhead. On Friday mornings, an armada of party boats—the Vol Navy—docks near the stadium, turning the Tennessee River into a floating parking lot, over which bright orange UT flags fly in the mountain breeze. On Saturday, an orange mass, one hundred thousand people strong, descends onto campus and packs into Neyland Stadium. Jeff Friedman loved the whole wild, scruffy scene and all the memories it brought back.

After graduating from UT, Friedman had willed himself into a great trial lawyer, to the surprise of more than a few of his fraternity brothers, whose memories of him tended to involve woozy nights at the Lambda Chi house. Now, whenever Friedman ate at The Club, a private restaurant that overlooked downtown Birmingham—one of his go-tos—he would still drink a Manhattan and a not-insignificant quantity of red wine with his steak. His daughters disapproved of his diet; a heart attack had killed his father at forty-three, after all. But, all told, Friedman walked a straight line. He attended church. He and his wife, Anise, had raised three successful children. He served on the board of charitable organizations. Still, when Jim Scott called and asked to meet, Friedman couldn't pass up a chance to drive to Knoxville in the middle of football season, in the middle of all the fun. He agreed to meet Scott at 10 a.m. on Friday, October 13, 2017, at Gourmet Market, a breakfast-and-sandwich place a few miles from campus. The Vols would be playing the South Carolina Gamecocks the next afternoon, and Friedman had season tickets.

Friedman's willingness to meet with Scott owed only partly to football. Over the summer, Jamie Satterfield, the reporter who'd covered Scott's victory in the Sixth Circuit almost three years earlier, had published a lengthy front-page story in *The Knoxville News Sentinel* about the workers' case—the first major piece about the suit in a local or regional paper. (Dupree and Scott had met Satterfield for lunch that spring and nudged her to investigate.) Satterfield's story recounted the most severe allegations against Jacobs: that its staff forbade the workers from wearing dust masks, that it swore the fly ash posed no serious health risk. "These men were treated like collateral damage," Janie Clark told Satterfield for the story, "and they fell between the cracks in this toxic place."

The online version of the article included Mike McCarthy's "cock" video, which Satterfield had somehow obtained, along with another, equally explosive video that a worker had surreptitiously recorded. This second video showed a Jacobs staffer knocking part of a personal air monitor against a table, presumably clearing out ash from the filter before having it analyzed for hazards.

Until Friedman read Satterfield's story, he had failed to realize how brazenly Jacobs had acted in denying the workers respiratory protection and how sick they were as a result. Seventeen workers had already died, according to Satterfield's reporting, and there would surely be more. Friedman's disdain for bullies had drawn him to the TVA land cases. Now challenging Jacobs held a similar appeal. He didn't like that Scott's team had missed a major deadline with their expert reports, nor did he like that Scott's attention to detail was wanting. But Friedman respected Scott's unwavering belief in the workers, his brass in taking on Jacobs, and his refusal to quit after Judge Varlan had thrown out the case.

Friedman arrived at Gourmet Market dressed in a blazer and a white button-down shirt, his customary outfit. When the COVID-19 pandemic broke out a few years later, Friedman's law practice shifted to working remotely; he nonetheless kept showing up to the empty office every day dressed in a suit.

Keith Stewart and Tyler Roper accompanied Scott. (John Dupree was busy with another appointment.) After Friedman greeted them, the four lawyers settled into wooden chairs around a large table to the right of the front door and ordered coffee. The restaurant had red walls and a checkered black-and-white-tile floor; customers flowed in and out.

After the attorneys ordered, they traded stories for a while. Friedman talked about his years as a young trial lawyer. Once, he said, after he won a case in some small backwater town, another attorney, an old-timer, tried to shake him down for his fee, grabbing his arm and telling him, "Son, this is my town—you get half, I get the other half." The story got a few laughs. Friedman said he'd had a jury trial in at least half of Alabama's sixty-seven counties and that he'd learned how to win over Southern juries.

When the conversation at last turned to the workers' suit, Friedman agreed that it would be difficult for Jimmy Sanders and the rest of the defense team to explain away the plaintiffs' evidence, especially the videos. But Friedman said they needed more experts, a lot more experts, if they hoped to reach trial, especially with an exacting federal judge like Thomas Varlan. The trouble, Friedman said, was that "academics don't want to rush."

Scott, confident in the case he'd built, had little patience for pessimism. "Look," he said, eyes fixed on Friedman, "you are the only one we want to try this case. You got the knowledge, you got the background, we like the way you practice law, and you can identify with our workers."

Friedman thought for a moment. Scott took a slow breath. "From time to time," Friedman said, "I work with a lawyer in Asheville by the name of Gary Davis." Friedman sat forward in his chair. "I will get in this case and help you and fund it and try it and pour my heart out. But I need Gary Davis."

"Hell, no," Scott said. He knew Davis, an environmental engineer-turned-lawyer in his mid-sixties. Davis had worked on the land cases with Friedman. During lunch breaks during depositions, the gregarious Scott had found it impossible, almost tortuous, to carry on a conversation with the stiff, analytical Davis. Scott doubted that Davis would get along well with the workers or sparkle in front of an East Tennessee jury, and they needed sparkle. Scott told Friedman as much.

Friedman conceded that Davis wasn't the most dynamic, or warmest, attorney he'd ever known, but he couldn't try the case without him. There was no way, Friedman said, not under such crushing time constraints. Davis would dig into the science, write about it clearly, and argue pretrial motions before Varlan. And, ultimately, Friedman said, Davis would do whatever was needed to win. "I got to have him," insisted Friedman, growing annoyed.

This was Scott's case. Friedman would bring their team to five attorneys. Did they really need Davis, too? Then again, what choice did he have? He knew, without question, that he needed Friedman, for his trial skills and for his deep pockets.

The same fall day that Friedman notified the court that he intended to appear in the case on the plaintiffs' behalf, Gary Davis submitted the same notice of his own.

On a cold November morning, Keith Stewart woke up before dawn, pulled on a pair of hiking shorts, and brewed a pot of coffee. Most days, he didn't roll into the office until nine-thirty or so, but he got up early anyway, a habit that had come with age: the dumbass, cocaine-dealing college kid was now nearly fifty-one and lived with his wife in Sequoyah Hills, about a mile from Jim Scott's house. Theirs was a tasteful two-story brick home overlooking the Tennessee River, with window boxes of flowers and a screened-in porch off the side. That morning, Stewart sat alone at a desk in the living room, sipping coffee from a Yeti tumbler, skimming emails, and occasionally glancing at a flatscreen TV above the fireplace, turned to the local news.

Stewart felt good about the workers' case, all in all. A month had passed since the meeting with Jeff Friedman, and they were still negotiating a formal agreement over how much money he would initially contribute to fund the case—$100,000 was the working number. They also needed to agree on Friedman's and Davis's share of the attorneys' fee if, by some miracle, their team won a recovery. Stewart proposed that, for most of the first two hundred or so cases, the four Knoxville attorneys would take 60 percent of the fees, while Friedman and Davis split the rest. That seemed fair to Stewart, and he felt sure they'd quickly reach an agreement (and they would). Then, Stewart hoped, once their team had six attorneys to write briefs and divide sundry other tasks, their workload would feel less akin to drowning. Like Scott, Stewart worked past twelve many nights, and he would often jolt awake once he dozed off, anxious about upcoming deadlines.

Adding to the team's momentum, shortly after the meeting with Friedman, John Dupree had filed the motion he'd been drafting to urge Judge Varlan to push back the start of the trial, owing to Jacobs's slow response to some of their document requests. To Stewart's relief, Varlan had rescheduled the trial for April 2018, about five months away now. He had also reset the deadline for expert reports, and the plaintiffs' team desperately needed the extra time. It was beginning to look as if, of the nine doctors or academics they had intended to put on the stand, only Paul Terry, the UT epidemiologist, might have time to complete a full study of the workers' health conditions before the trial. If he didn't, or if Varlan found his work unconvincing, their team might have to try the case without expert witnesses, which would spell certain defeat.

To head off such a calamity, Stewart had spent the past few days trying to arrange a phone call with Avner Vengosh, the Duke professor who, shortly after the Kingston disaster, had tested the fly ash and found that it contained potentially dangerous concentrations of arsenic, mercury, and radium. Vengosh would be the ideal expert witness to bring in alongside Terry. That Vengosh worked at Duke, one of the nation's most well-regarded universities, bolstered his credibility considerably. Tyler Roper, the collections attorney, had already sent Vengosh a novella of an email, praising his research and begging him to help them "to fight the good fight . . . for the workers who are sick and dying or have already died." Stewart felt sure that Vengosh would come through and manhandle whatever experts Jacobs rounded up for its defense.

At 6:12 that morning, as Stewart typed away, his cell phone rang. He seldom received calls at that hour, and he didn't recognize the number, but he answered anyway. "Hello?"

"This is KUB," a man said, referring to the Knoxville Utility Board, the local electric, gas, and water provider. "We've got you as the contact for 713 Market Street. Are you affiliated with that?"

"Yes, sir," Stewart said.

"Okay, uh, the fire line that goes into that building is ruptured and is leaking fairly significantly," the man said, a bit casually, before adding, "You've got water coming out your front door."

"Oh, God," Stewart said.

The dispatcher explained that a KUB employee was already on-site and needed to get inside the building to shut off the water. How fast could Stewart get downtown?

"Shit," Stewart said. "Five to seven minutes?"

"I'll let him know."

Stewart hung up, put on a fleece jacket and a Yankees baseball hat, and raced to his pickup. He reached the old three-story brick building within minutes and parked behind it near some garbage cans. The temperature hovered a few degrees above freezing. In Stewart's rush to leave the house, he'd slipped on flip-flops and hadn't changed out of hiking shorts. *Dumb move*, he thought, as he strode up the alley.

When he rounded the corner, a KUB employee was standing on the sidewalk watching as water streamed from the front door and cascaded into the street. Stewart bounded up the five stone steps to the entrance, stuck his key into the lock, and grabbed the brass handle. When he slung open the double doors, a foot-tall wave rushed out, covering his flip-flops. Smoke billowed into his face. "Oh, shit!" he yelled, as he retreated to the sidewalk. There was no ruptured pipe; the building's sprinkler system had gone off. This was a fire.

A fire engine arrived within minutes, throwing red light over the narrow downtown block. Two ladder trucks and three more engines followed, along with a rescue vehicle and a pair of command cars. Firefighters spilled into the road. They broke out the window to Tyler Roper's first-floor office and then, hoses in hand, charged into the heat. Heavy smoke met them on the first floor, where Roper and Jim Scott had their offices. The blaze was concentrated in the drop ceiling above the elevator on the first story, but flames had spread into the walls and floor of the second and third levels, burning structural supports and drywall. The firefighters chased the blaze through darkness and smoke, relying on flashlights to see. They smashed holes in the walls and axed the ceiling and ripped down acoustic ceiling tiles, exposing the flame and the wired guts of the building. Then they opened their hoses, adding to the inches of standing water already on the ground.

Stewart, shivering in his hiking shorts, stood on the sidewalk across the street. He dialed the other attorneys. "Man, get down here!" he told Dupree. "The place is on fire!"

As Stewart waited for the others, he watched as smoke streamed from the building's arched limestone entrance and curled from the second-story windows—his windows—into the blue dawn. He ran toward the building and followed a group of firefighters through a side door, which led to the top of a stairwell. He had to know how bad the fire was. He stepped inside and looked down the stairs toward the basement. He saw only water. It had risen nearly to the top of the stairs. *No, no, no!* he thought, as firefighters shooed him outside.

Within eighteen minutes, the fire company had doused the blaze and begun ventilating the space. Of the lawyers, John Dupree arrived first, followed by Roper. No one could reach Scott. Roper ran inside three times to salvage whatever he could. There was little point. The basement was a swimming pool. The four sprinklers had activated at 12:41 a.m., according to the building's alarm system, and then had run for nearly six hours unnoticed. The average sprinkler spews at least fifteen gallons a minute. That meant, Stewart quickly calculated, nearly twenty-two thousand gallons of water stood in the basement, though likely far more. Roper put the total closer to forty thousand, based on what a firefighter told him. Before the last fire engine left, at 8:42 a.m., two crew members stood outside the waterlogged, smoked-out building and drained their boots onto the sidewalk.

News of the fire moved quickly through Knoxville's legal circles, given the building's proximity to the federal courthouse. The attorneys fielded calls from concerned friends and clients in a parking lot across the street, trying to assure them that there was no reason to worry, though the lawyers had no idea whether that was true.

Once the building was deemed reasonably safe, the attorneys went from room to room, floor to floor, taking stock. The entire building would need gutting. A sooty, tar-like substance glazed the walls, furniture, computers, and printers. Papers on desks were entirely black on one side and remained white on the reverse. Stewart's particle-board file cabinets had swelled with so much water that he had to pry them open; by the time he managed to get inside, his documents had disintegrated into a soggy, inseparable mush.

No portion of the building was spared. A hole had formed in the floor leading to Dupree's office. On the wall inside hung a framed painting of two hunters and their dogs, now streaked with water. On his desk, grit blotted out framed family photos. The attorneys found small comfort in the fact that they'd scanned and backed up many of their documents on a cloud server. Their originals were gone, and they had no way of knowing which documents they might have neglected to back up digitally, and reprints would cost no small sum. They fumed, and grew suspicious.

An investigator deemed the fire an accident. In a one-paragraph report, he concluded that it had likely started in the ceiling near the HVAC room. "There were [sic] a lot of wiring running through this area," the investigator wrote, before promptly closing the case.

The attorneys rejected this conclusion. Roper and Stewart had recently spent a few thousand dollars on a new alarm system, which a security firm had inspected and signed off on six months earlier. The attorneys couldn't figure out why, then, the alarm system had failed to alert the fire department when the sprinklers had kicked on around one o'clock. Curiously, the alarm system also seemed to indicate that one of the manual pull stations, sometimes called a "T-bar," had been tripped inside the building. Had someone been inside and yanked it?

The lawyers lacked evidence but felt sure that TVA or Jacobs was somehow involved. "They tried to take us out," Roper said. "They're awful. They're not okay. They're not good people." Stewart agreed: this was a pro job. He suspected that an arsonist had disabled the alarm system, perhaps by snipping some wires or cables, and then pulled the T-bar to ensure that, once the blaze was lit, the alarm system wouldn't notify the fire department. Stewart maintained this position for years, though friends looked at him skeptically whenever he brought it up. He wasn't able to prove his theory, and never would, but he felt certain that he was right.* Both TVA and Jacobs had motive.

Stewart and the other lawyers would soon learn that, because of a

* Stewart later reiterated that, despite his suspicions, he had no evidence connecting TVA or Jacobs Engineering to the fire. In a statement to the author, an attorney for Jacobs denied the company had any involvement in the blaze and said it was "absurd and insulting" for anyone to suggest otherwise.

clause in Jacobs's contract with TVA, the agency would likely have to pay at least some of Jacobs's legal bills and at least some of whatever money it might pay the plaintiffs as a result of litigation. Perhaps a larger concern for TVA was the potential hit to its revenue if lawsuits or government action forced it to handle or store its fly ash with greater care or, worse, restricted TVA from selling its fly ash altogether. Was that a compelling enough reason to torch the attorneys' offices?

The team needed somewhere to go, and quickly, to stand any chance of regrouping before the trial. In the parking lot across from the smoldering building, Stewart called a property manager he knew by the name of John Trotter. Trotter answered, and said he'd already seen news reports about the fire. "If you've got any space," Stewart told him, "we're going to need somewhere to land." Trotter said that he did, at 625 Market Street, one block away from the attorneys' current office. Trotter asked, When do you want to see it? Stewart said right now.

Stewart, still in hiking shorts and flip-flops, met Trotter outside the building at around eleven o'clock that morning. The fifteen-story tower stood on the corner of Market Street and W. Church Avenue, and was, at the time of its completion in 1925, Knoxville's tallest building. Stewart and Trotter rode the elevator to the fourteenth floor. The attorneys would have the entire level to themselves, Trotter explained, as the two stepped into a small reception area. They walked through a set of double doors into a beige-carpeted bullpen. Five cubicles sat along a set of north-facing windows, while across the room, four doors led to private offices. There was a conference room near reception. With a one-year lease, Trotter told Stewart, rent would run $3,235.18 a month, including utilities and janitorial services. Stewart jotted down the number on a yellow legal pad and drew a square around it next to a list of office supplies he needed to buy: a wireless router, copy paper, a coffee machine, sticky notes. The attorneys' current office had markedly more charm than this available space, and it cost them $325 less than what Trotter wanted. But where else could they go if not here? Stewart thought for a few moments. "Fuck it," he told Trotter. "We'll do it."

Jim Scott never showed up the morning the office burned, and he didn't return John Dupree's calls or text messages, either, because he was in the Blue Ridge Mountains. He had driven up to spend a long weekend with his sons at the Chetola Resort, a wooded, forty-two-room lodge in Blowing Rock, North Carolina. He'd devised the trip specifically to avoid thinking about the case. With the trial approaching and his divorce proceedings dragging out, he needed a break from the endless phone calls and emails and the dizzying, free-falling sensation of it all. More important, he needed to reconnect with his sons, to remind them, amid his and their mother's divorce and the rush toward trial, that his affection for them hadn't waned, that he would always be there when they needed him most.

Scott succeeded in not thinking about work once that weekend, largely by ignoring his cell phone. He and his sons hiked mountain trails, swam in the lodge's heated indoor pool, and strolled the campus of Appalachian State University, in case Jack, fifteen now, wanted to apply one day. "It's going to break my heart when he goes to college," Jim later confided to a friend. On Saturday, he watched football with great pleasure.

The trip's highlight came the morning that Jim and his sons fly-fished in a creek near the lodge. Jack kept their guide busy, netting a dozen or more trout. For Jim, seeing Jack gain confidence and move with ease among the boulders and cold, clear pools justified the entire trip. Sam's lures had a way of snagging tree branches, but he was young and would learn in time. Jim was proud of his sons, for the young men they were becoming, for their resilience these past two difficult years. If he could transport himself back through time and space to that cold evening when Ansol Clark and the other workers first visited his office, he would still agree to take their case. His heart had been and remained, he hoped, in the right place. But, if he had a second try, he would do better by his sons. At the very least, he would warn them about what lay ahead. Not that he had had much idea himself in the case's early days. Without such a redo, he could hope only for their understanding and grace.

At the end of the trip, as Scott packed his bags and prepared to head home, John Dupree finally reached him with news of the fire. "Oh, shit!" said Scott, clenching his cell phone. "How the hell could this happen?" By this point, the other three Knoxville attorneys had fairly well agreed that TVA or Jacobs—somehow, someway—had had a hand in igniting the blaze. Dupree told Scott as much.

The theory struck Scott as far-fetched but not altogether insane. Was this what his friend, the former DOE staffer, had warned him about at Calhoun's that night soon after he filed the workers' lawsuit? And what might TVA or Jacobs do next? Days earlier, TVA's public-records officer had informed Scott that the agency no longer had in its possession videos that it had recorded of the Kingston cleanup site—videos it should have kept for at least ten years under federal Superfund guidelines. Scott had hoped that the tapes would show fly ash blowing and swirling around the jobsite, further undercutting Jacobs's claim that the site wasn't dusty and thus not dangerous. And the videos' disappearance, in Scott's view, constituted a criminal act. Did TVA really have the brass, and have such disregard for the judicial process, that it would destroy evidence it was required to preserve under federal law? Two days before the fire, he'd sent an email to Jim Chase, a senior TVA attorney, demanding to know why the agency had destroyed the footage; he would never get a straight answer.

Beyond the missing tapes, the fire brought to mind a story Scott had heard during the land cases and nearly forgotten about in the years since. In a deposition, a TVA senior manager named Melissa Hedgecoth had testified that, in July 2009, her supervisor had forced her to delete damning information about TVA from a report she'd written about the Kingston disaster. The same day Hedgecoth made the deletions, someone broke into her car as she picked up her son from daycare. The thief took her laptop, on which she'd saved an unedited version of her report, and Hedgecoth felt sure that TVA bore responsibility. "If it would have just been any old thug," she explained, "they would have certainly got my purse right there with [the laptop] in the back floorboard." More curious, since Hedgecoth's laptop contained government documents, it had a built-in tracking device in case it went missing, and yet TVA allegedly never recovered the laptop. According to Hedgecoth, a TVA police officer later told her that whoever stole the laptop surely knew about the tracking feature, and how to get around it. Hedgecoth testified that she was subsequently shut out of TVA's computer system and had her replacement laptop, employee badge, and company phone temporarily turned off.

Scott thought about the fire as he weaved out of the gray mountains on the drive back to Knoxville. If Hedgecoth's allegations were true and

Jim Scott (*left*) and Keith Stewart
in their law office at 625 Market Street

TVA was indeed willing to break into a car and steal a laptop, would it also lie about its involvement in denying the workers dust masks and respirators? Even before the fire, such questions had rattled around in his head, but now they were a klaxon blaring. He came to fear what TVA and Jacobs might try next.

The attorneys had no time to settle in. In their new office, they stacked boxes and set up bargain office furniture, either borrowed or newly purchased, wherever they could find space. After a glass-top coffee table they ordered arrived shattered, they left the golden base between a few faux-leather chairs in the foyer, as if it had come that way. Fortunately, Scott had kept many of his original case notebooks in an off-site storage locker, so the team still had many of the workers' medical reports, and Stewart had done a commendable job backing up other key documents on the server. Still, the fire and the move taxed the team nearly to the point of collapse.

When the four Knoxville lawyers finally had a chance to update Jeff Friedman, he was incredulous. He told the others that he wanted to hear no talk—not one word—of conspiracy. "Look," he said on speakerphone. "I can't allow my mind to go there. We have to get ready for trial." Any other concern had to wait.

Judge Varlan, in his recent ruling to push back the start of the trial, had stated that he would refuse to reschedule it again "absent extraordinary circumstances." He'd bolded the words for emphasis. But, in a hearing two weeks after the fire, he conceded that an extraordinary circumstance had indeed occurred, warranting further delay. He eventually slated the first trial to begin on October 16, 2018, less than a year away. Paul Terry, the plaintiffs' star expert witness, had still yet to complete his report on the workers' exposure to fly ash, and probably wouldn't by the fast-approaching, mid-December deadline the court had given him. But Varlan referred that and other expert issues to Magistrate Guyton, since he had a deeper understanding of that particularly knotty aspect of the case.

Not long after Janie and Ansol Clark got married, she quit her job at the Tennessee Theatre and began waitressing at the Journeyman's Table, a restaurant inside a Holiday Inn near the University of Tennessee campus. It had burgundy carpet and linen napkins and coffee cups turned down on the tables. Janie worked nights, and she liked that because Ansol did too. They could see each other after their shifts and watch *The Tonight Show*. But, in taking the job, she had stepped into an overwhelming new world populated by vacationers and business travelers, all of whom seemed impossibly sophisticated to her. She had just turned eighteen. She didn't know how to drive, and, even if she had known, she didn't have enough money to buy a car. (Ansol dropped her off and picked her up.) She didn't know how to wait tables, either, and she knew almost nothing about food, having survived mostly on canned soup as a child. She didn't know what shrimp looked like until she worked one of the restaurant's Friday-night seafood buffets.

Her manager gave her no training before sending her out into the dining room for the first time. She wore an orange dress and a white apron. The customers could order off the menu or help themselves at the buffet, where roast and fried chicken and country ham was kept warm under heat lamps. She learned how to dart between tables to refill drinks and take orders and, no less important, how to talk to businessmen. Once she mastered both skills, she warmed to the job. The diners spoke kindly to her and tipped her well, and she enjoyed joking around with the other waitresses, one of whom became a lifelong friend.

Janie hung on to the job for eight years, as she and Ansol saved up to buy her a car—a 1968 Chevy Malibu—and then to have a baby. When Janie got pregnant, in 1979, she knew that expecting mothers did not, as a rule, wait tables in Knoxville. It was taboo. But the money was good, and she would need it for their child, so she worked on. As her stomach swelled, she suspected that her boss, the innkeeper, would prefer to have a young, flirty waitress attending to the business travelers rather than a slow pregnant woman. But Janie decided that if her boss wanted her gone, he would have to fire her.

Two weeks before her due date, her boss summoned her to his office. The Pregnancy Discrimination Act, which prohibits discrimination against expecting parents, had passed a year earlier, but Janie doubted that the innkeeper cared much about that. *Oh, boy*, she thought, *this is the end.*

The meeting lasted only a few minutes. When Janie returned to the dining room, the other waitresses gathered around. "So," one asked, "did you get fired?"

Janie held out a yellow Winnie-the-Pooh onesie: "He said, 'My wife wanted you to have this.' "

Almost forty years later, Janie still laughed whenever she recalled that story. She felt she had somehow stood up for pregnant women simply by persevering. The experience taught her to be tough, and now she decided that she would be tough again.

On a cool December evening, about three weeks after the fire ravaged the lawyers' office, Janie and Ansol drove to a meeting in a long brick building in west Knoxville, eight miles from their home. They weren't activists. Sometimes they'd gone years without voting. But Ansol's illness had galvanized them to hold TVA to account, or at least try to. Janie couldn't fathom how TVA, a federal entity designed to improve the lives of simple, hardworking Southerners like her and Ansol, could show such disregard for human life. TVA had almost certainly exposed the workers to hazards, and its apparent willingness to do that shattered her view of the government. This was the United States of America. Such meanness shouldn't be tolerated here, she believed. TVA had sent the Kingston cleanup workers into a toxic wasteland with little or, more often, no respiratory protection, and now it refused to do anything about the consequences of its decision. Janie's mother and father had instilled in her the basic Christian principles of right and wrong, and TVA had violated all of them, she believed, and she thought the world ought to know it.

A fundamental problem with TVA, she'd realized, was that it almost entirely lacked accountability. The agency, since its inception, had been led by a board of directors, nominated by the U.S. president and confirmed by the Senate. The president could fire board members at will, and congressional committees lightly monitored TVA. But ever since TVA began self-financing its operations, in 1959, Washington mostly left it alone, unless a scandal emerged. The public, for its part, had no real say in TVA's operations. "TVA open board meetings are not real scrutiny," complained a member of an energy-industry committee that had investigated TVA in the late 1980s.

The meeting that December evening was held at the Knoxville office of the Tennessee Department of Environment and Conservation (TDEC), a state agency that had no direct influence over TVA but did regulate Tennessee's rivers. For reasons that the Clarks could not begin to understand, TDEC was considering whether to allow TVA extra time to bring the Kingston Fossil Plant into compliance with the EPA's 2015 coal-ash rules (the ones Jim Scott had found frustratingly weak). These regulations, as proposed by the Obama administration, capped the quantity of toxic metals and other contaminants that coal-fired power plants—believed to be the nation's largest industrial source of toxic water pollution—could discharge into rivers or ponds. The 2015 coal-ash rules also required power plants to monitor and repair leaking coal-ash holding ponds. But, in the spring of 2017, the EPA, now under Donald Trump's administration, had capitulated to pressure from energy-industry groups, of which TVA was a member. In short order, the EPA began rolling back many of its new coal-ash policies. These rollbacks would let states decide whether to enforce many of the new coal-ash regulations, or waive them altogether. That was the reason for the TDEC meeting.

Janie, wearing a red flannel shirt and a vest, and Ansol, in a green

Henley shirt, sat in the back row of a small meeting room. Three or four dozen people showed up. Once everyone found a seat, a TVA spokesman walked to a lectern at the front of the room and told the crowd that TVA was in compliance with its current water-discharge permit and that it didn't "make sense" for it to meet the EPA's new, stricter pollution limits by 2022, as TVA had already promised it would, since the regulatory guidelines looked likely to change under Trump. TVA, in other words, didn't want to reduce the quantity of toxic heavy metals it expelled into Tennessee's rivers if it didn't have to.

The meeting included a public-comment period. Janie hadn't planned to speak, but, enraged by TVA's position, she found herself walking to the front of the room. She put her right arm on top of the lectern and looked out at faces staring back at her. She hadn't talked publicly about Ansol's illness, but she knew this moment presented a rare opportunity: many TVA staffers were among the crowd. She first discussed the Kingston disaster, explaining that TVA had treated the cleanup workers as if they were expendable, as if their lives meant nothing. She explained how TVA and Jacobs had lied about the fly-ash monitoring. "I do not trust TVA," she said through tears. "They told us [the worksite] was safe then. Why should you believe them now [about the water]?"

The audience applauded. When she glanced back at Ansol, tears dampened his cheeks.

On New Year's Day 2018, ten months remained until the start of the trial. The six lawyers, still reeling from the fire, would need to sprint. John Dupree was worried, not just about the limited time constraints but also about the case's strain on his health, his nerves, his life. Attorneys have a habit of keeling over at the age of seventy-five or eighty while surrounded by case files and transcripts and grimy coffee mugs, faded diplomas hanging on the wall. But Dupree wanted to quit practicing law before he got old. He didn't know what he'd do instead, but twenty years of fighting other attorneys day in and day out had exhausted him. He wanted to stop bickering with people. Maybe he'd teach history. That wouldn't involve daily combat, and the stakes would be far lower; no one's health and well-being would be on the line.

The main reason Dupree wanted to change his profession, though, was to have more time to hunt and fish and spend time with his three children. He loved them, and not just in the obligatory way that hard-driving professionals often say they love their children. He really loved them, and he'd seen very little of them since Jim Scott had recruited him to help in the lawsuit against Jacobs. Dupree had seldom seen his own dad when he was a child, and he thought his kids deserved to have a present father.

One evening, as the case lurched toward trial, Dupree and his wife, Karen, called their kids into the kitchen of their home. He explained that preparing for trial would absorb nearly his every waking moment in the months ahead. He would only be around in the small hours of the morning or at night. So, they had to decide: did they want him to proceed, or should he back out while he still had a chance? His children, having read about the case in the news, understood its importance. He had to keep going, they decided. He had to do the right thing.

That was why, shortly after Jeff Friedman joined the team, Dupree made the four-hour drive to Birmingham. Dupree, having missed the meeting at Gourmet Market, knew almost nothing about Friedman. They planned to spend a few days going over the case and getting to know each other.

When Dupree pulled into the parking lot of Friedman's office, he didn't quite understand what he was looking at. The building, tucked into a patch of woods ten miles outside downtown Birmingham, had a flat, fortresslike stone facade, with no street-facing windows and an oversize wooden front door. In the rear, large windows overlooked a lush, manicured glade, with a long stone pond running down the middle.

"Is this a fucking castle?" Dupree asked when Friedman greeted him at the entrance. Friedman explained that he had bought the building from a developer who had money problems—perhaps no surprise, given the place's opulence.

Friedman led Dupree to a conference room. Two glass walls offered views of the surrounding foliage, making the room appear as if it were floating among the trees. Friedman took a chair with his back to the glass. Dupree, after taking in the sight, removed some case files from his bag and set them on the table. As the two dug in, Friedman broke out a large tobacco pipe. "You mind if I smoke?" he asked. At that moment, Dupree, also a pipe smoker, knew he and Friedman would get along fine.

The pair spent two days poring over evidence and filling up the conference room with smoke. Friedman applauded Jim Scott for believing the workers' stories when no one else had, but the case was an absolute mess, in his view. Paul Terry would be a strong authority on the witness stand, but Friedman stressed to Dupree that they needed more experts, ideally doctors or researchers with deep knowledge of coal ash who could write compelling reports to complement Terry's research. "Without that level of proof," Friedman explained, "you don't have the right, especially in federal court, to even present your case to the jury." He also stressed that they needed clear and ample proof that Jacobs had manipulated evidence on a grand scale with its dodgy-at-best air-monitoring practices.

Dupree and the other Knoxville lawyers had already planned to attack Jacobs's air-monitoring practices during the trial. Jacobs's air-monitoring results were "completely fucked," Tyler Roper, the collections attorney, had written to the team in an email. But, Dupree told Friedman, the case was "a monstrosity"—easily the most complex one he'd ever been involved in—and they had almost no time to prepare more experts, provided Judge Varlan and Magistrate Guyton even allowed them to bring in more. At a hearing after the fire, Keith Stewart had told Varlan that the plaintiffs wanted to introduce three additional expert witnesses, including, above all, Avner Vengosh, the Duke professor, whom they'd listed as a potential witness in an early filing. But the court had yet to decide on the matter.

The prospect that Varlan might deny the plaintiffs' request flooded Friedman with anxiety. Having only one witness, Terry, would be a major vulnerability, since it would be far easier for Jimmy Sanders to discredit one expert as opposed to multiple. And Friedman knew their team could expect no mercy from Sanders. Early in his career, Friedman had defended large companies and learned their tactics—how they dragged out cases seemingly forever, and how they aimed to "put plaintiffs in the poor house," as he described it. Jacobs seemed no different. "They want a pound of flesh from Jim Scott," Friedman said, and they wanted to punish the workers for bringing suits against the company.

For that reason, Friedman said, their team needed to plan for every conceivable thing that could go wrong, because a lot could.

Friedman's ambition to bring in more experts died quickly and painfully. First, in January 2018, Guyton ruled that, after several extensions, Terry needed to submit a full report on the workers' conditions by July 19, about six months away, or risk Varlan's barring his testimony. But the real blow came in March 2018, when Guyton determined that the "Plaintiffs had not acted diligently in seeking an extension of time [for expert disclosures]," nor had they demonstrated good cause for their delay. For these reasons, Guyton forbade them from bringing in new experts. He extended Scott's team one mercy: since they'd previously mentioned Vengosh as a potential witness, he gave them thirty days to submit a brief report outlining Vengosh's testimony and the scientific basis for his opinions. Once they did, Guyton or Varlan would decide whether to let Vengosh testify, based on the strength of his work.

The issue was soon moot. Stewart had felt sure, based on phone calls and emails with Vengosh, that he was eager to participate in the case. But when Stewart reached out to the professor again, he told Stewart that he'd received a grant to study in China and would be unable to testify as a result.

Dark clouds fell over Scott and the rest of the team. The odds of the workers' case reaching trial had grown improbably slim. The case now hinged on Dr. Paul Terry.

Two months after the court barred Scott's team from bringing in new experts, Sanders filed a motion for summary judgment—a fresh attempt to kill the suit. In a status conference, Sanders had outlined the legal burden he believed the plaintiffs had to meet to proceed to trial. "Everybody knew that there was stuff in fly ash that was capable of causing health problems," he said. "Everybody admitted that. TVA admitted it. Jacobs admits it. That's not the issue." The issue, Sanders said, was "whether at this site it was at levels that could cause any of the plaintiffs the health problems they have." Sanders, in the defense's new motion, went further, arguing that the plaintiffs, who still lacked a true expert report, hadn't supplied evidence to prove that fly ash had caused the workers' medical conditions. This was why, he argued, Varlan should spare Jacobs the hassle of a trial.

Sanders's motion didn't leave Friedman with a rosy feeling. To overcome summary judgment, the plaintiffs' team would have to prove, with convincing evidence, that fly ash had almost certainly harmed the workers. Terry's still-unfinished report would serve as the basis for their response, which meant they had to do everything they could to ensure that he finished it—which was exactly why Friedman had insisted on adding Gary Davis to the team.

Scott tried not to worry about summary judgment. He felt sure the workers had the truth on their side, and he would appeal Varlan's decision to the Sixth Circuit if he killed the case again. What worried Scott was Sanders's bid to block Terry from testifying. Scott would have to trust that Davis would sort everything out.

Fifteen minutes before two o'clock one afternoon, Mary Scott, Jim's ex, turned her silver Mercedes station wagon onto a leafy residential street in Knoxville's Sequoyah Hills neighborhood and dialed the police. It was March 14, 2018, five days after Sanders filed the motion for summary judgment. When the dispatcher answered, Mary told the woman her name. "I have been court-ordered to have a police escort come to my home to remove my ex-husband," she explained, in an edgy tone.

By her home, she meant 3639 Talahi Drive, the white house that she and Jim and their children had shared until a judge ordered her to leave nearly three years earlier, after she smashed Jack's iPad and Nintendo. Jim had retained full custody of his sons ever since and stayed with them on Talahi. Mary, for her part, had moved in with her mother, who lived in a condo a street or two over. But, at a hearing that March morning, Mary had convinced a Knox County judge to make a dramatic decision that upturned the status quo. At her lawyer's urging, the judge had signed a restraining order that forbade Jim from entering the Talahi home "at any time, for any purpose, other than a prescheduled opportunity to gather his personal effects." The judge went further, transferring custody of Sam to his mother. "I have full custody of my son," Mary told the dispatcher as she drove, "so I need an escort to go over to my house."

The basis for the judge's bold ruling was a motion that Mary's attorney had written outlining Jim's alleged shortcomings as a caretaker.

Sam's grades in schools had plunged, and his attendance record was "littered with tardiness and absences," her attorney wrote. Moreover, the previous spring, a judge had ordered Jim to let Mary spend time with Sam some weekends, which Jim did for a while, until he didn't. Worse still, overwhelmed by work, he had fallen behind on taking Sam to court-ordered counseling sessions, and Mary alleged that he drove both sons to school, though a judge had ordered her to do it instead, in light of his drunk-driving charge, which at the time had yet to be downgraded to reckless driving. (Jim denied this accusation and said his parents drove the boys.) In court that spring morning, Mary had insisted that, in sum, Jim was purposefully preventing Sam from seeing her. She'd previously testified, "When [my sons] don't respond to me on the phone, they don't respond to me in a message, and they have no contact with me—that is alienation." The judge agreed.

On the phone with the dispatcher, Mary explained that she wanted an officer present when she picked up Sam. "I'm real nervous about it," she said. She turned onto Kenesaw Avenue and drove a quarter of a mile down the road to Sequoyah Hills Presbyterian, a church she had attended since the early 1990s.

She told the dispatcher that an officer could meet her there. "My house is just one street up." She reiterated that the court had ordered Jim to leave immediately. "He can take my oldest son with him," she said, adding, "I have control of my house. So I'm going to have to call a locksmith and change the locks and do all that." The dispatcher asked if Mary had paperwork confirming that she had been awarded custody of Sam, and she replied that she did.

Impatient, Mary pulled onto Talahi Drive. As she approached the family home, she spied Buddy Scott's car parked in the driveway. It was spring break, and the old judge was watching both her sons while Jim worked. She told the dispatcher that she wasn't going to wait for the police. "He might leave with my child," she said of Buddy.

She pulled into the driveway, blocking Buddy's car, and then climbed out of the Mercedes with the judge's order in hand.

Mary took Sam and demanded that everyone else leave the house. The judge had agreed to give her primary custody of Sam in an ex-parte, or one-sided, hearing, so Jim hadn't been present to defend himself. He raced home from work once he learned of the decision, but nothing could be undone. He and Jack had to get out. Blindsided and furious, they packed their things and drove to Jim's parents in Oak Ridge. Jack would sleep in Jim's childhood bedroom; Jim was to take the couch.

What the hell are we going to do? Jack asked his dad.

Jim said he didn't know. His mind pinwheeled. He couldn't fathom how a judge could think that ripping away Sam from everything—his brother, his father, his grandparents—was in his best interest. Sam clearly wanted to be with Jim, so why upend his world? "My dad has done nothing wrong," Sam told a county official about a week after the judge awarded his mother custody. "My mom has lied to the courts, and they've believed it. It's crazy."

A few years earlier, a psychologist had determined that neither Jack nor Sam should spend time with their mother. Another psychologist had concurred, writing that even "casual contact" at school or at church should be avoided.* Yet the judge had disregarded these opinions, along with Jim's assertion that he had stopped dropping off Sam for weekend visits only after Mary reneged on a promise to the judge to undergo a psychological evaluation, to determine whether she was fit to care for Sam alone. Mary denied this: "Everything the court ordered me to do, I did." And that, she said, was why she won custody of Sam; it was *Jim* who had not followed the court's directives.

Shortly after leaving the house on Talahi, Jim petitioned the judge to transfer custody of Sam to Jim's parents, Buddy and Mildred—the next-best thing to having custody of Sam himself. The judge briefly allowed this arrangement, but Mary would ultimately have primary custody of the boy.

Jim didn't love living with his parents in Oak Ridge. They nagged at each other, in the way old couples sometimes will, and they hardly ever slept. Though Jim had agreed to sell the Talahi house and split the proceeds with Mary, he hadn't yet received an acceptable offer, and he couldn't buy a new place until he did, lest he complicate his already messy divorce by purchasing a large asset—not that he had much cash

* Mary Scott later said she disagreed with these psychologists and claimed that Jim had swayed their opinions. She called any assertion that she wasn't fit to care for her sons absurd.

to spend anyway. The workers' case had drained his savings, and he would eventually pay his divorce attorney six figures in fees and all but give up fighting his ex in court.

He and Jack stayed with his parents throughout the spring and summer. Then Jim decided, with almost no warning, that he needed to move downtown for work. He and Jack bounced between hotels, switching places every few days, depending on whichever hotel had deals. Most nights, Jack, a sophomore with a heavy course load, would study and do homework in the suite, while Jim worked in the hotel lobby. He was tired—tired of the upheavals, tired of having no home, tired of the unending work. During his time as an assistant district attorney, he'd seen hellish cases—rapes, murders, child abuse. Any case involving an injured kid blew a hole of grief through his heart. But, in time, he'd learned to compartmentalize his work and his personal life, stuffing each case into a tiny box he could abandon in a corner of his mind. The workers' case had collapsed the two worlds together. He had no life outside the case.

As he toiled, he found himself longing for the warm, peaceful evenings when he would run or bike down the Sequoyah Hills greenway. He missed, too, the summer nights when he and Jack, still a little boy then, would walk up and down the neighborhood's dark streets, flashlight beams sweeping over the front lawns and the trees that swayed overhead. The workers' case and his divorce had brought an abrupt, bitter end to that gentle stage of his life, and he knew he would never get it back.

Gary Davis, meanwhile, focused his efforts on Dr. Paul Terry. Davis had significant experience working on reports of the sort that Terry needed to finish. When Davis was in his twenties, he'd taken a job in the administration of California governor Jerry Brown, working in an agency that developed and promoted environmentally beneficial technologies. Davis had focused on hazardous-waste dump sites, and, after he entered private practice, he took cases related to that specialty. He spent hours talking on the phone and emailing with Terry about his unfinished report. Davis didn't tell Terry what to write—the doctor wouldn't have listened even had he tried—but he wanted to ensure that every word Terry wrote was supported by fact, because Jimmy Sanders would surely seize on any that wasn't.

None of the lawyers knew whether Judge Varlan would allow the trial to commence, considering Jacobs's motion for summary judgment and Terry's unfinished research, but they had to prepare all the same. They exchanged countless emails and text messages about strategy, and they scheduled conference calls to discuss ideas. For days at a time, John Dupree decamped to Birmingham and took over Jeff Friedman's glass conference room, filling it with pipe smoke. There, he and Friedman storyboarded the trial on a whiteboard, plotting when to present key evidence to the jury.

Jim Scott, as part of his trial prep, watched the legal thriller *A Civil Action*, starring John Travolta, at least fifteen times, studying it for tips and to boost his enthusiasm for the trial. The team had agreed that Friedman would examine most of the witnesses, but Scott would still play a critical role in the proceedings.

Dupree suspected that, at times, Scott felt sidelined by Davis and Friedman, or at least less central to the team than he had been before. It didn't help that Friedman and Davis sometimes poked fun at Scott's disorderliness. But Scott had collected the team's best evidence and found Terry. The case was a mess, sure, but a winnable mess. Plus, Dupree gave Scott tremendous credit for agreeing to bring in Friedman and letting him lead their trial team. "When you have an attorney like Jeff Friedman, you got to let him get up there and shine," Dupree explained to a friend one morning. "And if you're smart, you sit and watch and learn."

Keith Stewart, for his part, tried to keep the six lawyers organized. On Saturday afternoons, after working on the case all week, Stewart would call Friedman to discuss their progress. "This case is going to mean one of two things," Stewart told Friedman once. "Bankruptcy or a private jet." The odds tilted toward the former, it seemed.

Tyler Roper, the former mountain-climbing guide, kept busy, too, though not in a way the other lawyers on the team expected. After Roper, who grew up in Nashville, graduated from law school at UT in

2001, he'd landed a position at one of Knoxville's largest law firms—a prime first job, had he been assigned to the litigation department. Instead, he got stuck in the health-care division, mostly doing compliance work. He compared the experience to being locked inside a tiny closet with copies of the tax code and Medicare laws and not being let out for a year and a half. He loathed it. He wanted to meet with clients and argue motions and take depositions and do all the fun stuff trial lawyers got to do.

But in that job Roper learned to embrace the simple, terrible fact that he had to read every mind-numbing page of every mind-numbing document to gain mastery of a subject. There were no shortcuts. After he joined the plaintiffs' team, he generally did as instructed by John Dupree and Jim Scott and attended the workers' depositions, but, whenever Roper had open time, he tried to learn everything he could about fly ash and about the Kingston cleanup. Over the years, Scott had pored over an untold number of documents and, in doing so, gained a strong understanding of the project, but Scott, true to his scattered nature, hadn't organized his findings for the other attorneys to reference. All the information rattled around in his head.

In the fourteenth-floor office, Roper rummaged through notebooks and binders that Scott had crammed with material and, fortunately, kept in an off-site storage locker, sparing them from the blaze. Roper knew the workers were sick, of course, but he wanted to understand what exactly had caused some of their rare illnesses, like Ansol Clark's polycythemia vera. He stayed late into the night reading papers. "What the hell are you doing up there?" his wife would ask when she called to check in. The answer was that he'd decided to learn all he could about radium, a cancer-causing radioactive metal found in coal ash.

Coal, like nearly every rock, naturally contains trace quantities of radium. After the Kingston disaster, TVA acknowledged that the spilled coal ash contained radium but claimed that the ash was "less radioactive than low-sodium table salt." But, as Roper had already learned, on three trips, between January 2009 and March 2009, Avner Vengosh's team at Duke had collected samples of the Kingston coal ash, and their analysis undercut TVA's salt claim, finding unacceptably high levels of radium in the ash. What Roper discovered, though, was that TVA had to confront the coal ash's radioactivity itself after some of the Kingston coal ash it shipped to the landfill in Uniontown, Alabama, was found to contain radium in levels well above the government's safety threshold.* Alabama authorities granted the landfill an exemption to store the coal ash on-site, but the EPA ordered the workers who unloaded the train cars to wear hazmat suits, along with respiratory protection. There was more: in a 2011 report, TVA disclosed that the radium levels in the Kingston coal ash exceeded acceptable safety standards twofold, meaning it was just as dangerous as the ash in Uniontown; it was, after all, the same ash. But the EPA bowed to pressure from Jacobs's staff, who insisted that hazmat suits would be "a significant hazard" in the summertime and that the dust levels at Kingston didn't warrant such protective clothing anyway. The EPA, in turn, decided not to require the Kingston workers to wear protective attire like that of the Alabama workers. (Weeks after one Jacobs staffer, Sean Healey—Tom Bock's supervisor—encouraged the EPA to adopt this policy, he promised a crowd at a public meeting that Jacobs would provide workers who "routinely contact[ed] ash" with "[hazmat] coveralls if necessary.")

That TVA's and Jacobs's own documents made this narrative clear almost made Roper dizzy. How, he wondered, could the EPA, TVA, and Jacobs justify denying the Kingston workers hazmat suits when the EPA insisted that Uniontown workers wear such protection? But he realized soon enough that the naturally occurring radium in coal ash likely accounted for only a portion of the danger the workers faced. In poring over documents, he grew convinced that the workers hadn't just breathed in regular coal ash, which would have been nasty enough, but that they'd likely breathed in an ultra-contaminated variety, a floating cocktail of arsenic and mercury and uranium.

When Roper explained his theory to Scott, he didn't doubt it, and he didn't have to guess where the radioactive material originated. He grew up there.

* Vengosh's team detected radium at eight picocuries per gram in some Kingston samples, while the Uniontown samples contained as much as ten picocuries per gram. The federal government's safety threshold is five picocuries per gram. Jacobs says it had no involvement in radiation-exposure issues at Kingston and that evidence shows that the workers were not exposed to radiation in levels exceeding health standards.

• • •

At a little past eight in the morning on August 6, 1945, an American B-29 bomber appeared in the skies above Hiroshima, Japan. The aircraft flew at thirty-one thousand feet. When it reached the heart of Hiroshima, at 8:15 a.m., it dropped its payload: an untested nuclear bomb. The weapon, nicknamed Little Boy, contained one hundred and forty-one pounds of highly enriched uranium, nearly all such material in existence at the time. It fell five and a half miles in forty-three seconds. When the bomb was six hundred yards above the ground, a hollow "bullet" of uranium inside of it shot forward and struck another piece of uranium. A white flash flooded the city. Then the boom came, and the world underneath went flat. Little Boy, the first nuclear bomb used in wartime, and the fires it created destroyed almost 70 percent of Hiroshima. Between eighty thousand and one hundred and forty thousand people are believed to have died. A roughly equal number were injured.

The day after the attack, *The New York Times* carried a front-page story with the news. "First Atomic Bomb Dropped on Japan," the banner headline shouted. The paper devoted the better part of ten pages to Hiroshima's destruction, with lengthy statements by President Harry S. Truman and Secretary of War Henry L. Stimson. Almost as surprising as the news of Little Boy was a front-page story in the same edition about three "hidden cities" where the U.S.'s nuclear bombs had been secretly built. One lay on the New Mexico mesa, another in the scrub desert of Washington State. The third—"the most remarkable of the towns and heart of the entire project," the *Times* reported—lay in East Tennessee and had a quaint name that had never appeared on any local map: Oak Ridge.

Almost three years earlier, in October 1942, the U.S. Army had begun clearing a tract of rugged, hilly territory along the Clinch River near the village of Clinton, Tennessee, twenty-five miles northwest of Knoxville and twenty miles upstream from Kingston. The War Department selected the site, with the help of TVA staff, in part owing to its proximity to two TVA hydroelectric dams, Norris and Watts Bar, which could supply the government's bomb factories with power. The territory measured seventeen miles long and seven miles wide and comprised fifty-nine thousand acres—an area ten thousand acres larger than Acadia

National Park, in Maine. The Army constructed a barbed-wire fence around the sprawling property, and seven guarded gates controlled who went in and out. Over the next three years, Oak Ridge would grow into the fifth largest city in Tennessee, with a peak population of eighty thousand people. The governor didn't know it existed.

To create a viable bomb, the Americans needed to separate natural uranium, a rare metal, into two parts: the abundant and mostly useless U-238 isotope and the rare and fissile U-235 isotope. The Army built two primary enrichment complexes to produce this bomb fuel. The first, on the eastern end of what became known as the Oak Ridge Reservation, was called Y-12. By the end of the war, its nine main process buildings would cover an area equivalent to twenty football fields. The second primary complex, the K-25 Gaseous Diffusion Plant, was on the opposite end of the reservation, near the Clinch River. At the time, the Ford Motor Company's Willow Run plant, in Michigan—converted

The K-25 Gaseous Diffusion Plant, in Oak Ridge, Tennessee, was, at the time of its completion in 1945, the largest building in the United States.

to make B-24 bombers during the war—was generally considered the U.S.'s largest factory and, for that matter, the nation's largest building by area, boasting two and a half million square feet of floor space. K-25 had more than twice that footage.

To house Oak Ridge's workers—very few of whom had any idea what they were producing—the Army built eighty-nine dorms, forty-two barracks, three apartment buildings, and nine thousand prefabricated homes (some designed by TVA). It also shipped in thirty-eight hundred trailers and fifteen hundred hutments. Housing still ran short. Twenty thousand workers commuted from outlying towns each day. By the war's end, Oak Ridge boasted eight elementary schools, seventeen different churches or religious buildings, multiple theaters, a hospital, a dentist's office, a singing society, and a symphony orchestra, plus one hundred and sixty-five retail stores. A hot-dog stand sold Coney Island franks for ten cents.

By the time Jim Scott was growing up in Oak Ridge, in the 1970s, the guard gates around the city had come down, but the town's central mission remained the same. After the war, Y-12 and K-25 continued to enrich uranium to grow the U.S.'s atomic-weapons stockpile. Today Y-12 is the country's only industrial complex dedicated to producing and storing weapons-grade uranium. Every U.S. nuclear warhead includes uranium fabricated at the complex.

When Scott was a teenager, he often water-skied at Melton Hill Lake, a vast TVA reservoir on the Clinch River. The Oak Ridge Reservation ran along the lake's western bank. Forested hills hid from view the industrial sprawl of Y-12 and K-25, but Scott saw signs along the shore that warned against eating fish from the reservoir. Years earlier an underground tank on the reservation had sprung a leak, contaminating the ground with radioactive cobalt and cesium.

As Scott entered high school, stories of Oak Ridge's pollution became a fixture of local newspaper coverage. In 1983, when he was fifteen, the Department of Energy, which had taken charge of the reservation in the 1970s, admitted that more than two million pounds of mercury had gone "missing" from Y-12 over several decades. Hundreds of thousands of pounds of it had ended up in a narrow stream that winds through the reservation and through Oak Ridge's main commercial district before it empties into the Clinch. The rest of the mercury was either released into the air or spilled on the ground or was entirely unaccounted for.

The disclosures kept coming. When Scott was seventeen, the DOE revealed that between 1954 and 1983 fifty-one million pounds of uranium had been buried at Y-12. In a sixty-five-acre burial plot, crews had dug canyonlike trenches where they'd dumped wastewater sludge, scrap metal, and uranium shavings. Over time, rainwater filled the trenches, which a state official later referred to as "witches' cauldrons," and the radioactive runoff mixed with and contaminated the groundwater. Fifty-two settling ponds, filled with nearly three million gallons of acid and nuclear waste, added to the contamination.

The K-25 Gaseous Diffusion Plant, on the other side of the reservation, had its own burial yards, where staff had also dumped vast quantities of radioactive waste. The complex had released thirty-five thousand pounds of uranium into the air. For a while in the 1950s, drinking milk from cows grazing anywhere within twenty-five miles of Oak Ridge meaningfully increased one's cancer risk.

The cool streams that weaved and curved through the reservation suffered some of the worst pollution. Over three decades, Y-12 released an estimated two hundred and eighty thousand pounds of depleted uranium into two creeks, Bear and East Fork Poplar. Water samples taken from East Fork Poplar Creek in 1968 found that the water contained at least fifty-four times more radioactive particles per liter than EPA regulations would later allow. Radioactive cesium, cobalt, and strontium ran into another creek, White Oak, which also flowed into the Clinch River. Frogs bred in the water and became radioactive nuisances. Deer had high levels of radioactive strontium in their bones. An estimated three hundred thousand people ate contaminated fish, courtesy of Oak Ridge. Commercial clammers unwittingly dug up and sold toxic mollusks from the Clinch.

By the time Scott started college, in the late 1980s, Oak Ridge's reputation had morphed from that of a wartime miracle into a bleak B-movie punchline. During his freshman year, when he told classmates where he grew up, a typical response went: *Oh, you're from Oak Ridge. How come you're not glowing green?* He probably heard that joke sixty times before summer break.

The full extent of Oak Ridge's pollution was, and remains, impossible to know. A fire in 1957 destroyed waste-disposal records at one major research lab, and "we know we had some midnight dumping," a DOE contractor told *The Tennessean* in 1997. One retired Oak Ridge chemist claimed that he and other workers had regularly driven to area ponds, thrown in barrels of radioactive waste, and then shot the containers with rifles until they sank. Another Oak Ridge worker alleged that for decades he'd dumped radioactive materials into the Clinch River. "We knew it was bad stuff, but we didn't worry about it," a retired worker once explained.

Scott had lived in Oak Ridge long enough to have heard such stories, so when the Kingston cleanup workers told him about the "hot stuff," he knew what they meant. He had asked about radiation in some depositions. To his disbelief, a TVA supervisor named Gary MacDonald had told him, "I know that there's radioactive material in the Clinch River." MacDonald said he'd heard about it being dredged and piped out of the river, adding, "I assume it would have all been captured somewhere and put in the [ash] stack." Billy Isley, in the deposition before his death, said that he saw crews remove and haul out a boat's dredge head—the suction nozzle on one of the underwater vacuums—after it hit radioactive material in the river. The dredge head was loaded onto a barge. "The next morning we come in," Isley said, "the barge was gone."

The trouble for Scott was that, with his focus on fly-ash exposure and on simply keeping the case alive, he had little time to search for evidence to back up the workers' stories. Roper had the time. He searched government reports posted online. He worried that, since the EPA didn't consider fly ash hazardous waste, Jacobs might use that fact to discredit the workers' case, and Roper wanted to be able to prove that Jacobs had exposed them to other hazards.

One of the first things he learned was that, in the early 1990s, TVA, the EPA, the Army Corps of Engineers, and the DOE had studied the radioactive pollutants in the rivers around Oak Ridge. In a report, written by none other than Jacobs Engineering, the four federal agencies determined that the sediment at the bottom of the Clinch and the lower Emory contained such large quantities of radioactive waste and posed such a threat to public health that they forbade any activity that would disturb the river bottom, such as building a dock, without a special permit. Moreover, the four federal agencies presumed that any sediment dredged from the waters would contain at least some radioactive material, and they vowed to avoid any activity that would disturb the sediment. But in 2008, the coal-ash disaster had done just that, overwhelming the Emory River and stirring up the river bottom.

Following the disaster, TVA had raced to remove fly ash from the Emory. But Roper learned from documents that, before crews got to work, TVA had submitted a dredging plan to the EPA, the U.S. Fish & Wildlife Service, and several other state and federal agencies. In written responses to this plan, an EPA employee and a U.S. Fish & Wildlife employee both warned of "legacy" contaminants from Oak Ridge in the river. TVA, in reply, insisted that its dredging operations would "not disturb river sediments or resuspend potential legacy contaminants," and stated that it would collect and analyze sediment samples as a precaution. TVA followed through, though it initially didn't test for cesium-137, one of the primary radioactive pollutants released from Oak Ridge, and one of the pollutants that made the Chernobyl disaster in Ukraine in 1986 incredibly deadly.

TVA knew from the studies it had participated in during the 1990s that sections of the Emory were highly contaminated. At a community college six months after the Kingston disaster, TVA, EPA, and state officials had even explained to residents that TVA didn't want workers to dredge the lower section of the Emory River because of radioactive contamination. "If we go down there and start dredging," one state employee explained, "we could make a bigger mess than we ever wanted to make." Yet, around this same time, TVA published a report in which it concluded, "There is no evidence that past contamination of sediments would have any impact on TVA's dredging of ash from the Emory River." Tom Kilgore, TVA's chief executive at the time, told members of Congress something similar.

This, Roper realized, was the great lie behind the project's early phase: that dredging wouldn't disturb the river sediment. Of course it would, and did. Two years into the coal-ash cleanup, TVA had released a five-hundred-plus-page report about the project's first major phase. Roper read the entire thing. In it, TVA disclosed that between December 2009 and January 2010 dredging crews had experienced "difficulties" after they encountered high levels of cesium-137—which TVA had evidently begun testing for—near where the Emory River met the Clinch. A 1984 study had detected cesium near the confluence of the rivers at levels thirteen times higher than what TVA and other federal agencies considered safe. (TVA claimed that its testing found cesium-137 in the sediment up to seventeen picocuries per gram, six picocuries per gram above the agencies' agreed-upon limit.) The fly ash had "co-mingled" with this radioactive material, according to one document. Given the high risk of trying to remove the radioactive material, the dredging crews left in place nearly seven hundred thousand tons of ash, spread over some two hundred acres of the river bottom.

An EPA staffer would later testify that, though the discovery of cesium had caused "a lot of discussion" within TVA and the EPA, she had no knowledge of any work stoppage resulting from radioactivity. The workers had told Jim Scott a different story.

One man, Rick Samson, spent time on a debris-removal barge. He alleged that at about three-thirty one winter morning, he and two other guys took a johnboat across the cold, black Emory River to clear a boat's dredge head. The dredge head had teeth that spun and sometimes got clogged as it sucked up ash. In the darkness, the three men watched as the dredge head rose dripping from the water. Stuck in its teeth was a rusted, leaking barrel. "Back the boat up!" one man yelled. They had all taken hazardous-waste training; they recognized the hazard placard on the barrel's side. "That was a radioactive drum," Samson recalled the men saying as the johnboat whined through the water to shore. The dredging boat dropped the barrel back into the water to avoid exposing anyone, and the three men reported the incident to their foreman. Over the next week, they watched as divers, sporting protective suits, hauled to shore dozens of similar-looking barrels. At about three-thirty one morning, a few days after the divers dragged the barrels to shore, Samson, early to his shift, watched as a forklift loaded the barrels into an unmarked dump truck. Once the job was done, the dump truck promptly left the site, and he never saw it again.

The two men with Samson on the boat that night later submitted sworn statements that supported his account; Clint Mannis, a dredge operator, recalled an almost identical story. The barrels, he believed, contained cesium-137.

Another man, Brian Thacker, who worked on a dredging boat,

alleged that on at least two occasions he alerted Jacobs staff that his crew had hit hot stuff in the river. Jacobs staff told him it was harmless, and he believed them until blisters and sores formed on his arms. In the spring of 2013, Thacker filed a report with a TVA office that investigated employee concerns. In it, he alleged that, over a year and a half's time, he had been exposed to radiation eight to ten times per shift but supervisors had insisted to him that the radiation dose was "no more than an X-ray."

Edwin Small, TVA's chief litigator, helped to draft a response to Thacker's complaint. It was Small who had, in not so many words, called the Kingston landowners rednecks in the Knoxville Convention Center years earlier during mediation in the land cases, and, by the time Thacker came forward, Small was already aware that sickened cleanup workers had contacted Jim Scott for representation. TVA responded to Thacker a month after he submitted his complaint. "Your concern was found to be unsubstantiated," TVA's email read. The message explained that one hundred and ninety-three samples had been taken in the exclusion zone, the ground zero of the disaster, and not one had detected cesium-137. But TVA's email to Thacker didn't mention that one hundred and fourteen samples taken from the river sediment, not the exclusion zone, had, in fact, detected cesium-137. TVA's response was, in Roper's view, a deception and a lie.

Roper outlined his findings in long emails to Friedman, Scott, and the other lawyers. He wanted to educate everybody about "what the fuck was actually going on," as he put it in one message. He felt certain that contaminated fly ash from the river had been sucked to shore and set out to dry, then become airborne. "Everyone [at TVA and Jacobs] knew if it got in the air, people would start dying," he wrote.* He explained that once the workers inhaled the fly ash, "the radioactive contaminants [proceeded] quickly into the bloodstream and then into the bones." He added, "This is not conjecture. This is fact."

Scott read Roper's emails with great interest. In his opinion, one of the more compelling connections between the Kingston disaster and the Oak Ridge radiation was a man named Steve McCracken, a DOE

* Jacobs claims that it had no role in evaluating or addressing radiation-exposure issues during the cleanup project.

manager. After reports surfaced of Oak Ridge's contamination in the early 1980s, the DOE had launched a decades-long cleanup project. McCracken had overseen this effort beginning in 2003. Oddly enough, days after McCracken announced his retirement from the DOE, in 2009, TVA hired him as general manager of the Kingston cleanup. Why, Scott wondered, would TVA hire someone with experience in radioactive contamination to run a coal-ash cleanup?* The question seemed to answer itself: coal ash wasn't TVA's chief concern, or at least not its only one.

Roper and Scott agreed on the significance of the radioactive sediment and thought their team should focus on it at trial. The lawyers debated the idea in Keith Stewart's office. Large windows looked out over downtown Knoxville; the TVA Towers stood a few blocks away. Scott sat at a table near the door. "Radiation is something people understand," he said, especially with Y-12 and K-25 a short drive from Knoxville, whereas the jurors likely knew nothing about coal ash.

Roper, who had dark hair and retained something of a mountain climber's build, sat on a couch near Scott. In his view, Jacobs's and TVA's failure to protect the workers constituted criminally negligent homicide. The site was radioactive, he said. Vengosh's studies and TVA's own documents proved it. "Why don't we just blow this whole thing wide open with the radioactive content now?" he asked. It would help their team in the second stage, when they would fight over damages.

John Dupree found Roper's findings interesting, but the case their team had built centered on coal ash, not radiation, and he felt bound by the facts they'd entered into the record. Let's keep the focus on fine particulate matter—on dust—he told the others. They needed to focus on what they had. Besides, Dupree added, Roper and Scott hadn't recruited any expert to support their theories.

"Radiation is like stepping in dog shit!" Roper said. "It gets everywhere." And it had clearly gotten all over the workers.

Stewart, Roper's oldest and closest friend in the office, was unmoved. "There's evidence of it in the ash," he agreed. "But we don't have it nailed down." They needed an expert to link radiation exposure to the workers'

* Stephen McCracken left TVA after three years and later took a job with Jacobs Engineering.

diseases. They didn't have one, Stewart said, and until they did, "we can't prove it."

Jeff Friedman shared Stewart's view and grew annoyed with Roper's repeated emails. Friedman discussed the matter one evening with Davis, in town for work, as they drove through Birmingham in Friedman's Toyota pickup. Why, Friedman asked Davis, if Roper and Scott thought radionuclides posed such a danger, hadn't they included it in the case already and found experts who could testify about it?

Davis had the same questions. Friedman and Davis sided with Dupree and Stewart and outvoted Roper and Scott about the direction of the trial. Their team had good evidence about coal ash, Friedman told the others. And coal ash needed to remain their focus. That was their case, for better or worse.

One hundred and fifteen miles separate Asheville, North Carolina, and Knoxville, and the highways that curve and wind between them lead up and over the Blue Ridge Mountains and down through the big green woods of the Cherokee National Forest, a mountain wilderness of severe slopes, narrow valley streams, and cool blue swimming holes. In June 2018, four months before the scheduled start of the Jacobs trial, Gary Davis made the drive.

Davis and the other plaintiffs' attorneys still had no idea whether the trial would commence. But, to Davis's relief, Dr. Paul Terry had met the court's final deadline, submitting a ninety-five-page report in late April of that year. Now Davis needed to convince Magistrate Guyton why he and Judge Varlan should allow Terry to testify. Hence the Knoxville trip.

The hearing began at 9:30 a.m. John Dupree and Jim Scott joined Davis at the plaintiffs' table. As Davis waited for Guyton to take his place at the bench, he knew the main issue he'd have to address: though Terry had met the court's filing deadline, he hadn't completed a full epidemiological study but merely a review of scientific literature. Initially, Scott had planned to have Terry produce a lengthy epidemiological report in which he compared the workers' health with that of a sample group. But, once Davis got involved, he realized that Terry would never be able to complete such a rigorous study in time for the trial. At Davis's urging, Terry had instead analyzed seventy academic studies on fly ash's constituents. In doing so, he'd concluded that fly ash had at least a causal relationship to cancer and other diseases. Davis hoped Guyton would be convinced.

Jimmy Sanders approached the lectern first that morning. "Your Honor, may it please the Court," he said. Terry, Sanders said, hadn't completed an epidemiological study, as he'd promised, but had instead written something completely different. And it was a "poor substitute . . . because all it is is a literature review," Sanders said. The plaintiffs, Sanders went on, were "trying to prove something that cannot be proved scientifically valid." There was no evidence that proved that fly ash's constituents had been absorbed into the workers' bodies, only conjecture. And because of that, Sanders argued, no jury would be able to find Jacobs liable for harming the workers.

When Davis stepped up to the lectern, he knew the entire case hinged on this hearing. He had been practicing environmental law for thirty-five years and had had cases thrown out because of weak expert reports. This case couldn't be allowed to fall into that category, he told himself. A jury had to hear this case.

Speaking in a deep, dry monotone, Davis conceded that an epidemiological study would be "the gold standard" in a case of this nature. But Terry wasn't a professional witness, Davis said, and "it was a bit naive on his part" to think he would be able to complete such a study in time. But his literature review still addressed the all-critical question of whether coal ash was capable of injuring the workers, and that was the plaintiffs' sole requirement at this stage of litigation. Davis told Guyton there was plenty of general evidence to suggest that the plaintiffs had inhaled fly ash. "We've got photographs of [workers] just totally covered with coal ash from head to toe, every orifice practically," Davis explained. "I mean, these guys were breathing it in day in and day out. They breathed clouds of it."

In Guyton's ruling, issued a month later, he agreed with Sanders that Terry's literature review was unlike the study he'd promised to produce. But Guyton decided that Terry's literature review was "harmless" to the defense and admissible under the so-called *Daubert* standard, a hurdle, established by the U.S. Supreme Court, that scientific evidence must clear to be admitted in a courtroom. For these reasons, Guyton concluded, the court would allow Terry to testify.

Then, less than a month before the scheduled start of trial, Judge Varlan brought a sledgehammer down on Jimmy Sanders. Varlan, in a thirty-one-page ruling, disagreed with Sanders's argument that in the first trial phase each worker had to prove precisely how much coal ash they were exposed to. Varlan also disagreed that Terry's literature review failed to establish fly ash's hazards. On the contrary, Varlan wrote, Scott's team had "put forward evidence from which a reasonable jury could find that plaintiffs' exposure was capable of causing the complained-of diseases." In fact, Varlan added, the evidence was "legion."

Jacobs's motion for summary judgment was denied. The two parties could proceed to trial. Jeff Friedman read Varlan's ruling carefully. He had never seen a judge use the word "legion" in such a context, so he pulled up a dictionary to make sure he understood. *Legion*, an adjective: very large in size, numerous, many, multiple. Friedman had just found his new favorite word.

On the morning of October 16, 2018, Jim Scott put on a cheap dark suit. He never dressed too sharply for trial; he never wanted a jury to think he was different from them. After months of bouncing between hotels, Scott had recently bought a two-bedroom condo across the river from downtown Knoxville, though he'd hardly had time to settle in. The case left no room for other concerns. Nearly six years had passed since the autumn evening when the workers first visited his office on Kingston Pike; since that time, more than two hundred former coal-ash workers had fallen ill, and thirty had died. Scott worried that Ansol Clark might be next. Janie had recently asked him to deliver the eulogy at Ansol's funeral, whenever the day came. Ansol struggled to get out of bed some mornings, she explained. He had debilitating spells; and his mind slipped. Scott told Janie that of course he would speak at Ansol's funeral. In the meantime, though, Scott needed to focus on the task at hand, because today, at long last, Jacobs would have to answer for its actions.

At about eight o'clock, Scott met Keith Stewart, Tyler Roper, and John Dupree at their office on the fourteenth floor of 625 Market Street. They'd agreed to walk to the courthouse together in solidarity. For Scott, knotted with adrenaline and nerves, the two-block stroll from the office to the federal courthouse was a blur.

The trial concerned only the lead case—*Adkisson et al. v. Jacobs Engineering*—that Scott had first filed against the company. But the jury's verdict would likely be applied to the other cases Scott had filed afterward on behalf of some two hundred additional cleanup workers and their family members. As he rode the elevator to the courthouse's fourth floor, he felt confident in the case his team had built. He knew that the facts and law tilted in the workers' favor, and yet the stakes still felt crushingly high. The case centered on Ansol and the other plaintiffs and Jacobs's actions against them, of course. But it was also about whether the working class could beat the C-suite; whether "hillbilly lawyers," as Dupree called them, could beat elite corporate defense attorneys; and about whether strong evidence could beat fat pocketbooks. Perhaps above all, though, the case was about whether the federal government had failed its people.

There were nearly seven hundred and fifty coal-ash ponds spread throughout the United States, from Massachusetts to Washington State and nearly everywhere in between. The EPA had not only let power companies fill these ponds with toxic coal-ash slurry that it knew could harm millions of people, but it had also maintained publicly that coal ash posed no significant health threat. This policy failure, this deception, had allowed TVA, in turn, to pollute the rivers and the air and the dirt of the Southeast while telling the people who lived there that it had come to save them, to deliver them from the evils of underdevelopment. The trial offered Scott a chance to unravel this fiction: a coal-ash exposure case had never reached trial in a federal court, as far as he or anyone else knew. This was his astronaut moment, his opportunity to achieve something improbable and grand. If Scott's team prevailed in this first all-important trial phase, they might be able to win a billion dollars or more for the workers, or so they hoped. But, if the jury sided with the defense, all his work would amount to nothing, a possibility he couldn't consider. He was a speck hurtling through the sky. Now he needed to bring the shuttle back down to Earth.

With the full strain and heaviness of the day pressing down on him, Scott strode into courtroom number 4 a few minutes before nine o'clock. Dark green carpet covered the floor of the cavernous courtroom, and large white pillars held up the high ceiling. Jamie Satterfield, of *The Knoxville News Sentinel*, sat in the gallery on a wooden bench. The local

NBC affiliate had sent a reporter as well and would run a segment about the trial during its evening broadcast. Workers and their spouses and paralegals and attorneys—including Stewart, Roper, and Dupree—filled the remaining benches. Throughout much of the trial, Stewart sat next to Sandy Sharp, the lawyer who'd paid Scott's salary for two years and who, as a result, had a small financial stake in the case.

As Scott worked his way down the aisle toward the front of the courtroom, he made a point to shake hands with Jimmy Sanders, who warmly returned the gesture. Scott, despite his rage at TVA and Jacobs, liked Sanders; he was chatty and easy to get along with. That a jury might feel similarly wasn't comforting.

Scott took his place at the wooden counsel table between Jeff Friedman and Gary Davis. Scott didn't lack confidence in a courtroom. Judges had told him he was among the best trial lawyers they'd seen. Still, their team had agreed that Friedman, easily the best orator among them, would deliver the opening statement for their side.

Everyone rose when Judge Varlan, in his black robes, stepped into the courtroom a few minutes after nine o'clock. "Good morning, everyone," he said, as he settled behind the bench. "All right," he said. "Based on preparing your openings, I think, Mr. Friedman, you're doing the opening."

"Yes, Your Honor," Friedman said.

"Mr. Sanders," Varlan said, turning to the defense, "are y'all still in the forty-five-minute range now that you've prepared more?"

Sanders said that was correct.

"All right," Varlan said.

After a ten-minute recess, the jury was led in. During the jury-selection process a week earlier, Friedman and the rest of the plaintiffs' team had tried to pick Knoxvillians who would likely extend sympathy to the workers, like teachers or union members, and they tried to avoid rich businessmen, who might favor Jacobs. Over Sanders's objections, the plaintiffs managed to get a nurse seated, a win for their side, since she might be able to explain the medical science to the other jurors when the time came to debate a verdict.

Once the jurors had found their seats in the jury box, on the right side of the room, Varlan explained that the trial would run three or four weeks. He thanked them for their willingness to sit through it.

"Mr. Friedman," Varlan said, after another recess, "you may proceed with opening statements on behalf of the plaintiffs."

Friedman stood at the lectern facing the jury. Crisp shirt, neatly combed hair, warm smile: he looked just as he had the last time he'd tried a case involving the Kingston disaster. That trial, seven years earlier, was important. People had lost their homes, fled their city, feared for their children. But none of them had collapsed on their bedroom floors, or coughed up blood, or wondered if they'd live long enough to see the birth of their grandchildren. None of the homeowners, more to the point, had died. The workers had. The cases didn't compare.

Friedman had an outline of his remarks next to him, but he didn't look at it. A jury would never rule in his clients' favor, he believed, if he read from notes instead of talking to them person to person. He didn't want to overpromise explosive evidence, but he did want to hit the defense right away.

He looked squarely at the ten men and women seated in the jury box—all eyes on him, everyone waiting for his words.

"Ladies and gentlemen," he began, in a sure voice, "my name is Jeff Friedman. It's my honor to address you here today." He said he was going to tell them a story, a story about a disaster. "Disasters leave scars," he said. "They leave scars that live on—scars on the people, scars on the communities. Nowhere, ladies and gentlemen, is that more true than what happened in Kingston . . . on December 22nd of 2008."

It's a cliché that trial lawyers are actors who preform for a ten- or twelve-person audience as opposed to the public. Friedman didn't act. He believed deeply in the workers' cause, and he spoke to the jury with the sort of earnestness and the moral seriousness usually reserved for close friends. He explained that the coal-ash disaster had destroyed people's homes and wrecked the environment. But, he said, in a clear, confident tone, "the illnesses and the health problems that our clients are suffering from are every bit as real as the [coal-ash] disaster itself. It was what we refer to as a second disaster."

Dupree, positioned at a projector next to Friedman, pulled up an aerial photo of the Kingston site. The disaster had made headlines across the country, Friedman explained. "TVA had to move fast," he said, and because of that, it "gave huge financial incentives to contractors, most notably Jacobs Engineering." Jacobs alone stood to earn $1.5 million on top of its $64 million fee if it kept the cleanup project moving. But, Friedman said, the on-site air-monitoring devices presented Jacobs with a big problem. The results, had they been accurately recorded, would have revealed that the workers were being exposed to dangerous quantities of fly ash, and that would have required Jacobs, and TVA, to take extra, time-consuming precautions to protect the workers. To avoid this, said Friedman—eyes still locked on the jury, his voice still sure—Jacobs staff often deployed the air monitors when the fly ash was wet from rain, since less of it was airborne then. Jacobs was now using the manipulated data, Friedman said, to claim that it hadn't harmed the workers.

Friedman promised the jury that the evidence would show that the workers suffered "significant and repeated exposure to fly ash." He added that the evidence would illustrate, clearly, that Jacobs had failed to provide the workers with respiratory protection. And, Friedman said, "we believe Dr. Terry's testimony will support the claims in this case on behalf of the plaintiffs."

For many years, the law firm Neal & Harwell occupied the twentieth floor of 150 Fourth Avenue North, in downtown Nashville. People called it the R2D2 building, because of the *Star Wars* character it resembled. Jimmy Sanders's office had a blue-and-salmon-pink oriental rug and windows that overlooked the wide, dull Cumberland River. His computer monitor faced the door. In the weeks leading up to a trial, other attorneys walking by would often notice him playing solitaire for hours on end. After these attorneys tried a case with him, they realized that, as he played, he was stewing on the facts and deciding which documents to focus on and which to ignore. "If it's not a home run," he would tell associates when reviewing evidence for trial, "why the hell do you have this document in here?" Sanders didn't expect to win every case. "I know . . . the verdict could be awful," he once told an interviewer. But sometimes his job, like in the *Exxon Valdez* case, was to lose less, to limit the damage for whichever company had hired him. And to do that he wrote detailed examination outlines and hired jury consultants to inform his strategy. He wanted to know, as he once put it, "What's going to resonate? What's not going to work? What should we say? What issues will hurt us?"

He'd clearly put the same degree of rigor into preparing Jacobs's defense. In the Knoxville courthouse, after Judge Varlan signaled that Sanders could now give the opening statement for Jacobs, he crossed the green carpet to the lectern and faced the jury. Sanders's legal mentor had been Jim Neal, a famed trial lawyer whom Robert F. Kennedy had tapped, in 1961, to lead the Justice Department's prosecution of the labor leader Jimmy Hoffa. Neal went on to defend the Ford Motor Company in suits over the design flaws in its Pinto subcompact. Before Neal's death, in 2010, he had often advised younger trial attorneys, like Sanders, to "stay out of the capillaries and stay in the arteries" while in court. His protégé had clearly internalized this advice.

"This is not a complicated case," Sanders told the jury. "It may sound complicated, but it's simple." Five and a half years' worth of air-monitoring data proved that the coal ash was "incapable of causing the harm" alleged by the workers, he said. Of course, Sanders went on, Jeff Friedman and Jim Scott and the rest of the plaintiffs' team would argue otherwise. But, he said, the EPA and state environmental officials had time and again signed off on reports that Jacobs's monitoring data was accurate.

Sanders said the workers' allegations against Jacobs were lies. They had lied about Jacobs denying them respiratory protection, and they had lied about being deceived about coal ash's potential dangers. Besides, the coal ash wasn't dangerous anyway, at least not at the levels present at Kingston.

Sanders conceded that Tom Bock had told the workers that they could eat a pound of fly ash a day and be fine, but that, Sanders said, was "a gross exaggeration to make a point." And Bock's point was that, based on samples collected by state and federal agencies, the workers would need to ingest a pound of coal ash every day for the rest of their working lives for the arsenic it contained to cause them harm. "That was no lie," Sanders said. Then Sanders addressed the workers' requests for dust masks and respirators: the prescriptions signed by the workers' family doctors meant nothing, he said. That was because an "independent doctor"—provided by TVA—had to evaluate whether the workers were healthy enough to wear a dust mask or respirator, and many were not.

After a brief recess following Sanders's opening statement, Friedman wasted no time calling to the stand one of the plaintiffs' strongest witnesses—Robert Muse. Muse, a former TVA safety coordinator, had a round head and a goatee and wore a light-orange polo shirt. He was the only TVA employee, former or current, who had volunteered to testify on the workers' behalf.

Friedman knew that Muse had contacted Scott about testifying because he'd spent significant time with the cleanup workers in the exclusion zone, the ground zero of the disaster, and he felt that TVA and Jacobs had ignored their health concerns, some of which he shared. While preparing Muse for the trial, Scott and the plaintiffs' lawyers had told him to answer Sanders's questions honestly, no matter what. They'd also advised him against wearing a red shirt, since jurors sometimes responded poorly to the color. They suggested he wear a light color instead, but neither white nor tan, since those were boring, hence Muse's light-orange polo.

Whenever Friedman asked a question during an examination, he would face the ten jurors, focusing their attention, then he would turn back to the witness to await their answer. Muse was no exception. Friedman began by asking some biographical questions. Muse, clearly nervous, explained that he had worked in Roane County for two decades as a paramedic and a firefighter before he took a job at Kingston.

"What was your job title?"

"I was brought in as a field safety coordinator," Muse said. He made sure "people were obeying the safety rules." He said he split his time between Trailer City, where Jacobs and TVA kept offices, and the exclusion zone. Working in the latter, Muse said, "was like going to a very nasty beach every day." Fly ash clung to his clothes and his shoes and got in his nose.

Friedman asked what he understood Jacobs's role to be at Kingston concerning safety.

"They were the overseer of safety for the entire site," said Muse.

Friedman wanted the jury to hear this as early as possible: that Jacobs headed up safety, not TVA or the EPA or anyone else, and that TVA's own safety staff—Muse—had taken cues from Jacobs. (The next day, Tom Heffernan, TVA's head of safety at the cleanup, whom the plaintiffs forced to appear through subpoena, also testified that Jacobs had largely overseen site safety.)

Friedman asked Muse whether he'd ever discussed the need for respiratory protection with members of Jacobs's staff.

Muse explained that, within his first week at Kingston, he'd met with a Jacobs staffer, who told him that "the public perception was that the site was dirty."

"He's saying that to you?" Friedman asked.

"Yes," Muse said. "And he said, at that point in time, we do not want to give the appearance that there is an issue here."

Muse said that Tom Bock had told him much the same, explaining that respiratory protection, hazmat suits, and other such protection would "give the public the impression that we were working with a dirty material," which was "not the direction we wanted to go."

"How did you take the statement?" Friedman asked.

"As a direction," Muse said.

This was the exact sort of anecdote that Friedman hoped would smolder in the jury's mind for the rest of the trial, coloring all other testimony, which was why Friedman had wanted to put Muse, though not the most eager or confident witness, on the stand first.

Friedman shifted direction: "Were there dust masks kept on-site?"

Muse said there were some in a tool room for a short time, but he'd heard from someone else that Bock had ordered them to be removed. But Muse said that when he confronted Bock about throwing out the masks, Bock had reiterated that workers in masks "would give a bad impression to the public."

Friedman understood the importance of giving a jury clear characters to pull for and root against. Bock likely hadn't hatched the scheme to endanger the workers. (Scott had some guesses about which TVA or Jacobs employee might have, but only guesses.) Bock was a yes-man. Still, Bock had treated the workers cruelly, in Friedman's view, so he and Scott and the others had decided to make him their villain.

At Friedman's urging, Muse explained that, as part of his job, he had handed out personal air monitors to workers to wear. Muse said that, at first, he had given workers across the jobsite the devices, so the resulting samples would be representative of the entire cleanup area. But that "stopped after a short period," Muse told Friedman. "We started getting some very high readings [for fly ash]." Muse said that Bock called him into his office one day to discuss the problem. "He told me we wanted to start pulling workers [to wear the monitors] from areas that were less dusty and the wetter areas," Muse said. He also alleged that Bock told him that he planned to "disqualify" the high readings, because he believed the workers hadn't used the air monitors correctly. "He didn't feel that there was that much dust," Muse said.

Muse said at first he didn't think twice about such comments, "because they"—Jacobs—"were leading the safety push and I worked under them."

Then Friedman asked Muse whether he had seen a Jacobs staffer tap out the filter from one of the air monitors, as captured in the video that Jamie Satterfield had posted to *The Knoxville News Sentinel*'s website with one of her articles. "I would not call it tapping," Muse said. "I would call it more of a banging it against the side of the counter."

Judge Varlan excused the jury members at 5:05 p.m. Their day had begun early, and Varlan told the courtroom that he thought it best to begin fresh in the morning. Jeff Friedman and Gary Davis had rented rooms at the old Farragut Hotel, a nine-story brick structure on Gay Street, three blocks from the federal courthouse. After court, the six plaintiffs' attorneys walked over together, as they would almost every evening throughout the trial. They found seats around a table near the bar. In 1933, TVA's first board of directors had held some of its first meetings at the Farragut, and the hotel remained, thanks to some recent remodeling, arguably Knoxville's finest lodging. That explained why Jimmy Sanders and the two Neal & Harwell attorneys he'd brought with him from Nashville were staying there too. As Scott and Friedman and the others ordered drinks and laughed and talked about the promising first day of trial, Sanders marched past silently toward his room.

Scott, buoyant, said he thought Friedman's opening statement soared compared with Sanders's. And Muse had done well, too. "It's going the way it should," Scott added. "They won't win."

Friedman hardly ever felt at ease during a trial, and he certainly didn't now. Sanders hadn't cross-examined any of the workers yet, and Friedman worried how well they would hold up once he did. Friedman always carried such worries with him throughout a trial, and, though he'd been practicing law for decades, examining witnesses sucked the life out of him. During the multi-week showdown in the land cases against TVA, he couldn't reliably drive a vehicle after spending all day in the courtroom; he lacked the energy and focus. And that trial, for all its stress, had centered on property damage. Now people's health, their lives even, were at the center of litigation, which raised the pressure a hundredfold.

After Friedman finished a sandwich, he said goodnight to the others and retired to his room. He would be asleep by eight o'clock. He and Gary Davis planned to meet back in the lobby at five in the morning and prepare for the day ahead.

After dinner and drinks, Dupree, Stewart, Roper, and Scott walked through the darkening streets of Knoxville to the office, where they worked late into the night. They needed to call and prepare the witnesses slated to testify in the coming days and read over their depositions again, to anticipate tough questions the defense might ask.

When deciding who to put on the witness stand, Scott and the rest of the team tried to pick witnesses who could relay different parts of the narrative they wanted to convey to the jury. Ansol Clark knew a lot about the case, but he didn't have any unique knowledge about the site, as Muse did. But the attorneys agreed that a worker's spouse would add a beneficial perspective, which was why Scott had asked Janie to testify. She was on the schedule for the next morning.

"Tell the truth," Scott told her on the phone that night, "because you'll get caught if you don't. And, if you don't understand a question, by God, tell them." He gave a similar spiel to the other witnesses. What he didn't do with Janie, as he did with others, was tell her the questions he planned to ask. He suspected that she might respond more sincerely if he didn't, and he wanted her to be as sincere and honest as possible. That was the main reason why the team wanted her to testify.

The next morning, Ansol and Janie rode the elevator to the lawyers' office. Ansol wore jeans, but Janie had dressed up: a periwinkle long-sleeve shirt, a matching jacket, black slacks. She'd steeled herself for the day ahead. Unlike most of the other workers or their spouses, she had been in federal court once before, in April 1957, shortly before she turned five. She could still recall it vividly. After the slate dam collapsed and killed her two young aunts—the angel-like girls she saw in their caskets—her grandparents had sued the mining company that had built the makeshift barricade. Janie and her mother sat with her grandfather in the courtroom while Janie's grandmother waited in the car. After less than a day in court, the two sides settled for $20,000, a far cry from the $400,000 the family had hoped for. Now, six decades later, Janie didn't want to settle for a similarly small sum, because she knew that money was the only way Jacobs would feel pain, and she wanted the company to suffer.

In the office, Janie and Ansol talked with the attorneys. They had missed the opening statements the previous day, but they planned to sit in the gallery throughout the remainder of the trial. That morning, though, the lawyers told them that Ansol should wait in the office while Janie testified. They didn't want him to distract her or add stress to the moment. Janie said that was okay with her.

Janie was scheduled to testify second, in what would prove to be one of the most significant days of the trial. The lawyers needed to be at the courthouse before she did for other testimony, so shortly before nine o'clock, Scott, Dupree, and Stewart gathered their bags and prepared to leave. As they did, Janie stood up and called Scott over. She took a tiny cross from her pocket. It had given her comfort before her mother's death. She didn't say anything to Scott and simply set the cross in his hand. He looked down at it for a moment, then closed his fist around it.

After an hour or so, Janie kissed Ansol on the forehead, then rode the elevator down to the street with Stewart's longtime legal assistant, Bridgette, and Roper. The three walked the two short blocks to the federal courthouse, passing the lawyers' burned-out office, with their names still written in golden type above the door.

Market Street dead-ends at the federal courthouse, and its clock tower, slender and copper-domed, seems to stand in the middle of the road; it loomed over Janie as she approached. The trio passed through an arched stone entryway at the base of the tower and crossed into the courthouse's grassy yard, bathed in subdued autumn sunlight. Once through security, Janie waited with Roper in an antechamber on the fourth floor. She had Bible verses jotted on notecards, including the well-known verse Philippians 4:13: "I can do all things through Christ who strengthens me." She tried to read, but, as she sat on a couch, her mind couldn't focus. In the courtroom on the other side of the door, a lawyer and a witness seemed to be yelling at each other. *Oh, my Lord*, she thought as she listened, *those lawyers are going to kill me.* The witness, she later learned, was Muse, who had been called back for cross-examination.

Jimmy Sanders had begun the morning's questions easily enough, asking Muse, who today sported a baby-blue polo, to clarify some details about his work experience. Then he asked Muse about an orientation booklet, produced by Jacobs, that everyone who worked at Kingston, including Muse, had received. Sanders gave Muse a copy for reference, and Muse thumbed through it. "Have you got the page," Sanders asked, "where there's a listing of 'activities and hazards'?"

"Yes, sir," said Muse.

Sanders had the page projected onto a screen. "And do you see in the middle of the page," Sanders asked, " 'We avoid these hazards through training, planning, and awareness.' Right?"

"Yes, sir."

"And then the very first one after that is 'handling fly ash.' Right?"

Sanders was clearly trying to illustrate that, contrary to the plaintiffs' allegations, Jacobs had given the workers notice of fly ash's potential dangers. Then Sanders asked why, if Muse thought fly ash posed such a danger, hadn't he done more to implement safety protocols? He was a TVA safety coordinator, after all.

"Obviously, we did know that we had a problem with dust," Muse said. It was clearly a risk. At the outset, he assumed that the water trucks, with their big spray cannons, would be able to suppress the fly ash. But when summer came, the water trucks clearly failed to keep the ash from drying and blowing around the jobsite. Muse said he and other workers had called for water trucks two or three times a day at one point, but they did little good.

Sanders, denying Muse a chance to elaborate, next tried to undercut the witness's credibility by bringing up the personal air-monitoring results that Bock had allegedly shown him, and which, in Sanders's words, Muse "thought" were high.

"No," Muse. He hadn't said that.

"Okay," said Sanders, apparently a bit confused.

"It wasn't *thought*," Muse said, growing irritated. "I saw it." The results were high.

Sanders, briskly moving on, asked about the dust masks that Tom

Bock had allegedly thrown out. Why hadn't Muse told anyone about that? Sanders asked.

"I didn't have to tell anyone else," Muse shot back. "It was general knowledge on the site."

"Mr. Muse, please answer the question," Sanders said. "You told no one, right?"

"No, sir."

And, Sanders asked, Muse knew that a dust mask could have been used to protect against excessive fly-ash exposure, right?

"It could have been," Muse said.

Sanders asked for and got confirmation that Muse had told no one about Bock destroying or altering air-monitoring results and that he had told no one that Bock had banged out the air-monitor filters on a table. And didn't he say yesterday that Bock's "eat a pound a day" comment was a running joke?

"Yeah, a very sick joke," Muse said.

And you were fired for falling asleep in your truck, isn't that right?

"Yes, sir," Muse said.

Friedman, on redirect, clarified with Muse that Jacobs's orientation booklet failed to mention several of fly ash's carcinogens, including beryllium and cadmium, and that it didn't specify that inhaling these hazards could cause breathing problems, among other health issues. With these questions, Friedman hoped the jury would see that Jacobs had not, as Sanders was suggesting, warned the workers of fly ash's dangers. Friedman also had Muse explain that he had seen water trucks spray around some of the stationary air monitors, presumably to manipulate their results.

Sanders, on recross, attacked Muse's credibility for his claim about the water trucks. "That's another thing you didn't tell anybody about, right?" Sanders said.

Muse, ready now, replied, "I went to my higher-ups, which would be in Jacobs. And they were aware of it going on."

"But . . . you didn't tell the TVA safety officers, right? You didn't tell them about this?"

"No," Muse said, ". . . we worked under Jacobs."

After Muse's testimony, Varlan called for a twenty-minute recess.

When Janie stepped into the courtroom during the break, Scott and Friedman were standing toward the back talking. She went to Scott's side. He slid his arm around her for a moment, which put her at ease, after having heard Muse's testimony through the door.

Then she took her place on the witness stand. The chair swiveled, and she turned back and forth as she scanned the courtroom, still in recess and not terribly full yet. She and Ansol had waited for this day for more than five years, and it felt surreal now that it had arrived. She spied Jamie Satterfield, the reporter, who had become a friend, seated in the gallery. Their eyes found each other, and Janie tapped her heart with a closed fist, as if to say, *Love you.* Satterfield did the same. Then Janie's gaze drifted toward the defense table and Jimmy Sanders, snappily dressed, with his long white mustache and long white hair. She wanted to hold her own against him, to make him regret ever deciding to represent a company like Jacobs Engineering. She wouldn't raise her voice like Muse had, but she would stand firm in her own way.

After a deputy called the court back into session, at 10:46 a.m., Varlan asked for the jury to be let back in. Janie watched as they filed into the box, directly to her left. The ten men and women looked like normal people, middle-aged or older, mostly. People like her and Ansol. These were her neighbors, essentially her brothers and sisters.

After Janie was sworn in, Scott approached the lectern. Little lightning bolts seemed to course through him. To Janie, he seemed taller somehow, more confident, stronger even. His dark eyes peered straight into hers, as if to say, All right now, *here we go*, then he began: "Good morning, Ms. Clark."

"Good morning," Janie said.

He asked her to tell the jury a little about her marriage.

Well, she said, she and Ansol had been married for forty-six and a half years. They met in high school, after he returned from the Navy. "I've spent my whole life taking care of my husband, pretty much," she said, "and my son." She faced the jurors as she spoke, looking them in the eyes, then she turned back to Scott as she awaited his next question.

"Ms. Clark," Scott said, "could you tell the ladies and gentlemen of the jury about your hobbies—and, in particular, the one I'm most fond of?"

She knew what he meant. "Well," she began, "one of my hobbies is I bake and I cook, and I like to read books. But my main interest is cooking for my husband."

Scott lobbed her another softball: "Can you tell the ladies and gentlemen of the jury what it's like to have been married to Mr. Clark all this time?"

"Well," she said, almost smiling, "he's the best man you'd ever want to meet." She couldn't imagine life without him, she said. "He's my best friend." She described his work schedule during the first year of the cleanup, how he would leave at five and usually not return home until eight-thirty or nine at night. When he arrived, he would be covered in mucky coal ash. It was in his nose, in his ears, in his eyebrows.

"And we've talked about baking," Scott said, pivoting. "What do you bake besides dinners?"

"Cakes, cookies, and cupcakes," she said.

Scott, who had unbuttoned his jacket, asked what she used to measure her ingredients: "Measuring cups, teaspoons, tablespoons?"

All those, she said.

"If you can," Scott asked, would she describe to the jury, using measuring cups, how much coal ash Ansol would have clinging to him when he arrived home?

"Well," she said, "the thickest part was caked on his boots when he came in." The ash would fill two cups, she guessed. "It was terrible." His blue jeans probably held about a cup's worth of muck and his shirt another half a cup. He would take off his boots and clothes in the garage, and the ash would fall to the floor. "It ruined his truck," she added. "The ash at the spill, when it was dry, would settle on his truck, on his hood, and it rusted it a lot." As Janie talked, she could feel the eyes of the jury on her. She had them.

Janie spent the rest of the examination describing Ansol's slow decline. She told Scott that, in the five years Ansol had worked at Kingston, his appearance had changed. "He honestly looks like he was poisoned," Janie said. "And that's the only way I know to describe it." Before he fell ill, even on his days off, he would wake early to work in the yard. Now, she said, he sometimes slept until eleven o'clock. And if he did try to rise early, "there's a chance he would probably fall," she said. "He gets dizzy when he wakes up."

"No further questions at this time, Ms. Clark," Scott said.

As Janie stood to leave, she mouthed the words *Thank you* to Judge Varlan.

During trials, Jimmy Sanders usually brought along at least one other partner from Neal & Harwell, plus a trial tech or two, maybe a few paralegals, and three or four associate attorneys to prepare cross-examination outlines, which could sometimes fill an entire large three-ring binder. Sanders hardly ate or slept during trials; he mostly reviewed these outlines when not in court. In recent years, his trial team tended to include his son Isaac. He was in his early thirties, and, like his father, he had graduated from Vanderbilt Law School and had a compact build; he weighed one hundred and twelve pounds as a high-school wrestler. The two often ate lunch together, and Isaac, who clearly idolized his dad, threw himself, fully and without complaint, at whatever task Jimmy assigned him. Jimmy was something of an asshole but a brilliant trial lawyer, whereas Isaac was kind but no courtroom genius, not yet anyway. That kindness perhaps explained why he was assigned to conduct Janie Clark's cross-examination.

In many toxic-exposure trials, corporate defense attorneys try to prevent the jury from sympathizing with injured plaintiffs, to reduce the odds of the jurors doling out a hefty reward. But sympathy is often inevitable, especially if the sickened plaintiffs include hardworking members of a community, like Janie and Ansol Clark. Isaac Sanders certainly recognized that it would not bode well for Jacobs if he beat up on little Janie. After a few introductory questions, he asked her, delicately, to clarify whether Ansol had arrived home caked in fly-ash muck during his entire five years at Kingston.

Janie could tell that Isaac was trying to minimize, or at least call into question, Ansol's exposure to fly ash. He hadn't come home covered in wet muck for the entire five years, she said, because in the summers the fly ash had dried and become dusty. But, she said, "he was still dirty."

"So, the whole time he was there," Isaac said, "he would come home and he hadn't washed his face or his hands?"

"He might have wiped them off with a paper towel," she allowed. But, racing to get home, he never cleaned himself off well, she said, and he drove thirty-five miles covered in ash.

Did Ansol ever tell her about any risks on the jobsite?

"No," she said firmly. "What he mainly talked about was how they told him [the fly ash] was safe."

Jim Scott examined the day's next witness, a Roane County commissioner, who described the morning the coal-ash dike failed. He testified that, in the years following the disaster, the wind had carried fly ash from the cleanup site onto his parents' property and into their home. "You could tell the dust was on [the] countertops," he said. The next witness proved more critical: Danny Gouge.

Gouge took the witness stand at one-thirty in the afternoon, wearing his work clothes. Scott, seated at the plaintiffs' table, had waited for this moment all day. He had a hunch that the jury would appreciate some levity, and he hoped Gouge would supply it.

Gouge was something of a local legend in Roane County. He lived on a farmhouse near Kingston, where he kept twelve dogs, thirteen head of cattle, two hundred chickens, and an eighteen-hundred-pound bull named, appropriately, Bully, which followed him around almost like a puppy. Over the years, he'd also owned binturongs, camels, emus, ostriches, rheas, and zebras. During discovery, John Dupree had visited Gouge's home; Gouge told him that he'd known Tom Bock since the mid-1990s, when they worked together at a steel mill. "[Bock] was just a kid," Gouge said. And after they both took jobs at Kingston—Gouge was an equipment operator—they talked often.

Since Dupree had visited with Gouge during discovery, he would conduct the examination. At the lectern, Dupree asked Gouge some simple biographical questions. Gouge's answers failed to arouse the jury's interest much until Dupree asked about Gouge's pet ape.

"Name was Kayo," Gouge said.

"Tell us about Kayo for just a minute," Dupree said.

"I can tell you so much," Gouge said. "I learned him how to fish, learned him how to ride a four-wheeler. He rode on my Harley with me back in the day, never contained."

Scott glanced at the jurors. They were smiling, clearly warming to the witness, just as he'd hoped. Ideally, the jury would not only believe the workers but also like them. And how could anyone not like hearing about a grown man's pet primate?

Gouge explained that he'd rescued the little ape from a "bad home" and took care of him for nineteen years. He had never lost a child, he said, but he imagined the experience was comparable to when the little ape finally died.

Dupree shifted directions before Gouge could get too emotional and asked about a more germane topic: Gouge's friendship with Bock. Gouge said that he and Bock usually talked before the morning safety meetings. Gouge said that, after he'd worked at Kingston for some time, Bock looked at him one day and said, "Man, if these people knowed what was in this ash, they'd quit." Gouge said Bock hadn't explained why he'd said that.

Why did you not quit after Bock told you such a thing? Dupree asked.

"I got a family to feed," Gouge said. "I didn't even think about quitting."

Dupree brought up the personal air-monitoring devices the workers had sometimes worn. Gouge told the jury that he had sometimes worn one clipped to his belt, and that it would invariably be covered in fly ash by the end of his shift. But, Gouge said, on several occasions, when he turned in the device, Bock told him, "Danny, what did you do? Leave it in the floorboard all day long?" Gouge said Bock had accused him of trying to sabotage the results. Then, according to Gouge, Bock took out the filter, threw it out, and insisted that Gouge redo the test another day.

Jeff Friedman flipped the pages of *The Knoxville New Sentinel* in the lobby of the Farragut Hotel as he sipped his coffee. It was Friday, October 19, the final day of the first week of trial, and Friedman had been up since before dawn to prepare. Nearly every day that week, the newspaper had carried a lengthy front-page story by Jamie Satterfield about the trial. The hotel staff, having read the reports, talked about the case with Friedman and Gary Davis each morning, rooting them on. To Friedman's satisfaction, that Friday morning the paper had run another story about the trial. The piece recounted the testimonies from the day before and included an insightful tidbit unrelated to the trial: a year earlier, the government of Hong Kong had temporarily banned Jacobs's China division from bidding on new projects, after twenty-one of its employees were arrested for faking concrete test reports, risking the structural integrity of a bridge under construction. (Twelve were found guilty in 2019.) Friedman had a hunch that, with Tom Bock set to take the stand, that day's testimonies would provide Satterfield with her most colorful material yet.

Court convened at nine o'clock. First, Dupree questioned Michael Robinette, a laborer foreman, who testified that Bock had reprimanded him for handing out dust masks to a group of workers. In Robinette's telling, Bock had insisted that he throw out the dust masks, because if he didn't, the EPA might ratchet up the site's federal Superfund classification to a more serious level and require the workers to follow additional, time-consuming safety precautions. During cross-examination, Sanders tried to muddle the matter—one of his go-to tactics throughout the trial—by suggesting that Bock would have violated the "Site Wide Safety and Health Plan" had he allowed the workers to wear a dust mask without receiving medical testing first. The jury seemed unmoved.

Next, Keith Stewart examined Jeff Brewer, the part-time Baptist preacher. After TVA fired Brewer, he was diagnosed with obstructive lung disease, a chronic breathing condition. Given the trial's two-phase structure, Judge Varlan largely forbade the plaintiffs' attorneys from asking questions that would reveal the severity of the workers' conditions; another jury, in the phase two trial, would hear about their specific illnesses. But Brewer couldn't hide his failing health. As he recounted driving trucks at Kingston, he coughed hard, mid-sentence, and he couldn't stop. After several moments, he stood up and turned his back to the jury, hacking until the fit subsided after a minute or so. He collected himself and sat again. Varlan told him, "If you need a break, let us know."

"Oh, no," Brewer said. "That's an everyday thing."

Isaac Sanders's cross-examination of Brewer didn't finish until after two o'clock. Then, at long last, it was Bock's turn to testify. Bock crossed the green carpet to the witness stand and took the oath, as every previous witness had, then sat in front of a small microphone.

This was Friedman's moment. The wolf, at least the one he'd created in the jurors' minds, had stepped out of the dark woods into the light. So far, as best as Friedman could tell, the jurors had believed the workers' testimonies. Now Friedman needed them not only to mistrust Bock but to loathe him. Friedman had to orchestrate that.

At the lectern, Friedman, confident and collected in a dark suit, first asked Bock some background questions about his work experience and his duties at Kingston. Then he asked Bock to read the part of his deposition where he'd told Jim Scott, in effect, that the most important document at the cleanup site was not the "Site Wide Safety and Health Plan" but his paycheck.

"Sir," Bock said, "I believe that was said tongue in cheek, if you understand. I was making light of that statement at that time."

Silence filled the room. Friedman looked at the jurors, to ensure that they'd fully registered Bock's comment. "All right," he said after several long moments. "Let me help you with this in my questions: I'm not asking for any humor. Understand?"

"Yes, sir," Bock said.

Bock seemed almost cavalier, as if he couldn't grasp how poorly his comments might be perceived.

Friedman didn't let up. During discovery, while digging through boxes, one of the lawyers had found an email Bock had received in 2009. In it, Sean Healey, Bock's supervisor at the time, instructs him not to use the word *decon* (that is, decontamination) in reference to the cleanup. "The site control efforts we undertake are primarily for the benefit of public perception," Healey wrote, "and given what we know about fly ash are not based on any type of occupational health risk." The sentence, or at least the first part of it, was one of the most damning pieces of evidence the plaintiffs had found. (Another was Mike McCarthy's "cock" video, which the attorneys would play for the jurors a few days later.) Friedman had Healey's email projected on a screen for the courtroom to see. Then he asked Bock, "How would site-control efforts be for the benefit of public perception?"

"I don't know, sir," Bock said. "That's not me writing that."

"Well, it's your boss writing to you?"

"Yes, sir."

"So, did you ever inquire of him: 'Hey, what do you mean, Mr. Healey? I'm a safety man. What do I know about public perception?' "

Bock said he couldn't recall whether they had talked about it. Friedman then asked what, if anything, did worker safety have to do with public perception. Bock said he didn't believe it did, but he added that he could probably explain why Healey had used that phrase in that context.

Friedman denied him the chance: "My question was: Did you ever ask him why he was using ['public perception']?"

"I don't know if I did or not," Bock said.

"Does public perception have anything to do with worker health and safety?" Friedman asked.

Jimmy Sanders, at the defense table, objected: "Asked and answered."

"If I asked it, I missed it," Friedman said, turning his gaze from Bock.

"Go ahead," Varlan said. "I'll overrule it."

Friedman refocused his attention on the witness: "Does public perception have anything to do with worker health and safety?"

"In my opinion, no, it doesn't," Bock said.

Friedman then read another part of Healey's email, in which he reminds Bock that "a worker would have to ingest about one pound of fly ash per day just to get to the allowable occupational arsenic body burden."

Friedman stopped. "Have you ever told a worker at the Kingston site that they could eat a pound of fly ash a day and it wouldn't hurt them?" he asked.

Bock said he'd told workers something along those lines during every site safety orientation he'd conducted between roughly 2009 and 2010. But he insisted that he wasn't encouraging anyone to eat fly ash. "It was an analogy," he said, "so folks could understand the amount it would take to accumulate arsenic in your system to be hazardous for you."

After such a response, Friedman guessed that, if the jurors didn't hate Bock already, they probably did now. Bock, not helping his case, also maintained that he had never told the workers that the fly ash was safe. Jacobs, he said, had kept the fly ash "below the action levels"—that is, levels that would have required Jacobs to shut down the site until the fly ash was controlled and not hanging in the air.

At three-thirty, Varlan recessed the court for a break. Scott was impressed with Friedman's examination of Bock, who was proving to be a disaster for the defense. His testimony seemed to have sincerely shocked the jury. And it didn't help Bock's case that, at different points throughout the day, he appeared to roll his eyes when sickened workers hobbled into the gallery. Did he think they were faking their illnesses? Scott wondered.

The court resumed at ten minutes before four o'clock, giving Friedman about an hour to give the ten jurors vivid testimony to think about over the weekend.

When pressed by Friedman, and later on cross-examination, Bock denied all the major allegations against him: that he had destroyed or tampered with the air-monitoring results, that he had banged the filters against a table, that he had threatened to fire anyone who requested a dust mask or a respirator. When Friedman asked Bock whether he had demanded that Michael Robinette, the craft foreman who had testified earlier in the day, throw away dust masks he'd handed out, Bock said, "I may have. I don't know. I mean, this is how many years ago?"

When the court reconvened Monday morning, Friedman picked up with Bock as if no time had passed. On Friday, Friedman had undercut Bock's credibility. Now he needed to convince the jury that the air-monitoring data that Jacobs used to insist that the site posted no safety risk was unreliable, if not total junk.

Gary Davis, manning the projector, displayed a calendar onto the screen for the jury to see. It was dated January 2012, and, like the other calendars Scott and the other Knoxville lawyers had found during discovery, it noted, in green, the days when Jacobs had handed out personal air monitors to workers and it noted, in blue, the days when it had rained.

Friedman asked Bock if he had helped to prepare the calendar, and he said he had. Then Friedman asked, "If you count the green boxes in January 2012, you've got seven test days; is that correct?"

"Yes, sir," Bock said.

Friedman went through each of the seven days: January 3 was dry, he said, but it rained on the 5th and on the 10th. Then "you've got the 17th—you tested on a rain day," he said, and "on the 24th, you tested after you got an inch and a quarter of rain; is that right?"

"Yes, sir," Bock said.

"And on the 31st, you have a dry day. So, by my count, you have basically two dry ash days in that month?"

"Yes, sir," Bock said.

Friedman explained that his team had cross-referenced government weather data to verify the calendar's precipitation levels, which had checked out. Then he went through the rest of the year, asking Bock to confirm the days Jacobs had tested the air for hazards based on the calendars. It took a while. When Friedman finished, he turned to Bock. "Okay," he said. "Now, the reason I pulled that up is: You said that Jacobs's testing of fly ash in the elements wasn't dependent upon what the weather was doing; is that right? Do you remember testifying to that Friday, or words to that effect?"

Bock agreed that he had.

"Okay," Friedman said. If Bock and Jacobs really wanted to determine how much fly ash was in the air, their best chances of finding out was on dry days, right?

"Sir," Bock shot back, "we were trying to sample representative of what the site conditions were. So, if you've got fifteen days of rain, it's going to be wet." They had a testing plan, he insisted, and they had followed it.

Friedman, ready for such a response, said, "Would it surprise you that two-thirds of the time that you were testing out there in 2012 the ash was wet?"

"Objection," Sanders said from the defense table. What was the definition of "wet"? Varlan overruled him.

Friedman repeated the question for Bock: Would he be surprised to learn that two-thirds of the test days corresponded with rainfall?

After stammering a bit, Bock said, "I don't have an opinion either way, sir."

Okay, Friedman said. What about the twenty-five workers, or thereabouts, who complained of breathing issues in 2013 because of the fly ash—was that why Bock had put together these calendars?

Bock said it was. At TVA's request, after the workers came forward with their health complaints, he'd prepared a document recapping the air-monitoring tests and data that Jacobs had conducted from 2010 to 2013.

Friedman knew, of course, that TVA and Jacobs had used this data to justify denying many of the workers respiratory protection. He asked Davis, still at the projector, to show the jury a chart from Bock's document. It listed the results of five hundred and fifty different air-monitoring tests. Friedman pointed out that three hundred and sixty-eight—"the vast majority of them"—had detected fly ash. And the tests weren't just positive, he said, but some showed fly-ash levels at half of the site's acceptable exposure limit. Wasn't that right?

"Yes, sir," Bock said.

Friedman was ready to connect the threads and hang Bock with them. "And so," he said, ". . . even with moist conditions or rain conditions, y'all are still getting hits in your respiratory monitors three hundred and sixty-eight out of five hundred and fifty times, right?"

"Objection!" Sanders said from the defense table. "That's just so vague and misleading." Friedman was clearly trying to suggest that, had Bock and Jacobs tested on more dry days, the air-monitoring results would have been even higher and revealed that the cleanup site was more dangerous than they'd let on.

"Let's just see if the witness can answer," Varlan said.

Bock explained that the chart indicated that no action was needed from Jacobs or TVA: the fly-ash levels fell below the permissible exposure limit, based on air tests.

Friedman shot back: "Do you have an opinion as to what . . . those tests would look like if you tested under dry conditions all the time?"

"I don't have an opinion, sir," Bock said. Even on dry days, Bock insistened, the water trucks kept the fly ash suppressed (a claim contrary to the workers' testimonies, to photos taken of the jobsite, and to the testimony of an environmental consultant the plaintiffs had subpoenaed to testify).

Friedman, after asking several more questions, pointed out the irony that Bock, of all people, had investigated the workers' initial complaints that fly ash had caused their breathing problems: "You were the same person who told all these workers that fly ash was safe and they could even eat it, right?"

"Sir," Bock said, "I stated that you could eat a pound of ash a day. You would need to eat a pound of ash a day to be able to reach the body burden of arsenic."

"But you went on record as saying it was safe," Friedman said.

"Yes, at the levels that they were exposed."

On cross-examination, Jimmy Sanders had Bock clarify that TVA and the EPA, as well as the U.S. Coast Guard, had ultimate oversight of the cleanup site, not Jacobs. Bock also pointed out that another TVA contractor had collected air-monitoring data in the first few months of the cleanup and that its testing days also corresponded with rainfall, as if that might excuse Jacobs's behavior.

• • •

Dr. Paul Terry struggled to sleep. He shifted and turned in bed. He worked in Knoxville, at the sprawling campus of the University of Tennessee Medical Center, but he lived in Maryville, a town of about thirty thousand people at the base of the Great Smoky Mountains National Park. It was the night of Tuesday, October 23, and he was expected to testify the next morning. As the hours crawled by, he ran over in his mind precisely how he needed to present himself in court. He hadn't attended any of the pretrial hearings about the sufficiency of his reports or whether he possessed the qualifications to testify, but the lawyers had told him, of course, that he was the subject of much fighting, and it was not the sort of attention he enjoyed.

Over the past few weeks, Terry had spent most evenings preparing for his testimony in a small conference room at the attorneys' office. Gary Davis, seated across the table, had gone over the questions that he intended to ask on direct examination. Don't over-answer, Davis cautioned, and don't get ahead of yourself. Answer only one question at a time. Davis explained to Terry that he had carefully ordered his queries and that he would get to all of Terry's major findings in time. He just needed to be patient.

Before Terry agreed to participate in the case, he'd decided that he wouldn't omit or downplay any fact that reflected poorly on the workers' suit against Jacobs; he would be honest no matter what. And, to Terry's relief, while preparing for trial, Davis never encouraged him to say anything that went against his research or scientific fact. Davis did coach Terry on how to clearly articulate his conclusions from the research and data he'd reviewed. Even with such preparation, Terry fretted about his testimony. Whenever he gave talks at academic conferences, several minutes passed before he could relax and speak confidently. He knew that the defense attorneys could easily make a fool of him if he didn't articulate his points well.

On Wednesday morning, Terry woke up early and climbed out of bed. The evening prior, before all the tossing and turning, he and his wife had driven to a Belk department store and picked out a new belt for him. She wanted him to look nice on the witness stand, but Terry had put on some weight and his old belt fit poorly. They had settled on a brown replacement. He put it on, along with pants, a jacket and tie, and a nice pair of shoes.

Once downtown, he parked in a paid lot near the courthouse. After passing through security, he met Davis outside the courtroom. Davis asked Terry if he felt ready, and Terry said that he did. Rather than pass time in the antechamber, where Janie Clark had sat, Terry found a seat in the back of the courtroom and waited for his turn. The defense needed to finish cross-examining another witness, the truck driver Brad Green, before the plaintiffs called on Terry.

He surveyed the courtroom. He'd never testified in a trial before, and the lawyers had stressed the importance of his role: the jurors had to believe it was scientifically possible that the fly ash had harmed the workers. Several workers and their wives sat near Terry in the gallery; some had oxygen tanks. He assumed that the workers had no idea who he was, and he didn't know them, either. But seeing the workers stirred something in him. No one should have to live like that, not on account of a job anyway, not because somebody decided to risk their health.

At nine-thirty, Davis called Terry to the stand. First, Davis asked about Terry's professional history. For the past fifteen years or so, Terry said, he had been a professor at the University of Tennessee and at Emory University, in Georgia, where he taught medical students. Before that, as a postdoctoral fellow at the Centers for Disease Control and Prevention in Atlanta, he'd studied the effects of weather and pollution on children with asthma. He worked alongside medical doctors, but he was, at his core, a researcher. He told the jurors that he'd agreed to study the Kingston workers out of a sense of public duty. "I am at a public university," he explained, "and I guess my salary is paid for by the university but ultimately by the people of Tennessee." He had requested no money from Scott: "I figured [my university salary] was enough."

Terry, growing more comfortable, explained that, at first, he'd asked for the workers' medical records and had drafted a health questionnaire for them to fill out. That way, he could compare their responses to a control group's and determine whether fly ash had likely contributed to or caused their illnesses. But the study didn't work out, Terry said, because the number of questionnaires he received back—about one hundred in all—was too small for him to draw "a very solid conclusion." That was why, he said, "I went to the literature." This approach had problems, too, he acknowledged, since there weren't "really any studies out there of people who were exposed [to fly ash] the way the Kingston coal-ash workers were exposed." But—crucially—plenty of studies *had* examined fly ash's constituents. For example, "ionizing radiation in [fly ash] can cause leukemia and other hematologic malignancies," he said, and PM2.5, microscopic particulate matter found in fly ash, was able to penetrate deep into the lungs and "actually be absorbed into the bloodstream from there."

Terry faced the jurors as he answered Davis's questions, and he was glad he did. They looked attentive, if not intrigued, which bolstered his confidence. He told the jurors that, based on the hundreds of studies he'd read, he could conclude, with a reasonable degree of certainty, that coal ash was capable of causing hypertension, coronary artery disease, lung cancer, and leukemia, along with damage to the nervous system—all health issues from which the workers suffered.

Davis asked, "Did you include any of these conclusions in your report unless you felt that the bulk of the evidence supported you?"

"I felt that the bulk of the evidence supported me in every case," Terry said.

Jimmy Sanders opened his cross-examination of Terry at 11:16 a.m., and quickly tried to undermine his credibility and objectivity. Sanders brought up the fact that Terry had not studied the on-site air-monitoring data collected by Jacobs—the exact sort of data an epidemiologist would normally want to review—only because the plaintiffs' lawyers had told him it was unreliable, not because he had independent knowledge of its accuracy.

Terry conceded that, yes, he'd taken the attorneys' word that the data was faulty. Next, Sanders accused Terry of being unable to accurately conclude whether a constituent of fly ash—lead, for instance—had harmed the workers. A toxin might be present at the site, Sanders said, but Terry had no data regarding how much each worker had inhaled. Sanders had made variations of this argument since he joined Jacobs's defense team, and Terry partially conceded the point. But he explained that Avner Vengosh, of Duke, and other researchers had measured the toxins in the Kingston ash, so he could strongly "infer" that the toxins had entered the workers' bodies—he'd seen photos of the dusty worksite. "But you can't prove it," Terry said, of the workers' exposures.

"Very good point," Sanders said. "And that is my point."

As for the worksite photos, Sanders added, how did Terry know the dust in the images was fly ash? What if it were fog or some other sort of dust?

"I did see fly-ash dust," Terry said. The workers were exposed "significantly" to it—more than a billion gallons of coal-ash sludge had flooded the landscape, after all. But, he said, "I can't tell you exactly what the exposure was."

At twelve-fifteen, Judge Varlan dismissed the court for lunch. Terry, despite his nerves and poor night of sleep, had held up well on cross-examination. Sanders had tried to smother the workers' stories in doubt and whataboutisms, but the jury had loved Terry, at least as far as Davis could tell. When the court reconvened an hour later, Sanders told Varlan he had no further questions for Terry. Sanders had likely realized that attacking Terry, clearly beloved by the jurors, would only hurt Jacobs's standing in their eyes.

Over the next several days, the defense called its own experts to testify. The most compelling among them was Scott Phillips, a medical doctor and a partner at an environmental consulting firm. He'd reviewed data from the stationary air monitors around the site's perimeter—around the so-called donut of death—and produced a fifty-page report for the defense. On the stand, Phillips told Sanders that the samples collected by the stationary air monitors suggested it was highly unlikely that fly-ash exposure had caused the workers' illnesses. There just wasn't enough arsenic and silica and other harmful constituents in the air, he said. Moreover, Phillips had evaluated blood and urine samples provided by eight workers, including Ansol Clark and Jeff Brewer. The samples, he stated, did not contain high levels of arsenic, mercury, lead, cobalt, thallium, or cadmium, further suggesting that the site posed no major health danger.

Jeff Friedman and Gary Davis had declined to depose the defense's experts so they could instead ambush them on the stand. Now Davis did just that. First, he obliterated Phillips's credibility by having the doctor admit that, unlike Terry, he wasn't an epidemiologist; that he and his company had professional ties with the mining, oil, and gas industries; and that he testified in four or five cases a year. The implication: he was, in lawyer-speak, a whore—a professional expert, a scientist for hire. When asked about pay, Phillips admitted that Jacobs was paying him $450 an hour. Davis pointed out that if he spent one hundred hours writing his report and testifying—which would not be hard—he would earn $42,500. "He is in it for the money," Friedman would later tell the jury. "His testimony is bought and paid for."

Davis also called attention to the fact that the stationary air monitors Phillips had put so much stock in stood thousands of feet away from the exclusion zone, and that water trucks had likely skewed their results. The EPA had even thrown out several months' worth of the monitors' data for being unreliable, Davis pointed out, and, at any rate, the "Site Wide Safety and Health Plan"—the site's bible—stated that, as a rule, data from the stationary air monitors shouldn't be used to evaluate the workers' exposure levels.

Then Davis sprang a trap. "Would you agree," he asked Phillips, "that lead, arsenic, radium, and other constituents are found in fly ash, and that those substances can, in certain doses and under certain circumstances and through certain avenues of exposure, cause the types of health issues alleged in this case?"

"No," Phillips said, "I wouldn't agree with that."

"What if I told you that Jacobs wrote that statement to the judge?" Davis asked.

Phillips floundered: "I have no way of knowing yes or no."

"Well," Davis said, "I'm representing to you that Jacobs did that, and Jacobs further said that issue was not contested."

Phillips reiterated, lamely, that he didn't agree with the statement.

By the time Phillips finished testifying, shortly before three-thirty that afternoon, Davis and Friedman not only had made Jacobs's air-monitoring data seem like junk, but they also had made the defense's lead expert witness object to scientific facts that not even Jacobs had disputed, no doubt damaging his credibility.

Jimmy Sanders tried to hit back in week three, when the defense called a surprise, last-minute witness: William Cheung, an engineer for Mesa Labs, a company that makes personal air monitors of the sort the workers had worn. On the stand, Cheung said that tapping out a monitor's filter, as Bock had allegedly done, wouldn't affect the results—which, if true, undercut the plaintiffs' case, since that would mean that Jacobs's air-monitoring data had perhaps been somewhat accurate. One of Sanders's co-counsels asked Cheung about the surreptitiously recorded videos that showed a Jacobs staffer hitting part of a personal air monitor against a table. The employee, Cheung said, appeared to be clearing out a piece of the device known as the grit pot, which captured large airborne particles that posed no health concern. Cheung said that tapping out the grit pot wouldn't have affected the filter cartridge that collected the tiny, dangerous airborne particles, so nothing about the staffer's action seemed improper to him. On cross-examination, Cheung conceded that if someone had hit the air monitors against a table "technically, yeah . . . I'm sure something will fall from the filter, but it will still be inside [the sealed filter]." Much to Scott and Friedman's relief, however, Cheung couldn't confirm whether Jacobs had actually used his company's air monitors at Kingston.

On the morning of November 6, closing statements were set to begin. Mike McCarthy, the worker who filmed the "cock" video, arrived dressed in a blue Columbia fishing shirt. Of the jury, "I hope they see the truth first off," he told a local news crew in the courtyard. He got choked up. "We need medical care," he went on. "We need the treatment. Not every doctor can handle what we were exposed to; they just don't know about it. So we need to get to the right doctors, and our families need to get to the right doctors, too, because they were affected just as bad as we were."

At eight-thirty, Judge Varlan called the court to order and discussed a few housekeeping items. After a brief recess, he called in the jury. The evening prior, as the plaintiffs' team discussed strategy at the hotel bar, Jeff Friedman had proclaimed that he was tired of talking about science and data and academics. "I want the jury to see the faces of the guys who drove hours to work each day to clean up this mess," he told the others. "I want them to know our people and to know their stories." Now, standing before a packed gallery, Friedman tried to make the workers' stories unforgettable. He recounted major moments from the testimonies, referring to blown-up photos of the workers, including Jeff Brewer and Danny Gouge. Friedman also recalled how Jacobs staff had demanded air-filtration systems for the trailers where they worked, to ensure that *they* weren't breathing in fly ash, because it was dangerous.

Avner Vengosh's study, which had come up throughout the trial, had made this point clear. "Jacobs couldn't get far enough away from that study," Friedman told the jury. Even one of Jacobs's own expert witnesses had agreed that the ionizing radiation in fly ash could cause leukemia and other blood cancers.

For the defense, Sanders insisted that the plaintiffs' case was based on "alternative reality." He said that, according to the EPA, the site wasn't hazardous. And, based on the air-monitoring results, there was no way the coal ash was dangerous. Sanders reminded the jurors that Scott Phillips, the defense's star expert witness, had evaluated lab tests for eight of the forty-eight plaintiffs and determined that the workers did not have high levels of arsenic in their blood or urine, undermining their exposure claims. (Urine tests would later show that other workers did have unusually high levels of aluminum, cadmium, lead, mercury, and uranium in their systems.) Sanders also pointed out that, though some workers had indeed been denied a respirator—ostensibly because they'd flunked a medical exam due to their poor health—other workers had passed the test. "Guess what?" Sanders asked the jury. "They wore their dust masks on the site." That simple fact, he said, unraveled the plaintiffs' entire conspiracy theory.

At two o'clock, Varlan dismissed the jurors to deliberate, then recessed the court at six after they failed to reach a verdict. Scott and his team felt relieved at having finished the trial, but waiting for the verdict brought a fresh wave of anxiety.

The next morning, Scott's team, along with a few plaintiffs, met at their office to await a text message to report to the courtroom for the verdict. The workers sipped coffee and water and tried their best to pass the time. Scott felt good about their odds. The testimonies had gone as well as he could have hoped, but juries are notoriously unpredictable, so he tried to temper his expectations. Friedman, unable to tolerate the tense mood in the office, left to do paperwork alone in his hotel room. He changed out of his customary dark suit and pulled on a broken-in gray sports coat, khakis, and a pair of brown leather shoes.

The text message arrived shortly before lunch. As the attorneys walked down Market Street and entered the courthouse grounds, Keith Stewart wore a sickened look, nervous that at least one juror doubted the workers' testimonies.

Varlan called the court to order at ten to noon. To reach a verdict, the ten jurors had to check "yes" or "no" to twelve questions, accepting or rejecting whether Jacobs's actions could have possibly sickened the workers with leukemia, lung cancer, and coronary artery disease, among other illnesses. Both parties stood for the verdict. Scott could sense the workers behind him in the gallery. He could feel their eyes on him, and almost hear their hearts pounding. His thoughts jumped to Ansol and Janie Clark and all the plaintiffs who'd sat through the trial and to those who hadn't, like Billy Isley and Mike Shelton. All sound fell away, just as the cheering crowds had when Scott played football as a boy. He clenched a fist.

Then came twelve "yes" replies in a row.

A tear formed in Scott's eye. Friedman wrapped him in a hug, but they said nothing. Federal courts do not permit noise in the gallery, much less cheering, so the workers quietly sobbed to themselves.

The Clarks, unsure of when the jury would return, missed the reading of the verdict, but they followed the news at home. When Janie

The plaintiffs' team after the reading of the verdict. Front row from left: Gary Davis, Jeff Friedman, paralegal Stephanie Johnson, Jim Scott, John Dupree. Back row from left: Ellis "Sandy" Sharp, Tyler Roper, Keith Stewart

learned of the results, she ran into the living room, where Ansol was sitting in his armchair. "We won! We won!" she screamed, jumping and jumping. Ansol sprung to his feet. They had seen the best of humanity and the worst of it in this case, Janie later explained. They had hung on only because Scott had given them reason to.

On December 22, 2018, ten years to the day after the Kingston disaster, and about a month after the jury delivered its verdict, some three hundred people, many of them former Kingston cleanup workers, including Ansol Clark, gathered at soccer fields built over a portion of the old disaster site. A bright, winter-blue sky hung over the leafless trees that covered the nearby hills. In the distance, the rebuilt holding pond, smoothed and covered with grass, resembled a soft-sloping hill, just as it had before it collapsed. The day before, Ansol had planted a white cross in the ground near the entrance to the soccer fields. It bore the words "First Responders Gave All." Janie snapped photos. To TVA and Jacobs, these workers' lives meant nothing, she believed, and she doubted the trial had changed that. She called the workers "the Expendables," because that was how Jacobs and TVA had treated them.

At least two truck drivers in attendance that day had matching sores on their faces that they attributed to coal ash. Some of the workers relied on canes. Most struggled to walk far without fighting off a cough and carried inhalers in their pockets. Jeff Brewer, the part-time preacher, was among them. "What they've done to us, it angers me," he told a reporter. He pointed toward the Kingston Fossil Plant, about a mile away. Gases rose from a smokestack and drifted over the countryside. "To sit there and lie knowingly," Brewer said. He stopped himself, hands stuffed in the front pockets of his jacket. "That's the thing," he said, "they know'd it was dangerous. Now we've got thirty-one that've done passed away because of lung issues, all kinds of cancer issues, leukemia."

Brewer was one of the fortunate ones who had health insurance. Some 40 percent of the plaintiffs didn't. But he worried that if his health declined further, he might get fired from his current job, driving trucks for a company named Holland Freight, and lose coverage. Though the plaintiffs had won the first trial phase, they would have to wait until the second phase was decided to receive damages. He had no idea when that might be.

Jim Scott stood at the edge of the soccer fields and addressed the crowd. The workers, he said, had stepped up in the face of disaster to the benefit of their neighbors. "That's a great American story," he said. But "they slaved for us in an environment they didn't realize was dangerous," and that was unacceptable. By being present today on those soccer fields, he said, "you're not only honoring the ones that [died] and the ones who are sick, but you are honoring a work ethic."

After Scott and a few other speakers finished their remarks, the workers stood together for a photo. The verdict they'd won against Jacobs Engineering marked a first in the history of American civil litigation: no plaintiffs had ever convinced a federal jury that coal ash could sicken them. This meant the workers had proved to the jury that TVA, the EPA, and the coal lobby were wrong, and dangerously so, about coal ash. It *was* a hazardous waste. It could hurt and kill a person. But the workers' win, as monumental as it was, had yet to spur any real change.

After the jury handed down its verdict, neither TVA nor Jacobs admitted any wrongdoing. Jacobs continued to insist that air-sampling data proved that the workers were not exposed to excessive concentrations of airborne particulate, and it maintained that its staff hadn't improperly discarded or tampered with any air samples. Moreover, it denied that its staff had violated the "Site Wide Safety and Health Plan" when processing the workers' requests for respiratory protection, and that any worker had been inappropriately not allowed to wear a dust mask.

TVA took a slightly softer approach, conceding in a statement that "troubling testimony" had been presented during the trial regarding Jacobs's safety record. Yet TVA continued to work with the company. TVA also asserted that coal ash posed no serious health risk to the workers and that it had been transparent throughout the cleanup process. "TVA has acknowledged the constituents in coal ash for decades, including trace amounts of radium," Scott Brooks, a TVA spokesman, said in a statement to reporters. "Coal ash is not considered a hazardous waste by the EPA, and is handled and stored as such." Shortly after the ceremony that December day, Jamie Satterfield reported in *The Knoxville News Sentinel* that, because of indemnity provisions in Jacobs's contract,

TVA would perhaps have to cover some of the company's expenses resulting from the workers' lawsuit and that TVA would pass that cost on to its ratepayers.

Then, as now, TVA fell partially under the jurisdiction of the House Transportation and Infrastructure Committee. Following the trial, Representative Peter DeFazio, a Democrat from Oregon who served as the committee chair, promised to inquire further into TVA's handling of the Kingston cleanup. Nothing came of it. DeFazio and other members of his committee accepted campaign donations from Jacobs Engineering in the months after the federal jury's verdict in the workers' case, as did Tennessee representative Chuck Fleischmann, whose district included the city of Kingston. The Senate also did nothing. The EPA did nothing, the White House did nothing, the state of Tennessee did nothing. The Tennessee Bureau of Investigation said it would launch an investigation but, in the end, did nothing.

Judge Thomas Varlan did do something. In January 2019, less than a month after the ceremony at the soccer fields, he ordered both parties to participate in mediation, in the hope they would settle the case out of court. The two sides agreed to let a Louisiana attorney named Daniel Balhoff serve as the mediator.

In March 2019, Janie and Ansol Clark celebrated their forty-seventh wedding anniversary. She decided to cook Ansol's favorite meal at home: fried chicken, gravy, mashed potatoes, biscuits, green beans. She knew that, with Jacobs sure to play tough in mediation and contest the outcome of the next trial if mediation failed, any hope of justice was likely years away. And, should justice come, it would hardly suffice for the damage that Jacobs and TVA had caused. She had no idea how much time Ansol might have left. He was sixty-seven. Would he reach seventy? She couldn't escape the thought that they might not have another anniversary together. That was why she decided to cook for Ansol: she wanted him to feel loved, to enjoy as many of her meals as he could.

Oftentimes, on hot summer nights, when the sun slouched beneath the hills, Jim Scott would stroll down to the river from his condo and throw rocks into the current, just as he'd done when he lived on Talahi

Drive. One Sunday night in August by the river, he ate a bag of Skittles and thought about life, about work, about everything. Almost a year had passed since the jury sided with the workers in federal court, and the lawyers for the plaintiffs and the defense were finally scheduled to meet at Scott's office the next morning to begin mediation. He'd spent weeks preparing, reading up on relevant laws and reviewing letters that doctors had written at the workers' requests, drawing correlations between fly ash and their diseases. He hoped, for the workers' sake and his own, such documentation would help the two sides quickly reach an agreement. That way, Ansol and the others could get the medical care they needed, and he could spend more time with his sons. He tried to be optimistic, but he worried that the jury's verdict might have only hardened Jacobs's resolve to fight.

He hated this part of litigation—the negotiation phase—and he especially hated it in Tennessee, a state with notorious anti-worker laws and increasingly odious political leaders. One particularly devious statute imposed a cap of $750,000 on noneconomic damages—that is, pain or suffering from the loss of a spouse or family member—in civil lawsuits. It was a pathetic amount of money for many cases, in Scott's opinion, and Tennessee law put similar restrictions on punitive damages. These caps gave Jacobs a clear advantage. If the two sides returned to trial, Jacobs would do so knowing there was almost no risk of a jury handing out a multibillion-dollar judgment against it, as in the *Exxon Valdez* case. Without such a risk, Jacobs would have little motivation to settle quickly. For such reasons, the company would soon inform shareholders, in a filing with the U.S. Securities and Exchange Commission, that it did not expect that resolving the workers' lawsuits would have "a material adverse effect" on its business, financial condition, or cash flows.

On Monday morning, Jimmy and Isaac Sanders drove in from Nashville, and Jacobs's in-house counsel flew in from California. At the Market Street office, the plaintiffs' team—Scott, John Dupree, Gary Davis, Jeff Friedman, Keith Stewart, and Tyler Roper—sat in Stewart's office, while Jacobs's attorneys (there would be seventeen in all throughout mediation) took a conference room on another floor. The mediator relayed messages between them. Jimmy Sanders and the other defense attorneys hadn't been agreeable throughout discovery or the trial, so it came as no shock to Scott that they weren't during the mediation conference, either.

The defense team offered the forty-eight workers named in the original suit filed against Jacobs a $10 million settlement. *That's a crock of shit*, Scott thought after the mediator shared the figure. He had settled a single murder case for nearly as much money, and it involved one dead person. Now there were almost fifty dead Kingston workers. Stewart was irritated because he knew that the surviving workers were growing desperate: they called his law office daily, asking for updates. "Clients are losing their homes, talking about suicide, and the cancers are multiplying," Stewart reminded the other attorneys. Some might consider taking Jacobs's offer, depending on their financial needs.

As part of any agreement, Sanders and the defense team wanted the plaintiffs to vacate the 2018 jury verdict—that is, absolve Jacobs of any wrongdoing. The defense also insisted that Scott's team destroy all their files, including expert reports and whatever documents they'd obtained in discovery. Fuck no, Scott said. If they agreed to vacate the verdict won by the first forty-eight workers, the two hundred or so other plaintiffs, including Jeff Brewer, in the subsequent, connected cases against Jacobs wouldn't be able to use it to negotiate a settlement. "Vacating the verdict should not even be on the table," Roper said. The other attorneys didn't disagree, but they thought they should weigh all their options before deciding anything.

The parties argued for two days over details of a potential settlement without reaching a tentative agreement. Over the next few months, the plaintiffs' team mostly corresponded by email. Friedman told the others that he thought Jacobs would come up to at least $40 million for the two hundred and fifty total plaintiffs if they agreed to vacate the verdict. Roper said he thought they should consider nothing less than $50 million. If Jacobs didn't agree to that, he said, they should take some of the individual cases to trial and "pop" Jacobs in the chin, then try mediation again. Stewart agreed; others were cooler to the idea.

Scott found the entire back-and-forth maddening. "With the stuff I continually learn," he wrote in one email, "there is not a bat's chance in hell I back off $50 million. I don't care if the tornado jumps up and down on my balls 50x." What's more, he considered it unethical for

Jacobs's lawyers to even propose that they destroy their files, especially since he'd learned that the district attorney in Roane County was weighing whether to pursue a criminal case against Jacobs. And, though nothing would ultimately come of the inquiry, if Scott destroyed his files, it would amount to destroying potential evidence, in his view. The other attorneys agreed: they wouldn't do that. But they believed they had a duty to the first forty-eight clients to let them hear Jacobs's $10 million offer, along with a rough estimate of their individual share of the settlement. Friedman said the attorneys should also try to secure a settlement for the other two hundred plaintiffs; that way, they wouldn't be left with nothing if the first group vacated the verdict. Most would get "some nice settlement money," Friedman wrote in an email. But, he added, if the first forty-eight workers didn't agree to Jacobs's settlement offer, "we move on to the trial plan."

Janie and Ansol Clark met with the mediator on the afternoon of March 3, 2020. Ansol wore a plaid shirt, Janie a denim jacket. As they rode the elevator to the lawyers' office, Janie could tell that Ansol's mind had wandered into dark territory. He, like most of the workers, always seemed to know precisely how many of his friends and former coworkers had died. This grim tally—growing month after month, year after year—was not just a number but *the* number. It was there in the morning when he woke up and there at night when he tried to sleep. He tracked its growth—*forty-seven, forty-eight, forty-nine.* What would his own death bring the total to?

They sat at a long table across from the mediator, Daniel Balhoff, in a conference room with glass doors. They didn't know what to expect; Scott had told them nothing. Balhoff, before sharing the settlement offer, told the Clarks that he thought the number was reasonable, and he clearly wanted them to consider accepting it. But he explained that Jacobs insisted that the workers vacate the verdict as part of the deal and that, under the terms of the settlement, the workers would have to reimburse Medicare or their insurance providers for any medical bills they had paid resulting from their illnesses. (This is typical procedure in civil-action lawsuits, under what are known as subrogation laws.) Then Balhoff told the Clarks the offer was $10 million.

That's terrible! Janie said. They had waited more than a year after the verdict for this? Once the attorneys subtracted their fees and expenses, the forty-eight plaintiffs would each get *maybe* $125,000. But Jacobs's request to vacate the verdict was the true offense. "I've never been sitting here waiting for a pile of money," Janie said. "I want accountability."

Ansol shook with rage. The entire mediation was a "sham," he said.

Scott, standing outside the conference room, stepped inside. "Don't stroke out, Ansol," he told him. "Stay calm."

Janie collected her things. "Let's get out of here," she told Ansol.

They left and drove to a soft-serve stand called Freezo, where they ordered tamales with chili on top. They needed to treat themselves after such an insult, Janie said. They'd left the meeting without even hearing their individual settlement estimate. Janie didn't want to know.

Jeff Brewer and his wife, Tammy, also met with the mediator, who told them that, if they agreed to the terms, the lawyers would go through his medical records, then decide the exact size of his individual settlement. "It's not about the money," Jeff said. "It's about what has been done." He added, "I'll go to my grave before I sign something that Jacobs isn't guilty." Then he and Tammy stood up and left.

Mike McCarthy refused to sign any settlement agreement that didn't include the specific amount he'd receive, as opposed to an estimate. "[Jacobs] ain't got no heart," he told the mediator through tears, his voice growing hoarse. "They don't care if they kill us. They don't care if they shorten our lives. They don't care if they take away a dad from their family. They don't give a *fuck*."

Some workers, after learning of the settlement offer from friends, refused to meet with the mediator. "I'm not fucking coming," one told Scott over the phone. "It's fucking crazy." Scott had to explain that, if they didn't participate, Jacobs might argue that they hadn't mediated in good faith, which stood to hurt them. The surviving relatives of one worker, Jean Nance, at first thought the $10 million was just for her, only to be insulted when they learned otherwise.

In the end, about twenty workers accepted $10,000 individual settlements from Jacobs and dropped their complaints against the company. Those who did were mostly workers in the later rounds of the ten consolidated cases against Jacobs—not in the lead *Adkisson* suit—who might have struggled to prove damages if the parties had returned to trial. After the vast majority of the workers refused to accept Jacobs's deal, the company retracted its offer entirely and refused to make another.* Gary Davis was furious. Jeff Friedman was furious. All the plaintiffs were furious. Then, after Jamie Satterfield published Jacobs's confidential $10 million settlement offer in *The Knoxville News Sentinel*, Jacobs was furious, too. "Jacobs used the [mediation] process to try to delay," Scott told a friend, after mediation collapsed. "They thought the memory of what they had done would fade." Friedman felt similarly, and believed that, had Jacobs come to the negotiating table in good faith, both sides would have been able to come to terms, saving everyone a lot of time and money. But, with Jacobs no longer willing to talk about money, the case seemed destined to return to trial. And Friedman suspected that Judge Varlan would rush it back as quickly as possible. "This is going to move," he told a friend over the phone.

Then COVID-19 swept Tennessee.

The district court in Knoxville suspended all jury trials because of the pandemic. As Jim Scott and his team weighed how to proceed, they began to doubt they had enough money to fight Jacobs in a second trial phase. Jeff Friedman estimated that he'd already spent half a million dollars on the case, and the other attorneys had together contributed a similar sum. The six lawyers had almost entirely stopped working on other cases in the run-up to the 2018 trial, and they needed to bring in money to stay afloat, because the workers' case was still surely years away from a resolution. John Dupree said he hoped his children would one day get his share of the attorneys' fee, because he would probably be long gone by the time Jacobs agreed to settle. He was only sort of joking. Scott shared his concern. His sons urged him to back off, to let another attorney take the lead, to focus on their family instead of work. "I don't care how much money you make on these cases," Jack told him. "I want my dad." Those words echoed in Scott's head.

Jeff Friedman realized that the next trial phase would demand that he move to Knoxville for a year or more, given how often he would need to be in court. He wasn't willing to do that, to uproot his law practice and life. Gary Davis wasn't willing to, either. In the spring of 2020, Davis

* The group of twenty workers still received their agreed-upon $10,000 settlements after Jacobs retracted its offer to the larger group.

called a Knoxville lawyer by the name of Greg Coleman. Coleman had brilliant white teeth, tan skin, and an angular beard. He drank coconut water, and had a habit of punctuating sentences with "brother"—as in, "all right, here's the deal, brother." Coleman was aware of the workers' suit. "It's an incredibly righteous case," he said, and he told Davis he was interested in getting involved. He didn't have unlimited resources like Jacobs, but he had enough money to put up a fight. He also had a track record of beating major corporations, including Volkswagen and the Aluminum Company of America (ALCOA). But Coleman told Davis, "You're talking about several million dollars in cost outlay." He said he needed to talk to his team before he agreed to anything, and he asked Davis to broach the idea of his coming aboard with John Dupree, Scott, and Keith Stewart, who didn't know about Davis's call to Coleman.

Davis obliged, and arranged for his colleagues to meet with Coleman at his office, on the eleventh floor of a glass tower on Gay Street. Large windows offered views of the Smokies' highest summit, Clingman's Dome, more than thirty-five miles away. Coleman told Scott and the others that his team could carry the case and track down qualified experts to produce reports to prove the workers' exposures. But, Coleman said, if they agreed to let him run with this phase of litigation, he wanted to be the captain. He said he would consult Scott and the others, but he believed such an involved case demanded a strong leader, and he wanted that job.

Scott liked Coleman—he'd known him for years. Also, Scott had gained some perspective in the year and a half since the jury delivered its verdict; he could admit to himself now that he hadn't been prepared, personally or financially, to fight Jacobs. For the workers to stand any chance of winning damages, he needed to back off. He had to let go, to concede that he had done all he was able to. He hadn't earned a dollar from the case yet, and he had to find other work to avoid going totally broke. He and the other five plaintiffs' attorneys agreed to split their fee with Coleman and let his team lead the second phase of litigation.

Over the next few months, Coleman's team raced ahead, because they had to. A literature review had sufficed in the first trial phase, but, to prove damages in the second phase, they needed qualified expert witnesses to analyze Jacobs's air-monitoring data and other evidence and then clearly explain how the company's actions had endangered the workers. These experts would also need to assess each worker's exposure to fly ash and determine whether it had harmed them.

Coleman's team sought out the most well-credentialed experts it could find. One report they commissioned was by Michael Ellenbecker, a professor emeritus at the University of Massachusetts, Lowell, who had previously taught at the Harvard University School of Public Health. In a merciless, thirty-seven-page report, Ellenbecker criticized Jacobs for its "abject, indefensible failure" to protect the workers. He explained that Jacobs's air-monitoring data made clear that it had infrequently and inconsistently sampled the air for arsenic, silica, or metal. And much of the data Jacobs had collected, Ellenbecker added, was "oddly uniform," even though variation is expected when sampling is done correctly. The "significant" overlap between rainy days and the days Jacobs's staff had sampled the air further undercut the data's reliability. "Jacobs's failures allowed an environmental disaster to become an unnecessary occupational disaster," Ellenbecker concluded, adding, "It cannot be seriously disputed that Jacobs understood the dangers posed by human exposure to coal fly ash."

An independent researcher in no way involved in the lawsuit offered further criticism of the air-monitoring data. This researcher analyzed regional emissions and air-quality data that local industry sources, including the aluminum giant ALCOA, had reported to the EPA. In doing so, he found that the data TVA and its contractors had collected did "not even come close to agreeing" with this third-party data in terms of the concentration of harmful particulate matter in the air around Kingston. There was far more tiny, potentially harmful particulate matter in the air than TVA or its contractors had let on, he argued.

But perhaps the biggest boon for the plaintiffs was a report written by Elizabeth Ward, a researcher at the American Cancer Society and the chair of the World Trade Center Scientific Advisory Committee, a group created by Congress. In that role, she'd advised the federal government on the cancer risks faced by first responders at the site of the September 11 terror attacks in New York. In her report about Kingston, she accused the defense and its experts of attempting to create a "roadblock" seemingly "calculated to deny plaintiffs the ability to recover damages" by claiming that the sampling data proved that the workers hadn't inhaled harmful quantities of particulate matter or airborne toxins when photos clearly showed "high visible dust levels at the site." Air monitoring had failed to detect airborne toxins at the World Trade Center site, too, Ward explained, but first responders and cleanup workers suffered significant health problems from their exposures there.

Jacobs hired its own experts, who tended to work for independent consulting firms and whose conclusions, predictably, opposed those of the plaintiffs' experts. "I feel confident that the [air-monitoring] samples were collected and analyzed properly," one industrial hygienist wrote. There was also "[no] evidence to support the contention that there was a bias to collect samples on rainy days so the results would be lower." In fact, the expert claimed, the bulk of the samples that Jacobs had collected were from *dry* days. Another expert commissioned by Jacobs reached similar conclusions. Jacobs's attorneys argued that these findings proved that its staff hadn't focused sampling on rainy days, contrary to the narrative that Jeff Friedman and Jim Scott had spun in the courtroom and contrary to the many falsehoods the workers had told.

On an April morning in 2021, Janie Clark woke up and decided to bake biscuits. After a bleak winter marked by a surge in COVID deaths, spring had finally reached East Tennessee. In the Smokies outside Knoxville, cool winds flowed through the towering old-growth timber, glowing green with fresh leaves, while brook trout darted torpedolike in the streams that wrinkled through the mountains, some of the same streams where Ansol and his siblings had splashed as children. But, despite the weather's pleasant turn, Janie and Ansol seldom stepped outside. Ansol's pet turkey, Junior, had died a few months earlier. Ansol had wrapped the bird in a blanket and had him buried. "Ansol looked so pitiful," Janie recalled to a friend on the phone shortly thereafter. "A lot of people would laugh about being upset about a turkey, but it was his world."

After Junior's death, Ansol had withdrawn further into his own shrinking universe. He had little reason to venture into the backyard now, and any outing beyond quick errands risked his catching COVID. Janie doubted he would survive if he were infected. So Ansol spent his days in his favorite maroon armchair, watching *Andy Griffith Show* reruns and the History channel. "My memory is going fast," he told a friend one day. "I can't remember jack." Indeed, Janie noticed that he seldom knew what day it was or when to take his medications. She could no longer trust him to answer the phone, either, for fear he might talk with someone he shouldn't—a reporter, or maybe a Jacobs or TVA goon. Or that was Janie's fear, anyway. She did her best to keep the house clean, the bills paid, and the two of them fed.

Still, despite Ansol's condition, Janie could tolerate only so much time indoors. A few days earlier, they'd attended a Workers Memorial Day ceremony. And, with COVID cases on a sharp decline, Janie was glad they had. The Church of the Savior, in west Knoxville, had hosted the event, which honored dead Kingston workers and other locals who had died from fatal jobsite injuries. A few other former Kingston workers, including Jeff Brewer, showed up, and Janie always liked seeing them. Afterward, to the Clarks' delight, Brewer had given them a jar of wildflower honey he had bought somewhere out in the country. Janie asked Ansol if he would like her to bake biscuits to eat with it. "I'd like that mighty fine," he'd said, in the old-fashioned way he talked whenever he felt pleased. But when they got home and she checked the fridge, she found no buttermilk. And why even bother making biscuits without buttermilk? So she put off the biscuit plan for a few days until she was able to swing by the grocery store. And now that she had the missing ingredient, biscuit day had come. She would bake them for supper, she decided. Ansol would like that.

As much as Janie had enjoyed the Workers Memorial Day ceremony, Ansol had looked exhausted the entire time, and he hadn't recovered from the outing in the few days that followed. She hated to imagine life without Ansol, hated to imagine herself alone on this side of heaven without him, but she found it impossible not to think about this possibility now. They'd recently visited the cross they had planted at the former cleanup site, near the soccer fields, and Ansol had lacked the strength to walk up the small hill to see it. Jim Scott had met the Clarks there. "Ansol won't be with me the next time I come out here," Janie had told him, as they stood together at the cross. Ansol seemed to believe the same. "I've had a good life," he said on another trip to the former cleanup site, hinting that he knew his time might be limited.

In Janie's more optimistic moments, she considered going to college. She could enroll at almost no cost, thanks to a state program, and attending classes would fill a good chunk of her time. Or maybe she would write a children's book, like *The Giving Tree*, one of her favorites. She learned almost everything she knew from library books, and she liked to imagine a little boy or a little girl reading a story she'd written and discovering something new about the world. Just as often, though, she doubted whether she would be able to carry on after Ansol died. What was the point?

Greg Coleman's team, after filing the plaintiffs' expert reports, had spent the past year racing to complete discovery for the second trial phase, which involved deposing some two hundred and fifty workers and their families about their medical conditions. But, a month earlier, in March 2021, Judge Varlan had dealt Coleman's team a sharp blow by agreeing to let Jacobs return the case to the Sixth Circuit Court of Appeals, stalling the case further. In 2019, shortly after the workers beat Jacobs in trial, the Supreme Court had ruled against TVA in an unrelated case. In 2013, a fisherman had been killed, and nearly decapitated, when the boat he was riding in collided with a power line that TVA workers were raising from the bottom of the Tennessee River. The Court's decision stripped TVA of automatic sovereign immunity when its actions were of a commercial, rather than governmental, nature, including when it generated power. Jacobs argued that the ruling somehow made it immune from suit after all, despite the Sixth Circuit's previous decision. Judge Varlan seemed skeptical of Jacobs's argument but let it appeal anyway, explaining that, if the company were in fact immune somehow, it would save everyone "substantial . . . time and resources" if the Sixth Circuit killed the workers' case now, rather than after both sides had slogged through a lengthy second trial phase.

Varlan's decision rocked Janie. "The whole system is stacked against the workers ever getting justice," she emailed a friend after learning of Jacobs's appeal. "They have been betrayed on every side." So far, she hadn't been terribly impressed by Coleman, and she worried whether his team would beat Jacobs in the Sixth Circuit, as Scott had. Scott still called her and Ansol about once a week, and she appreciated the gesture, but she hated that he had run out of money and backed away from the case. As far as she was concerned, he was still their lawyer, not Coleman, but neither she nor Ansol nor any other worker had any real say in the matter. A letter showed up in the mail one day informing them that Coleman was now leading the case.

At one-thirty in the afternoon on that April day, before Janie began making biscuits, she sat in a rocking chair in her bedroom, as she often did after lunch. It was in this same bedroom where she and Ansol had been sleeping the December morning when his general foreman had called about the Kingston disaster. As Janie gazed out the window, she heard a loud thud through the open door to the kitchen—the familiar, solid thud of flesh meeting floor. She flew through the kitchen into the living room. Ansol was face down in front of his armchair. He'd split his head falling onto the hardwood floor. Blood poured from the wound. His glasses were twisted and broken.

Janie rushed for him and screamed his name. Bergan, hearing the commotion, darted into the room and dialed 911. "Yes, my father is having a medical emergency," he sputtered to the operator. "He's passed out on the floor." Bergan rattled off his name and the family's address.

Janie shrieked, *"Ansol!"*

"Okay, don't hang up," the operator told Bergan. "I'm going to let you speak to EMS."

"Okay," Bergan said, then added, "Okay, he's foaming at the mouth." But no one seemed to be listening. He took three long, anxious breaths.

After some dialing, a second operator came on and asked Bergan to repeat all the information he had already shared.

Janie was hysterical: *"ANSOL!"*

"Okay, I'm getting a lot of static," the operator said. Bergan repeated his phone number, fighting to be heard over his mother, over the screams.

"Sir! Sir!" the operator said. "Let me finish what I was saying. I have your phone number confirmed."

At that, Bergan dropped the phone.

First responders reached the Clarks' home within minutes. Bergan was performing CPR on Ansol, who was still alive but unconscious. An emergency crew loaded him into an ambulance and raced him to Parkwest Medical Center. His heart had stopped beating, and his brain had stopped receiving oxygen. Janie was told that he needed immediate emergency surgery to stand any chance of survival.

Janie entered a great, gray fog. A fugue state, she later called it. Things were happening to her, but she wasn't in control. Doctors and nurses talked to her, but their words carried no meaning. The noises of the hospital whirred around her. In her delirium, in the blinding mist, she knew, with absolute certainty, with terrible, pure clarity, that Ansol had left her. Once, while doing yard work, he had collapsed. Janie had backed her car out of the driveway, loaded him in, and helped him inside, then put him in a cold bath. That revived him. But this time, as doctors rushed him into the operating room, she knew that no amount of effort would bring him back.

Janie considered Jamie Satterfield, the reporter, one of her closest friends, and, even in her fugue state, she had the wherewithal to answer the phone when Satterfield called. Bergan had texted Satterfield about Ansol. She asked if Janie wanted her to come to the hospital for support. Janie said she appreciated the offer but said no. The hospital, Janie said, was too far from Satterfield's home outside Knoxville. Plus, with COVID, Satterfield probably wouldn't be able to come inside anyway.

Throughout the night, Bergan texted updates to Satterfield, who shared the news with a small circle of the Clarks' friends. Among them was Jim Scott. He was driving down I-40, heading home after finishing some work in Loudoun County, when he received a text message about Ansol. He pulled off at the Watt Road exit, found a truck stop, and parked. He said a prayer, and then he cried. He didn't want to badger Bergan with follow-up questions. He knew that Janie was a private person when it came to Ansol's health, so he called Satterfield and asked what she thought he should do. "Just pray," she told him. Ansol probably wouldn't survive surgery, she said.

Scott took his sons out for Italian food that night. He had known this day was coming for years, yet the news still overwhelmed him. His sons felt the weight. "Is Ms. Clark going to be okay?" asked Sam. Jack said Jacobs's staff ought to go to jail.

Scott had meant to call Ansol that afternoon—they hadn't talked in three or four days, which was longer than usual—and he desperately hoped they could speak one more time. Scott wanted to tell Ansol everything he'd learned from him since the evening, nearly a decade earlier now, when he and the other workers first stepped into his law office on Kingston Pike. "That guy has been through complete and total hell," Scott said. And yet, even as Ansol's body failed, he never complained, never seemed to be in a foul mood, never said anything to suggest that he felt sorry for himself. Even after Ansol's health largely confined him indoors, whenever Scott called, he would say cheerfully, "Hey, James"—Ansol always called him that—"I'm just sitting here in my chair." The only thing that seemed to bother Ansol was the harm coal ash had caused to his friends and their families.

Parkwest hugs Interstate 40, and trucks howled past late into the night, awash in the orange glow of highway lights. Ansol remained in surgery until after nine o'clock, as doctors put stents into his heart. He survived surgery, to Jamie Satterfield's surprise, but he remained in critical care in an induced coma. Janie sat by his bed and held his hand. His eyes were closed, and she felt grateful for that. "Ansol, it's me," she said. His leg flinched. "He does that," an attendant interjected, dashing Janie's momentary hope that Ansol had recognized her voice. Spontaneous movements are common among brain-injury patients.

On April 30, two days after Ansol collapsed, doctors checked his brain function and concluded that he wouldn't regain consciousness. Janie didn't need to be told. She didn't want to keep Ansol on life support, but, for Bergan's sake, she let him remain on it for the rest of the day.

Early the next morning, Janie and Bergan returned to the hospital. They pulled up chairs on either side of Ansol's bed and squeezed his hand and said their goodbyes. His eyes were open now. The nurses explained that, once they began shutting off the ventilator and the other machines that sustained him, he would exhale a final time, then breathe no more. Ansol did just as the nurses promised.

Ansol Dwain Clark died on May 1, 2021, twelve years, four months, and nine days after the December morning he responded to the Kingston spill. He was seventy years old. He had grown up on a farm without indoor plumbing, served his country during wartime, married the woman he loved, raised a son, built a home, joined a union, and took action when a disaster visited his community. He was a good man, by all accounts.

The Kingston workers had a private Facebook page where they shared news and case updates. The day after Ansol's death, Bergan posted a photo of his father. He wore a green hard hat and yellow reflective safety vest and held a white dove, with an amused smile spread across his face. "In loving memory of ❤ Ansol Clark ❤," the post read. "The best father and husband in the world. We want to thank everyone for all of the love and support."

When Janie returned home from the hospital, everyone she knew seemed to call, but she felt there was only one person she could speak with candidly. She dialed Jamie Satterfield's number. Satterfield said she had been expecting to hear from Janie. Satterfield's husband had passed away six years earlier, and she described to Janie what she said would be the longest journey of her life: that of a widow. Satterfield encouraged Janie to remember that the Lord had called Janie and Ansol for this path, to fight for the Kingston workers. She added that, not long before Ansol died, she had told him, "I know that you worry about Janie. But I want you to know she's going to be taken care of." Satterfield said she believed that was true: Janie would carry on. She had to. As Janie held the phone to her ear, listening closely, a wave of peace rolled over her. A righteous peace. Janie believed she would carry on, too, and that Ansol wouldn't forsake her.

A dream later convinced her of this. It was twilight, and she was in her bedroom when Ansol appeared. His body was not sickly and exhausted, full of cancer, full of hurt; it was his thirty-year-old frame, strong and healthy. His young, taut skin seemed to glow. She ran to him and wrapped him in a hug. "Does this mean you can stay?" she asked. No, he told her. But he was able to see her from the other side of this life, he said, and she should find comfort in that truth.

A haze, dense and black, rolled over Jim Scott. A few days after Ansol died, he went hiking with some friends near Tellico Plains, a mountain town an hour's drive from Knoxville. As he followed the trails through the shimmering spring woods, his mind returned to Ansol's body hitting the thick hardwood floor. Scott had learned about the fall shortly after Ansol's death, and he couldn't shake the image. Whenever his thoughts did briefly turn from Ansol, he fixated on Jacobs's absurd renewed appeal to the Sixth Circuit. The company seemed to believe it was immune from killing people. Could you read the appeal any other way?

Amid the gloom of Ansol's death and Jacobs's new appeal, a new, much-needed bright spot had twinkled alive in Scott's life: he had a girlfriend. Her name was Lisa Niles. He'd known her since his days as an assistant district attorney. She was the chief judicial aide for the Loudoun County courts, and he liked her so much that he hoped his crazed work hours wouldn't push her away. The risk was real.

On the night of Saturday, May 8, Niles came to Scott's condo. At around ten o'clock, as they watched a movie in the den, Scott felt tingling in his face and in one leg. Soon, numbness. A few days earlier, he'd received his second COVID vaccine shot, which had left him fatigued and thirsty. He'd filled a cooler with water and drank one bottle after another as he worked that week, tossing the empties on the floor next to his bed. The water had helped, he thought, so when his face went numb, he poured a glass in the kitchen. Over the next twenty minutes, the numbness spread, then the muscles in his face pulsated and tightened. His hands and fingers stopped working. What was happening? Jack, now a high-school senior, was watching *Curb Your Enthusiasm* in his bedroom. Scared, Jim called for him, and together Jack and Lisa loaded Jim into her Jeep and sped him to Parkwest.

After Jim described his symptoms, nurses hurried him from triage to the emergency room, which frightened him. Doctors and nurses swarmed his bed, checking his vitals. The color had drained from his face. His blood pressure, usually high, had plummeted.

Doctors ran through a battery of tests. In doing so, they realized that the right side of Jim's brain was damaged. He had suffered a transient ischemic attack, or TIA, often referred to as a ministroke. A blockage had interrupted the blood flow to his brain, causing him to lose control of his face and extremities. All the water he drank might have contributed to the problem, doctors said, by throwing off his sodium levels. But stress provided a more likely explanation. A TIA usually doesn't cause lasting brain damage, but it can signal a full stroke ahead. He needed to take care of himself, doctors warned. They advised that he eat no more than forty grams of protein a day. That, and he needed to rest.

When Jack visited his dad the next morning, Jim looked and felt fine, but doctors wanted to keep him in the hospital for another day for observation. Though he had no choice, he felt guilty for not being available for Janie after Ansol's death.

Lisa stayed with him, working on her laptop as he slept and rested. He had a lot of time to think. The workers had overcome every legal hurdle so far, had proved time and again that the law was on their side, and yet their case was *still* unresolved. Though Greg Coleman was now leading the plaintiffs' team, many of the Kingston workers still called Scott whenever they had questions or, just as often, complaints about Coleman. They didn't like that they often struggled to get an attorney on the phone whenever they called his office, nor did they like that case updates were sporadic. Plus, they hadn't hired Coleman. They'd hired Scott. He was their attorney, many felt, and he still acted like it, by fielding their calls. One friend noticed that Scott seemed to resent having to let other attorneys run with the case.

The ministroke changed Scott's perspective. Niles told him that all the stress had caught up with him, and he agreed. He had worried too much about the workers, he said, and let it beat him down. He had to move on, for his sons' sake and for his own. He had to trust that Coleman, a fine and decent lawyer by all measures, would hold Jacobs to account and secure the workers an acceptable recovery. Scott was later referred to a grief counselor to help him cope, which embarrassed him. But the more he thought about the suggestion, the more he understood: letting Coleman run with the case was a grievous loss.

Scott's hospital stay afforded him the best rest he'd had in years. Tyler Roper visited Scott after he returned home and said he looked like a new person. His brain still felt fuzzy from whatever medicine and vitamins doctors had put in his IV drip, but he said he was happy. "I'm not going to let this stuff"—the workers' case—"bother me like it used to," he said.

Over the next three weeks, Scott still felt fatigued, but he gradually regained control of his face and felt as though he was on the mend. On the last Sunday in May 2021, he woke up before seven and turned on his bedroom TV. It was a long holiday weekend, with Memorial Day on Monday. He clicked on the History channel. One segment, in a program about American foods, focused on M&M's. Scott, a candy fiend, had tried, and tried earnestly, to eat healthy in the weeks following his ministroke: grilled chicken, light pasta, smoothies. But, as he watched, sweets beckoned. He retrieved a bag of peanut M&M's he had stashed in his condo and, returning to bed, shoved a handful into his mouth—the only true and decent way to eat peanut M&M's, in his view. But when he swallowed, a sharp pain stabbed his chest. He breathed in, but it wasn't easy. He coughed and tried to vomit but couldn't force anything out. Panicked, he reached for his phone and asked Lisa to come over. "I can't breathe well," he said.

When Lisa arrived, about forty-five minutes later, Scott was still struggling for air. He tried to explain that an M&M, or part of its hard sugar shell, had gone down his windpipe. But he couldn't talk well enough to be understood. He was choking. Hit my back, he indicated to Lisa. She did, several times. Then she lay on the bed and kicked his back. Nothing helped. "We're calling 911," she said.

"My boyfriend, who is fifty-three, is experiencing difficulty breathing," she said after the dispatcher picked up. He was eating M&M's, she explained, and now some were in his lungs. He was dizzy and weak.

Almost twenty minutes passed before an ambulance arrived, and by the time it did, Scott had collapsed onto the floor.

EMTs loaded Jim onto a gurney and hurried him to the University of Tennessee Medical Center, four miles away. When he reached the emergency room, his body temperature had plunged; not enough oxygen was circulating through his body or to his brain. Doctors and nurses crowded around his bed and put him on oxygen and wrapped him in a silver warming blanket attached to a heating unit. "I'm *hurting*," he moaned. "I'm *hurting*. I'm *hurting*."

From the ER, Lisa dialed Jack, who'd stayed the night with a friend. "There's been an event," she said abruptly when he answered. His dad's condition was dire, far more dire than it had been with the ministroke.

When Jack strode into the hospital thirty minutes later, Lisa met him in the lobby and led him to his father's room. A ventilator mask, pulled over Jim's nose and mouth, forced air into his lungs. When Jim saw Jack enter, he tried to yank off the mask to talk. "You cannot take this off, Mr. Scott," a doctor insisted. His blood oxygen levels had fallen by around 40 percent. "You're seconds away from being intubated," the doctor said.

Jim, dazed and frightened, fought the X-ray machine, but doctors managed to see that the M&M had infected his lungs. He had double pneumonia, and the infection was spreading. A CT scan revealed that his kidneys were shutting down. His body was entering septic shock.

The hospital staff seemed unable to reconcile his dire condition with the M&M story. It seemed ridiculous to Jack and Lisa, too. How had a piece of candy put his life in jeopardy?

Jim, hooked to monitors and an IV drip, bobbed in and out of consciousness. Doctors made it clear to Lisa and Jack that they needed to prepare for the possibility that he might not survive. Jack, eyes reddening, excused himself from the room after staff withdrew a large sample of blood from Jim's wrist. An hour passed before Jim relaxed and fell into a long, uneasy sleep.

That afternoon, with Jim's odds of survival still uncertain, doctors transferred him to the hospital's critical-care unit. Before doctors could remove the candy from his lungs, they needed to raise his blood oxygen levels and control his infections, and that took time. Jim's son Sam, who had been with Jim's ex-wife all day, visited the hospital that evening, in case Jim didn't last through the night.

Jim had moments of semi-lucidity that evening, but he didn't fully wake up until the next day. When he blinked and opened his eyes, he was hooked up to monitors and, by his count, four different IVs, plus a ventilator. His brain felt scrambled, and fluids had puffed up his body. His stomach was swollen, too, though he hadn't eaten anything in at least a day.

During his first day and a half in critical care, he mostly slept, or tried to. Every two or three hours, day or night, nurses drew blood or checked his vitals, which made uninterrupted rest all but impossible. Whenever he was awake, he didn't feel like talking. His chest and sides screamed in pain whenever he moved or spoke; he had torn muscles coughing and strained his lungs.

After three days, Jim showed improvement and was moved to another floor for further observation. Jack visited every day. As Jim's mind gradually sharpened, he could tell that his health scare had spooked Jack, and he was glad when Jack started teasing him again. Jim had once considered himself abnormally fortunate. He would misplace a $20 bill, then find another on the sidewalk or in an old coat. Jack joked that he was now the unluckiest man on Earth. Divorce, money problems, a life-consuming case, two freak health crises.

Jim spent the better part of two weeks in the hospital. He decided against surgery to remove the candy in his lungs, since the procedure would require that he stay on a ventilator for an extra week, and he wanted to go home, even if it prolonged his recovery.

Jim needed to remain on oxygen twenty-four hours a day until his lungs began to heal. Lisa bought him a portable oxygen tank from a medical-supply store and helped him to get settled into his condo. During his first week at home, he slept for fifteen hours a day. He had always felt empathy for the Kingston workers, but his bout of double pneumonia thrust him, for the first time, into the hell of having bad lungs. The entire episode was a nightmare, he told a friend over the phone. He couldn't imagine the torture that Ansol, not yet dead a month, had endured. After his ministroke, Jim had planned to take it easy. Now his body would force him to.

Scott recovered slowly. He slept until three-thirty p.m. some days. His voice gained a slight rasp, and his feet took uneasy steps across the floor of his condo. Doctors told him that he might need four to six months to recover. As he regained his strength, he accepted new cases, ones that had nothing to do with TVA or coal ash. One involved a young electrician gravely burned on a jobsite. Mostly, though, he spent time with Lisa. By November 2021, six months after he swallowed the near-fatal M&M, he felt well enough to fly with her to New York for a long weekend. They saw *The Lehman Trilogy* on Broadway and ate steaks—the best Scott had ever had—at Sparks, on East Forty-sixth Street. When they walked past the M&M's megastore in Times Square, she badgered him to take a photo in front of it. He kept walking.

He took three weeks off work for the holidays that December, a first in all his years practicing law. He and his sons watched movies, ate at Aubrey's, played trivia. Jacobs's appeal to the Sixth Circuit had stalled the coal-ash case again, and he hated that for the workers and their families, but he tried not to let the appeal dominate his thoughts. He tried to be happy. He told himself that Greg Coleman's team would stomp Jacobs just like he had. He had to move on, and, as the months crawled by, other people involved in the litigation gradually moved on as well.

Jeff Friedman and Gary Davis took other worthy cases, including water-pollution suits in north Georgia and Alabama.

John Dupree, tired of sharing an office with the other attorneys, relocated to a different building a few blocks away. He talked about wanting to retire and teach high-school history, but instead he kept practicing law.

Keith Stewart did one thing he thought he'd never do—he joined a local law firm. He bought a house in the country. He played more golf.

Tyler Roper spent more time with his wife and young daughters. He grew disenchanted with work and stopped coming into the office much.

Jeff Brewer met his first grandchild, one of his greatest hopes in life. He and his wife babysat on weekends when he wasn't driving trucks.

Mike McCarthy took a job at Y-12, in Oak Ridge. He raised his two children alone with help from some neighbors.

More workers died: Tommy Johnson, Doug Bledsoe, Jackie Paul Bunch.

Buddy Scott died, too, at the age of eighty-three. Shortly before he passed, he told Jim that he was proud of him, for his work on the Jacobs case and for the two fine sons he'd raised.

Jack Scott enrolled at the University of Tennessee. Sam would begin classes at Belmont University, in Nashville, a few years later.

Jamie Satterfield continued to investigate the Kingston cleanup. In doing so, she revealed that, in 2009, at the very start of the project, the Tennessee Department of Environment and Conservation had detected high levels of radium and uranium in the coal ash. But, shortly after this data was posted online, state officials replaced the figures with ones that were lower by as much as 98 percent—clearly suggesting some sort of cover-up. TDEC, in response to Satterfield's reporting, didn't deny that the data had been altered, but a spokeswoman said the agency didn't know which employee, all those years ago, had changed it. At Satterfield's request, Avner Vengosh, of Duke, analyzed samples of the Kingston coal ash and corroborated her reporting, finding that the uranium in the ash exceeded the levels reported by TDEC and TVA by at least threefold. And it was likely not innocuous. A Columbia professor retained by Coleman's team produced a report in which he concluded that radioactive contamination at Kingston had greatly increased the workers' risk of lung cancer, leukemia, and other cancers. Jacobs should have known, based on ample scientific literature, about coal ash's radiological hazards, the professor wrote. Instead, he added, "information, data, and procedures for proper monitoring . . . were negligently or recklessly disregarded."

Satterfield, digging further, discovered that, in 2009, the Occupational Safety and Health Administration had received an anonymous complaint that the Kingston workers were overexposed to radiation. But, rather than investigate, OSHA asked TVA to look into the matter itself. When a TVA employee reported back to OSHA a month later, he claimed that TVA had provided respirators to the workers during the first few months of the cleanup, a generally untrue statement. TVA also told OSHA that, based on air-monitoring data, the workers were exposed to "radium at safe levels"—the reason it hadn't required respirators throughout the cleanup project's duration.

One evening, in the middle of Satterfield's reporting, she attended a public meeting held by the government of Anderson County, a municipality a few miles from Kingston. She'd learned that a playground next to a TVA coal-fired power plant there called Bull Run had been built atop a coal-ash pile. Vengosh had tested the soil and confirmed that it contained coal ash. He told her, "The kids that are playing there would be exposed every time dust is kicked up or they are playing in sand there or whatever kids do."

At the meeting, Satterfield, overcome by Ansol's death and her discoveries about Kingston, warned county leaders of the risk of letting children play on the equipment. She stood at a microphone. "The problem is that when you breathe [coal ash] in, then this radiation is in the body," she said, hitting her hands against her chest. The Kingston cleanup workers, like Ansol, were exposed to coal-ash dust for years, she said, and "their bodies are proof of what it does."

Welling with tears, she told the county leaders that she had recently visited the playground and talked with a mother there. "She brought her kids there every day!" Satterfield yelled. "She's a good momma! And when I gave her the right information [about coal ash], she quit bringing her kids!" A buzzer went off, signaling that Satterfield's time had expired. "I'm sorry," she said, a hand pressed against her heart. "You all can protect children starting today, and you can hold TVA accountable! Hell, yes, there ought to be a law against this stuff!" But right now, she said, when it came to coal ash, "the EPA doesn't have a standard." She finished by saying that she might need a donation, because "I'm going to get fired for doing this. But I had to. God required it."

She guessed right about being fired. *The Knoxville News Sentinel* terminated her days after she spoke at the meeting, briskly ending her twenty-seven-year career at the paper. She had broken journalism norms by expressing her views so freely and with such righteous anger. When she moved out of her office, she took her documents related to her TVA investigation, some of which she kept in an overstuffed red folder. She stuck a yellow sticky note on the front and scrawled on it in pen "Kingston Expendables Murder Book."

In the weeks to come, Satterfield, devastated but determined to hold TVA and Jacobs to account, tried to convince a grand jury to bring criminal charges against certain TVA and Jacobs personnel, including Tom Bock. Janie Clark helped her prepare a presentation. But an agent with the Tennessee Bureau of Investigation persuaded the grand jury not to recommend charges, on the basis that federal, not state, authorities should investigate Jacobs or TVA, since the disaster site was under federal jurisdiction. Satterfield suspected that, in truth, state investigators wanted the Kingston disaster out of the headlines. A month after she was fired from the *Sentinel*, the Ford Motor Company announced that it would spend nearly $6 billion to build a mammoth new factory outside Memphis, a major coup for the state. TVA had reportedly worked with Governor Bill Lee to help lure Ford to Tennessee, with promises of reliable, low-cost electricity. When Satterfield had a chance to ask Governor Lee about the workers' case, he told her, "I support TVA."

On March 11, 2022, thirteen years after the Kingston disaster and three years after the jury rendered a verdict in the workers' favor, Jacobs Engineering again argued its case, via video conference, before the Sixth Circuit. The defense lawyer representing Jacobs, Theane Evangelis, contended that the Supreme Court's decision in the case involving the dead boater changed how the court should analyze Jacobs's immunity. Evangelis rehashed many of the arguments the defense had made throughout litigation: that cleaning up the Kingston coal sludge was part of TVA's governmental duties and that, since Jacobs had helped to oversee the cleanup, it should share in TVA's immunity. The trouble with the workers' suit, Evangelis told the three-judge panel, was that it attacked "TVA's choices, its policy judgment, [and its] standard of care," and interfered with TVA's ability to carry out its governmental duties.

The Sixth Circuit disagreed. In an opinion issued two months after oral arguments, one of the judges wrote, "TVA would not have been immune from suit" on the grounds that the workers' case interfered with its governmental duties, because its power operations were of a commercial, not governmental, nature. And since that was true, Jacobs couldn't claim that it had acted as an extension of the government at Kingston. Besides, the judge noted, the facts of the case suggested that Jacobs had violated its contract with TVA by failing to honor the workers' dust-mask prescriptions, by neglecting to tell TVA of repeated worker complaints about the coal ash, and by selectively distributing the personal air monitors. Jacobs's appeal was denied.

The Sixth Circuit's decision narrowed Jacobs's options. It would either need to settle or have its name in the press for another three or four years, at minimum, as it fought every worker's individual complaint in court. It chose the former, and would soon rename itself Jacobs Solutions and spin off its government-contracting divisions into a separate company, called Critical Mission Solutions.

In September 2022, Jacobs's defense team resumed negotiations with Greg Coleman's firm and submitted a new settlement offer, and by January 2023, the two sides had reached a tentative agreement. Jacobs would pay two hundred and twenty-one workers a total of $77.5 million. Once the attorneys took their fees—about $26 million—and subtracted their expenses, the workers would be left with roughly $49 million, or about $222,000 each. From that sum, they would have to reimburse their insurance companies whatever money they'd spent to cover their medical expenses. The sickest workers, as a result, would likely end up with very little cash. Another problem was that Jacobs insisted on a global settlement, meaning that all two hundred and twenty-one workers had to accept the deal or none would receive anything.

The settlement was shit, in many of the workers' opinion. It was just less shitty than Jacobs's previous offers. Coleman's team urged the workers to take the deal anyway, because returning to trial would cost untold sums and carried no promise of victory.

Another wrinkle: Jacobs had appealed the case to the Tennessee Supreme Court in an attempt to boot forty plaintiffs off the lawsuit, under a little-known, pro-business state law that limited workers' ability to sue their employers over exposure to silica, a mineral common on construction sites. Jacobs argued that, since silica was fly ash's most abundant constituent, state law barred the plaintiffs from suing the company. The Tennessee Supreme Court had yet to rule on the matter, but the possibility that it might side with Jacobs further incentivized the workers to accept Jacobs's deal.

The workers had gone to trial in 2018 with strong-willed attorneys, strong evidence, and strong scientific facts. Yet, in the end, none of it seemed to matter. What mattered was that Jacobs had more money than they did. A few months before the company issued its final settlement offer, it announced that it had made $644 million in profit in 2022. Its settlement offer amounted to about 12 percent of that haul. With all that money, Jacobs could prolong the case, with delay after delay, until the plaintiffs capitulated. "It was never about [settlement] money to me; it was about the principal," Jeff Brewer told a friend one Saturday morning, as he babysat his infant granddaughter. "No matter how much money they give anybody, it'll never bring back Ansol or Mike Shelton, and it won't bring back our health." He added, "The judicial system and Judge Varlan have been unfair to the working people." But, Brewer said, at least if he accepted Jacobs's offer, the case would at last be over. Many of the other workers felt similarly. But Brewer vowed to keep fighting for the working man, because no one else seemed to be.

The same month the two sides reached a tentative settlement agreement, Jim Scott and Lisa Niles flew to Paris. They arrived in the early morning and wandered the awakening city, bathed in cold, golden light. They passed the Arc de Triomphe and reached the Eiffel Tower by nine-thirty. The top floor, with the best views, was closed, so, while on the second floor, almost four hundred feet above Paris, Jim retrieved a ring from his pocket. Forgetting to kneel, he told Lisa he'd been looking for a woman like her his entire life. They married a little over a month later, in the little white sanctuary of the Cumberland Presbyterian Church in Loudon, Tennessee, where Lisa lived.

Two days later, the newlyweds flew to the island of Anguilla. Jim had visited before, but more than a decade and a half had passed since his last trip. The white sand and clear water had lost none of their magic in the intervening years. He and Lisa lay on the beach and watched as the breeze pulled a catamaran through the water. After a while, it lowered its sail and bobbed in the tide. How, Jim wondered, had he come out on the other side of this case alive? More than fifty Kingston workers had died, simply because they were, in most cases, blue-collar guys who took hard, manual jobs to provide for their families. They deserved better endings, and they deserved more money, but Jim hoped their settlements would help somewhat. As far as his payment went, once the attorneys divided up their fee, he would probably take home $2 million, perhaps even $3 million. He didn't know for sure yet.

He felt relieved that the case was settling—almost a decade of litigation was long enough—but the outcome left him unsatisfied. He had done his best to expose Jacobs's wrongdoing, but TVA had faced no real reckoning. He tried to maintain hope that one day it would. Three Tennessee representatives had recently cosponsored a bill called the TVA Transparency Act, which aimed to increase public involvement in the agency's decision-making process. The bill didn't call for a total overhaul of TVA, but perhaps one bill would lead to another, then Congress would one day pass meaningful reforms. Until then, the workers' case had, at the very least, turned public opinion sharply against TVA, or so it seemed to Jim. He'd noticed that whenever he mentioned the case to someone in Knoxville—a bartender, a waiter, an old friend—they had a remarkably similar reaction: *It's awful what TVA did to those workers*. The injustice was clear. Still, Jim wondered, and wondered sincerely, whether the case had been worth almost a decade of his life and all the personal turmoil that came with it. If he had the option to do it all again, to start from zero and build the case from nothing, he sometimes questioned whether he would. He hadn't had a choice, though. No one else would have taken the case had he declined to. No one else would have saved it on appeal. No one else would have wrecked their life for it. And the case demanded that and more. So, in the end, he thought he would take the case again. He would have to.

• • •

In the months that followed, streaks of light pierced the clouds. In the spring of 2023, Michael Regan, the administrator of the EPA, strode onto a stage at the University of Maryland and took his place in front of a clear lectern. He was fit and handsome in his mid-forties with a sincere, good-natured smile. Four American flags flanked him, and a banner to his back read, TACKLING THE CLIMATE CRISIS. Regan, the first Black man to lead the EPA, had been tapped for the job by President-elect Joe Biden in 2020. Before that, he'd served as the head of the North Carolina Department of Environmental Quality, where he had ordered Duke Energy, a power company with a larger generation capacity than TVA's, to dig up and dispose of eighty million tons of coal ash from six sites across the state.

Regan had not let up on power companies since joining the EPA. He quickly set about restoring some of the hundred-plus environmental regulations that Donald Trump's administration had rolled back during its four years in power. Most notably, the EPA had proposed a rule that would force power plants to reduce their discharges of toxic pollutants into lakes and streams, reversing the Trump administration's efforts to relax such standards. Janie and Ansol Clark had advocated against this policy change before the 2018 trial.

At the University of Maryland, Regan began his remarks by applauding young people for demanding action on climate change. "We hear you," he said, "and I know for certain that President Biden does, too." That was why, he said, "we're proposing new technology standards that will significantly reduce greenhouse-gas emission from fossil-fuel-fired power plants." When finalized, he explained, these new standards would avoid an estimated six hundred and seventeen million metric tons of carbon-dioxide pollution by the year 2042. "Folks," he said, "that's equivalent to the annual emissions of one hundred and thirty-seven million cars or passenger vehicles." And these reduced emissions would prevent as many as thirteen hundred premature deaths annually.

Days after Regan's speech, the EPA went further, announcing that it would close a loophole that had exempted at least two hundred and sixty-one inactive "legacy" coal-ash dump sites from regulation. Under existing EPA rules, power companies were able to let their abandoned, unlined dump sites pollute groundwater with no consequence. The

EPA's new amendment would require power companies, like TVA, to monitor groundwater near their unlined coal-ash dumps and to clean up any contamination.

The New York Times published a story about the EPA's new coal-ash amendment, noting that the Kingston spill—"one of the largest industrial disasters in U.S. history"—had helped to spur the first federal coal-ash rules, in 2015. The story included a photo, taken in December 2008, of the East Tennessee countryside smothered in gray coal muck. What the *Times* story didn't include was any mention of the men and women who had suffered and died because of the disaster.

On the March afternoon in 2023 that would have been Janie and Ansol's fifty-first wedding anniversary, she stayed at home, talking with friends on the phone and piddling around the house. She'd kept busy in recent months. First, with the help of a local congressman, she'd arranged to have a flag flown over the U.S. Capitol in the workers' memory—a symbolic gesture that moved her a great deal. Then, in December 2022, to commemorate the fourteenth anniversary of the Kingston disaster, she'd worked with some other workers' families and with the local Sierra Club chapter to run messages on four billboards throughout the greater Knoxville area. They read, THANK YOU TO ALL KINGSTON COAL ASH CLEANUP WORKERS. Next to these words was an illustration of a white dove.

At about five o'clock on the day of the anniversary, she sat down in her bedroom to eat a Snickers candy bar. She was interrupted by a phone call from a friend, a writer she'd gotten to know over the past five-odd years. She'd been updating the house, she explained. She was there all the time, so why not? She painted the walls and bought new pillows and throw blankets. The writer knew the room well and said he could picture it. She and the writer had met shortly after he and his wife had learned they were expecting their first child. Now they had two beautiful daughters. Janie took delight in hearing about them, in knowing of their girlhood joys. Good things were still happening in this world, magical things even. She had to remind herself of that.

Bergan, she told her friend, believed that she had many good years ahead of her. She said he had asked her to consider downsizing and buying an apartment in a community with other folks her age. She would need to think about it. This was her and Ansol's home.

Janie mentioned that August would mark ten years since Jim Scott had filed the workers' suit against Jacobs Engineering. She wasn't sure she'd do it again if given the option, she said. She reminded her friend that when Ansol had first told her about meeting with Scott she had discouraged the idea. She eventually agreed that they should sue Jacobs, and some good things had come out of the lawsuit, like her friendship with Jamie Satterfield and some of the other workers' wives. But now, she said, she sometimes wondered whether she should have trusted her initial impulse and avoided the case. She would always hold Jim Scott in her heart, but he and the lawyers had disappointed her. For all their pride and relief in the settlement, they operated in a dirty system, and this system had forced them to make an unjust compromise. They should have taken Jacobs back to court and beaten them in the second trial phase, to teach Jacobs and TVA and the rest of corporate America that they couldn't treat blue-collar workers the way Ansol had been treated. She wanted to defeat Jacobs publicly. But there would be no second trial. Every lawyer involved in the case had underestimated Jacobs and TVA, she believed. They had all thought that their side would prevail with facts and evidence and compelling testimony. But they had deceived themselves.

She hadn't yet met with Greg Coleman's team to learn precisely how much money she'd get if she accepted Jacobs's settlement offer. Maybe a couple of hundred thousand dollars. But even a billion dollars wouldn't change anything. The case was about more than money for her. It was about justice, and that justice had been thwarted.

She believed that the story of Ansol and the other Kingston workers had, in almost every respect, ended in tragedy. But she said she refused to let the story end without some goodness. She and Ansol were just average working people before he got sick. They'd heard about bad things happening in the news—environmental disasters, legal injustices, government failures—but it took Ansol's failing health to awaken them to the hideous truth that almost no one in a position of power looked out for working men and women. Maybe Janie could convince other working-class families to care about jobsite safety, and to demand better from TVA and state agencies and the federal government before tragedy visited their homes and wrecked their lives. Maybe that was God's plan for her. She and several other Kingston widows had already formed a coalition. "We're going to see that this doesn't happen again," she said.

She told her friend about an upcoming public meeting hosted by TVA. She planned to attend, she said, and she did. A few weeks later, dressed in a black cardigan and matching black pants, she would stand at a lectern and tell TVA's current CEO, Jeff Lyash, that, in denying the Kingston workers respiratory protection, TVA and Jacobs had denied them "their own basic fundamental right to life." In a sharp tone, she would demand that TVA employ honest, competent contractors. "Workers must be protected," she would insist, adding that "from now on, people will *always* remember Kingston."

She told her friend that, beyond the meeting, she had another plan, a private one. She had decided that, no matter how much or how little money she received from Jacobs, she would go with Ansol—or at least his ashes—to the ocean, just as they had long intended. North Carolina, with its white, semi-wild beaches, lay on the other side of the Great Smoky Mountains. She could make the trip in a day. Maybe Bergan would drive her. They would weave through the big lush mountains, climbing and climbing, and then flow out of the hills into the hot, honeyed sunlight of the piedmont and roll on to the coast. She didn't know which beach she would visit, she said, but she would go. That was certain. She would find a quiet spot among the grassy dunes, nowhere near sunbathers or partiers, and then walk toward the water's edge, sun and waves and gentle winds whipping. Then she would scatter Ansol's ashes into the sea. She had made a life with him. A sweet life, a gentle life. TVA and Jacobs had taken almost everything from her. But they couldn't rob her of that—all those years of goodness and light. Once Ansol's ashes had mingled with and disappeared into the ocean, she would walk out into the surf and let it roll over her ankles and her calves and feel the cool goodness of the water against her skin and try to feel clean again.

Acknowledgments

I wouldn't have been able to write this book without the full faith and (almost) endless patience of my wife, Caroline. Neither of us suspected that it would take me five years to complete it, and it's to her tremendous credit that she put up with me as I reported and wrote it. Janie Clark once told me that I'm the luckiest man alive, and with a wife like Caroline, I cannot disagree. She's a saint of saints, and she has my whole heart.

My oldest daughter was born at the beginning of the reporting process, and my second was born as I raced to finish a manuscript for Knopf. The babies didn't make the reporting or writing easier, but they made life sweeter. So thank you for that, Miller and Margot. I owe my parents, Leigh and Curtis Sullivan, and my in-laws, Taylor and Marie Morris, a tremendous debt of gratitude. They bought me precious writing time by watching my daughters, especially during the pandemic. I thank all my family, especially my sister and her husband, Kirby and Clayton Ginn, who let me stay at their home, in Knoxville, on my many reporting trips there. Clayton also obtained an important transcript for me.

I feel absurdly lucky to be publishing my first book with Jonathan Segal at Knopf. He's a legend, and I am certainly not, but he took my work seriously and edited my manuscript with rigor, thoughtfulness, and speed; I owe him much for that. I also feel absurdly lucky that my agent, Elyse Cheney, took me on as a client and that she and Alice Whitwham helped me shape my book proposal.

I learned how to write largely by editing other people, and I learned from some of the best: Jessica Camille Aguirre, Rick Bass, Matthew Bremner, Devin Gordon, Bill Heavey, Hal Herring, Ben Mathis-Lilley, T. Edward

Nickens, Nick Paumgarten, Anna Peele, David E. Petzal, Sarah Rieger, David Sedaris, Nico Walker, Stacey Woods. The list goes on for miles. Thank you all for showing me how it's done.

I appreciate the camaraderie and the guidance of the editors I've worked with at various magazines and publications: Kat Angus, Taylor Bruce, Greg Emmanuel, Dave Hurteau, Larry Kanter, Matthew Karasz, Marjorie Korn, Ryan Krogh, Natalie Krebs, Anthony Licata, Russ Lumpkin, Peter Martin, Nate Matthews, Jean McKenna, Donna Ng, Alex Robinson, Sal Vaglica. Last but most important: Devin Friedman and Colin Kearns. Thanks, y'all.

In 2016, Lizzie Widdicombe accepted a cold pitch I sent her for a Talk of the Town story and sort of changed my life by letting me write for *The New Yorker* for the first time. After that, Anthony Lydgate edited a few short pieces I wrote for the magazine's website, and his edits were incredibly instructive. I owe them both a lot.

I'd be remiss if I didn't also thank, for various reasons, Elizabeth Alexander; Sybil Baker; Charles Bethea; Houston Cofield; Pamela Colloff; Rebecca Cook; Quynh Do; Austyn Gaffney; Ann Harris; Maureen Hill, of the National Archives in Atlanta; Hugh Inman; Laura Kim; Gilbert King; Rebekah Lockwood; Meaghan Maguire; John McNamara; Molly Moore and Appalachian Voices; Phillip Rhodes; Isabel Ribeiro; Hayden Shafer; and Joel Tomlin, of Landmark Booksellers. Thank you.

Sara Black McCulloch and Ambrose Martos fact-checked portions of this book, and Sam Kestenbaum checked my original *Men's Journal* story about the workers' case. I thank them all, and I bear the blame for any errors that slipped through.

Kristen Lombardi, of the Center for Public Integrity, was the first reporter outside Tennessee to interview the Kingston workers and Jim Scott. She deserves much credit for her early, solid reporting on the case. Jamie Satterfield owned the Kingston story for the better part of four years, and some of her pieces in *The Knoxville News Sentinel* go deeper on certain aspects of the workers' case than this book does. I grew up in Tennessee (and live there again now), and I remember watching news coverage of the Kingston disaster on TV, but I wouldn't have known about the workers' lawsuit had it not been for her reporting. I appreciate her for that, and for the fact that she encouraged the workers to talk with me early on. She didn't have to do that, but she did, and I won't forget her kindness.

Last and most crucial, I'm grateful for every lawyer and every worker who spoke with me. I am especially appreciative of Janie Clark, Ansol Clark, and Jim Scott. This book would have been impossible to write without their cooperation. They trusted me and let me into their lives, answered the phone nearly anytime I called with questions, and imposed no conditions on me in exchange for their participation. I feel privileged that I got to know Ansol. A few months before his death, I called to tell him that Knopf had agreed to publish this book. "You've got the ball," he told me. "Now run with it." I hope I've done that.

Notes

I began working on this book in December 2018 after I attended a ceremony commemorating the tenth anniversary of the Kingston disaster. I describe this scene in the text. I was in East Tennessee visiting my sister, and I went to the ceremony on a lark. There I met Jeff Brewer, Tyler Roper, and Keith Stewart. In February 2019, I flew from New York, where I lived at the time, to Knoxville and interviewed Ansol and Janie Clark, Mike McCarthy, Jim Scott, Stewart, and Roper. These interviews, along with a phone call with Jeff Friedman, provided the basis of a magazine story I published about the workers' lawsuit in the September 2019 edition of *Men's Journal*, where I was an editor. This book greatly expands on that article.

I conducted hundreds of interviews over five years to build this narrative. I also relied heavily on deposition, trial, and hearing transcripts, along with court filings, documents obtained through records requests, books, and historical sources. The archives of *The Knoxville News Sentinel* were an invaluable resource, especially the many stories written by Frank Munger and Jamie Satterfield. They're easily two of the finest journalists that Tennessee has produced, and they did much good on the public's behalf.

Any scene set before December 2018 is a reconstruction, as I did not witness the events described firsthand. I used transcripts and documents whenever I was able to build these scenes; I've listed my sources in the Notes that follow. When it came to private conversations between the lawyers or the workers, I often had to rely on recollections, which I cross-checked with multiple sources when I was able to. Where memories diverged, I went with the account that best aligned with my understanding of events and seemed the most plausible. There was some approximation involved. If I attribute a feeling or thought to a character, it's because the person described that feeling or thought to me or, in rare cases, a source close to the person did. If you encounter a quotation or detail in the text with no corresponding note, you can assume that the material comes from an interview I conducted with a source. Generally, I cited interview sources only when a piece of information originated from a single person or if it felt important to make clear where I got a detail.

It was understood from the start that the plaintiffs' lawyers would not have the right to read or revise the manuscript before publication. Jim Scott's one request was that I not divulge some sensitive details about his sons, who were still minors when I began reporting. I honored this request, and I spoke with Jack and Sam Scott about sections of the book that concern them before I submitted the manuscript to Knopf. Mary Scott disputes much of my reporting, though I drew heavily on a deposition she gave in 2017. Mary Scott is not her real name. I gave her and two other minor characters, Greg Jones and Tim Henry, pseudonyms at the request of these individuals.

Neither TVA nor Jacobs Engineering (now Jacobs Solutions) cooperated with my efforts to research this book. I interviewed several employees of both organizations on background (that is, not for attribution), but many key figures within TVA or Jacobs declined to speak to me or did not respond to interview requests; I was unable to contact a few people. A partial list of these individuals: Tom Bock, Raymond B. Biagini, Josh Chesser, Karen G. Crutchfield, Kurt Hamrock, Sean Healey, Melissa Hedgecoth, Tom Heffernan, Gary MacDonald, Steve McCracken, Rebecca Murray, Kathryn Nash, Anda Ray, Isaac Sanders, James F. Sanders, Alex L. Sarria, Kenneth Schrupp, Edwin Small, and Joseph Welborn. Moreover, during the fact-checking process, I asked TVA if it would make the following individuals available for an interview, and it did not: Tom Heffernan, Gary MacDonald, Tom Kilgore, Jeffrey Lyash, Anda Ray, Edwin Small. I also asked Jacobs Engineering if it would make Tom Bock or Kurt Hamrock available for an interview, and it did not. This book would have greatly benefited from the participation of these individuals.

Fortunately for me, many Jacobs and TVA employees testified in depositions or in the 2018 trial, so I relied heavily on their testimony transcripts. (In the Notes, in almost every instance where I cite a trial or deposition transcript, the case in question is *Adkisson et al. v. Jacobs Engineering*, unless I state otherwise; I cite a few other cases and provide the full annotation when the case is first mentioned.) Also, throughout the Notes, I cite public meetings held by TVA; the transcripts of these meetings can be found by searching TVA's website on the Internet Archive's Wayback Machine.

The U.S. Attorney's Office in Knoxville declined to comment on whether it was investigating Jacobs's handling of the Kingston cleanup. The EPA also declined to comment.

I worked with a deep commitment to the truth. The competing facts presented by both sides of the *Adkisson* lawsuit did not make this easy. Generally, I included details from documents and testimony that I found the most convincing and that best aligned with other source material. I'll admit that I, like the federal jury in the 2018 trial, found the plaintiffs' case stronger than Jacobs's. That said, much of the evidence that the plaintiffs presented was circumstantial—that is, there was no single smoking gun that proved, without a hint of doubt, the conspiracy to deny the workers dust masks or respirators. Jacobs presented plenty of evidence that it believes undermines the plaintiffs' case, and I tried to present accurately and fairly the central arguments its defense team made based on this evidence.

Jacobs Engineering disputes much of my reporting. In the fact-checking process, I sent the company a twenty-five-page document listing allegations and details I planned to include in this book. An attorney representing Jacobs sent me a twenty-one-page response. The company did not address my fact-checking queries point by point, because, according to the lawyer, "The false and inaccurate statements in your memorandum are so numerous that it is not possible to address all of them in this letter." But the lawyer said that Jacobs takes issue with the "falsehoods" that "impugn the honesty, attitudes and competence of Jacobs and its employees." The company believes that my characterization of its staff is not true and "contradicts Jacobs'[s] ethos." In the Notes, and in footnotes in the text, I have incorporated the company's views to the best of my ability, but, in the interest of transparency, I've included the central thrust of Jacobs's response to me here.

Jacobs denies that its staff manipulated air-monitoring data, improperly discarded air-monitoring samples, or violated the "Site Wide Safety and Health Plan" when processing the workers' requests for respiratory protection. It denies that its staff inappropriately denied any worker a dust mask. It denies that the workers were exposed to harmful levels of particulate matter, and it denies that the airborne samples collected by its staff had concentrations of any metal, including arsenic, that exceeded the site's occupational exposure limits. It denies that its employees concealed the potential hazard of arsenic in fly ash and called any such allegation "provably false," since this information was included in the "Site Wide Safety and Health Plan." Moreover, Jacobs says there is no evidence proving that the workers were instructed to spray water near the stationary air monitors, and it says its staff was not responsible for directing work activities at the jobsite anyway, or for selecting personal protective equipment for the workers. The company says it had no role in evaluating or addressing radiation-exposure issues (but maintains that radionuclides in the fly ash posed no danger to the workers, based on samples collected by another contractor). Similarly, it says that its staff had no role in testing river sediment for radionuclides, but it called the workers' claims about potentially being exposed to contaminated sediment "false."

I stand by my reporting and the contents of this book.

As with Jacobs, I gave TVA a chance to respond to the allegations and facts that appear here. But it did not address my specific queries, either. Instead, TVA said through a representative that it "disagree[d] with some of the characterizations and portrayals of the information" and sent me a statement that read, in part:

> In the aftermath of the Kingston event, TVA committed to becoming an industry leader in the safe, secure management of coal ash, which was noted in a pair of 2014 TVA Office of the Inspector General reports. Today, TVA has fulfilled that promise by implementing best practices years before they were required by the 2015 federal coal ash rule and [by] continuing to pioneer new technol-

ogy to ensure our coal ash sites are safe, secure, and protective of the environment and public health.

TVA also said that it has "one of the best performing nuclear fleets in the country, and these plants are at the peak of their performance over the 50-year life of the industry."

I believe that there are people within TVA who know more about the Kingston cleanup project beyond what I've reported in this book and beyond what was brought to light by the workers' lawsuits. I encourage these individuals to contact me if they'd like to talk. They can reach me through my website, jr-sullivan.com.

PART I

3 On December 22, 2008: The scenes from the morning of the spill are drawn from interviews with Ansol and Janie Clark, along with Tim Henry. Ansol also discussed the morning of the spill in an April 2017 deposition. Other people who spoke with me for this section include Troy Beets, Chris and DeAnna Copeland, Randy Ellis, Mike Farmer, Annie Harrell, Joshua Harrell, Chuck Head, Jill Murphy, Jeff Spurgeon, and Carlan Tapp. James Schean died before I had a chance to speak with him. Tim Henry is a pseudonym.

4 completion in 1954: "New Unit Swells T.V.A. Power Load," *New York Times*, March 21, 1954.

4 fourteen thousand tons: TVA, "How a Coal Plant Works," https://www.tva.com/.

4 one hundred and forty train cars: Ibid.

4 seven hundred thousand homes: TVA, "Kingston Fossil Plant," https://www.tva.com/.

4 a thousand tons: TVA OIG, "Inspection Report: Kingston Fossil Plant Ash Spill Interim Report," June 12, 2009, p. 2.

4 In the 1950s: Ibid.; AECOM, "Root Cause Analysis," p. 3.

4 swimming hole: Sean Flynn, "Black Tide," *GQ*, April 30, 2009.

4 sixty feet tall: Ibid.

4 eighty-four acres: *Adkisson et al. v. Jacobs Engineering*, Docket no. 56, p. 42, U.S. District Court, Eastern District of Tennessee.

4 and bulldozers: Flynn, "Black Tide."

5 *The Year Without a Santa Claus*: TV listings, *Knoxville News Sentinel*, December 21, 2008.

5 14 degrees Fahrenheit: Mansfield, "TVA Dam Breaks; Homes Damaged."

6 at least fifty feet high: AECOM, "Root Cause Analysis," pp. 15, 19.

6 through a dam: Flynn, "Black Tide."

6 into the peninsula: EPA, "TVA Kingston Ash Recovery Project, Roane County, TN, Project Completion Meeting, June 4, 2015," slide no. 3.

6 six million tons: TVA, "TVA Kingston Fossil Fuel Plant Release Site On-Scene Coordinator Report," p. ES-2.

6 forty-foot-deep channel: Flynn, "Black Tide."

6 nearly three million tons: How I arrived at this number: TVA states that 2,293,000 cubic yards of ash were removed from the sloughs. (See TVA's "Kingston Ash Recovery Project Completion Report," p. 3-2.) Elsewhere, TVA states that 3,096,000 cubic yards of ash weigh about 4 million tons. By that measure, 2,293,000 cubic yards weigh about 2,960,000 tons.

6 hurling fish forty feet: Scott Barker, "TVA Working to Repair Damage to Area," *Knoxville News Sentinel*, December 25, 2008.

6 soccer fields were smothered: Randy Ellis trial testimony, October 17, 2018, p. 227.

6 The wave first: AECOM, "Root Cause Analysis," p. 15.

6 James Schean: Mansfield, "TVA Dam Breaks; Homes Damaged."

6 a thundering boom: Ibid.

6 knocking over Christmas presents: Ibid.

6 an hour or more: TVA OIG, "Review of the Kingston Fossil Plant Ash Spill Root Cause Study," p. 10.

7 The first 911 calls: Barker, "One Year Later"; TVA OIG, "Inspection Report: Kingston Fossil Plant Ash Spill Interim Report," p. 5.

7 By 1:06 a.m.: Ibid.

7 police had blocked off: Troy Beets interview; *Blanchard et al. v. TVA*, Gary Wallace deposition, July 15, 2009, p. 63, U.S. District Court, Eastern District of Tennessee.

7 The TVA staffers: Wallace deposition, p. 48.

7 A shift supervisor: Ibid., p. 52; AECOM, "Root Cause Analysis," pp. 13–15.

7 fell upon a deer: Wallace deposition, p. 56.

7 "This is unbelievable": *Blanchard et al. v. TVA*, James Settles deposition, June 19, 2009, pp. 151–52.

7 later tell reporters: J. Scott Holladay, "No More Excuses: The Economic Case for Coal Ash Regulation," policy brief, Institute for Policy Integrity, NYU School of Law, June 2009, p. 4.

8 sixty-five feet: AECOM, "Root Cause Analysis," p. 19.

8 concrete blocks: WBIR, "Historic Disaster: 10 Years After the Ash Spill," December 21, 2018.

8 the dog itself: Chris Copeland interview. The dog did not die, as some news outlets initially reported, but it did get swept away.

9 The house popped and cracked: WBIR, "Historic Disaster."

9 crust over with ice: Barker, "One Year Later."

9 helicopters whirled overhead: TVA OIG, "Inspection Report: Kingston Fossil Plant Ash Spill Interim Report," pp. 5–6.

9 single largest industrial disaster: Bob Tuke, "Consider All Costs Connected to Spill," *The Tennessean*, May 21, 2009; "Inside the Tennessee Coal Ash Spill," *Newsweek*, July 17, 2009.

9 Empire State Building: The Kingston spill released 5.4 million cubic yards, or

145,800,000 cubic feet, of ash. The Empire State Building contains 37 million cubic feet of space, according to a fact sheet by the Empire State Realty Trust.

9 trapped in the ash: TVA background source.

9 would soon pile up: Photo provided to me by a worker.

9 nearby community college: Mansfield, "TVA Dam Breaks; Homes Damaged."

9 twenty-six homes: TVA OIG, "Inspection Report: Review of the Kingston Fossil Plant Ash Spill," p. 10.

9 twenty-two people: Cheremisinoff, *Handbook of Pollution Prevention*, p. 119.

9 reserved hotel rooms: Tom Kilgore responses to the U.S. Senate Committee on Environment and Public Works, "Follow-Up Questions for Written Submission, Questions for Kilgore," January 8, 2009, p. 43.

10 "scruffy little city of 180,000": Leon Daniel, "What If You Gave a World's Fair and Nobody Came?," UPI, June 4, 1981.

10 wrapped in frost: Weather report in *The Tennessean*, December 22, 2008.

10 contempt of court: Matt Lakin, "Buddy Scott, Longtime Anderson County Judge Who Oversaw Houston Brothers' Trials, Dies," *Knoxville News Sentinel*, May 15, 2019.

11 Knoxville public schools: Knox County School Calendar 2008–2009.

11 The local news: Earthjustice, "Coal Ash Contaminates Our Lives: Tennessee Interview," YouTube video, uploaded on April 20, 2010, 3:17, https://www.youtube.com/watch?v=F1bOED1XcLg.

11 *Roane County News*: Terri Likens, "TVA Mudslide Forces Swan Pond Evacuation," *Roane County News*, April 6, 2009.

12 "It is a chore": Tyler Roper interview.

12 "He's a mess": Background source.

13 gold, coins, and collectibles: Real-estate records; archival Google Maps images.

13 insular and cliquish: Background Roane County source.

13 coloring book and a Coke: Lisa Niles interview.

14 a hysterical mother: Ann Harris interview.

14 perhaps autism as well: Sam's autism is a point of dispute among the Scott family. I obtained an email in which a Knoxville doctor states that Sam has autism. Mary denies that Sam has the disorder, though a record of a call she made to Knox County 911 in March 2018 suggests that she told a dispatcher Sam was on the spectrum. Sam told me that neither parent told him he had autism and he doubted he did. What's true is that Jim believed Sam had autism and that, I felt, was an important part of the story.

14 called B. R. Ladd: Ladd corroborated Scott's account.

14 coal-fired power stations: U.S. Energy Information Administration, "Count of Electric Power Industry Power Plants, by Sector, by Predominant Energy Sources Within Plant, 2008 Through 2018," accessed in April 2020, https://www.eia.gov/.

14 thirty-six hundred times a minute: Cheremisinoff, *Handbook of Pollution Prevention*, p. 110; TVA, "How a Coal Plant Works," https://www.tva.com/.

15 one hundred and thirty-six million tons: American Coal Ash Association, "2008 Coal Combustion Product (CCP) Production & Use Survey Report," https://acaa-usa.org/.

15 large holding ponds: Interview with Elizabeth Southerland, who previously led the EPA's Office of Water.

15 fifty other men: Danny Gouge trial testimony, October 17, 2018, p. 238.

15 poorly constructed and maintained: TVA OIG, "Inspection Report: Review of the Kingston Fossil Plant Ash Spill," p. 32.

15 by hand at times: Danny Gouge trial testimony, October 17, 2018, p. 238; Mike McCarthy trial testimony, October 23, 2018, pp. 1262–63.

15 fifteen or so people: Troy Beets interview, corroborated by photos.

15 toxicity of the ash: Tetra Tech, "Final Comprehensive Environmental Response," Appendix E.

15 No one knew: Troy Beets interview.

15 The Coast Guard: Shaw Environmental, Inc., for TVA, "Phase 1 Emory River Dredging Plan Kingston Fossil Plant Ash Recovery Project, Tennessee Department of Environment and Conservation Commissioner's Order, Case No. OGC09-0001," February 2009, p. 2-2.

15 sample water intakes: Tetra Tech, "Final Comprehensive Environmental Response," p. D-1.

15 building a weir: TVA, "TVA Kingston Fossil Fuel Plant Release Site On-Scene Coordinator Report," p. 1–13.

15 Union representatives: Danny Gouge trial testimony, October 17, 2018, p. 236; interviews with Mike McCarthy and Ansol Clark.

15 Come to Kingston: My descriptions of the workers in this paragraph are drawn from extensive interviews with and observations of the workers.

15 nine hundred workers: Jamie Satterfield, "TVA Coal Ash Spill: 5 Things to Know on 10-Year Anniversary," *Knoxville News Sentinel*, December 20, 2018.

16 Ernest Hickman: Jessica Waller interview; "Separation Notice: Ernest Hickman," State of Tennessee Department of Labor and Workforce Development.

16 Danny Gouge: Danny Gouge trial testimony, October 17, 2018, p. 235.

16 President George W. Bush: "Transcript: President Bush's Speech to the Nation on the Economic Crisis," *New York Times*, September 24, 2008.

16 logged similar hours: Danny Gouge trial testimony, October 17, 2018, p. 240.

16 had coal reserves: Tetra Tech, "Final Comprehensive Environmental Response," Appendix E.

16 amphibious track hoes: Barker, "TVA Working to Repair Damage to Area"; Danny Gouge trial testimony, October 17, 2018, p. 240.

16 nearly four days: Tetra Tech, "Final Comprehensive Environmental Response," D-1.

16 almost two weeks: Ibid., p. C-31.

17 private construction outfit: *Love v. G-UB-MK Constructors*, Memorandum and Order, November 15, 2016, U.S. District Court, Eastern District of Tennessee.

18 "I don't need your apologies": Shaila Dewan, "Coal Ash Spill Revives Issue of Its Hazards," *New York Times*, December 24, 2008.

18 TVA had few answers: Jill Murphy interview.

18 Anne Thompson: "Toxic Mess," *NBC Nightly News*, December 26, 2008.

20 "Son, you can't beat that money": Jim Scott interview. Buddy Scott died before I had a chance to interview him.

20 airport parking lot: Sam Scott told me he had no recollection of this, though he would have been very young when it occurred.

20 "you have to know somebody": annebonnylives, "TVA Coal Ash Disaster TVA Roadblocks 12-27-09," YouTube video, uploaded on December 27, 2008, 9:11, https://www.youtube.com/watch?v=ujSElW0iG74.

21 fifty-two-year-old trial lawyer: This section is primarily drawn from interviews with Friedman and Jeff Hagood and from my own interactions with Friedman.

21 It regularly sparred: "E.P.A. to Join Lawsuit to Reduce Pollution," *New York Times*, July 13, 1977.

21 the state of North Carolina: *North Carolina v. TVA*, Opinion, July 21, 2006, U.S. District Court, Western District of North Carolina.

21 deaths of some fourteen hundred people: "TVA Ordered to Install Pollution Controls near N.C.," AP via *Star News Online*, January 14, 2009.

22 Friedman's father: "Ralph Friedman Dies at Home," *The Tennessean*, May 30, 1960; "Ralph Friedman Buried Today in Nashville," *Leaf-Chronicle*, May 30, 1960.

22 shopping center burned: "Midway Shopping Center Leveled by Spectacular Fire," *Leaf-Chronicle*, March 21, 1962.

23 60 percent of its power: Duncan Mansfield, "TVA Agrees to Pursue Renewable Energy Purchases," AP, April 2, 2009.

23 consent to be sued: *Adkisson et al. v. Jacobs Engineering*, Opinion of the U.S. Court of Appeals for the Sixth Circuit, June 2, 2015, p. 5.

23 On a map: My description of the Tennessee River and Valley is primarily drawn from Lilienthal's *TVA: Democracy on the March* (pp. 10–11); James Agee's "Where Did the Tennessee Valley Authority Come From?," *Fortune* (1933); Frome's *Strangers in High Places*; and Owen's *The Tennessee Valley Authority*. I also know the area well, having spent most of my life in the Tennessee Valley.

23 feet above sea level: Owen, *The Tennessee Valley Authority*, p. 57; U.S. Geological Survey, "Introduction to the Upper Tennessee River Basin," https://pubs.usgs.gov/circ/circ1205/introduction.htm.

23 Great Smoky and Unaka Mountains: Frome, *Strangers in High Places*, pp. 14–18, 59.

23 the rings of Saturn: According to NASA, Saturn's rings formed from 10 million to 100 million years ago. Academics generally believe that the Appalachians formed around 200 million to 300 million years ago. See following note and NASA, "NASA's Cassini Data Show Saturn's Rings Relatively New," January 17, 2019, https://www.nasa.gov/.

23 three hundred million years: Brown University, "Scientists Reconstruct Formation of the Appalachians," November 21, 2016, https://www.brown.edu/.

24 fifty-five miles wide: H. C. Amick, "The Great Valley of East Tennessee," *Economic Geography* 10, no. 1 (January 1934): 35–52.

24 In the 1770s: Munzer, *Valley of Vision*, pp. 6–7, 60.

24 a wasteland of the valley: Ibid., p. 19.

24 survived in crude shacks: Ibid., p. 27.

24 three or four to a bed: Ibid., p. 31.

24 Malaria was endemic: Owen, *The Tennessee Valley Authority*, p. 19.

24 lacked indoor plumbing: Kevin Baker, "Where Our New World Begins," *Harper's* (May 2019).

24 In 1867: Munzer, *Valley of Vision*, pp. 22–23; Steve Johnson, "150 Years Ago: Tennessee River Rose 58 Feet Above Normal, Submerging Chattanooga," *Chattanooga Times Free Press*, March 5, 2017.

24 Six million acres: Owen, *The Tennessee Valley Authority*, p. 83.

24 $317 a year: Moore, *The Economic Impact of TVA*, p. 51; Owen, *The Tennessee Valley Authority*, p. 19. Similar information in Chandler, *The Myth of TVA*, p. 48.

25 crushing poverty challenged: U.S. Office of War Information Overseas Branch, *Life in the Tennessee Valley in the 1930s & 1940s*, 1944 documentary; David E. Lilienthal remarks, TVA MoMA Exhibit, April 29, 1941.

25 Roosevelt's expansive vision: Hargrove, *Prisoners of Myth*, pp. 20–21; Caro, *The Power Broker*, p. 261.

25 "social and economic welfare of the Nation": "Roosevelt Urges Shoals Project," *New York Times*, April 11, 1933.

25 only 3 percent of farms: Owen, "For the Progress of Man," p. 338; Lilienthal, *TVA: Democracy on the March*, p. 22. Chandler, *The Myth of TVA*, p. 57, states that 4 percent of farmers had power in 1930.

25 some forty thousand workers: The number of workers said to have built the TVA dams varies widely between sources. TVA states on its website ("Power to Win") that 28,000 people worked on the dams in 1942, while other sources put the number at around forty thousand, which is what I went with. These sources include Owen, *The Tennessee Valley Authority*, p. 84; Grant, *TVA and Black Americans*, p. 21; and Kevin Baker, "Where Our New World Begins," *Harper's* (May 2019). David Lilienthal writes in *TVA: Democracy on the March*," p. 103, that by 1944, two hundred thousand workers had helped to build the dams, but I think his math, like his politics, is liberal.

25 men from across the valley: Lilienthal, *TVA: Democracy on the March*, p. 105.

25 almost all white: Munzer, *Valley of Vision*, pp. 91–93; Wheeler, *Knoxville, Tennessee*, p. 134.

25 completing sixteen dams: Hargrove, *Prisoners of Myth*, p. 60.

25n During the first: John P. Davis, "The Plight of the Negro in the Tennessee Valley," *The Crisis* (October 1935); Grant, *TVA and Black Americans*, pp. 20–21.

26 eleven thousand miles: The two figures listed here are my calculations based on

data from TVA's website about the size of its reservoirs. Moore, *The Economic Impact of TVA*, p. 151, includes similar figures. Various TVA webpages state its reservoirs have eleven thousand miles of shoreline.

26 around the Great Lakes: State of Michigan, "Learn About the Great Lakes," https://www.michigan.gov/.

26 twenty thousand families: U.S. National Archives, "TVA: Displacement," https://www.archives.gov/atlanta/exhibits/tva-displacement.html.

26 praise in the South: J. Percy Priest, "Writer Finds Dreams Come True Along Tennessee," *Nashville Tennessean*, August 20, 1939.

26 "should make one prouder": Lewis Mumford, "The Sky Line," *New Yorker*, June 7, 1941.

27 BUILT FOR THE PEOPLE OF THE UNITED STATES: David E. Lilienthal remarks, TVA MoMA Exhibit, April 29, 1941.

27 not just to electrify: Shlaes, *The Forgotten Man*, pp. 10, 11.

27 mobile-library service: Lilienthal, *TVA: Democracy on the March*, p. 141.

27 state and county parks departments: Ibid., p. 145.

27 thirteen thousand demonstration farms: Chandler, *The Myth of TVA*, p. 103.

27 It built bunkhouses: Munzer, *Valley of Vision*, pp. 99–100.

27 chimneys and cedar shingles: TVA, "Norris: An American Ideal," https://www.tva.com/.

27 TVA outproduced: Hargrove, *Prisoners of Myth*, p. 60.

27 a tenth of the electricity: Ibid.

27 sole producer of tritium: Congressional Research Service, "The U.S. Nuclear Weapons Complex: Overview of Department of Energy Sites," updated February 3, 2020, p. 23.

27 Per capita income rose: Chandler, *The Myth of TVA*, p. 7; Moore, *The Economic Impact of TVA*, p. 51.

28 The Cold War: Hargrove, *TVA: Fifty Years of Grass-Roots Bureaucracy*, p. 70.

28 eleven of the world's largest: TVA, "Plants of the Past," https://www.tva.com/; Owen, "For the Progress of Man," pp. 74–75; Chandler, *The Myth of TVA*, p. 121.

28 coal-fired power stations: Chandler, *The Myth of TVA*, p. 116.

28 Republicans in Congress: Hargrove, *Prisoners of Myth*, p. 4; TVA, "The Great Compromise," https://www.tva.com/.

28 roughly half of TVA's power: TVA, "Annual Report of the Tennessee Valley Authority for the Fiscal Year Ended June 30, 1959," pp. 34–36.

28 In 1959, Congress: Chandler, *The Myth of TVA*, p. 5.

28 "the most liberal": Bill Donahue, "Can Antioch College Return from the Dead Again?," *New York Times Magazine*, September 16, 2011.

28 an electricity behemoth: Wheeler and McDonald, *TVA and the Tellico Dam, 1936–1979*, pp. 6–12.

28 largest power system by output: Hargrove, *Prisoners of Myth*, p. 60; Robert Greene, "TVA's Life Continues Turbulent," AP via *El Paso Times*, May 11, 1958; Owen, *The Tennessee Valley Authority*, p. 201.

28 largest coal consumer: Lisa Friedman, "Largest Federal Utility Chooses Gas, Undermining Biden's Climate Goals," *New York Times*, March 18, 2022; Congressional Record—House, 1963, vol. 109, p. 8797; Owen, "For the Progress of Man," p. 318.

28 soot blackened: Interviews with Chattanooga locals.

28 handkerchiefs: Owen, "For the Progress of Man," p. 104.

28 the nearest TVA power plant: TVA Division of Health and Safety, "Air Pollution Studies TVA Steam Plants Calendar Year 1956," April 1957, p. 5.

28 Widows Creek Fossil Plant: Nat Caldwell, "Toothless Air Pollution Bill Causes Few Worries," *The Tennessean*, April 30, 1967.

29 federal government ranked: "3 Tenn. Cities in Air Pollution Report," *Knoxville News Sentinel*, August 4, 1970.

29 In the months: This section is primarily drawn from interviews with Ansol and Janie Clark, along with Jeff Brewer, Mike McCarthy, Clint Mannis, and several other workers.

29 the air would sparkle: Jeff Brewer trial testimony, October 19, 2019, p. 580.

29 four million tons: TVA, "TVA Kingston Fossil Fuel Plant Release Site On-Scene Coordinator Report," p. ES-2.

29 from migrating downriver: TVA, transcript of public meeting, June 23, 2009, Roane State Community College, Harriman, Tennessee, p. 100.

29 six or seven mobile officers: Background TVA source who worked on-site.

30 a mix of operators: Jeff Brewer trial testimony, October 19, 2018, p. 590.

30 met for a safety meeting: TVA, "Site Wide Safety and Health Plan," prepared by Jacobs Engineering, June 2009, p. 14-1.

30 U.S. government contractors: "2009 Top 100," *Washington Technology*, 2009.

30 fifty-three thousand people: These numbers are from the Jacobs Engineering 2009 annual report, pp. 6, 17.

30 mining and recovering potash: Jacobs, *The Anatomy of an Entrepreneur*, p. 122.

30 from the U.S. Army: "Jacobs Engineering Wins Army Contract," *Los Angeles Times*, May 15, 2002.

30 NASA: Michael White, "JPL, Engineering Firm to Commercialize Technologies," AP via *Daily Press*, August 12, 1998.

30 government of Jordan: John Getze, "Jacobs' Boss Still Running to Get Ahead," *Los Angeles Times*, December 25, 1977.

30 "environmentalists": Jacobs, *The Anatomy of an Entrepreneur*, p. 86.

30 at least ten states: Ibid., p. 266.

30 including Tennessee: DOE, "History of the Oak Ridge EM Program," Oak Ridge Environmental Management Program, 2015.

30 the EPA: Jacobs, *The Anatomy of an Entrepreneur*, p. 266.

30 almost $64 million: Jack Howard trial testimony, October 24, 2018, pp. 1706; Gaffney, "They Deserve to Be Heard." TVA stated in 2019 that it expected to pay Jacobs closer to $40 million and that it did not pay the company any safety or environmental incentive under its contract provisions.

30 $1.2 billion: This is a widely reported figure; Bill Poovey, "TVA Ash Spill Trial Begins in Knoxville," AP via *The Tennessean*, September 16, 2011.

30 about a dozen employees: Tom Bock deposition, August 12, 2016, p. 74.

30 Tom Bock: As I state in a footnote, Bock declined to respond to a request for comment I sent him in 2019, when I was working on the magazine story from which this book grew. In June of that year, however, Bock wrote me the following email: "Thanks for all of the questions. Here is what I can tell you. I'm a safety professional and take my work extremely serious. The TVA Coal Ash spill was a large and complicated job. Throughout the duration of the project the Kingston Cleanup Safety team worked hand in hand with TVA, EPA, and TDEC to accomplish worker safety and health. The coal ash spill was a huge environmental incident and has been a challenge for everyone involved. There have been many false accusations and much misinformation published about worker protection, but I think the Kingston Cleanup safety team did a great job. Sincerely, Tom Bock."

31 pound of fly ash: Kevin Thompson trial testimony, October 18, 2018, p. 435; interviews with Ansol Clark, Jeff Brewer, and many others. Billy Isley testified that Tom Bock told him fly ash was safe unless he breathed it; see Isley deposition, August 22, 2017, p. 39.

31 *Don't worry, man*: Billy Isley deposition, August 22, 2017, pp. 39–40.

31 clips on social media: Photos posted on Bock's Facebook page in January 2021.

31 Marshall University: Tom Bock deposition, August 12, 2016, p. 22.

31 "I've got a wife and kids": Ibid., p. 125.

31 air-quality tests: TVA, "Kingston Ash Slide: Air Quality Information," March 31, 2011, captured on October 11, 2012, by the Internet Archive, https://www.tva.com/.

31 "aggressive dust suppression": Ibid.

31 Billy Isley: Interview with Lena Isley; Billy Isley deposition, August 22, 2017, p. 21; *Adkisson et al. v. Jacobs Engineering*, Docket no. 337-4, p. 10.

31 tattoo of an eagle: Regional Forensic Center, Knox County, "Autopsy Final Report: William Franklin Isley," May 4, 2019.

31 thought he was an asshole: Interviews with Jason Williams and Mike McCarthy.

31 eighteen of these trucks: Steve Cherry deposition, August 4, 2016, p. 72. Tom Heffernan, of TVA, guessed, in a July 2016 deposition, that the number of water trucks on-site ranged from three to fifteen.

31 migrating off-site: Steve Richardson email, April 6, 2010, obtained through FOIA.

32 "Dust suppression": Ibid.

32 Isley mentioned to Ansol: Ansol Clark interview.

32 orders came from Jacobs: Billy Isley deposition, August 22, 2017, p. 45.

32 basically innocuous: Ibid., p. 39.

32 "you'd have to eat it": Shaila Dewan, "Tennessee Ash Flood Larger Than Initial Estimate," *New York Times*, December 26, 2008.

32 "It's primarily sand": TVA, transcript of public meeting, May 20, 2010, at Roane County High School, p. 65. Leo Francendese declined to be interviewed for this book.

32 famously ugly town: Eugene Kinkead, "Notes from a Gazetteer: XXV—Knoxville, Tenn.," *New Yorker*, December 31, 1978.

32 an old Cherokee trail: Rule, *Standard History of Knoxville, Tennessee*, p. 272.

33 everyone called Spoon: James Weatherspoon interview.

33 "He would hammer us": John Dupree interview.

33 James Crichton: James Crichton interview; *Crichton v. TVA*, Docket no. 36-1, James Crichton deposition, March 5, 2010.

33 seventy-one properties: "Utility Rejects Many Requests as It Buys Land Tainted by Tennessee Coal-Ash Spill," AP via *New York Times*, April 11, 2009.

33 one hundred and eight more properties: Duane W. Gang, "Kingston Coal Ash Spill: 5 Years, $1 Billion in Cleanup and No Regulations Later," *The Tennessean*, December 21, 2013.

33 But far more locals: "Utility Rejects Many Requests."

34 "we have found": Ibid.

35 evening of October 1, 2009: This scene is drawn from the transcript of the public meeting and from interviews with Steve Scarbrough, Randy Ellis, Jill Murphy, and Mike Farmer.

35 CLEAN COAL IS A MYTH and CLEAN COAL: "Tennessee Toxic Spill Woes," CBS News, YouTube video, uploaded on December 29, 2008, 1:49, https://www.youtube.com/watch?v=3i-gzhW10WA&t=48s.

35 church's family center: Mike Farmer interview.

35 Anda Ray: Ray did not respond to an interview request in 2019; my subsequent attempts to reach her were unsuccessful.

35 "eminent-domained the shit": Background Roane County source.

36 "the city of New York": Thurman, *A History of the Tennessee Valley Authority*, p. 27.

36 pumped four hundred and fifty tons: TVA Division of Health and Safety, "Air Pollution Studies TVA Steam Plants Calendar Year 1956," April 1957, pp. 2, 7, obtained from the National Archives.

36 seven hundred tons of sulfur dioxide: Ibid.

36 blew through clotheslines: Ibid., pp. 2–3, 14.

36 blanketed rivers and streams: Ken Ellis interview.

36 a five-year-old boy: Ken Ellis interview; TVA memorandum from C. L. Karr to G. O. Wessenauer, "Complaints About TVA Steam Plant Operations," May 13, 1957, National Archives in Atlanta, Power Manager Box 801–802.

36 contributed 53 percent: Chandler, *The Myth of TVA*, p. 135. Various newspapers report that TVA had 2 million residential customers in 1973 at a time when the U.S. population was around 211 million.

36 half-heartedly addressed: Randy Ellis interview.

36 speculated that public pressure: TVA Division of Health and Safety, "Air Pollution Studies TVA Steam Plants Calendar Year 1956," pp. 14–15.

36 the president and Congress: Owen, "For the Progress of Man," p. 122; Hargrove, *Prisoners of Myth*, p. 267.

36 senator Barbara Boxer: U.S. Government Publishing Office, "Hearing Before the Committee on Environment and Public Works, United States Senate, One Hundred Eleventh Congress, First Session, January 8, 2009," S. Hrg. 111-1177.

37 On a living room shelf: The section about Janie's childhood is mostly drawn from interviews with her and, to a lesser degree, Ansol. She showed me the photos described in the text. Janie asked that I not contact other members of her family, out of respect for their privacy, and I honored that request, since I could corroborate much of her story with public records and newspaper clips.

38 married less than a year: Marriage Record: Claiborne County, Tennessee, signed November 3, 1957: Joseph D. Palmer and Margaret Henderson.

38 young women customarily married: Syrett, *American Child Bride*, chapter 8.

38 A Baptist reverend: *Hancock County News*, November 7, 1951; *Baptist and Reflector: Organ Tennessee Baptist Convention*, September 17, 1936, p. 14.

38 worked for Southern Railway: Tennessee Department of Public Health, Division of Vital Statistics, Certificate of Death, File No. 66-007053, March 14, 1966.

38 "I don't know why": "Victims' Sister Had Premonition," *Knoxville News Sentinel*, March 23, 1955.

38 sat in a narrow valley: The failed-dam scene is drawn from these stories: "2 Sisters Drowned in Claiborne Flood," *Knoxville News Sentinel*, March 23, 1955; Henry Basham, "Second Flood Victim's Body Found in Debris," *Knoxville Journal*, March 24, 1955; "Double Service Held for Girls," *Knoxville News Sentinel*, March 24, 1955; "Couple Asks $400,000 in Flood Suit," *Knoxville Journal*, April 5, 1957; "$400,000 Suit on 1955 Flood Scheduled Today," *Knoxville Journal*, April 10, 1957.

39 taken to St. Mary's Hospital: Tennessee Department of Public Health, Joe Palmer Certificate of Death, file no. 66-007053.

40 sixty-five years old: Joe Palmer tombstone.

40 Woodlawn Cemetery: Joe Palmer Certificate of Death.

40 had a gold-painted ceiling: Tennessee Theatre website, https://www.tennesseetheatre.com/.

40 had been in decline: Wheeler, *Knoxville, Tennessee*, pp. 129–31.

40 Smoke and soot: Carson Brewer, "Trash Dribbles Out Into the Streets," *Knoxville News Sentinel*, February 9, 1969.

40 President Lyndon B. Johnson: "President Spurs Drive on Poverty in Six-State Tour," *New York Times*, May 8, 1964.

40 state and federal employees: Jack Neely, "Can We Learn from the TVA Headquarters Experience?," *Scruffy Citizen*, May 4, 2016; Wheeler, *Knoxville, Tennessee*, p. 136.

40 Veterans: "Korean Veterans, Your Knoxville Evening . . . ," *Knoxville News Sentinel*, June 16, 1952.

40 working mothers: Lloyd V. Jeffers, "Dropout Leads Grads at City Evening High," *Knoxville News Sentinel*, May 21, 1967.

40 recent immigrants: "English Usage Taught Adults in Evenings," *Knoxville News Sentinel*, December 26, 1970.

42 Two Whoppers: I failed to find historical Whopper prices in Maryville, but the Whopper was regularly advertised for fifty-nine to sixty-nine cents throughout the U.S. in that period, so I took Janie's word on the price.

43 wasn't as expressive: This section is primarily drawn from my observations of and interviews with Ansol Clark, along with a timeline of his health problems and work history, typed by Janie Clark for Jim Scott and later given to me.

43 Jacobs's staff assured him: Janie Clark interview.

44 "Ansol won't be in today": Janie's memory is fuzzy when it comes to whether she or Ansol talked to his foreman on the phone. Because she later made similar calls for Ansol, I feel it's reasonable to assume that she did the talking. Ansol's general foreman declined to speak with me on the record for this book.

45 nine in the morning: Dr. Craig Rylands, Summit Medical Group exam form for Ansol Clark, March 3, 2010.

45 X-ray, blood tests: Ibid.

45 atrial fibrillation: Ibid.

45 "Diagnosis": Ibid.

46 The same month: This section about Brewer is primarily drawn from interviews with him, along with his deposition and trial testimonies, April 11, 2017, and October 19, 2018, respectively.

46 line up for drug tests: Kevin Thompson corroborates that he also received a drug test; Kevin Thompson trial testimony, October 18, 2018, p. 433.

46 "The Lord broke my heart": Jeff Brewer deposition, April 11, 2017, p. 19.

46 Men in rubber boots: Randy Ellis trial testimony, October 17, 2018, p. 222.

47 By the spring of 2010: EPA, "Kingston Coal Ash Release Site: Project Completion Fact Sheet," December 2014.

47 four million tons: TVA, "TVA Kingston Fossil Fuel Plant Release Site On-Scene Coordinator Report," p. ES-2.

47 allowed it to be reopened: Craig Zeller of the EPA, "TVA Kingston Ash Recovery Project, Roane County, TN, Project Completion Meeting, June 4, 2015," slideshow, p. 6.

47 three hundred and seventy miles southwest: TVA, "TVA Kingston Fossil Fuel Plant Release Site On-Scene Coordinator Report," p. 221.

47 eighteen hours: Ibid., p. 2-27.

47 nearly all of them Black: *Census Reporter*, Uniontown, Alabama, https://censusreporter.org/.

47 one of the poorest counties: U.S. Census Bureau data for Perry County.

47 Over a year and a half: EPA, "Ecological Revitalization of Contaminated Sites Case Study: TVA Kingston Case Study," EPA 543-F-16-003, April 2017.

47 forty-one thousand railcars: Bob Fowler, "EPA Calls Ash Spill Cleanup Complete," *Knoxville News Sentinel*, June 5, 2015.

47 thirteen-hundred-acre dump: Arrowhead Environmental Partners website, accessed in August 2021, https://arrowheadenvironmentalpartners.com/.

47 bed of Selma chalk: Shaila Dewan, "Clash in Alabama over Tennessee Coal Ash," *New York Times*, August 29, 2009.

47 into the groundwater: EPA, "Municipal Solid Waste Landfills," https://www.epa.gov/landfills/municipal-solid-waste-landfills.

47 "You're taking that": NowThis, "How Uniontown, Alabama, Became Victim of Environmental Injustice," YouTube video, uploaded on October 14, 2017, 10:01, https://www.youtube.com/watch?v=lNik_ZLBsWc&t=241s.

48 bumped to $25.86: Jeff Brewer deposition, April 11, 2017, pp. 22–23.

48 Jacobs's staff discussed: TVA, "Site Wide Safety and Health Plan," p. 14-1.

48 One afternoon in: This section is primarily based on interviews with Jim Scott and corroborated by court documents. Walter Goolsby and Gilbert Pickel had both died by the time I was reporting.

48 May 2011: *TVA Ash Spill Litigation*, William Walter Goolsby Sr. deposition, July 13, 2011, p. 93.

49 more than sixty complaints: Duane W. Gang, "TVA to Pay $27.8M to Settle Coal Ash Lawsuits," *The Tennessean*, August 2, 2014.

49 shouldn't be immune: *Larry Mays v. TVA*, Docket no. 699 F, U.S. District Court, Eastern District of Tennessee; Scott Barker, "Ash Suits Against TVA Allowed," *Knoxville News Sentinel*, March 27, 2010.

49 six hundred thousand pages: *Larry Mays v. TVA*, hearing transcript, March 25, 2010, p. 16.

49 at least thirty-five people: This number is based on deposition transcripts I received via FOIA from TVA's Office of the Inspector General.

49 a hundred plaintiffs: Jim Scott interview; *George Chesney et al. v. TVA*, transcript of hearing, November 19, 2012, p. 28, U.S. District Court, Eastern District of Tennessee.

49 motion for summary judgment: *James Crichton v. TVA*, Docket no. 58, U.S. District Court, Eastern District of Tennessee.

49 successful real-estate firm: William Walter Goolsby Sr. obituary, Kyker Funeral Homes, https://www.kykerfuneralhomes.com/.

49 Gilbert Pickel: Gilbert DeRieux Pickel obituary, *Knoxville News Sentinel*, April 15, 2018.

50 blew onto his land: Pickel later testified that he had not seen fly ash blow onto his property firsthand but felt sure that it had. See *Gilbert D. Pickel v. TVA*, Pickel deposition, May 20, 2010, p. 80, U.S. District Court, Eastern District of Tennessee.

50 in their backyard pool: Poovey, "Hundreds Wait for Ruling on Ash Spill."

50 "we are just stuck": Ibid.

50 White steam: My observations of Pickel's property.

50 blue-green tint: TVA, "TVA Kingston Fossil Fuel Plant Release Site On-Scene Coordinator Report," p. ES-2.

50 boating or swimming: Poovey, "Hundreds Wait for Ruling on Ash Spill."

50 spherical, floating clumps: Gary MacDonald deposition, August 11, 2016, p. 20.

50 under Pickel's dock: *Gilbert D. Pickel v. TVA*, Walter Goolsby deposition, July 13, 2011, p. 98; Gilbert Pickel deposition, May 20, 2010, p. 49.

50 large coal-ash plumes: Jill Murphy interview.

50 seven hundred thousand tons: TVA, "TVA Kingston Fossil Fuel Plant Release Site On-Scene Coordinator Report," p. ES-2, 7-11 (according to TVA, 0.769 cubic yards of coal ash is equal to one ton of fly ash); TVA, "Kingston Ash Recovery Project Completion Report," p. 6-2.

51 at least 26 percent: Walter Goolsby, "Marketability Report on Properties Affected by the TVA Kingston Fossil Plant Coal-Ash Spill on December 22, 2008. Kingston, Roane County Tennessee," June 2, 2011, p. 18.

51 55 percent: Walter Goolsby, "Goolsby Property Diminution Summary," 2011.

51 "couldn't give land away": "Inside the Tennessee Coal Ash Spill," *Newsweek*, July 17, 2009.

51 more than $600,000: Matt Lakin, "Knox Attorney's License on Line over Handling of Money," *Knoxville News Sentinel*, January 10, 2018.

51 "all the hallmarks": Jamie Satterfield, "Former Law Partners Meet in Court," *Knoxville News Sentinel*, September 8, 2010.

51 Michael Pemberton: I tried several times to contact Pemberton but was unsuccessful. The attorneys of Pemberton & Scott generally challenged the accusations Daniel made against them.

51 Tennessee Bureau of Investigation: Natalie Neysa Alund, "Knoxville-Based Lawyer Under Investigation over Allegations of Fraud," *Knoxville News Sentinel*, May 13, 2011.

52 Howard J. Baker Jr.: This section is primarily drawn from interviews with Jim Scott, Beth Alexander, and Jeff Friedman, along with John Agee and Gary Davis. All the quoted dialogue in the trial scene comes from the official transcript, *George Chesney et al. v. TVA*.

52 looking disheveled: James Crichton interview.

52 courtroom 3C: *Larry Mays v. TVA*, Docket no. 97.

52 two consecutive rounds: *George Chesney et al. v. TVA*, transcript of hearing, November 19, 2012, p. 29; *George Chesney et al. v. TVA*, transcript of proceedings, September 19, 2011, pp. 3–4.

53 dark-gray suit: Bill Poovey photo for the AP.

53 $4 million: "TVA Triples Kilgore Pay," *Chattanooga Times Free Press*, November 20, 2010.

53 Columbus, Georgia: "Manufacturer Ordered to Pay City $20 Million for Air Pollution," *Lawyers Weekly USA*, September 27, 2004; *Action Marine Inc. et al. v. Continental Carbon Incorporated*, March 21, 2007, Federal Reporter, 3d Series, p. 1302, U.S. Court of Appeals, Eleventh Circuit.

54 "slimes" layer of silt: TVA, "Kingston Ash Recovery Project Non-Time-Critical Removal Action Embayment/Dredge Cell Action Memorandum, 2010," p. 12.

54 improved its policies: Ed Marcum, "TVA CEO Admits No Blame," *Knoxville News Sentinel*, September 22, 2011.

54 complaints about the resulting pollution: Owen, "For the Progress of Man," pp. 233, 260, 265, etc.

54 thirty thousand Americans: Freese, *Coal: A Human History*, p. 175. Similar figures here: Clean Air Task Force, "Dirty Air, Dirty Power: Mortality and Health Damage Due to Air Pollution from Power Plants," June 2004.

54 new federal emissions rules: Hargrove, *Prisoners of Myth*, pp. 177–78, 182; Thurman, *A History of the Tennessee Valley Authority*, p. 37.

54 production capacity: TVA, "Nuclear Power in the Tennessee Valley," pp. 4, 10.

54 largest nuclear-power system: Hargrove, *Prisoners of Myth*, p. 223.

54 seventeen reactors: Steve Holland, "TVA Users Seen Footing Nuke Reactor Fuel Bill," UPI via *The Tennessean*, December 22, 1981.

55 throughout New Mexico: Walter Pincus, "TVA in Uranium Mines," *Washington Post*, September 17, 1981.

55 billion dollars' worth: Holland, "TVA Users Seen Footing Nuke Reactor Fuel Bill."

55 Casper, Wyoming: Keel Hunt, "TVA Goes West in Uranium Hunt," *The Tennessean*, November 21, 1976.

55 using a lighted candle: Nuclear Regulatory Commission, "Fire at Browns Ferry Nuclear Plant, TVA, March 22, 1975. Final Report of Preliminary Investigating Committee," May 7, 1975, p. 9.

55 largest nuclear-power plant: "T.V.A. Lays Off Hundreds over Nuclear Plant Safety," *New York Times*, January 24, 1984.

55 $100 million: Center for Land Use Interpretation, "Browns Ferry Nuclear Power Plant," https://clui.org/.

55 the most serious accident: TVA, "Nuclear Power in the Tennessee Valley," p. 15.

55 some five hundred: "Business Digest," *New York Times*, January 24, 1984.

55 its nuclear plants: Matthew L. Ward, "TVA Shuts Down Last Nuclear Plant," *New York Times*, August 24, 1985.

55 "What we are seeing": William E. Schmidt, "T.V.A., Once Model Agency, Now Swamped by Troubles," *New York Times*, June 11, 1986.

55 90 percent: Rebecca Ferrar, "TVA Tops List of Informing by Workers," *Knoxville News Sentinel*, October 12, 1989.

55 "Our program": Tom Kilgore, "Why We Still Need Nuclear," *New York Times*, July 29, 2011.

55 two-thirds: TVA, "Fossil-Fuel Generation," captured by the Internet Archive on October 13, 2011, https://www.tva.com/.

55 two hours: Bill Poovey, "TVA President Calls Ash Spill Avoidable," AP via *The Tennessean*, September 22, 2011.

56 "red flags": TVA OIG, "Inspection Report: Review of the Kingston Fossil Plant Ash Spill," p. i.

56 "litigation strategy:" Ibid., pp. 15–17.

56 "a major factor": AECOM, "Root Cause Analysis," pp. 4, 35.

56 difficult for TVA to detect: TVA OIG, "Inspection Report: Review of the Kingston Fossil Plant Ash Spill," p. i.

56 suspiciously "fortuitous": Ibid.

57 "That was not done": Tom Kilgore testified that he was unaware that TVA had given the consultant such strict limitations.

58 finished high school: Keith Stewart interview.

59 "Nobody would talk about nothing": Mike McCarthy interview.

59 "There's plenty of people": Billy Isley deposition, August 22, 2017, p. 51.

59 five hundred: OSHA, "Case File Diary Sheet, Nashville Area Office: TVA—Kingston," case file number 202046892, Labor Inspection Narrative 301512539, p. 64.

59 out of a job: *Cox v. G-UB-MK Construction*, Brad Green deposition, July 9, 2015, p. 152, U.S. District Court, Eastern District of Tennessee; *Adkisson et al. v. Jacobs Engineering*, Docket no. 256-22, Michael Robinette affidavit.

59 "a complete blackout": Kevin Thompson trial testimony, October 18, 2018, pp. 443–44.

59 had offices upstairs: Danny Gouge trial testimony, October 17, 2018, p. 245.

59 their clothes, their hair: Jeff Brewer trial testimony, October 19, 2018, p. 585.

59 got in their sandwiches: Donald Vangilder deposition, August 4, 2020, p. 94.

59 constant cough and skin lesions: Billy Isley deposition, August 22, 2017, p. 36.

60 service the guy's wife: TVA, "TVA Documentation of Counseling with Dwayne Rushing," June 21, 2013; *McCarthy v. G-UB-UK*, Dwayne Rushing deposition, August 5, 2016, p. 58, U.S. District Court, Eastern District of Tennessee.

60 wash his clothes: Jeff Brewer deposition, April 11, 2017, p. 53.

60 Gibson and Ansol: Ibid., p. 30.

60 a little red barn: Ibid., pp. 156–58.

60 hosing off: Ibid., p. 160.

61 asked to do the job: Ibid., p. 30.

61 had similar hunches: Billy Isley deposition, August 22, 2017, p. 44; Brad Green deposition, July 9, 2015, p. 35.

61 the main gravel road: Jeff Brewer trial testimony, October 19, 2018, p. 616; a background TVA source corroborated Brewer's claim.

61 Geiger counters: Jeff Brewer deposition, April 11, 2017, p. 49. The workers widely claim that Geiger counters were ignored by Jacobs and TVA staff. A foreman, who spoke to me on the condition of anonymity, corroborated the workers' stories. In the 2018 trial, Sean Healey, of Jacobs, testified that he had heard about radioactive material in the river but said, "I didn't get too involved with the details of that." Jacobs denies that the workers were exposed to harmful radioactive material.

61 Jim Scott's office: The scene of the first three workers meeting Scott is mostly drawn from interviews with Ansol Clark, Scott, and another worker. Billy Gibson told me he didn't remember much about the meeting. No one could recall exactly when the meeting was or produce calendars to confirm it, but Ansol and Scott were confident that the meeting occurred in the fall. Billy Isley recalled a larger meeting in the spring of 2013. See his deposition on August 22, 2017, p. 28.

61 twelve-foot maroon sign: Archival Google Street View photos.

61 three pickups: Jeff Brewer text message.

61 Serita Phillips: Phillips died before I had a chance to speak with her. Two members of her family, Tammy Gosnell and Tori England, corroborated Jim Scott's story.

61 CERCLA: EPA, Region 4, "Administrative Order and Agreement on Consent, May 11, 2009," TVA respondent, CERCLA-04-2009-3766.

62 hazardous-waste training: Brad Green deposition, July 9, 2015, p. 19; *McCarthy v. G-UB-MK*, Gary MacDonald deposition, August 11, 2016, p. 48; TVA, "Site Wide Safety and Health Plan," prepared by Jacobs Engineering, January 2013 revision, p. 3-1.

62 renovated department store: "Former Watson's About Ready for Use," *Knoxville News Sentinel*, February 6, 1994.

63 the agency only discussed: Background source.

63 "run off the site": *Adkisson et al. v. Jacobs Engineering*, Docket no. 698, Billy Gibson Supplemental Responses. Scott confirmed to me that Gibson told him this.

63 "inert dust": TVA, "Class 'F' Fly Ash: Material Safety Data Sheet, No. BP—001," June 2001.

64 On the Appalachian Trail: "Snow, Ice Don't Stop Smokies Hikers," *Knoxville News Sentinel*, October 30, 2012.

64 three-foot drifts: *High on LeConte*, blog, October 31, 2012, http://www.highonleconte.com/.

64 McGhee Tyson Airport: "Knox Business Deal with Hurricane," *Knoxville News Sentinel*, October 30, 2012.

64 Mountain communities: Steve Keighton et al., "Northwest Flow Snow Aspects of Hurricane Sandy," *Weather and Forecasting* (February 2016).

66 performed an ultrasound: Letter by John D. Arnett, of Parkwest.

66 shock Ansol's heart: Ibid.

67 Personal-injury attorneys: The first paragraph in this section is partly drawn from the following study: David A. Hyman, Bernard Black, and Charles Silver, "The Economics of Plaintiff-Side Personal Injury Practice," *University of Illinois Law Review*, August 21, 2015.

67 as many as 99 percent: Ibid., p. 1586.

69 more than thirteen thousand: U.S. DOE Oak Ridge Office, "2013 Annual Workforce Analysis and Staffing Plan Report," January 2014, p. 1.

69 thousands of those jobs: State of Tennessee, "FY2013 Economic Impact: Department of Energy Spending," p. 15.

69 risked getting blackballed: Clint Mannis interview. Other workers told me similar things.

69 Vengosh's team: Avner Vengosh, "Survey of the Potential Environmental and Health Impacts in the Immediate Aftermath of the Coal Ash Spill in Kingston, Tennessee"; Vengosh, "The Tennessee Valley Authority's Kingston Ash Slide: Potential Water Quality Impacts of Coal Combustion Waste Storage," a testimony to the Subcommittee on Water Resources and Environment, U.S. House of Representatives, March 31, 2009, p. 2.

70 formed dust devils: Photo provided to me; Kevin Thompson trial testimony, October 18, 2018, p. 437.

70 twenty-seven countries: AES, "The AES Corporation Fact Sheet, as of March 31, 2013."

70 eighty-two thousand tons: Sharon Theimer, "Dominican Republic Seeking $80M from U.S. Utility," AP via *Telegram & Gazette*, March 15, 2006.

70 ten barge loads: *Government of Dominican Republic v. AES CORP*, Memorandum Order, December 5, 2006, U.S. District Court, Eastern District of Virginia; Frances Robles, "Lawsuit Highlights Coal Ash Debate," McClatchy via *The Tennessean*, November 8, 2009.

70 "When I was pregnant": Frances Robles, "A Scourge Unsettled," *Miami Herald*, November 9, 2009.

70 Dominican government filed: *Government of Dominican Republic v. AES CORP*, Memorandum Order, December 5, 2006.

70 $6 million: UPI, "Dominican Republic Dumping Case Settled," April 14, 2007.

70 a potential irritant: TVA, "Class 'F' Fly Ash: Material Safety Data Sheet, No. BP—001," June 2001.

70 Mike McCarthy stopped by: This scene is drawn from interviews with Scott and McCarthy, except where noted; McCarthy and Scott met several times, and their memories were somewhat fuzzy regarding at which meeting McCarthy showed Scott the images.

72 In the clip: Video provided to the author.

73 toy elves: "Downtown Window Decorations Part I and Part II," *Inside of Knoxville*, December 17, 2012, https://insideofknoxville.com/.

73 a temporary ice rink: "Regal Festival of Lights 2012 . . . And More," *Inside of Knoxville*, November 26, 2012, https://insideofknoxville.com/.

73 Sequoyah Presbyterian Church: Sequoyah Presbyterian website, November 2012, accessed through the Internet Archive, https://www.sequoyahchurch.org/.

73 his wife, Mary: My description of Jim and Mary Scott's relationship is drawn mainly from court documents in their divorce case, from interviews with Jack and Sam Scott, and from a deposition Mary gave over two days in June 2017. The deposition was thorough; the transcription ran 240 pages. Still, in the fact-checking process for this book, Mary said my descriptions of her and of her relationship with Jim were "dead wrong." She said that Jim tried to cast her as an angry woman and a bad mother in court documents—characterizations she vehe-

mently disputes. She said she cares deeply about her children and was a great mother. Mary is a pseudonym.

73 $252,000: Knox County property records.

74 home economics: *Scott v. Scott*, No. 189567-2, Mary Scott deposition, June 5, 2017, pp. 12–13, Chancery Court for Knox County, Tennessee.

74 sat on the PTA: Mary Scott deposition, June 5, 2017, p. 115.

74 dozen years of marriage: *Scott v. Scott*, Divorce Complaint, May 7, 2015.

74 resented him: Mary Scott interview.

74 O'Charley's: O'Charley's Annual Report for the fiscal year ended December 28, 2003, SEC filing, Form 10-K, p. 9; "Lawsuit Against O'Charley's Amended," AP via *Johnson City Press*, November 15, 2003.

74 care for their sons: Mary Scott interview.

74 best use of his time: Jim Scott interview.

74 need a new roof: Mary Scott emailed statement.

74 Eddie Daniel debacle: Jim Scott interview.

74 kept Mary in the dark: Mary Scott deposition, June 5, 2017, p. 91.

74 "too much money": Ibid., p. 98.

74 $60,000 in back taxes: Ibid., p. 107.

74 medical bills: Ibid., p. 93.

74 borrow $97,000: Jim Scott interview.

74 blowing through $1,800: Mary Scott deposition, June 5, 2017, p. 141.

74 "absolutely absurd": Ibid., p. 98.

75 seven figures in fees: Jim Scott interview.

75 the main landing page: TVA, "Kingston Recovery," captured by the Internet Archive on October 11, 2012, https://www.tva.com/.

75 project plans: TVA, "Administrative Record Documents Available for Public Review and Comment," captured by the Internet Archive on January 10, 2013, https://www.tva.com/.

76 four million tons: TVA, "TVA Kingston Fossil Fuel Plant Release Site On-Scene Coordinator Report," p. ES-2.

76 backwater sloughs: Ibid., pp. ES-2, 1-11; TVA, EPA, TDEC, transcript of quarterly public meeting, December 8, 2011, at Roane County High School, p. 6.

76 three million tons: TVA's "Kingston Ash Recovery Project Completion Report," p. 3-2.

76 a rebuilt, reinforced version: EPA, "Kingston Coal Ash Release Site: Project Completion Fact Sheet," December 2014.

76 A third, concurrent phase: TVA, EPA, TDEC, transcript of quarterly public meeting, p. 8.

76 long-term ecological risks: Ibid., p. 7.

76 seven hundred thousand tons of ash: TVA, "TVA Kingston Fossil Fuel Plant Release Site On-Scene Coordinator Report," p. ES-2, 7-11 (according to TVA, 0.769 cubic yards of coal ash is equal to one ton of fly ash); TVA, "Kingston Ash Recovery Project Completion Report," p. 6-2.

76 "Site Wide Safety and Health Plan": TVA, "Site Wide Safety and Health Plan for the TVA Kingston Fossil Plant Ash Release Response," prepared by Jacobs Engineering Group, June 2009.

76 six toxic constituents: Ibid., p. 4-12.

76 selenium, cadmium, boron, thallium: Ibid., p. 3-1.

76 twenty-three heavy metals: TVA, "Site Wide Safety and Health Plan," prepared by Jacobs Engineering Group, January 2013, pp. 4–14, 4–19.

77 needed to halt operations: Ibid., pp. 15-5, C-7-4; Jeff Friedman opening statements in October 2018 trial.

77 hazmat suit: TVA, "Site Wide Safety and Health Plan," prepared by Jacobs Engineering Group, June 2009, pp. 6-1, E-27. Jacobs disputes that the workers needed to wear a hazmat suit on the jobsite.

77 couldn't keep up: The scenes in this section are drawn from interviews with Janie Clark, Ansol Clark, and Mike McCarthy.

78 brick Baptist church: "Ernest Tate Heads Teamsters Local 519," *Knoxville News Sentinel*, March 10, 1979.

78 his retirement application: Ansol Clark interview, corroborated by retirement information on the Central States Pension Fund website, https://mycentralstatespension.org/.

78 March 15, 2013: Ansol Clark deposition, April 17, 2017, p. 100.

79 Birmingham attorney: This chapter is drawn from interviews with four attorneys who were present for Edwin Small's monologue; one plaintiff, Bob Delaney, was also there and shared his recollections with me. Rodney Max, one of the two mediators, spoke with me, but I've cited his contributions individually. Pamela Reeves, the other mediator, died before I had a chance to interview her.

79 mid-1970s: "Massive TVA Moving Job to New Offices Nearly Done," *Knoxville News Sentinel*, April 4, 1976.

79 taking his photo: Jim Scott corroborated Friedman's recollection of the ID badges.

80 TVA had failed: *Tennessee Valley Authority Ash Spill Litigation*, Memorandum Opinion and Order, August 23, 2012, pp. 72–73.

80 February 2013: The conference was on February 20–22, 2013, per one attorney's time sheets.

80 two court-appointed mediators: Rodney Max interview.

80 ten different law firms: "Rule 31 Continuing Mediation Education Accreditation Request Form: TVA Coal Ash Spill Class-Action Lawsuit," Tennessee Supreme Court, October 1, 2019.

80 nine hundred plaintiffs: *George Chesney et al. v. TVA*, transcript of hearing, November 19, 2012, before Judge Thomas A. Varlan, pp. 14, 19.

81 "gone to war": Ibid., p. 9.

81 top-ranked law schools: Charles W. Crawford, "Oral History of the Tennessee Valley Authority Interview with Charles McCarthy," Oral History Research Office, Memphis State University, October 30, 1969, pp. 4, 13–15, 20.

81 "I'm not sure": Ibid., p. 14.

81 freak geological events: Ed Marcum, "Expert Rebuts Plaintiff Claim," *Knoxville News Sentinel*, October 8, 2011.

82 mediation was premature: *George Chesney et al. v. TVA*, transcript of hearing, November 19, 2012, before Judge Thomas A. Varlan, p. 25.

83 private jets and helicopters: "TVA Decides Not to Buy or Lease Jet," AP via *Courier-Journal*, January 5, 1998; TVA OIG, "Request for Final Action—Audit 2017—15470—TVA's Fixed-Wing Aircraft," March 29, 2018.

83 multimillion-dollar salaries: TVA Fiscal Annual Report 2012.

83 government salary limits: Dave Flessner, "TVA Salaries Keep Climbing," *The Tennessean*, March 26, 2012.

83 $94 million in bonuses: "TVA Triples Kilgore Pay," *Chattanooga Times Free Press*, November 20, 2010.

83 $2.7 million: TVA Annual Report 2010, SEC filing, Form 10-6, p. 153.

84 crooks or incompetents: Elizabeth Alexander interview.

84 won their trust: Interviews with Rodney Max, along with several plaintiffs' attorneys.

84 "matrix": *George Chesney et al. v. TVA*, transcript of hearing, November 19, 2012, before Judge Thomas A. Varlan, p. 50.

84 90 percent: Yun-chien Chang and Daniel Klerman, "Settlement Around the World: Settlement Rates in the Largest Economies," Center for Law and Social Science Research Paper Series, No. CLASS21-8, February 22, 2021, pp. 10, 30–31; similar findings in Theodore Eisenberg and Charlotte Lanvers, "What Is the Settlement Rate and Why Should We Care?," *Journal of Empirical Legal Studies* (2009); Jonathan D. Glater, "Study Finds Settling Is Better Than Going to Trial," *New York Times*, August 7, 2008.

84 at least four times: From a lawyer's time sheets.

84 remained cordial: Rodney Max interview.

84 rejected the plaintiffs': Gary Davis interview.

84 didn't explain *why*: Ibid.

84 later complimented Small: Rodney Max interview.

85 five-bedroom mansion: *Armes v. TVA*, Docket no. 1, p. 4, U.S. District Court, Eastern District of Tennessee.

85 should pay $20 million: Ibid., p. 15.

85 less than $10 million: Background interview with one plaintiff's attorney.

PART II

89 On a bright: The *Challenger* scene is drawn from the following sources, in addition to interviews with Jim Scott: NASA STI Program, "STS 41-G: Mission Highlights," YouTube video, uploaded October 25, 2011, 50:01; Frank Yacenda, "Third Time Is a Charm for Crippen," *Florida Today*, October 14, 1984; Anders Gyllenhaal, "Challenger's Landing Is a Perfect 10," *Miami Herald*, October 14, 1984; live-coverage footage by NBC Cape Canaveral, "NBC News Coverage of

the STS-41-G Landing," YouTube video, uploaded by zellco321, on January 18, 2010, 5:35.

90 Thompson: My account of Kevin Thompson's termination is drawn from the testimonies of Kevin Thompson, David Thompson, Jeff Brewer, and Brad Green, as well as from interviews with Jim Scott, Kevin Thompson, and Ansol Clark. In the 2018 *Adkisson* trial, Tom Bock denied any wrongdoing, and said he sent Thompson to a TVA doctor and denied him permission to wear a respirator only as a matter of protocol. (Jacobs told me something similar, explaining that Thompson was directed to TVA's medical director for a "proper" health evaluation, which determined that he didn't meet the health requirements to wear a dust mask.) Bock also alleged that Thompson was not laid off for asking for a dust mask and claimed, in a 2014 affidavit, that Jacobs would have violated federal safety rules had the company allowed Thompson to wear a dust mask. Jacobs also maintains that permitting Thompson to use a dust mask would have violated federal rules and the "Site Wide Safety and Health Plan." But, as I detail later in the book, Tom Heffernan, of TVA, testified in 2016 that Jacobs staff should have honored respirator and dust-mask prescriptions written by the workers' own doctors. Similarly, in a 2021 order, Judge Varlan noted that there was evidence that Jacobs should have honored the prescriptions. See *Adkisson et al. v. Jacobs Engineering*, Doc. 759.

90 "they're trying to send me home": Kevin Thompson told me couldn't recall whether he called Jim while on the jobsite or at a later point, but testimony in several depositions suggests that he was at the jobsite, and that's what Jim Scott recalled.

90 "he turned real red": Kevin Thompson trial testimony, October 18, 2018, pp. 462–63.

91 "They said they didn't have nothing": Ibid., p. 466.

91 visited Scott's office: Kevin Thompson interview.

91 hit his head: Dave Thompson trial testimony, October 18, 2018, p. 390; Kevin Thompson trial testimony, October 18, 2018, p. 462.

91 "They came in and told me": Kevin Thompson trial testimony, October 18, 2018, p. 461.

91 He was fired: In an August 2016 deposition (p. 93), Gary MacDonald, of TVA, who did not respond to my interview requests, said Thompson no longer worked at Kingston because "the project [was] over."

92 *The New England Journal of Medicine*: C. Arden Pope III et al., "Fine-Particulate Air Pollution and Life Expectancy in the United States," *New England Journal of Medicine*, January 22, 2009, pp. 376–84.

92 relationship had deteriorated: Mary Scott deposition, June 6, 2017, p. 4.

92 credit cards: Mary Scott deposition, June 5, 2017, p. 91.

92 which Scott denied: Jim Scott interview.

92 job at Hallmark: Mary Scott deposition, June 5, 2017, pp. 108, 110. Jim later said he couldn't recall urging Mary against taking a job at the store.

93 marriage counselor: Mary Scott deposition, June 6, 2017, pp. 59–60.

93 about sex, about alcohol: These are recurring themes in Mary Scott's June 5 and June 6, 2017, deposition.

93 both enjoyed wine: Mary Scott deposition, June 5, 2017, p. 63.

93 could overdo it: Ibid., p. 100; June 6, 2017, p. 10.

93 amplified their bickering: Mary Scott denies that she had a drinking problem, though in her 2017 deposition she acknowledged that she did for a time. Jim said he began drinking too much around 2017 but has since stopped.

93 could also be erratic: James K. Scott affidavit, June 15, 2015; Sam Scott interview.

93 screaming at him: Mary Scott interview. She later told me that she yelled and screamed at Jim because she believed he was "living a double life."

93 "frat daddy": Mary Scott interview.

93 having said that he was: Email from a Knoxville physician.

94 Tom Bevill: Sue Sturgis, "Big Energy vs. Coal Ash Regulation," *Grist*, May 27, 2010; Max Blau, "The Coal Plant Next Door," *ProPublica/Georgia Health News*, March 22, 2021.

94 Jeff Brewer had: This scene is primarily drawn from interviews with Brewer, along with his 2018 trial testimony. Brad Green corroborated much of Brewer's account in a July 9, 2015, deposition. Bock, who didn't grant an interview for this book, acknowledged in the 2018 trial that Brewer, along with Ansol and many others, complained to him that fly ash had made him sick. See Tom Bock trial testimony, October 19, 2018, p. 735.

94 night crews: Jeff Brewer trial testimony, October 19, 2018, p. 590.

95 "I'm not a pharmacist": This sentence is taken from Tom Bock's August 26, 2016, deposition, p. 166; Jeff Brewer recalls Bock telling him the same thing verbatim, which is why I thought it was appropriate to quote Bock here.

95 "We don't do that": Jeff Brewer trial testimony, October 19, 2018, pp. 636–37.

95 "You can't wear a respirator": Ibid., p. 637.

95 N95 dust mask: Tom Bock later signed an affidavit stating that Brewer didn't need a prescription to voluntarily wear an N95, nor did any worker, provided they followed the protocols outlined in the "Site Wide Safety and Health Plan."

95 was fitted for one: Jeff Brewer trial testimony, October 19, 2018, pp. 638, 646. Tom Bock corroborated much of Brewer's story in a deposition on August 26, 2016, pp. 93–96, 129–30, and in his trial testimony, pp. 734–35, 848.

96 twenty-five workers: *Adkisson et al. v. Jacobs Engineering*, Docket no. 200-8.

96 most were told no: Tom Bock deposition, August 26, 2016, pp. 96–104, 121.

96 their doctors were wrong: Brad Green deposition, July 9, 2015, p. 98.

96 public might see them: Brad Green deposition, July 9, 2015, p. 57.

96 dust masks or respirators: Jacobs denies that its staff improperly handled any request for respiratory protection.

96 Kathryn Nash: Nash declined to speak with me.

96 "a plan of attack": Tom Bock email to Douglas Mills, May 6, 2013, obtained through FOIA.

96 "a unified front": Tom Bock email to Gary Draper, August 19, 2013, obtained through FOIA.

96 build a defense: Christopher M. Williams email, June 7, 2013, obtained through FOIA.

96 Calhoun's barbecue: The Calhoun's scene is based on interviews with Jim Scott and Greg Jones. Neither could verify exactly when the dinner took place—Scott said after the Sixth Circuit; Jones said before. I've placed it before the Sixth Circuit, since that timing aligns with the nature of their conversation at that point in the case. Greg Jones is a pseudonym. This person asked to speak on background for professional reasons.

97 $11.5 million: TDEC, "Environment and Conservation Issues $11.5 Million Penalty to TVA for Kingston Coal Ash Spill," press release, June 14, 2010, https://www.tn.gov/environment.html.

97 $11 billion in revenue: TVA SEC filing, Form 10-K, for fiscal year 2010, p. 8.

97 front-page story: Bob Fowler, "Lawsuit: Company Covered Up Coal Ash Danger," *Knoxville News Sentinel*, August 23, 2013.

98 "non-adversarial": Corroborated by John Agee interview.

98 didn't have to fight the DOE: Matthew L. Wald, "U.S. Outlines Plan to Settle Claims of Nuclear Bomb Plant Workers Who Became Ill or Died," *New York Times*, April 13, 2000; EEOICPA, "The History of EEOICPA," https://www.eecap.org/.

98 presumed to be the cause: Frank Munger, "Ruling Helps Ex-Y-12 Workers on Claims," *Knoxville News Sentinel*, December 7, 2011.

98 largest construction-law practice: Smith, Cashion & Orr's website, November 2013, accessed through the Internet Archive, https://www.smithcashion.com/.

98 middle-aged attorney: U.S. Index to Public Records.

98 Joseph Welborn: Welborn did not respond to interview requests for this book.

98 "Don't be a dick": John Dupree interview.

99 one-hundred-and-ninety-pound senior: Pete Wickham, "Lynx Count on Maturity of Welborn," *Memphis Commercial Appeal*, September 3, 1987.

99 quarterback sneaks: Larry Rea, "Welborn Makes Big Play in Rhodes' Win," *Memphis Commercial Appeal*, October 26, 1986.

99 in his mid-thirties: Smith, Cashion & Orr bio.

99 painted-brick home: Davidson County, Tennessee, property records.

99 Al Gore owned: Iain Murray, *Stealing You Blind* (Washington, DC: Regnery Publishing, Inc., 2011), p. 2.

99 federal law generally shielded: *Larry Mays v. TVA*, Memorandum Opinion and Order, March 26, 2010.

99 made an exception: "Judge Affirms TVA Negligence Led to 2008 Coal Ash Spill," *Knoxville News Sentinel*, August 26, 2012.

99 two Roane County cases: The case is *Larry Mays v. TVA.*

99 second Roane County case: The case is *George Chesney et al. v. Tennessee Valley Authority*. See the order and opinion filed on March 22, 2011; *Adkisson et al. v. Jacobs Engineering*, Opinion of the U.S. Court of Appeals for the Sixth Circuit, June 2, 2015, pp. 4–5.

100 critique this characterization: Interviews with several corporate defense attorneys who previously worked for Neal & Harwell.

100 commended his knack: John Agee interview.

101 Judge Thomas Varlan: The several paragraphs about Varlan are drawn from interviews with six former interns, clerks, or classmates of the judge, all of whom, except one, Andrew Folkner, requested to speak on background, given that the *Adkisson* case was still ongoing when I was reporting.

101 grown up in Oak Ridge: "Father of Judge Varlan Dies at 90," *Knoxville News Sentinel*, May 12, 2010.

101 defended the city: Tim Burchett, Senate Joint Resolution 189, Tennessee General Assembly, March 19, 2003.

101 "truly my life's goal": Jamie Satterfield, "Varlan Takes Judge's Oath," *Knoxville News Sentinel*, May 10, 2003.

102 left-leaning attorneys: Elizabeth Alexander interview.

102 since N95s: Brewer deposition, April 11, 2017, p. 124.

102 took orders from TVA: Brad Green deposition, July 9, 2015, p. 35.

102 passersby wouldn't see him: Brewer deposition, April 11, 2017, p. 124.

102 One humid Friday: Ibid., p. 22.

102 retaining wall: "TVA Completes Retaining Wall Around Coal Ash," AP via *Jackson Sun*, March 7, 2014; EPA, "Kingston Coal Ash Release Site: Project Completion Fact Sheet," December 2014.

103 thousands of trees: Ibid.

103 layoff papers: Brad Green, a foreman and Brewer's manager, described the layoff process in detail in a deposition on July 9, 2015, p. 107.

103 Mike McCarthy: In court filings, GUBMK, the TVA contractor that employed McCarthy, denied that his termination was retaliatory and maintained that TVA had picked him and thirty-four others as part of a workforce reduction. In 2017, Judge Varlan dismissed a wrongful-termination case McCarthy brought against GUBMK, on the grounds that TVA, not GUBMK, had decided to lay off McCarthy, and since McCarthy had little evidence to support that his termination was retaliatory. Given the testimonies of other workers, however, along with Chris Eich's "cock" comment to McCarthy, I find his allegation credible, which is why I included it. See *McCarthy v. G-UB-MK*, Docket no. 137.

103 air-monitoring results: Billy Isley deposition, August 22, 2017, pp. 22, 40–43.

104 "The only thing": Robert Muse interview.

104 bring him documentation: Craig Wilkinson interview.

104 "It is in my opinion": Letter by Dr. John D. Arnett, July 18, 2013.

105 urinary analysis: Dr. Kalpana D. Patel, urinary analysis report for Craig Wilkinson, May 5, 2014, Buffalo, New York.

105 coughed up blood nightly: *Wilkinson et al. v. Jacobs Engineering Group, Inc.*, Docket no. 15, U.S. District Court, Eastern District of Tennessee.

105 Wilkinson's physician: *Wilkinson v. Jacobs*, Docket no. 16-2, letter by Dr. Diana Vakante, May 26, 2015.

105 Tommy Johnson: Interviews with Tommy Johnson and Jim Scott.

105 "I'm concerned": TVA, transcript of public meeting, June 23, 2009, Roane State College, Harriman, Tennessee, p. 47.

105 "desire to have the coveralls": Ibid., p. 52.

105 much less a hazmat suit: In a memo, a lawyer representing Jacobs told me, "The assertion by the workers that they should have been provided protective clothing is wrong. Most workers sat inside sealed, air-conditioned vehicle cabs with filtered air. Providing Tyvek suits could have been harmful, just as providing dust masks could have been harmful." This is a disputed point.

106 One cold evening: This scene is drawn from interviews with Jeff Brewer; from transcripts of Brewer's deposition on April 11, 2017; and from an interview with a background source. Other workers—including Craig Wilkinson, Brian Thacker, Rick Samson, S. T. McCollum, and Roger Griffith—later shared similar stories that corroborated Brewer's account. TVA and Jacobs documents had also noted the presence of radioactive material in the river, as detailed later in the book.

106 "low-sodium table salt": TVA, "Radioactivity Analysis of Ash Samples, January 7, 2009," uploaded to TVA.com in 2009, captured by the Internet Archive, https://www.tva.com/.

106 *stop everything:* Craig Wilkinson interview.

107 The friend: This person, whom I interviewed, asked for his name to be withheld for fear of retaliation.

107 a urinary analysis: Dr. Kalpana D. Patel, urinary analysis report for Craig Wilkinson, May 5, 2014, Buffalo, New York.

107 hurt their property values: My description of the plaintiffs' position during mediation is drawn from interviews with Gary Davis, Jim Scott, and another plaintiffs' attorney who spoke to me on background.

108 represented individuals pro bono: Senate Judiciary Committee, transcript of confirmation hearings on federal appointments part five, September 25, October 30, and November 6, 2013.

108 poor treatment of women: *Knoxville News Sentinel*, August 20, 2006, and July 20, 2008.

108 felt sure they knew why: Background interviews with several plaintiffs' attorneys. TVA did not respond to a query about its decision to settle the land cases.

108 TVA tentatively agreed: A tentative settlement was reached in late 2013, according to Gary Davis, who reviewed his documents from this period for me. The lawyer Matt Conn told reporters that final terms were reached the week of the

deal's announcement. See Bob Fowler, "TVA Spill Settlement: $27.8M," *Knoxville News Sentinel*, August 2, 2014.

108 all nine hundred or so: Rodney Max interview.

109 less than $30,000: The exact sums that TVA paid the plaintiffs were kept secret. I arrived at $30,000 by subtracting a third from the total settlement offer to account for the lawyers' fees, then dividing the remainder by the number of plaintiffs. Lawyers involved in the cases agreed that this was a decent way to arrive at the average amount each plaintiff took home.

109 "Look": James Crichton interview.

109 Scott Brooks: "TVA to Pay Kingston Coal Ash Spill Victims $27.8M," WBIR, August 1, 2014.

109 "For us": Jessica Dye, "U.S. Court Approves $27.8 Million Deal for Toxic Tennessee Spill," Reuters, August 5, 2014.

109 Scott called Jeff Friedman: Jeff Friedman interview; Scott would later say he didn't remember calling Friedman at this particular time.

110 Thirteen circuit courts: United States Courts, "Court Role and Structure," https://www.uscourts.gov/.

110 Kentucky, Michigan, Ohio, and Tennessee: U.S. Court of Appeals for the Sixth Circuit, "About the Court," https://www.ca6.uscourts.gov/.

111 the nation's elite colleges: "The Echo Chamber," Reuters, December 8, 2014; Center for American Progress, "Pipelines to Power: Encouraging Professional Diversity on the Federal Appellate Bench," August 13, 2020, www.americanprogress.org; " 'We Need to Lose Our Addiction to Yale and Harvard.' Judge Urges Congress to Diversify Federal Courts," *National Law Journal*, July 12, 2021.

111 Harvard Law graduate: *Bloomberg*, Judge Gilman bio.

111 At two o'clock: The date was November 19, 2014, according to the Sixth Circuit docket.

111 meet with a mediator: My account of the mediation is primarily drawn from interviews with Ansol Clark; a few other workers present or familiar with the negotiations; and, to a lesser degree, Jim Scott. The mediator for the Sixth Circuit, Paul Calico, declined an interview request. See *Adkisson et al. v. Jacobs Engineering*, United States Court of Appeals for the Sixth Circuit, Docket nos. 3 and 6.

111 16 percent: Colter Paulson, "Reversal Rates in the Sixth Circuit, AKA, the Importance of an Excellent Brief," *Sixth Circuit Appellate Blog*, November 4, 2010, www.sixthcircuitappellateblog.com/; this source gives an overall reversal rate of 14 percent for circuit courts: Corey Lazar and Lindsay Murphy, "Survey: Circuit Court Treatment of Documents Commonly Submitted in CPC Asylum Claims," *Immigration Law Advisor* 3, no. 6 (June 2009).

111 $100,000: Ansol Clark recalled the number being closer to $50,000. Jacobs did not respond to a query about its settlement offer.

112 relationship with his sisters: Jim Scott interview; Mary Scott deposition, June 5, 2017, p. 69. Dana Pemberton and Annie Duncan both declined interview requests. I was unable to reach Michael Pemberton.

112 Ellis "Sandy" Sharp: Sandy Sharp didn't respond to interview requests. My description of him is based on conversations with two background sources.

112 assistant city attorney: "Miss Elda Brown Becomes Bride of Sandy Sharp," *Knoxville News Sentinel*, April 15, 1979.

113 Early in Ansol's: The scenes of Ansol's stroke and subsequent doctors' visits are drawn from interviews with Ansol and Janie, along with a detailed timeline of Ansol's medical issues that Janie drafted. Ansol also discussed his medical problems in a deposition on April 17, 2017, and his medical examinations are mentioned in various court filings.

113 fell out of the boat: Ansol Clark deposition, April 17, 2017, pp. 131–32.

116 One April night: I was unable to reach the officers who responded to the domestic-disturbance call at the Scott home, so my account is drawn mostly from an incident report they wrote; from interviews with Jim Scott, Jack Scott, and Sam Scott; from Mary Scott's deposition testimony; and from the couple's divorce filings. Mary Scott disputes some aspects of the couple's fight as I've portrayed it. As I've previously stated in these notes, Mary believes that Jim tried to cast her as an angry woman and a bad mother, a characterization she disputes. She also said my reporting was "incorrect on so many levels."

116 cursed at her: Mary Scott emailed statement.

116 "She punched the shit out of Dad": Jack Scott interview.

116 Mary, crying and upset: Mary Scott emailed statement.

116 to flee from the police: *Scott v. Scott*, James K. Scott affidavit, June 15, 2015.

117 "bogus": Mary Scott interview.

117 "non-husband": Ibid.

117 denied that she hit Jim: Mary Scott deposition, June 6, 2017, p. 55.

117 "I told [the boys] I was very sorry": Ibid., p. 37.

117 She wasn't accustomed: Mary Scott emailed statement.

117 then seldom at all: Mary Scott deposition, June 6, 2017, p. 80.

117 workers' lawsuit against Jacobs: Ibid., pp. 59–60.

117 fumed, drank: Ibid., p. 79.

117 keep paying their bills: Mary Scott interview.

117 "very serious, complex": *Adkisson et al. v. Jacobs Engineering*, Docket no. 26, U.S. Court of Appeals for the Sixth Circuit.

117 seventy-three-page brief: Ibid.

118 The Sixth Circuit Court: The Sixth Circuit courtroom scenes are drawn from interviews with Jim Scott, along with Emily Taylor and Keith Wesolowski, two attorneys present that day. I directly quote Scott's and Joe Welborn's arguments from an audio recording made by the court. Welborn didn't respond to interview requests. Joshua Bond, another attorney who represented a small number of the Kingston workers and who was also present in the courtroom, declined to speak with me since the workers' case hadn't yet been resolved.

118 conservative institution: Rewire News Group, "The Republican Takeover of the Federal Courts Should Terrify You," April 16, 2019; SCOTUS Blog, "Sixth Cir-

cuit: Now, a Split on Same-Sex Marriage," November 6, 2015, www.scotusblog.com/.

118 Republican appointees: Ballotpedia, "United States Court of Appeals for the Sixth Circuit," March 21, 2015, accessed via the Internet Archive, https://ballotpedia.org/.

118 had upheld bans: SCOTUS Blog, "Sixth Circuit: Now, a Split on Same-sex Marriage."

118 one dissenting judge: Dan Sewell, "Court Backs Ohio Antiabortion Law," AP via *Philadelphia Inquirer*, March 13, 2019.

118 reported to the clerk's office: *Adkisson et al. v. Jacobs Engineering*, Docket no. 33 and 38, U.S. Court of Appeals for the Sixth Circuit.

118 "hot bench": Keith Wesolowski interview.

119 scheduled to be heard second: Sixth Circuit, Oral Argument Calendar, April 27, 2015–May 1, 2015.

119 "had a lot of coffee": Emily Taylor interview.

121 Mild shock: Jim Scott interview.

122 the workers spray water: A lawyer representing Jacobs Engineering later said there was no evidence that the workers were ordered to spray around the air monitors and that Jacobs's staff was not responsible for directing the workers' activities.

122 family-law attorney: *Scott v. Scott*, Complaint for Divorce, May 7, 2015.

122 "Irreconcilable differences": James K. Scott affidavit, June 15, 2015.

123 elaborate sand fort: Interviews with Jim Scott and Jack Scott.

123 safety and well-being: *Scott v. Scott*, James K. Scott affidavit, June 22, 2018.

123 prefer that arrangement: Jack Scott interview; Knox County 911, audio recording of call by Sam Scott, March 25, 2018.

124 On Sunday: The Kilgore anecdote is drawn from two sources: CBS News, "Tennessee Toxic Spill Woes," YouTube video uploaded on December 29, 2008, 1:49; and J. J. Stambaugh, "TVA Not Holding Its Head Up High," *Knoxville News Sentinel*, December 29, 2008.

124 Craig Zeller: Craig Zeller professional bio.

124 environmental review board: Roane County Environmental Review Board: Meeting Minutes: June 4, 2015.

124 little fanfare: "Cleanup Complete, but TVA Ash Spill's Legacies Will Linger," *Knoxville News Sentinel*, June 10, 2015; Bob Fowler, "End of Mission Meeting Wraps Ash Spill Cleanup," *Knoxville News Sentinel*, YouTube video uploaded on June 4, 2015, 2:04, https://www.youtube.com/watch?v=Gs7aZ3RRZHk.

124 EPA's top staffer: TVA et al., transcript of quarterly public meeting, September 23, 2010.

124 clicked through a presentation: Craig Zeller, of the EPA, "TVA Kingston Ash Recovery Project, Roane County, TN, Project Completion Meeting, June 4, 2015," slideshow.

124 button-down shirt: Fowler, "End of Mission Meeting."

125 "an unacceptable risk": TVA et al., transcript of quarterly public meeting, May 20, 2010, Roane County High School, Kingston, Tennessee, pp. 31, 83–84.

125 "Adequately protecting the workers": TVA et al., transcript of quarterly public meeting, September 23, 2010, Roane County High School, Kingston, Tennessee, pp. 30–31.

125 reconsider its energy mix: Gold, *Superpower*, p. 147.

125 had decommissioned two: TVA, "Plants of the Past," https://www.tva.com/.

125 coal-fired power stations: U.S. Energy Information Administration, "Count of Electric Power Industry Power Plants, by Sector, by Predominant Energy Sources Within Plant, 2008 Through 2018," https://www.eia.gov/.

125 environmental nonprofits: David Drake and Jeffrey G. York, "Kicking Ash: Who (or What) Is Winning the 'War on Coal'?," University of Colorado Boulder, February 21, 2021; Michael Grunwald, "Inside the War on Coal," *Politico*, May 26, 2015.

125 top source of emissions: Hannah Ritchie and Max Rose, "CO_2 and Greenhouse Gas Emissions," OurWorldInData.org, updated in 2021.

125 "exceptional environmental controls": TVA, presentation slides from "Tennessee Valley Authority Regional Energy Resource Council, Chattanooga, Tennessee, February 2 and 3, 2015," p. 14.

125 halted since 1988: "Work Halted on 2nd Unit at Watts Bar," AP via *Memphis Commercial Appeal*, December 3, 1988.

125 36 percent: TVA, presentation slides from "Tennessee Valley Authority Regional Energy Resource Council, Chattanooga, Tennessee, February 2 and 3, 2015," p. 43; U.S. Energy Information Administration, "TVA Is the Largest Government-Owned Electricity Provider in the United States," August 13, 2021, https://www.eia.gov/.

126 down from 60 percent: Duncan Mansfield, "TVA Agrees to Pursue Renewable Energy Purchases," AP, April 2, 2009.

126 average of 20 percent: U.S. Energy Information Administration, "U.S. Primary Energy Production by Major Sources, 1950–2021," accessed July 2022, https://www.eia.gov/.

126 millions of dollars: Jeffrey Lyash, letter to Diana DeGetter, chair of the Subcommittee on Oversight and Investigations, House of Representatives Committee on Energy and Commerce, April 25, 2019. TVA maintained that its donations were not used to lobby or litigate on its behalf, but, after an investigation, TVA's Office of the Inspector General was unable to determine whether that claim was true.

126 fought Tennessee regulators: *State of Tennessee et al. v. TVA*, Consent Order, June 13, 2019, the Chancery Court for the State of Tennessee Twentieth Judicial District, Davidson County.

126 six-foot-five: Gold, *Superpower*, p. 198.

126 almost as much coal: John Murawski, "Is 'Clean' Coal the Answer?," *Raleigh News and Observer*, January 27, 2007.

126 compounded the distrust: David Wasilko, "TVA Coal Ash Spill's Legacy Is Distrust," *Knoxville News Sentinel*, June 21, 2015; interviews with various Kingston locals.

126 "Ash spill workers get 2nd crack": Jamie Satterfield, *Knoxville News Sentinel*, June 5, 2015.

127 *Dateline NBC*: "A Deadly Triangle," transcript published online on July 16, 2007, www.nbcnews.com/.

128 coal-ash disposal rules: EPA, "Hazardous and Solid Waste Management System; Disposal of Coal Combustion Residuals from Electric Utilities; Final Rule," *Federal Register* 80, no. 74, April 17, 2015, p. 21325.

128 there were some seven hundred and fifty: Earthjustice, "Mapping the Coal Ash Contamination," November 3, 2022, https://earthjustice.org/.

128 four thousand miles: Interview with Betsy Southerland; Lisa Friedman, "EPA to Roll Back Rules to Control Toxic Ash from Coal Plants," *New York Times*, October 31, 2019.

128 monitor: EPA, "Hazardous and Solid Waste Management System," pp. 21301–501.

128 "special waste": EPA, "Special Wastes," accessed in January 2023, https://www.epa.gov/.

129 several hundredfold: EPA, Office of Solid Waste and Emergency Response, "Human and Ecological Risk Assessment of Coal Combustion Wastes," draft document, April 2010, pp. ES-5, ES-7; Barbara Gottlieb et al., "Coal Ash: The Toxic Threat to Our Health and Environment," Physicians for Social Responsibility and EarthJustice, September 2010, p. vii; Shaila Dewan, "Hundreds of Coal Ash Dumps Lack Regulation," *New York Times*, January 6, 2009.

129 A report that contained: Ibid.

129 coal lobby: ProPublica, "Politics and Lobbying Influence EPA Rules on Coal Ash Wastewater," August 7, 2014; ProPublica," Lobbyists Bidding to Block Government Regs Set Sights on Secretive White House Office," July 31, 2014.

129 more than half of which: American Coal Ash Association, "2015 Coal Combustion Product (CCP) Production & Use Survey Report," https://acaa-usa.org/.

129 billions of dollars: MarketsandMarkets, "Fly Ash Market Worth 5.97 Billion USD by 2021," April 4, 2017.

129 *Are you interested yet?*: Interview with Jeff Friedman. Jim Scott's recollection of his correspondence with Friedman differs slightly, in that Scott says the conversation came about because of a case involving a train derailment.

130 were substantially similar: *Adkisson et al. v. Jacobs Engineering*, Docket no. 35.

130 ten lawsuits: Jacobs Engineering Group, SEC Quarterly Report for the quarterly period ended December 31, 2021, Form 10-Q, p. 33.

130 lesion on his face: Billy Isley deposition, August 22, 2017, p. 186.

130 suffered three strokes: Lena Isley interview.

130 Mike Shelton: Interviews with Angie Shelton, Jim Scott, and Janie Clark. Also: *Adkisson et al. v. Jacobs Engineering*, Docket no. 213-7, p. 26, and no. 766, p. 11;

Kristen Lombardi, "Former Cleanup Workers Blame Illness on Toxic Coal Ash Exposures," Center for Public Integrity, July 20, 2016; Jamie Satterfield, "Kingston Coal Ash Spill Workers Treated as 'Expendables,' Lawsuit by Sick and Dying Contends," *Knoxville News Sentinel*, July 21, 2017.

131 "lose Mike": Jim Scott interview.

131 soccer and basketball teams: Jeff Brewer deposition, April 11, 2017, pp. 174–76.

131 Glen Avon, California: Tom Gorman, "Final Settlement Is Approved in Waste Dump Case," *Los Angeles Times*, November 18, 1994.

131 more than three decades: Dan Lawton, "Stringfellow Acid Pits: The Toxic and Legal Legacy by Brian Craig," *California Litigation* 33, no. 2 (2020), p. 58.

132 Supreme Court: *Adkisson et al. v. Jacobs Engineering*, Docket no. 44-1, U.S. Court of Appeals for the Sixth Circuit.

132 ten had cancer: Lombardi, "Former Cleanup Workers Blame Illness on Toxic Coal Ash Exposures."

132 bickering over a condo: *Scott v. Scott*, James K. Scott affidavit, November 9, 2015.

133 John Dupree was: My description of John Dupree's backstory is drawn from interviews with Dupree, Keith Stewart, and Jim Scott, along with a family history provided to me by Dupree.

133 wittiest boy: Red Bank High School yearbook, 1986.

135 Dupree wasn't surprised: Jim Scott's and John Dupree's recollections of Dupree joining the case differ slightly in that, according to Scott, Dupree was eager to join the case, whereas Dupree said he needed some convincing.

136 nine in the morning: Elizabeth Henderson confirmed the swim-practice time.

136 had given Jim sole custody: Interviews with Jack and Sam Scott; Mary Scott deposition, June 5, 2017, pp. 52, 133; *Scott v. Scott*, Plaintiff's Motion Requesting Restriction of Visitation of Defendant and Request for Ex Parte Order, June 22, 2018; letters by Dr. Peter B. Young and Dr. Laurie T. Williams.

137 the names of a dozen: *Adkisson et al. v. Jacobs*, Docket no. 88-1.

138 a thousand dollars: *Adkisson et al. v. Jacobs*, Docket no. 88-3.

138 decided to part ways: Letter by Sandy Sharp, *Adkisson et al. v. Jacobs*, Docket no. 76-1.

138 "You come over here": Jim Scott interview.

139 died of cancer: "Helen Stewart," *Kingsport Times-News*, September 27, 1986.

139 in October 1987: My account of Stewart's arrest is drawn from interviews with Stewart, as well as from three newspaper stories by Emily Morse for *The Advocate-Messenger*: "Students Arrested for Cocaine Trafficking," October 16, 1987; "3 Former Students Held to Grand Jury on Cocaine Charge," October 29, 1987; "Plea Bargain Discussed in Cocaine Case," December 17, 1987.

139 "I was the worst drug dealer": I was the acquaintance Stewart told this to.

140 deep Baptist guilt: Keith Stewart, "Keith Gets a Haircut," essay shared with author.

140 After a divorce: *Robin Stewart v. Keith D. Stewart*, Opinion, March 20, 2001, Court of Appeals of Tennessee at Knoxville.

140 "Say what you want": Jason H. Long, "Annual Meeting Diary," *DICTA* (January 2017).

141 "a good lick": In 2022, Stewart sent me a four-page summary of his initial involvement in the case. This and several other details come from that document.

141 on July 12: This meeting scene is drawn from interviews with Jim Scott, Keith Stewart, and John Dupree, which I corroborated with various documents and photos.

141 drew four or five: TVA, "Air Monitoring Information: Particulate Monitoring Stations," July 9, 2009–August 8, 2009. Craig Zeller, of the EPA, explained in a public meeting that the stationary air monitors were around the perimeter of the site: TVA et al., transcript of quarterly public meeting, September 23, 2010, pp. 30–31.

141 across the river: Brad Green deposition, July 9, 2015, p. 45; TVA, "Early Emergency Response Air Monitoring," page saved on July 13, 2013, by the Internet Archive, www.tva.com/.

141 ash had to be dry: Craig Zeller, of the EPA, said the ash needed to be dry before it was shipped out: TVA et al., transcript of quarterly public meeting, May 20, 2010, p. 19. Corroborated by Jeff Brewer deposition, April 11, 2017, pp. 119–20, and Mike McCarthy trial testimony, October 23, 2018, p. 1270.

141 *not* to water down: John Cox trial testimony, October 23, 2018, pp. 1119–24. Jacobs says there's no evidence that the water trucks were instructed not to water around the stationary air monitors.

142 closely associated with TVA: *Love v. G-UB-MK Constructors*, Memorandum and Order, November 15, 2016, U.S. District Court, Eastern District of Tennessee.

142 "TVA people": Brad Green deposition, July 9, 2015, p. 35.

142 "if them monitors spiked": Ibid., p. 76.

142 the latency period: *Adkisson et al. v. Jacobs*, Docket no. 727-3; Norman J. Kleiman, "Human Health Concerns Related to Exposure to Radionuclides Found in Fly Ash."

143 third of the contingency fee: Keith Stewart memo.

144 fly ash blew around: Brad Green deposition, July 9, 2015, pp. 44–45, 50.

144 Tom Bock: Ibid.

144 soon after it stopped: Ibid., p. 130.

144 "pretty much do whatever": Ibid., pp. 90–91.

144 "a big lawsuit": Ibid., p. 124.

145 July 21, 2016: Many details from this scene, and all quoted dialogue from Heffernan's testimony, come from the official transcript. Other details are primarily drawn from interviews with Scott, Stewart, and Dupree. Kurt Hamrock did not respond to interview requests.

146 eight hundred and fifty lawyers: Covington & Burling website, May 2016, accessed via the Internet Archive, https://www.cov.com/.

146 Union Bank of Switzerland: Jeffrey Toobin, "Holder v. Roberts," *New Yorker*, February 17 & 24, 2014, issue.

146 Guantánamo Bay detainees: Brian Foster and David Parker, "Should All Gitmo Detainees 'Rot in Hell'?," *The Hill*, February 16, 2015.

146 Tom Heffernan: Tom Heffernan declined an interview request, but, in a brief phone call, he said he had no memory of what he wore to his deposition. This detail comes from interviews with the plaintiffs' attorneys.

147 took his job seriously: Background TVA source.

150 catch a flight: *Adkisson et al. v. Jacobs*, Docket no. 88-2, Kurt Hammock email to Karen S. Taylor, August 1, 2016.

150 at least ninety-five times: *Adkisson et al. v. Jacobs*, Docket no. 94, p. 5.

150 eight more key depositions: *Adkisson et al v. Jacobs*, Docket no. 88.

151 fly ash was safe: *McCarthy v. G-UB-UK*, Dwayne Rushing deposition, August 5, 2016, p. 41.

151 The contractor: Eugene Meredith deposition, August 3, 2016, pp. 14, 21, 46, 56.

151 John Parker: John Parker deposition, August 9, 2016.

151 two dozen times: *Adkisson et al. v. Jacobs*, Docket no. 94, p. 5.

151 "How did you find Kurt?": John Parker deposition, August 9, 2016, p. 136.

151 sworn declaration: *Adkisson et al. v. Jacobs*, Docket no. 65-4.

152 contracts and procurement: Jamie E. Keith deposition, August 10, 2016, p. 22.

152 simple yes-or-no questions: *Adkisson et al. v. Jacobs*, Docket no. 94, p. 5.

152 Do not answer that: Jamie E. Keith deposition, August 10, 2016, p. 23.

153 Bock's deposition: Tom Bock's deposition took place on August 26, 2016. It was especially long and convoluted, in part thanks to Jim Scott's erratic questions. For the sake of holding the reader's attention, I have greatly summarized what was said. All quoted dialogue from Bock's testimony comes from the official transcript. Additional scene-setting details come from interviews with Jim Scott, John Dupree, and Keith Stewart. Joe Welborn did not respond to multiple interview requests, and Bock, as previously stated, declined to speak with me. When I tried to contact Rebecca Murray, one of the other defense attorneys present, to ask about Bock's deposition, someone at her law firm told me that she had recently retired, and I failed to reach her with publicly listed phone numbers. Another defense attorney present, Karen Crutchfield, did not respond to an interview request.

154 "Tom Bock has a gift": Brad Green deposition, July 9, 2015, p. 98.

154 who got along with Bock: Danny Gouge interview.

155 "probably not the greatest example": Tom Bock trial testimony, October 19, 2018, p. 709.

155 energetic, enterprising: Background TVA source.

155 a bad guy: Interviews with a background TVA source and Robert Muse, a former TVA safety coordinator.

155 TVA elevated him: Tom Bock deposition, August 12, 2016, p. 78.

156 Greg Adkisson: Greg Adkisson deposition, p. 65.

156 "I'll check into it": Ansol Clark deposition, April 17, 2017, p. 98.

156 "There's nothing": Billy Isley deposition, August 22, 2017, p. 156.

156 largely denied: Jamie Satterfield, "Records: Safety Manager at Kingston Disaster Destroyed Proof of Fly Ash Danger to Workers," *Knoxville News Sentinel*, October 30, 2017.

157 said with a simper: Keith Stewart interview.

158 get "run off": Brad Green deposition, July 9, 2015, p. 50.

159 medical evaluation: Tom Bock trial testimony, October 19, 2018, p. 762.

159 physician's written opinion: "Site Wide Safety and Health Plan," prepared by Jacobs Engineering, June 2009, p. 9-1. Also see OSHA ordinance 29 CFR 1910.134.

159 Sean Healey: Healey testified on October 25, 2018, that, after he was made aware of the workers' exposure complaints, some trees were cut down on-site, since they contributed to the workers' exposures. See pp. 1897–99 in the trial transcript. Healey declined an interview request for this book.

160 Heffernan had said: Tom Heffernan deposition, July 21, 2016, pp. 18, 30.

160 GUBMK employee: Eugene Meredith deposition, August 3, 2016, p. 50.

160 Jacobs's decision alone: Jacobs maintains that it wasn't responsible for selecting their personal protective equipment for specific tasks; that job, it argues, belonged to TVA and other contractors. This was a disputed point in the litigation.

162 produce more evidence: *Adkisson et al. v. Jacobs*, Docket no. 86, p. 6.

PART III

165 The lawyers' redbrick: The following sections are primarily drawn from interviews with Keith Stewart, Jim Scott, and John Dupree. The production of documents occurred throughout late 2016 and 2017.

165 emails between: Email from Stephanie Johnson to Joe Welborn, November 20, 2016.

165 sixty-six thousand individual documents: *Adkisson et al. v. Jacobs*, Docket no. 200, pp. 6–7.

165 unreadable pages: Ibid., p. 5.

165 medical records: *Adkisson et al. v. Jacobs*, Docket no. 111-1.

165 twenty-four banker boxes: *Adkisson et al. v. Jacobs*, Docket no. 114-1.

165 eighty thousand pages: *Adkisson et al. v. Jacobs*, transcript of status conference proceedings before Judge Thomas A. Varlan, January 26, 2017, p. 16.

166 clumps of ash: Gary MacDonald deposition, August 11, 2016, p. 20.

167 cosmetics: Ibid.

167 bowling balls: Shaila Dewan, "Tennessee Ash Flood Larger Than Initial Estimate," *New York Times*, December 26, 2008.

167 concrete: Adeyemi Adesina, "Sustainable Application of Cenospheres in Cementitious Materials—Overview of Performance," *Developments in the Built Environment* 4 (November 2020).

167 "recovering" them a priority: TVA, "Site Wide Safety and Health Plan," prepared by Jacobs Engineering, June 2009, p. 1-1.

167 daily safety logs: *Adkisson et al. v. Jacobs*, Docket no. 200, p. 7; Docket no. 256, exhibit 48.

167 "Large quantities of dust": *Adkisson et al. v. Jacobs*, Docket no. 256, exhibit 48, p. 27.

167 forced a work stoppage: Ibid., p. 70.

167 had "never happened": Tom Bock deposition, August 26, 2016, p. 160.

167 "unacceptably high levels": Steve Richardson email, April 6, 2010, obtained through FOIA.

167 five to ten workers: Tom Bock trial testimony, October 22, 2018, p. 828.

167 "fish-aquarium vacuum": Jeff Brewer trial testimony, October 19, 2018, p. 583.

168 EnSafe: EnSafe declined to offer comment for this book.

168 about twenty-four hours: Tom Bock trial testimony, October 22, 2018, p. 815; Jeff Brewer trial testimony, October 19, 2018, p. 605.

168 EnSafe had handed out: Jacobs Engineering, "2009 Calendar of Sample Events Rains," exhibit number 85 in the fall 2018 *Adkisson* trial. During those proceedings, Tom Bock testified that he prepared the calendars for Jacobs; see pp. 811–16 of the transcript.

168 showed a significant overlap: *Adkisson et al. v. Jacobs*, Docket no. 772, exhibit 2, Michael Ellenbecker, "Report Kingston Coal Ash," December 7, 2020, p. 35.

168 In August 2011: Jacobs, "2011 Calendar of Sample Events Rains."

169 threatened to fine: EPA, "Administrative Order and Agreement on Consent: TVA Kingston Fossil Fuel Plant, TVA Release Site," May 5, 2009, p. 26.

169 $1.5 million: In 2019, TVA stated that it did not pay Jacobs any safety incentive under its contract provisions; a worker was killed in a jobsite accident. See TVA's memo "TVA Responds to Questions About Kingston Recovery Project, March 7, 2019."

169 almost $64 million: Jack Howard trial testimony, October 24, 2018, pp. 1706; Gaffney, "They Deserve to Be Heard."

169 "TVA didn't want": TVA background source who requested anonymity.

169 In the summer: Interviews with Larry Woody and Nick Sullivan; Bob Steber, "TVA an Ostrich in Ash? OH Pollution Increases," *Nashville Tennessean*, September 13, 1964.

169 accused TVA: Bob Steber, "TVA at Last to Study Environmental Needs," *Nashville Tennessean*, July 6, 1969.

169 TVA responded: Bob Steber, "Tubes at Gallatin Steam Plant's Discharge to Go," *Nashville Tennessean*, September 27, 1964.

170 "detrimental effects": Memo to L. J. Van Mol from Dr. O. M. Derryberry, "Fly Ash Fallout—Paradise Steam Plant and Village of Paradise, Kentucky," March 2, 1964, obtained through the National Archives, Power Manager Box 801–802.

170 fell over their gardens: Owen, "For the Progress of Man," pp. 310–11.

170 in a press release: Steber, "Tubes at Gallatin Steam Plant's Discharge to Go."

170 one hundred and forty-nine times higher: Josh Flory, "EPA Found High Arsenic Levels Day After Ash Spill," *Knoxville News Sentinel*, January 3, 2009.

170 one in fifty people: EPA Office of Solid Waste and Emergency Response, "Human and Ecological Risk Assessment of Coal Combustion Wastes," draft document, April 2010, p. ES-5; Environmental Integrity Project and Earthjustice, "Coming Clean: What the EPA Knows About the Dangers of Coal Ash," May 2007, p. 3.

171 two hundredfold: Max Blau, "The Coal Plant Next Door," *Georgia Health News/ProPublica*, March 22, 2021.

171 *60 Minutes* segment: CBS News, "Coal Ash: 130 Million Tons of Waste," October 1, 2009, https://www.cbsnews.com/.

171 comparing it to sand: TVA, transcript of public meeting, May 20, 2010, at Roane County High School, p. 65; Leo Francendese declined to be interviewed.

171 Jean Nance: Jamie Satterfield, "TVA Told Her the Coal Ash Was Safe. Now, She's Dead," *Knoxville News Sentinel*, December 22, 2018.

171 On a cloudy: The attorney Alex L. Sarria, then of Jacobs, who was present for the hearing, declined a request to comment on the hearing before Magistrate Bruce Guyton. Raymond B. Biagini, of Covington, did not return a voicemail, and Josh Chesser, then of Smith, Cashion & Orr, didn't respond to an email from me.

171 a senior partner: *Adkisson et al. v. Jacobs*, Docket no. 103. This filing lists Raymond B. Biagini, senior counsel for Covington, as present for the hearing.

172 motion to disqualify: *Adkisson et al. v. Jacobs*, Docket no. 94 and 110.

172 Bruce Guyton: Guyton did not respond to a request for comment or for an interview.

172 "Mr. Hamrock, would you come to the podium?": Transcript of motion proceedings, September 29, 2016, p. 24.

173 In Guyton's ruling: *Adkisson et al. v. Jacobs*, Docket no. 110.

173 bifurcated: Transcript of status-conference proceedings, January 26, 2017.

174 phase one trial: *Adkisson et al. v. Jacobs*, audio recording of status conference, February 22, 2017.

174 nine doctors or academics: *Adkisson et al. v. Jacobs*, Docket no. 234, p. 3.

174 "May it please the Court": All quoted dialogue in this scene comes from an audio recording of the hearing on May 18, 2017.

174 James F. Sanders: Sanders declined multiple interview requests for this book. In response to a fact-checking memo I sent him, he stated, "I find much of what you have said to be factually inaccurate and clearly biased," but he did not specify what information he considered incorrect or unfair when I asked him to. Much of the information I included about him was gleaned from interviews I conducted with eight defense lawyers who worked with Sanders at Neal & Harwell. These sources requested anonymity for professional reasons.

174 Jake Butcher: "Banker May Plead Guilty," *New York Times*, April 22, 1985.

174 showy three-piece suits: Interviews with several former Neal & Harwell employees, plus a 2017 photo taken when Neal & Harwell held an open house for their new offices.

175 "its most risky, sensitive jury cases": Coll, *Private Empire*, p. 388.

175 "very anti-establishment": Cosslett, *Lawyers at Work*, p. 19.

175 private-prison companies: Ibid., p. 25.
175 "I don't have moments": Ibid., p. 24.
175 close to the jury box: Scott Snyder interview.
175 "Niceness is his weapon": Ibid.
175 often apologized: Coll, *Private Empire*, p. 389.
175 thirty-two thousand fishermen: Robert E. Jenkins and Jill Watry, "Running Aground in a Sea of Complex Litigation: A Case Comment on the *Exxon Valdez* Litigation," *UCLA Journal of Environmental Law and Policy* 18, no. 151 (1999): 166; James Vicini, "*Exxon Valdez* $2.5 Billion Oil Spill Ruling Overturned," Reuters, June 25, 2008.
176 $287 million: "*Exxon Valdez* Jury Awards $287 Million," AP via *Pittsburgh Post-Gazette*, August 12, 1994.
176 $20 million: "Plaintiffs Say Exxon Owes More," AP via *Enterprise-Journal*, August 23, 1994.
176 "the largest ever": "Jury Hits Exxon for $5 Billion," *Chicago Tribune*, September 17, 1994.
176 "public purpose": *Grant Baker et al. v. Exxon Shipping Company et al.*, transcript of oral arguments, February 27, 2008, p. 80, U.S. Supreme Court.
176 The Court agreed: *Grant Baker et al. v. Exxon Shipping Company et al.*, Opinion of the Court, June 25, 2008.
176 The *Valdez* plaintiffs: Mark Thiessen, "Judge OKs First *Exxon Valdez* Oil Spill Payments," AP via *Santa Fe New Mexican*, November 24, 2008.
176 "completely arbitrary": Joni Hersch and W. Kip Viscusi, "Punitive Damages by Numbers: *Exxon Shipping Co. v. Baker*," *Supreme Court Economic Review* 18 (2010): 261, 280.
176 Justice Ruth Bader Ginsburg: *Grant Baker et al., v. Exxon Shipping Company et al.*, Justice Ginsburg opinion, June 25, 2008.
176 precedent for capping: *Ingram et al. v. Johnson & Johnson et al.*, Motion of the Chamber of Commerce of the United States of America and the Missouri Changer of Commerce and Industry for Leave to File Brief as Amici Curiae in Support of Defendants—Appellants, September 6, 2019, pp. 40, 44, Missouri Court of Appeals for the Eastern District.
178 On a cloudy: This scene is primarily drawn from interviews with Jim Scott, Sam Scott, and Keith Stewart, along with court documents in Scott's reckless-driving case.
179 Magistrate Guyton had decided: *Adkisson et al. v. Jacobs*, Docket no. 235, p. 4.
180 "The defendant could not": KDP Officer Kenneth Harrell, "Affidavit of Complaint," Case #1195174, General Sessions Court, Knox County, Tennessee.
180 Billy Isley: All of Isley's quoted dialogue in this scene comes from his deposition on August 22, 2017.
181 day-off uniform: Keith Stewart interview.
181 his wife's three strokes: Lena Isley interview.
181 "collegiately educated moron": Billy Isley deposition, August 22, 2017, p. 160.

181 inhale the fly ash: Ibid., pp. 39–40.

181 "They were above the limits": Ibid., pp. 40–43.

182 in the laundry room: The scene of Billy Isley's death is primarily drawn from several interviews with Lena Isley and from an incident report by the Campbell County Sheriff's Office, cited below.

182 on the walls: Offense Report, Campbell County Sheriff's Office, case #1901202255, January 20, 2019.

183 conducted an autopsy: Regional Forensic Center, Knox County, "Autopsy Final Report: William Franklin Isley," dated May 4, 2019.

183 exposure is known: Aimen K. Farraj et al., "Increased Nonconducted P-Wave Arrhythmias After a Single Oil Fly Ash Inhalation Exposure in Hypertensive Rats," *Environmental Health Perspectives* (May 2009).

183 pulmonary emphysema: Seung-Hyung Kim et al., "Herbal Combinational Medication of *Glycyrrhiza glabra*, *Agastache rugosa* Containing Glycyrrhizic Acid, Tilianin Inhibits Neutrophilic Lung Inflammation by Affecting CXCL2, Interleukin-17/STAT3 Signal Pathways in a Murine Model of COPD," *Nutrients*, March 27, 2020.

183 complicate Isley's case: In a 2020 court filing, Jacobs's attorneys urged Judge Varlan to rule in its favor in Isley's case, arguing that he hadn't been exposed to silica, a constituent of fly ash, for the minimum five years required under Tennessee law to bring a suit against the company. Jacobs also noted that Isley had a history of hypertension that predated his time at Kingston.

183 toxicological report: NMS Labs, toxicological report for Billy Isley, Patient ID 190121-73.

184 $250,000: Plaintiffs' co-counsel agreement, December 4, 2017.

185 to the surprise: Jeff Hagood interview.

186 October 13, 2017: Calendar provided by Keith Stewart.

186 lengthy front-page story: Jamie Satterfield, "Facing a Toxic Battle," *Knoxville News Sentinel*, July 23, 2017.

186 met Satterfield for lunch: Jamie Satterfield interview.

188 On a cold: The fire scene is drawn from interviews with the four Knoxville lawyers, along with photos and messages they provided to me. I also spoke with John Trotter. Beyond these conversations, I got much of the information for this scene from an investigation report by the Knoxville Fire Department and a dispatch record by Knox County 911. The fire was also covered in the local press.

188 $100,000: Plaintiffs' co-counsel agreement, December 4, 2017.

189 potentially dangerous concentrations: Vengosh, "Survey of the Potential Environmental and Health Impacts in the Immediate Aftermath of the Coal Ash Spill in Kingston, Tennessee"; Vengosh, "The Tennessee Valley Authority's Kingston Ash Slide: Potential Water Quality Impacts of Coal Combustion Waste Storage," a testimony to the Subcommittee on Water Resources and Environment, U.S. House of Representatives, March 31, 2009, p. 2.

189 "fight the good fight": Tyler Roper email to Avner Vengosh, November 2, 2017. Vengosh did not respond to my interview requests.

189 "Hello?": Knox County 911, audio recording of a call to Keith Stewart, November 14, 2017.

191 activated at 12:41 a.m.: *Cate Building Owners Association, Inc., et al. v. Gallaher Assoc., Inc.*, Complaint, November 10, 2020, Circuit Court of Knox County.

191 fifteen gallons a minute: Home Fire Sprinkler Coalition, "Understanding Water Supply for Home Fire Sprinkler Systems."

192 a security firm: *Cate Building Owners Association, Inc., et al. v. Gallaher Assoc., Inc.*, Complaint, November 10, 2020, Circuit Court of Knox County.

193 some of Jacobs's legal bills: TVA, 2021 Annual Report to the S.E.C., form 10-K, pp. 157–58. In 2021, in response to a records request, TVA acknowledged to me that it had in its possession invoices from Neal & Harwell, but it refused to release them or to disclose how much it had paid outside counsel. In 2023, a TVA spokesman wrote to me, "The disposition of the indemnity clause is still to be determined."

193 Knoxville's tallest building: "Tendency of Modern Buildings Skyward," *Knoxville Journal*, September 20, 1925.

193 $3,235.18 a month: Keith Stewart's contemporaneous notes.

195 TVA's public-records officer: Email from Denise Smith, of TVA, to Jim Scott.

195 at least ten years: Jamie Satterfield, "Video Key to Case of Sickened Kingston Spill Cleanup Workers Is Missing; TVA Mum," *Knoxville News Sentinel*, November 6, 2018. TVA did not respond to me when I asked, in 2019, about the missing video recordings; a TVA spokesman told Satterfield that its records didn't suggest that the videos had been destroyed or lost, but TVA was nonetheless unable to produce them.

195 email to Jim Chase: Jim Scott email to Jim Chase, November 12, 2017, obtained through FOIA.

195 Melissa Hedgecoth: *George Chesney v. TVA*, Melissa Hedgecoth deposition, June 6, 2011, pp. 139–41, 309; Ed Marcum, "TVA Manager: Superior Ordered Deletions to Report," *Knoxville News Sentinel*, October 5, 2011. Hedgecoth did not respond to an interview request.

197 Journeyman's Table: "Blount Terrace at Holiday Inn," *Knoxville News Sentinel*, May 27, 1977.

198 years without voting: *Knoxville News Sentinel*, public notice, Knox County Election Commission, February 7, 1978.

199 fire board members: Michael D. Shear, "Trump Dismisses 2 T.V.A. Board Members After Outsourcing Dispute," *New York Times*, August 3, 2020.

199 unless a scandal emerged: Hargrove, *Prisoners of Myth*, pp. 274–75; Reginald Stuart, "T.V.A. Swept by a Flood of Criticism," *New York Times*, January 12, 1975.

199 "TVA open board meetings": Hargrove, *Prisoners of Myth*, p. 275.

199 TDEC was considering: Brittany Crocker, "Small Group Turns Out at TDEC to Air Concerns About TVA Discharge Permit," *Knoxville News Sentinel*, December 7, 2017.

199 largest industrial source: Brady Dennis and Juliet Eilperin, "Trump Administration Rolls Back Obama-Era Rule Aimed at Limiting Toxic Wastewater from Coal Plants," *Washington Post*, August 31, 2020; interview with Elizabeth Southerland, former head of the EPA's Office of Water.

199 EPA began rolling back: Elizabeth Southerland interview; Margaret Talbot, "Dirty Politics," *New Yorker*, April 2, 2018; Reuters, "EPA Proposes Changes to Coal Ash Regulations," March 1, 2018.

202 "completely fucked": Email sent by Tyler Roper on October 25, 2017.

203 "Plaintiffs had not acted": *Adkisson et al. v. Jacobs*, Docket no. 279.

203 "Everybody knew": Transcript of status conference, November 29, 2017, p. 28.

204 Fifteen minutes before: This scene is primarily drawn from an audio recording of Mary's call to Knox County 911 on March 14 and related Knoxville Police Department incident reports. I also interviewed the four members of the Scott family and obtained audio recordings of calls that Jack and Sam Scott made to dispatchers at later dates.

204 ordered her to leave: Mary Scott deposition, June 5, 2017, p. 52.

204 retained full custody: Sam Scott interview; Mary Scott deposition, June 5, 2017, p. 52.

204 "at any time": *Scott v. Scott*, Ex Parte Order Transferring Custody to the Mother, March 14, 2018.

205 let Mary spend time: *Scott v. Scott*, Ex Parte Emergency Order, March 14, 2018; Jim Scott interview.

205 preventing Sam from seeing her: Jack Scott interview.

205 "When [my sons] don't respond": Mary Scott deposition, June 6, 2017, p. 123.

205 she had attended: Mary Scott deposition, June 5, 2017, p. 9.

205 It was spring break: Knox County Schools 2017–2018 calendar.

206 "My dad has done nothing wrong": Knox County 911, audio recording of a call made by Sam Scott, March 25, 2018.

206 a psychologist: Letter to the Chancery Court of Knox County, Tennessee, from Peter B. Young, September 29, 2016; *Scott v. Scott*, Petition/Motion for Emergency Termination of Mary Scott's Unsupervised Visitation, May 31, 2018.

206 even "casual contact": Laura T. Williams, PhD, affidavit, 2016.

206 "Everything the court": Mary Scott interview. She largely blamed Jim for their failures to resolve custody issues. "He's a trial lawyer, and he thinks he's above the law," she said on a March 15, 2018, phone call to authorities.

206 Buddy and Mildred: *Scott v. Scott*, Ex Parte Emergency Order Transferring Custody to the Paternal Grandparents, March 21, 2018.

207 six figures in fees: Jim Scott interview.

207 spring and summer: Jack Scott interview.

208 Tyler Roper: The details about Roper working in a law firm's health-care division

come from my interviews with him. There's some dispute among the lawyers about Roper's degree of involvement in the case.

209 "low-sodium table salt": TVA, "Radioactivity Analysis of Ash Samples, January 7, 2009," uploaded to TVA.com in 2009, captured by the Internet Archive, https://www.tva.com/.

209 high levels of radium: Vengosh, "Survey of the Potential Environmental and Health Impacts in the Immediate Aftermath," p. 6326; Ohio Department of Health, "NORM/TENORM Information Sheet," p. 5, https://odh.ohio.gov/. Kirk Whatley, previously of the Alabama Department of Public Health, told me that, though the Kingston coal ash continued to have high levels of radium, he did not believe it posed a public-health risk. TVA, for its part, has said that it was transparent about the radioactive content of the Kingston fly ash, while Jacobs maintains that one of its experts, Dr. John R. Frazier, who had also worked for the oil giant Chevron, determined that no plaintiff had been exposed to the metal in excess of established standards. One of the plaintiffs' experts, Norman J. Kleiman, of Columbia University, disputed Frazier's findings in a rebuttal report.

210 levels well above: TVA, "TVA Kingston Fossil Fuel Plant Release Site On-Scene Coordinator Report," pp. 3-6, 3-9; letter to Kirk Whatley of the Alabama Department of Public Health from Hodges, Harnin, Newberry & Tribble, June 22, 2009.

210 Alabama authorities: TVA, "TVA Kingston Fossil Fuel Plant Release Site On-Scene Coordinator Report," pp. 3-8, 3-9; Holly Haworth, "Something Inside of Us," *Oxford American*, November 10, 2013.

210 in a 2011 report: TVA, "TVA Kingston Fossil Fuel Plant Release Site On-Scene Coordinator Report," pp. 3-6, 3-9. This report states that the radium in the ash was as high as ten picocuries per gram, when, as Kleiman notes in the following citation, the regulatory health threshold was five picocuries per gram.

210 exceed acceptable safety standards twofold: *Adkisson et al. v. Jacobs*, Docket no. 763-2, "Rebuttal Report of Norman J. Kleiman, PhD, in Response to the Report of John R. Frazier, PhD, CHP," p. 6. Jacobs generally disputes Kleiman's research.

210 pressure from Jacobs's staff: The Shaw Group, "Summary of the 05-01-09 EPA Conference Call," May 2, 2009; Jamie Satterfield, "EPA Standards Different for Alabama, TN Workers," *Knoxville News Sentinel*, July 9, 2018. Jacobs takes issue with Satterfield's reporting.

210 "routinely contact[ed] ash": TVA, transcript of public meeting, June 23, 2009, Roane State College, Harriman, Tennessee, p. 50.

210 hazmat suits: As I state earlier in these notes, Jacobs disputes the assertion that the workers should have generally been provided protective clothing.

210 ultra-contaminated variety: Tyler Roper email to Avner Vengosh, November 2, 2017.

211 thirty-one thousand feet: *Enola Gay* flight log, August 6, 1945.

211 one hundred and forty-one pounds: Schlosser, *Command and Control*, p. 50.

211 nearly all such material: Ibid.

211 forty-three seconds: Atomic Heritage Foundation, "Bombings of Hiroshima and Nagasaki—1945," June 5, 2014.

211 six hundred yards: "In a Flash, a Changed World," Reuters, August 4, 2020.

211 Then the boom came: Rhodes, *The Making of the Atomic Bomb*, p. 717.

211 almost 70 percent: U.S. Strategic Bombing Survey, "The Effects of Atomic Bombs," p. 9.

211 eighty thousand: Ibid., p. 15.

211 one hundred and forty thousand: Selden and Selden, *The Atomic Bomb*, p. xxi.

211 roughly equal number: U.S. Strategic Bombing Survey, "The Effects of Atomic Bombs," p. 15.

211 "the most remarkable": Jay Walz, "Atom Bomb Made in 3 Hidden Cities," *New York Times*, August 7, 1945.

211 October 1942: Johnson and Johnson, *City Behind a Fence*, p. 17.

211 help of TVA staff: Compton, *Atomic Quest.*

211 Norris and Watts Bar: Johnson and Johnson, *City Behind a Fence*, p. 6.

211 seven miles wide: Rhodes, *The Making of the Atomic Bomb*, p. 486. The size of the Oak Ridge site would expand after Leslie Groves joined the Manhattan Project, but, in Arthur Compton's account, his team identified the general Clinch River area during its initial search of East Tennessee in the spring of 1942. See Compton, *Atomic Quest.*

211 fifty-nine thousand acres: Johnson and Johnson, *City Behind a Fence*, p. 6.

212 seven guarded gates: Rhodes, *The Making of the Atomic Bomb*, p. 487.

212 fifth largest city: Johnson and Johnson, *City Behind a Fence*, p. 26.

212 eighty thousand people: Ibid.

212 governor didn't know: Tennessee Virtual Archive, letter to Governor Prentice Cooper from Thomas T. Crenshaw, July 14, 1943, https://teva.contentdm.oclc.org/.

212 main process buildings: U.S. Atomic Energy Commission, *Manhattan District History*, 1948, Book V, Volume 3, p. S-2.

212 twenty football fields: Rhodes, *The Making of the Atomic Bomb*, p. 490.

213 largest building by area: The Pentagon was being built at the time, and though it would eventually top K-25 in square footage, it initially had 3,271,041 square feet of usable space, compared with K-25's 5,264,000 square feet. See "Charges Pentagon Operates at Loss," *New York Times*, March 7, 1944.

213 two and a half million square feet: Frank B. Woodford, "Ford Turning Out Bombers," *New York Times*, May 24, 1942.

213 more than twice that footage: Atomic Energy Commission, *Manhattan District History*, 1948, Book II, Volume 4, pp. 3.28–3.29.

213 some designed by TVA: Johnson and Johnson, *City Behind a Fence*, p. 100.

213 fifteen hundred hutments: Ibid., p. 25.

213 Twenty thousand workers: Ibid., p. 52.

213 eight elementary schools: Jay Walz, "Atom Bomb Made in 3 Hidden Cities," *New York Times*, August 7, 1945.

213 one hundred and sixty-five retail stores: Johnson and Johnson, *City Behind a Fence*, p. 35.
213 Coney Island franks: "A Visit to the Secret Town in Tennessee That Gave Birth to the Atomic Bomb," *New Republic*, November 12, 1945.
213 country's only industrial complex: Eric Schlosser, "A Break-in at Y-12," *New Yorker*, March 1, 2015.
213 an underground tank: Carson Brewer, "Decontamination Job Near Finish," *Knoxville News Sentinel*, March 23, 1975.
213 two million pounds of mercury: The Institute for Technology, Social, and Policy Awareness, "Impacts on Oak Ridge Landowners of Off-site Releases to the Environment from the Y-12 Plant and Associated Long-term Stewardship Issues," performed by Kapline Enterprises, Inc., March 31, 2005, p. xix.
214 The rest of the mercury: ATSDR, "Evaluation of Y-12 Mercury Releases, U.S. Department of Energy, Oak Ridge Reservation," March 2012, p. 57; John Huotar, "Construction on Y-12 Mercury Treatment Plant Could Start in 2018, Cost $146 Million," *Oak Ridge Today*, September 10, 2015.
214 fifty-one million pounds of uranium: Carolyn Shoulders, "51 Million Lbs. of Uranium Buried at Y-12," *The Tennessean*, June 26, 1985.
214 canyonlike trenches: Frank Munger, "Pollution Production," *Knoxville News Sentinel*, June 28, 1985.
214 dumped wastewater sludge: DOE Oak Ridge Operations, "Report on Historic Uranium Releases from Current DOE, Oak Ridge Operations Office Facilities," June 24, 1985; Frank Munger, "Uranium Buried in 65-Acre Cemetery," *Knoxville News Sentinel*, June 28, 1985.
214 "witches' cauldrons": Munger, "Pollution Production"; Dick Thompson, "Living Happily Near a Nuclear Trash Heap," *Time*, May 11, 1992.
214 Fifty-two settling ponds: "Oak Ridge Contamination Even Worse Than Feared," *The Tennessean*, August 17, 1997.
214 three million gallons: Thompson, "Living Happily Near a Nuclear Trash Heap."
214 dumped vast quantities: Frank Munger, "Tons of Uranium Polluting Earth, Air, Water," *Commercial Appeal*, June 27, 1985.
214 thirty-five thousand pounds: Tennessee Department of Health, "Oak Ridge Dose Reconstruction Project Summary," with ChemRisk, March 2000, p. 73.
214 milk from cows: ATSDR, "Public Health Assessment: Y-12 Uranium Releases," p. 22.
214 two hundred and eighty thousand pounds: Institute for Technology, Social, and Policy Awareness, "Impacts on Oak Ridge Landowners of Off-site Releases to the Environment from the Y-12 Plant and Associated Long-term Stewardship Issues," performed by Kapline Enterprises, Inc., March 31, 2005, p. xx.
214 at least fifty-four times: Here's how I arrived at this number: The EPA's max acceptable contaminant level for uranium in drinking water is 30 µg per liter, according to ATSDR. EAI Analytical Labs states that 30 µg/l of uranium is equal to about 20 pCi/l. And, according to ChemRisk, East Fork Poplar Creek con-

tained 1,100 pCi/l of uranium in 1968. See ATSDR, "Agency for Toxic Substances and Disease Registry Case Studies in Environmental Medicine (CSEM) Uranium Toxicity," May 1, 2009, p. 22; EAI Analytical Labs, "Dissolved Mineral Radioactivity in Drinking Water"; ChemRisk for the Tennessee Department of Health, "Uranium Releases from the Oak Ridge Reservation—A Review of the Quality of Historical Effluent Monitoring Data and a Screening Evaluation of Potential Off-site Exposures," July 1999, pp. 3-24.

214 Frogs: Frank Munger, "No More Nuclear Frogs at ORNL," *Knoxville News Sentinel*, October 25, 2003.

214 Deer: DOE, "Oak Ridge Reservation Environmental Report for 1988: Volume 1: Narrative, Summary, and Conclusions," May 1989, p. xiii.

214 three hundred thousand people: Oak Ridge Health Agreement Steering Panel, "Releases of Contaminants from Oak Ridge Facilities," December 1999, p. 11.

214 Commercial clammers: Clinch River Study Steering Committee, "Comprehensive Report of the Clinch River Study," April 1967, p. 82; D. J. Nelson, "Strontium, Strontium-90, and Calcium Analysis of Clinch and Tennessee River Clams," Oak Ridge National Laboratory, June 20, 1962, p. 3.

215 A fire in 1957: "Atom Burial Site Contents Not Known," *The Tennessean*, January 23, 1976.

215 "had some midnight dumping": "Oak Ridge Contamination Even Worse Than Feared," *The Tennessean*, August 17, 1997.

215 "We knew it was bad stuff": Janie Harper, "Secrets Revealed, Revelations Concealed: A Secret City Confronts Its Environmental Legacy of Weapons Production," *Anthropological Quarterly* 80, no. 1 (Winter 2007): 53.

215 "there's radioactive material": Gary MacDonald deposition, August 11, 2016, p. 105. MacDonald didn't respond to a letter I mailed him asking for an interview. I was unable to reach him through other means.

215 "The next morning we come in": Billy Isley deposition, August 22, 2017, pp. 140–41.

215 discredit the workers' case: Tyler Roper email, November 17, 2017.

215 such as building a dock: DOE, "Remedial Investigation/Feasibility Study Report for Lower Watts Bar Reservoir Operable Unit," 1995, p. 4-9; ATSDR, "Exposure Evaluation of the Clinch River and Lower Watts Bar Reservoir," 2006, p. 94.

216 federal agencies presumed: DOE, "Remedial Investigation/Feasibility Study Report for Lower Watts Bar Reservoir Operable Unit," 1995 p. 4-11; Austyn Gaffney, "A Legacy of Contamination," *Grist*, December 15, 2020.

216 written responses to this plan: TVA, "Phase 1 Emory River Dredging Plan and Ash Processing Area Construction and Operation Plan/Kingston Fossil Plant Ash Recovery Project Tennessee Valley Authority, February 20, 2009"; Gaffney, "A Legacy of Contamination."

216 didn't test for cesium-137: There's no mention of cesium-137 testing in TVA's "Kingston Ash Incident Evaluation of Potential Legacy Contamination in Local

Sediments," March 20, 2009. Moreover, on p. 30 of TVA's "Phase 1 Emory River Dredging Plan," the agency says it did not plan to conduct a radionuclide analysis of the dredged material, because it expected the fly ash in the river to have the same radiological activity as the ash on land, and that ash wouldn't have contained cesium. TVA did test for cesium eventually, but the internal documents I obtained suggest that it didn't begin until sometime in early 2010. See TVA, "TVA Kingston Fossil Fuel Plant Release Site On-Scene Coordinator Report," p. H-6.

216 "If we go down there": TVA, transcript of public meeting, June 23, 2009, Roane State College, Harriman, Tennessee, p. 101.

216 "There is no evidence": TVA, "Kingston Ash Incident Evaluation of Potential Legacy Contamination in Local Sediments March 20, 2009," captured by the Internet Archive, https://www.tva.com/.

216 Tom Kilgore: Tom Kilgore responses to the U.S. Senate Committee on Environment and Public Works, "Follow-Up Questions for Written Submission, Questions for Kilgore," January 8, 2009, p. 47.

216 experienced "difficulties": TVA, "TVA Kingston Fossil Fuel Plant Release Site On-Scene Coordinator Report," p. ES-2.

217 A 1984 study: The Emory River enters the Clinch at Clinch River Mile 4. A 1984 study notes cesium-137 at Clinch River Mile 1, three miles downstream of the confluence of the two rivers, at concentrations of 152 pCi/g. See DOE, "Remedial Investigation/Feasibility Study Report for Lower Watts Bar Reservoir Operable Unit," 1995, p. 3-27.

217 agencies considered safe: TVA, "Kingston Ash Recovery Project Time-Critical Removal Action Intake Channel Causeway Removal Work Plan, May 2011," No. RAWP-094, p. 1. This document states that 11 pCi/g was the interagency work group action level.

217 seventeen picocuries per gram: TVA, "TVA Kingston Fossil Fuel Plant Release Site On-Scene Coordinator Report," p. 7-11.

217 "co-mingled": Craig Zeller of the EPA, "TVA Kingston Ash Recovery Project, Roane County, TN, Project Completion Meeting, June 4, 2015."

217 seven hundred thousand tons: "TVA Kingston Fossil Fuel Plant Release Site On-Scene Coordinator Report," p. ES-2. See previous note about cubic-yard-to-ton conversion.

217 some two hundred acres: TVA, "Non-Time-Critical Removal Action River System Action Memorandum," Document no. EPA-AO-054, November 1, 2012, p. 3.

217 "a lot of discussion": *Adkisson et al. v. Jacobs*, Barbara Scott, EPA Region 4, trial testimony, October 30, 2018, pp. 2246, 2306.

217 Rick Samson: Interviews with Rick Samson and S. T. McCollum.

217 sworn statements: *Adkisson et al. v. Jacobs*, sworn declarations of S. T. McCollum and Roger Griffith.

217 Clint Mannis: Clint Mannis interview.

217 Brian Thacker: Brian Thacker interview.

218 Thacker filed a report: *Adkisson et al. v. Jacobs*, Docket no. 200-8, which includes Thacker's report and emails between TVA's Philip Davis and Ed Small.

218 one hundred and ninety-three samples: TVA, "TVA Kingston Fossil Fuel Plant Release Site On-Scene Coordinator Report," p. H-7.

218 one hundred and fourteen samples: Ibid., p. H-6.

218 "Everyone [at TVA and Jacobs]": Tyler Roper email, July 1, 2020. Jacobs denies that it knew about fly ash's radiation hazards or that it tried to conceal them from the workers.

218 "the radioactive contaminants": Tyler Roper email, October 27, 2018.

218 Steve McCracken: I spoke with a former TVA employee on background who worked closely with McCracken. McCracken did not respond to interview requests and died in May 2023.

219 McCracken had overseen: *Adkisson et al. v. Jacobs*, Stephen McCracken deposition, August 24, 2017, p. 26.

219 TVA hired him: Frank Munger, "McCracken Jumps from the Frying Pan to the Fire," Atomic City Underground blog, *Knoxville News Sentinel*, September 28, 2009.

219 in Keith Stewart's office: The direct quotes in this scene come from a 2019 interview I conducted with the lawyers.

219 criminally negligent homicide: Tyler Roper email, March 19, 2020.

219 Vengosh's studies: Roper email to Avner Vengosh, November 2, 2017.

220 Friedman discussed the matter: This conversation occurred in June 2021; I was with Friedman and Davis as they recalled Roper's urging their team to focus on radionuclides.

220 ninety-five-page report: *Adkisson et al. v. Jacobs*, Docket no. 253, exhibit 4, Paul D. Terry, "Coal Fly Ash: General Causation Analyses and Relevant Medical and Scientific Literature," April 30, 2018.

220 seventy academic: Transcript of Daubert motion proceedings before the Honorable H. Bruce Guyton, June 15, 2018, p. 25.

221 "Your Honor": Ibid.

221 constituents had been absorbed: *Adkisson et al v. Jacobs*, Docket nos. 237 and 302.

222 in a thirty-one-page ruling: *Adkisson et al. v. Jacobs*, Docket no. 302.

222 his new favorite word: Jeff Friedman interview; Jeff Friedman closing remarks, November 6, 2018, p. 3,000.

222 On the morning: All direct quotes in the trial scenes come from the official transcript of the jury trial proceedings before the Honorable Thomas A. Varlan, October 16, 2018, through November 7, 2018. I spoke with all the plaintiffs' attorneys, as well as the Clarks and many of the workers for these scenes.

222 thirty had died: Jamie Satterfield, "Former TVA Rep Refuses to Testify for Sickened Kingston Coal Ash Spill Workers," *Knoxville News Sentinel*, October 16, 2018.

223 seven hundred and fifty coal-ash ponds: Earthjustice, "Mapping the Coal Ash Contamination," November 3, 2022, https://earthjustice.org/.

223 Massachusetts to Washington State: Earthjustice, "Mapping the Coal Ash Contamination," November 3, 2022, https://earthjustice.org.

223 harm millions of people: Interview with Elizabeth Southerland, former head of the EPA Office of Water; Lisa Friedman, "EPA to Roll Back Rules to Control Toxic Ash from Coal Plants," *New York Times*, October 31, 2019; *Appalachian Voices et al. v. Lisa P. Jackson and U.S. EPA*, complaint filed April 5, 2012, U.S. District Court for the District of Columbia.

224 NBC affiliate: WBIR, "First Phase of Coal Ash Trial Begins," October 16, 2018, https://www.wbir.com/.

226 Jimmy Sanders's office: As stated earlier, I interviewed eight lawyers—associates and partners alike—who previously worked for Neal & Harwell. The details in this anecdote come from those conversations. Sanders declined interview requests for this book.

226 "the verdict could be awful": Cosslett, *Lawyers at Work*, p. 30.

227 "stay out of the capillaries": Mark Chalos interview.

227 based on samples: Tennessee Department of Health, "Public Health Assessment: KIF Coal Ash Release," July 5, 2011, pp. 16–18.

228 TVA safety coordinator: Robert Muse trial testimony, October 16, 2018, p. 66.

228 While preparing Muse: Robert Muse interview.

228 through subpoena: Jeff Friedman closing argument, November 6, 2018, p. 2,920.

228 largely overseen site safety: Tom Heffernan trial testimony, October 1, 2018, p. 280.

230 first meetings at the Farragut: Shlaes, *The Forgotten Man*, p. 181.

230 why Jimmy Sanders: Sanders did not respond to fact-checking queries. The plaintiffs' attorneys told me he stayed at the Farragut Hotel.

232 the two sides settled: Ibid.

237 usually brought along: Background interviews with two former Neal & Harwell attorneys.

237 as a high-school wrestler: Josh Ezzell, "Six Area Wrestlers Advance at State Tourney," *Daily News Journal*, February 16, 2001.

237 idolized his dad: Four former Neal & Harwell attorneys spoke with me about Isaac Sanders. He declined an interview request.

238 Danny Gouge: Danny Gouge interview; *Adkisson et al. v. Jacobs*, Docket no. 206-5, Danny Gouge affidavit; Danny Gouge trial testimony, October 17, 2018, p. 236.

238 wearing his work clothes: Danny Gouge interview.

238 kept twelve dogs: Danny Gouge trial testimony, October 17, 2018, pp. 233–35.

238 "[Bock] was just a kid": Danny Gouge interview.

238 They were smiling: Jim Scott interview.

239 "Man, if these people": Danny Gouge trial testimony, October 17, 2018, p. 248.

239 Jacobs's China division: Jamie Satterfield, "Worker Says Mask Request Led to His Firing," *Knoxville News Sentinel*, October 19, 2018; Nelson Moura, "Twelve Jacobs China Technicians Found Guilty of Faking HZMB Concrete Test Results," *Macau Business*, November 20, 2019.

240 EPA might ratchet up: Michael Robinette trial testimony, October 19, 2018, pp. 554, 562. Bock testified that he couldn't recall the incident Robinette described.

240 Bock would have violated: Robinette trial testimony, October 19, 2018, p. 565.

240 Judge Varlan largely forbade: Jamie Satterfield, "Roane County Commissioner Told Dust from Spill Was Safe," *Knoxville News Sentinel*, October 28, 2018.

240 stood up and turned: Ibid.

241 Silence filled the room: Keith Stewart interview.

241 Sean Healey: Healey declined an interview request for this book.

241 "The site control efforts we undertake": Tom Bock trial testimony, October 19, 2018, p. 694.

242 "below the action levels": Tom Bock trial testimony, October 19, 2018, pp. 731–33.

244 pointed out that three hundred and sixty-eight: *Adkisson et al. v. Jacobs*, Docket no. 347, Exhibit 98.

245 environmental consultant: Greg Schwartz trial testimony, October 10, 2018, p. 1,198.

246 Dr. Paul Terry: Most of the personal details in this scene come from an interview with Terry.

246 Don't over-answer: Gary Davis interview.

248 variations of this argument: *Adkisson et al. v. Jacobs*, Docket no. 295.

249 fifty-page report: *Adkisson et al. v. Jacobs*, Docket no. 237-7, exhibit G, declaration and report by Scott D. Phillips.

249 mining, oil, and gas industries: Scott D. Phillips trial testimony, October 29, 2018, p. 2095.

250 "in it for the money": Jeff Friedman closing argument, November 6, 2018, p. 3,000.

251 "I hope they see": "Kingston Coal Ash Workers Gather Before Closing Arguments," *Knoxville News Sentinel*, YouTube video, uploaded on November 6, 2018, 0:38, https://www.youtube.com/watch?v=ZH9aDRPIhSA.

252 Urine tests: Dr. Kalpana D. Patel, urinary analysis report of Craig Wilkinson, May 5, 2014. An attorney for Jacobs said in a letter to me that it is "false" that the workers had "high" levels of contaminants in their bodies, based on ten blood or urine tests that were taken at the site and later analyzed by one of their experts, Dr. John Kind. Patel's sample of Wilkinson's urine indicates otherwise, and two reports commissioned by the plaintiffs' lawyers cast doubt on the accuracy of Kind's work. See *Adkisson et al. v. Jacobs*, Docket no. 771, exhibit 13, Elizabeth Ward, "Rebuttal Report of Elizabeth Ward, PhD," February 5, 2021, and Docket

no. 772, exhibit 2, Michael Ellenbecker, "Report Kingston Coal Ash," December 7, 2020.

254 December 22, 2018: This scene is drawn from my firsthand observations and interviews I conducted that day.

254 Some 40 percent: Estimate by one of the plaintiffs' lawyers.

255 "That's a great American story": Jamie Satterfield, "Kingston Coal Ash Cleanup Workers Are Honored," *Knoxville News Sentinel*, December 23, 2008. I was there for the ceremony but missed Scott's comments.

255 American civil litigation: There have been several major cases involving coal-ash contamination, but a thorough search of archival newspaper clips and court records turned up no case in which a federal jury found that coal-ash exposure had likely harmed plaintiffs' health.

255 Jacobs continued to insist: Memo sent to me by Jeremy S. Smith, of Gibson Dunn, on Jacobs's behalf, October 2023.

255 "troubling testimony": TVA, "TVA Responds to Questions About Kingston Recovery Project," March 7, 2019.

256 some of the company's expenses: Jamie Satterfield first reported this in The *Knoxville News Sentinel*. I confirmed, through a FOIA request, that TVA had in its possession invoices from Neal & Harwell. As I stated previously, a TVA spokesman told me, "The disposition of the indemnity clause is still to be determined."

256 campaign donations: J. R. Sullivan, "T.V.A. Board Member Would 'Absolutely Not' Let Family Clean Up Coal Ash," *Men's Journal*, September 16, 2019. Chairman DeFazio's campaign manager told me in an email in response to my reporting for *Men's Journal*: "Chairman DeFazio engages with Jacobs Engineering on projects related to surface transportation and wastewater in Oregon. He has never spoken with Jacobs about their involvement in the T.V.A. spill cleanup."

257 notorious anti-worker laws: Cobb, *The Selling of the South*, pp. 208–60.

257 "a material adverse effect": Jacobs Engineering Group, Fiscal Year 2020 SEC filing, Form 10-K, p. F-60.

257 seventeen in all: Jamie Satterfield, "TVA Contractor Cannot Punish Workers over Mediation Leak," *News Sentinel* via *Daily News-Journal*, July 17, 2020.

258 fifty dead Kingston workers: Jamie Satterfield, "Coal Ash Keeps Killing," *News Sentinel* via *The Tennessean*, September 11, 2020; I was also provided a list of the dead Kingston workers by the plaintiffs' attorneys.

258 "Clients are losing their homes": Keith Stewart email, February 2020.

258 destroy all their files: Interviews with the plaintiffs' lawyers; an email from Diana M. Feinstein to Jeff Friedman, Gary Davis, Greg Coleman, and Keith Stewart on October 25, 2021, indicates that the plaintiffs believed Jacobs's lawyers had requested that they destroy their files.

258 "Vacating the verdict": Tyler Roper email, from a series of emails sent between the plaintiffs' attorneys, February–May 2020.

258 at least $40 million: Emails between the plaintiffs' attorneys, February–May 2020.

258 "With the stuff I continually learn": Ibid.

259 pursue a criminal case against Jacobs: As I describe later in the book, a grand jury ultimately decided not to charge Jacobs and TVA staff members with crimes connected to Kingston.

259 They sat at a long table: This and other details are drawn from interviews with various sources.

259 clearly wanted them: Ansol Clark interview. This is drawn from an audio recording, which was surreptitiously recorded, of a conversation another worker had with Balhoff in which he encouraged the worker to accept Jacobs's settlement offer, corroborating Ansol's account.

260 "waiting for a pile of money": Janie Clark told me this when speaking generally about the lawsuit. Janie, careful not to breach a confidentiality agreement regarding the negotiations, did not tell me how much money Jacobs offered the plaintiffs, and she told me nothing substantive about her conversation with Balhoff.

260 "Don't stroke out, Ansol": Jim Scott interview.

260 "It's not about the money": Jeff Brewer interview. He was speaking generally about the case.

260 "[Jacobs] ain't got no heart": Audio recording.

260 $10,000 individual settlements: Jamie Satterfield, "TVA Contractor's Latest Offer in Coal Ash Exposure Case," *News Sentinel*, May 1, 2020; background source.

261 "I don't care how much money": Scott related this to me.

262 called a Knoxville lawyer: Interview with Greg Coleman, Billy Ringger, Mark Silvey, and Adam Edwards.

263 thirty-seven-page report: *Adkisson et al. v. Jacobs*, Docket no. 772, exhibit 2, Michael Ellenbecker, "Report Kingston Coal Ash," December 7, 2020.

263 "not even come close to agreeing": Cheremisinoff, *Handbook of Pollution Prevention and Cleaner Production*, p. 154. Cheremisinoff establishes that more particulate was in the air around Kingston than TVA let on, because the air quality in the area remained relatively unchanged even though industrial pollution in the region fell drastically in 2009. This suggests that another, new source of air pollution—the Kingston disaster—caused air quality not to improve meaningfully. To arrive at this conclusion, Cheremisinoff relies on data from 2009, which was before Jacobs took over air-monitoring duties at Kingston. I think it's nonetheless relevant, because it establishes a pattern of seemingly questionable air-monitoring practices and reporting at the Kingston jobsite.

263 harmful particulate matter: Jacobs maintains that it did not conceal or misrepresent the presence of fine particulate at Kingston and holds that, based on an evaluation done by state officials, the Kingston fly ash was "nuisance dust" that had no greater toxicity than other airborne particles.

263 advised the federal government: David B. Caruso and Mike Stobbe, "Experts Say Science Lacking on 9/11 and Cancer," AP via NBC News, June 20, 2012.

263 In her report about Kingston: *Adkisson et al. v. Jacobs*, Docket no. 771, exhibit 13, Elizabeth Ward, "Rebuttal Report of Elizabeth Ward, Ph.D.," February 5, 2021.

264 "I feel confident": John F. McCarthy, "Report of John F. McCarthy," *Adkisson et al. v. Jacobs*, January 6, 2021, p. 4. This report was not submitted into the record; I received a copy from Jacobs's lawyers.

264 Another expert: William A. Huber, "Report: Greg Adkisson et al. vs. Jacobs Engineering Group, Inc.," January 6, 2021. This report was not submitted into the record; I received a copy from Jacobs's lawyers.

264 Jacobs's attorneys argued: Memo sent to me by Jeremy S. Smith, of Gibson Dunn, on Jacobs's behalf, October 2023.

266 deposing some two hundred and fifty workers: Interview with Greg Coleman, Billy Ringger, Mark Silvey, and Adam Edwards.

266 had ruled against: U.S. Supreme Court, Opinion of the Court, *Thacker v. TVA*, No. 17–1201, April 29, 2019.

266 "time and resources": *Adkisson et al. v. Jacobs*, Docket no. 759, p. 35.

266 "whole system is stacked": Janie Clark email to me, March 22, 2021.

267 "having a medical emergency": Knox County 911, audio recording and incident report, April 28, 2021.

267 *"Ansol!"*: Ibid.

267 "Okay, don't hang up": Ibid.

268 "Is Mrs. Clark going to be okay?": Jim recalled Sam asking him this.

269 Parkwest hugs Interstate 40: Janie Clark related most of the details in this scene to me shortly after Ansol died. When Ansol was in the hospital, I was staying at a hotel across the highway, so some scene-setting details come from my personal observations, and from a subsequent trip to the Smokies.

269 Satterfield: Satterfield corroborated Janie's recollections of their phone call.

270 A haze: This section is primarily drawn from interviews with Jim Scott, Jack Scott, Lisa Niles, Janie Clark, Tyler Roper, various Kingston workers, and a background source who asked not to be named. A nurse who works at UT Medical Center confirmed some details about the hospital.

272 One friend noticed: A lawyer told me this but asked not to be named.

273 "My boyfriend": Knox County 911, audio file and incident report, May 30, 2021.

276 She revealed that, in 2009: Jamie Satterfield, "Regulators Deleted and Altered Radiological Test Results on Coal Ash from Kingston Spill," *News Sentinel*, May 15, 2020.

276 TDEC, in response: Ibid.

276 Avner Vengosh: Jamie Satterfield, "Duke University Testing Shows Kingston Coal Ash Uranium at Triple Report Levels," *News Sentinel*, May 17, 2020.

276 A Columbia professor: *Adkisson et al. v. Jacobs*, Docket no. 771, exhibit 4, Kleiman, "Human Health Concerns Related to Exposure to Radionuclides Found in Fly Ash," May 17, 2021, p. 19.

277 "information, data, and procedures": *Adkisson et al. v. Jacobs*, Docket no. 771, exhibit 16, Kleiman, "Rebuttal Report of Norman J. Kleiman, Ph.D," p. 14.

277 "negligently or recklessly disregarded": Jacobs disputes Kleiman's findings and

holds that the workers were not exposed to radiation in excess of established standards, based on the calculations done by one of its experts, John Frazier.

277 an anonymous complaint: OSHA, "Notice of Alleged Safety or Health Hazards," February 11, 2009; Jamie Satterfield, "OSHA Officials Admit to Shredding Documents in Tennessee Valley Authority Coal Ash Case," *Tennessee Lookout*, April 12, 2022. I also interviewed Tommy Lucas, a former TVA employee who responded to the OSHA complaint.

277 provided respirators: TVA, "Employee Complaint Investigation 3.2.139-09 Kingston Fossil Plant—Ash Slide Exposures," p. 11.

277 "radium at safe levels": Ibid.

277 "kids that are playing there": Jamie Satterfield, "Toxic TVA Coal Ash on Claxton Playground Confirmed by Duke University Testing," *Knoxville News Sentinel*, July 26, 2021.

277 "The problem is that": Ansol Clark, "Anderson County Operations Committee 8 9 2021 Jamie Satterfield," YouTube video, uploaded on August 22, 2021, 7:29, https://www.youtube.com/watch?v=3XMoeBZXHOY&t=1s.

278 *Knoxville News Sentinel* terminated her: Jamie Satterfield interview.

278 "Kingston Expendables Murder Book": Jamie Satterfield, photo posted on Twitter, September 10, 2021. Satterfield's former editor at the paper did not respond to a request for comment.

278 convinced a grand jury: Russell Johnson, District Attorney General for the 9th Judicial District of Tennessee, statement posted on Facebook, November 16, 2021.

278 "I support TVA": Jamie Satterfield told me Lee said this to her. Lee's staff did not respond to a request for comment.

278 March 11, 2022: U.S. Court of Appeals for the Sixth Circuit, audio recording of proceedings in *Adkisson et al. v. Jacobs Engineering*, March 11, 2022; U.S. Court of Appeals for the Sixth Circuit, Opinion, May 18, 2022.

279 "TVA would not": U.S. Court of Appeals for the Sixth Circuit, Opinion, May 18, 2022, p. 20.

279 a total of $77.5 million: Interviews with six background sources.

279 roughly $49 million: Background sources.

280 Jacobs had appealed: Jacobs Engineering Group, "Motion of Amicus Curiae Coalition for Litigation Justice, Inc., for Permission to File Joint Brief in Support of Petitioner if the Court Accepts Judge Varlan's Certified Questions," *Jacobs Engineering Group, Inc., v. Greg Adkisson et al.*, in the Supreme Court for the State of Tennessee at Nashville.

280 forty plaintiffs: *Adkisson et al. v. Jacobs*, Docket no. 774.

280 pro-business state law: Tennessee "Silica Claims Priorities Act," Tenn. Code Ann. § 29-34-701.

280 $644 million: Jacobs Engineering, "Jacobs Reports Fiscal Fourth Quarter and Fiscal Year 2022 Earnings," press release, November 21, 2022, https://www.jacobs.com/.

281 $2 million: Because the settlement was confidential, Scott would not tell me the size of his fee. I arrived at this number by dividing the attorneys' fee by the number of attorneys involved in the case.

282 eighty million tons: North Carolina Department of Environmental Quality, "DEQ Secures the Nation's Largest Coal Ash Excavation of Nearly 80 Million Tons of Coal Ash," press release, January 2, 2020, https://www.deq.nc.gov.

282 set about restoring: Coral Davenport, "Restoring Environmental Rules Rolled Back by Trump Could Take Years," *New York Times*, January 22, 2021.

282 hundred-plus environmental regulations: "The Trump Administration Rolled Back More Than 100 Environmental Rules. Here's the Full List," *New York Times*, updated on January 20, 2021.

282 "We hear you": EPA, "Administrator Michael Regan, Remarks on Proposed Power Plant Regulations to Tackle the Climate Crisis, As Prepared for Delivery," YouTube video, uploaded on May 11, 2023, 59:25, https://www.youtube.com/watch?v=TXz77CrSR0w.

282 thirteen hundred premature deaths: EPA, "EPA Proposes New Carbon Pollution Standards for Fossil Fuel–Fired Power Plants to Tackle the Climate Crisis and Protect Public Health," press release, May 11, 2023, https://www.epa.gov/.

282 at least two hundred and sixty-one inactive: Timothy Puko, "Biden Seeks to Tighten Regulation of Toxic Power Plant Coal Waste Dumps," *Washington Post*, May 17, 2023.

283 EPA's new amendment: EPA, "EPA Announces Latest Action to Protect Communities from Coal Ash Contamination," press release, May 17, 2023, https://www.epa.gov/.

283 *The New York Times*: Lisa Friedman, "E.P.A. Announces Crackdown on Toxic Coal Ash from Landfills," *New York Times,* May 17, 2023.

283 On the March: I'm the writer Janie was talking with on the phone.

284 a couple of hundred thousand dollars: This number is based on my calculations, taking into account the total recovery, the lawyers' expenses and fees, and the number of plaintiffs. Janie Clark was prohibited from discussing the terms of the settlement with any reporter and didn't talk about it with me.

285 "own basic fundamental right": Bergan Clark, video of TVA listening session at Norris Middle School, May 9, 2023, posted on Facebook, 3:09.

Bibliography

AECOM. 2009. "Root Cause Analysis of TVA Kingston Dredge Pond Failure on December 22, 2008," submitted to TVA on June 25, 2009. Vernon Hills, Ill.: AECOM.

Barker, Scott. 2009. "One Year Later: Catastrophe in Kingston." *Knoxville News Sentinel*, December 20, 2009.

Caro, Robert. 1975. *The Power Broker.* New York: Vintage Books Edition.

Chandler, William U. 1984. *The Myth of TVA: Conservation and Development in the Tennessee Valley, 1933–1983.* Cambridge, Mass.: Ballinger Pub. Co.

Cheremisinoff, Nicholas P. 2012. *Handbook of Pollution Prevention and Cleaner Production* vol. 4: *Clean Electricity Through Advanced Coal Technologies.* Norwich, N.Y.: William Andrew.

Cobb, James C. 1982. *The Selling of the South: The Southern Crusade for Industrial Development, 1936–1980.* Baton Rouge: Louisiana State University Press.

Coll, Steve. 2012. *Private Empire: ExxonMobil and American Power.* New York: Penguin Press.

Compton, Arthur Holly. 2018. Kindle edition. *Atomic Quest: A Personal Narrative.*

Cosslett, Clare. 2012. *Lawyers at Work.* Berkeley, Calif.: Apress.

Freese, Barbara. 2003. *Coal: A Human History.* Cambridge, Mass.: Perseus Books.

Frome, Michael. 1986. *Strangers in High Places.* Knoxville: University of Tennessee Press.

Gaffney, Austyn. 2020. " 'They Deserve to Be Heard': Sick and Dying Coal Ash Cleanup Workers Fight for Their Lives." *The Guardian*, August 17, 2020.

Gold, Russell. 2019. *Superpower: One Man's Quest to Transform American Energy.* New York: Simon & Schuster.

Grant, Nancy. 1990. *TVA and Black Americans: Planning for the Status Quo.* Philadelphia: Temple University Press.

Hargrove, Erwin C. 1983. *TVA: Fifty Years of Grass-Roots Bureaucracy.* Edited by Erwin C. Hargrove. Urbana: University of Illinois Press.

———. 1994. *Prisoners of Myth: The Leadership of the Tennessee Valley Authority, 1933–1990.* Princeton: Princeton University Press.

Jacobs, Joseph J. 1991. *The Anatomy of an Entrepreneur.* San Francisco: ICS Press.

Johnson, Charles W., and Charles O. Johnson. 1981. *City Behind a Fence: Oak Ridge, Tennessee, 1942–1946.* Knoxville: University of Tennessee Press.

Langsdon, Phillip Royal. 2000. *Tennessee: A Political History.* Franklin, Tenn.: Hillsboro Press.

Lilienthal, David E. 1945. *TVA: Democracy on the March.* Pocket Book Edition. New York: Pocket Book, Inc.

Mansfield, Duncan. 2008. "TVA Dam Breaks; Homes Damaged." Associated Press via *Charlotte Observer*, December 23, 2008.

Moore, John R. 1967. *The Economic Impact of TVA.* Edited by John R. Moore. Knoxville: University of Tennessee Press.

Munzer, Martha E. 1969. *Valley of Vision: The TVA Years.* New York: Knopf.

Owen, Marguerite. 1973. *The Tennessee Valley Authority.* New York: Praeger Publishers.

Owen, Matthew D. 2014. "For the Progress of Man: The TVA, Electric Power, and the Environment, 1939–1969." PhD diss., Vanderbilt University.

Poovey, Bill. 2011. "Hundreds Wait for Ruling on Ash Spill." *The Tennessean*, December 26, 2011.

Rhodes, Richard. 2012. *The Making of the Atomic Bomb: 25th Anniversary Edition.* New York: Simon & Schuster Paperbacks.

Rule, William. 1900. *Standard History of Knoxville, Tennessee.* Edited by William Rule. Chicago: Lewis Publishing Company.

Schlosser, Eric. 2014. *Command and Control.* New York: Penguin Books.

Selden, Kyoko Iriye, and Mark Selden. 1989. *The Atomic Bomb: Voices from Hiroshima and Nagasaki.* Armonk, N.Y.: M. E. Sharpe.

Shlaes, Amity. 2008. *The Forgotten Man: A New History of the Great Depression.* New York: Harper Perennial.

Syrett, Nicholas L. 2016. *American Child Bride: A History of Minors and Marriage in the United States.* Chapel Hill: University of North Carolina Press.

Tennessee Valley Authority. 1978. "Nuclear Power in the Tennessee Valley." Pamphlet. Knoxville: TVA, January 1978. Available at the Williamson County Public Library, Special Collections, Franklin, Tenn.

———. 2011. "TVA Kingston Fossil Fuel Plant Release Site On-Scene Coordinator Report for the Time-Critical Removal Action, May 11, 2009, Through December 2010." Document No. EPA-AO-030.

———. 2015. "Kingston Ash Recovery Project Completion Report, TVA Kingston Fossil Fuel Plant Release Site." Submitted to the EPA on April 22, 2015. Document No. EPA-AO-064.

Tennessee Valley Authority, Office of the Inspector General. 2009. "Inspection Report: Review of the Kingston Fossil Plant Ash Spill Root Cause Study and Observations About Ash Management." TVA OIG, July 23, 2009.

Tetra Tech EM Inc. 2009. "Final Comprehensive Environmental Response, Compensation, and Liability Act (CERCLA) Emergency Response Report, Revision 0, Kingston Fossil Plant Fly Ash Response, Harriman, Roane County, Tennessee." Prepared for the U.S. EPA, Region 4, submitted on February 20, 2009. Duluth, Ga.: Tetra Tech EM Inc.

Thurman, Sybil. 1982. *A History of the Tennessee Valley Authority: 50th Anniversary Edition.* Edited by Sybil Thurman. Knoxville: S. B. Newman Printing Company.

U.S. Strategic Bombing Survey. 1946. "The Effects of Atomic Bombs." Washington, D.C.: U.S. Government Printing Office.

Vengosh, Avner, et al. 2009. "Survey of the Potential Environmental and Health Impacts in the Immediate Aftermath of the Coal Ash Spill in Kingston, Tennessee." *Environmental Science & Technology* 43, no. 16 (2009).

Wheeler, William Bruce. 2005. *Knoxville, Tennessee: A Mountain City in the New South.* Knoxville: University of Tennessee Press.

Wheeler, William Bruce, and Michael J. McDonald. 1986. *TVA and the Tellico Dam, 1936–1979.* Knoxville: University of Tennessee Press.

Index

Pages in boldface refer to illustrations.

Illustration Credits

5: Courtesy of Appalachian Voices/Dot Griffith; flight courtesy of Southwings

8: Courtesy of Appalachian Voices/Dot Griffith; flight courtesy of Southwings

19: Houston Cofield

26: Courtesy of the Library of Congress, Prints & Photographs Division, FSA/OWI Collection, LC-USW33-015709-C

37: Houston Cofield

103: (both) Houston Cofield

196: Houston Cofield

212: Courtesy of the U.S. Department of Energy; photo taken by Ed Westcott in 1947

253: Courtesy of the plaintiffs' counsel

A Note About the Author

Jared Sullivan formerly worked as a writer and editor for *Men's Journal* and *Field & Stream*. He has written for *The New Yorker*, *Time*, *Garden & Gun*, and *USA Today*. He lives in Franklin, Tennessee, with his wife and daughters.

A Note on the Type

This book was set in Adobe Garamond. Designed by Robert Slimbach, the fonts are based on types first cut by Claude Garamond (ca. 1480–1561).

Composed by North Market Street Graphics,
Lancaster, Pennsylvania

Printed and bound by Berryville Graphics,
Berryville, Virginia

Designed by Betty Lew